THE BIG BOOK OF

GARDENING SECRETS

THE BIG BOOK OF
GARDENING SECRETS

Charles W. G. Smith

STOREY
BOOKS

*The mission of Storey Communications is to serve our customers
by publishing practical information that encourages
personal independence in harmony with the environment.*

Edited by Gwen W. Steege
Cover design by Meredith Maker
Cover photographs courtesy of All-American Selections
Text design and production by Nathaniel Stout and Eileen M. Clawson
Line drawings credited on page 324
Indexed by Susan Olason, Indexes & Knowledge Maps

Printed in Canada by Transcontinental Printing

ISBN 1-58017-017-X

Dedication

This book is fondly dedicated to my mother, to Christine, and to the many other people who have shown me that every garden path and forest trail has a wonderful secret to tell; and to my son Nathaniel, for patiently listening as I try to pass on the lesson.

Contents

A World of Secrets to Discover

Years ago, when I was still an undergraduate taking classes in plant science, one lecture revolutionized the way I had always thought about plants. My professor described the results of some recent research concerning how trees in an oak grove reacted to having their leaves eaten by insects. The study analyzed the chemical content of the trees' leaves before and after they had been preyed on by insects. Now, most people think of plants as pretty passive things. After all, they can't get up and move if a wave of bugs comes their way. They just have to sit and take whatever comes. This study, however, demonstrated that plants are not just passive creatures after all, but quite dynamic. Here's what the research revealed:

When an insect begins to feed on a leaf, the tree responds by increasing the leaf's concentrations of acids and other substances distasteful to most bugs. This in itself is astonishing, but an even bigger surprise is that the tree also increases the concentrations of these chemicals in all its other leaves. So as soon as a bug starts chewing anywhere on the plant, it gets only a mandible full of distasteful leaf. Furthermore, the defensive response goes beyond this one tree. Soon the foliage of every tree in the grove has higher levels of these nasty tasting substances, and the concentrations on other trees increase *before* any insect has even taken so much as a nibble.

As a student listener I was spellbound by this much of the story, but the climax was still to come. Shortly after the grove of trees exhibited this concerted defensive response, the oak trees in a separate grove hundreds of yards away also showed elevated levels of these deterrent substances. What is the mechanism behind this seeming communication between isolated plants? In a nutshell, theories abound, but, as yet, nobody knows.

LESSONS FROM THE PAST

The natural world will always hold out secrets to us like a teamster holds a carrot on a stick before a donkey. It teases us forward into the unknown on an endlessly satisfying journey of discovery. And what is best of all, there are so many secrets out there that we will never run out of discoveries.

Plants and gardening have been revealing their secrets to the curious for literally thousands of years. The preferences and requirements, weaknesses and strengths of every crop ever grown had to be discovered by someone at sometime. This gradual revelation of knowledge literally enabled the creation of civilization as we know it. Until humans learned how to collect seed, sow it properly, and care for the plants those seeds produced, all the food people needed had to be gathered from the wild, a notoriously inefficient process. In places where people depend on gathering their food, it can take up to 20 square miles of land to feed just one person, depending on the climate. With so much space required for sustenance, the entire eastern hemisphere could support fewer than 10 million people before agriculture. With the development of agriculture, this same space now supports billions.

As early people observed how plants grew, they also began to learn how to select the best plants from what was grown. In the Americas, for example, a feeble grass that produced a few seed kernels atop a 4-inch terminal spike was transformed over thousands of years and by dozens of different cultures into a strong 4- to 6-foot-tall plant that produced kernel-filled ears in the leaf axils. This plant, now known as corn, has been so changed by humans that it is regarded as a completely different species from its now extinct wild

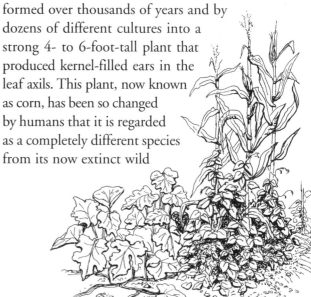

The "Three Sisters": corn, beans, and squash

ancestor. Over the last 500 years curious people have probed to discover even more secrets about corn. There are now hundreds of varieties, some over 8 feet tall that produce huge ears filled with super sweet kernels. Yet all the improvements of all the breeders of corn over the last five centuries do not equal the astounding changes introduced by thousands of anonymous Native American ancestors. Just how they accomplished what they did is in itself a secret.

SAVING TIME AND MONEY

The collection of secrets you hold in your hand comes from a number of sources, from backyard gardeners to commercial growers to universities and Agricultural Experiment Stations. Some, such as the methods of making a hotbed using livestock manure as a heating source, or of creating the same type of soil mix favored by English horticulturalists over a century ago, are as old as the hills. Others, including ways to thicken tomato stems by brushing your hand over the tops of the plants twice a day or warming the spring garden with the most modern warming mulch, are brand new. Some use modern technology, including methods to quickly dry herbs using a microwave oven or a frost-free refrigerator. Even research satellites have revealed secrets important to gardeners: for instance, data proved that spring comes to North America over a week earlier now than it did in the 1980s. Now that is an easy way to extend the growing season!

Then there are the secrets that can save folks a lot of time and money. In October of 1997 the central Rockies and Great Plains were hit by an early-season blizzard. The heavy, wet snow literally destroyed hundreds of silver maples in Omaha, Nebraska. This tragic loss could have been avoided by recognizing that of trees known to be prone to snow and ice damage, silver maple is one of the worst offenders. Discovering secrets like this can make your life more comfortable and more satisfying.

THE MYSTERY OF YOUR OWN GARDEN

When I was growing up, we had a garden in the side yard that my father plowed each spring. After the plowing, one more tradition was essential to complete before planting could begin. My mother, sisters, brothers, and I passed through the garden gate and began to slowly walk the newly turned earth. We weren't searching for the best place to plant corn or peas. We were looking for traces of the people who once also tilled this soil. We almost always discovered bits of white clay pipe left behind by the colonists who lived on the land about the time of the Revolution. Sometimes one of us found a small arrowhead chipped from white quartz, or a slightly larger one made of glassy flint. These stony reminders, much older than the bits of clay pipe, were made by the Native Americans who lived on the land 300 to 600 years ago. Near where they hunted, they also farmed. And near where they farmed centuries ago we grew our garden. A garden filled with squash and pumpkin, corn and beans — modern versions of an ancient tradition.

The secrets to growing tasty vegetables, berries, and fruit, or beautiful gardens, shrubs, and trees are exceedingly valuable, but for me, perhaps the most intriguing secret of all is the hidden link between the past and the future, represented in an unbroken chain of techniques and methods. Applying old-time gardening secrets allows you to grow the best antique roses, as well as the best of the super-hardy modern ones. Using time-tested techniques for growing standard varieties of vegetables and saving the seed translates effectively to growing the most vigorous and productive of the new hybrids. Enjoying the wild blueberries and strawberries that have grown in the woods and mountains for thousands of years goes hand in hand with savoring the modern varieties selected to thrive in your own garden.

Links to the past and paths to the future exist in everything we do. This book, filled with these secrets, seeks to keep the best of the past and the best of the present alive and well in your garden.

Acknowledgments

Among the items found on the cover of a book is the name of the author. There is usually just one name, and if the truth be known that is a bit of an injustice. A book is not the product of a single person, but of a team of people, and a large team at that. Some of those responsible for this book are the talented people at Storey Publishing, a company replete with topnotch editors, designers, sales, publicity, and support personnel. They not only do their jobs very well, they are genuinely good people as well. Another group of folks that deserve many thanks are those family members who put up with my eccentricities on a daily basis. (I don't think I am that difficult to live with — I'll bet everyone has raised an abandoned raccoon in the bathtub at least once.) Thanks to all those, living and passed on, who taught or otherwise shared the knowledge they have acquired in their travels through life. And special thanks to those who inspired as well as taught. The faith they exhibited is a gift that I carry with honor every day and everywhere.

Charles W. G. Smith
November 12, 1997

1

Amending Soil and Starting Right

Soil, of one type or another, covers most of the continents of our planet. This layer can run from just a few inches to over ten feet deep, but in any case it is essential to life. This thin, earthy skin is all that sustains every terrestrial plant and animal. Without it the continents of the earth would be nothing but desolate landscapes.

A garden is a fascinating interplay of plants and soil, roots and microorganisms; each is dependent on the others. Plants rely on the soil to supply nutrients and moisture, and the soil depends on decomposed plants for much of its fertility and structure. Some folks consider the soil of the garden just a growing medium — something for a plant's roots to hold onto. Others see a garden's soil for what it is, a thriving ecosystem of bacteria and fungi, earthworms and millipedes, woven into a matrix of minerals and organic matter — an ecosystem whose health and vitality determines the vigor and beauty of the plants and flowers in the garden.

Because soils are living ecosystems, they respond to the environment around them. For example, 150 years of deep plowing, monocultural planting, and tons of synthetic fertilizers have robbed many midwestern soils of as much as 40 percent of their nutrients. Just as important as our ability to destroy soils is our ability to rebuild them. Over the last 20 years many farmers across the Midwest have adopted no-till farming techniques, which have begun to restore to the soil nutrients that had previously been lost.

The soil in any backyard garden is just as dynamic as that of the corn, wheat, and soybean fields in the Midwest — and just as responsive to help. Great gardeners rely on dirty hands much more than green thumbs. Whatever soil you have, it can be made healthier and more vital. This means that no matter how beautiful your garden is now, improving the soil will make it even better.

Your sense of touch is a good gauge of soil texture.

1

Soil Texture

Soil is divided into many different types, depending on the size and amount of mineral particles it contains. These particles (sands, silts, and clays) have unique properties that are necessary for the proper growth of plants. *Sand* is principally composed of unweathered grains of quartz rock, the particles being about the size of individual grains of salt. It increases aeration and permeability in soils but retains little water and few nutrients. Particles of *silts* and *clays* are much smaller than those of sand and come from many different rock types. They hold nutrients and water well but drain slowly and have poor aeration. A good soil is therefore one that contains a balanced blend of sand, silt, and clay: about 50 percent sand, 30 percent silt, and 20 percent clay.

Of the many types of soil, the one generally regarded as the most desirable for gardens is sandy loam. The term *loam* refers to a soil that contains a mixture of sand, silt, clay, and organic matter.

A FIELD-TEST FOR TEXTURE

To make a quick field-test for soil texture, place a small amount of moist but not wet soil in the palm of your hand. Swirl it around with your fingers until you can feel its texture. Soil that feels gritty and rough is high in sand. (It's a feeling similar to that of rubbing salt between your fingers.) Soil that feels soft, however — like flour — is high in silt. Clay soils, in contrast, feel slippery-soft, like frozen butter.

Most soils are a blend of these three textures, so as you feel your soil, describe it beginning with the texture that seems dominant, followed by the other(s): a *sandy silt,* for example. This will give you a rough idea of your soil type.

HOW TO DETERMINE SOIL TYPE

The test most commonly used to determine soil type precisely is called a fractional analysis. To perform it, begin with a cylindrical jar, such as a small canning jar. Collect samples of soil from various parts of your garden and dry them on a sheet of newspaper for a few days. Then rub the dried soil between your fingers until no clumps remain. Fill the jar halfway with it. Add a few drops of Murphy's Oil Soap, then add water until the soil is saturated and the waterline about an inch above the soil. Tighten the lid and shake well.

After letting the jar sit for one or two minutes, mark it with a grease pencil to indicate the level of sand. Mark the level again after two hours to measure the silt content, and again after the water has become completely clear (usually one to three days later) to measure the level of clay. Record the thickness of each layer as well as their combined thickness (sand = A, silt = B, clay = C, combined = D). To determine the percentage of each particle type, multiply its thickness by 100 and divide by D. Then, to determine your soil's type, compare your percentages with those on the chart here.

TYPES OF SOIL TEXTURES

TEXTURE	CONTENT
Sand	0–10% clay; 0–10% silt; no more than 20% clay and silt combined; 80–100% sand
Sandy Loam	Up to 20% clay; up to 50% silt; no more than 50% but at least 20% clay and silt combined; 50–80% sand
Silty Loam	20% or less clay; 40–80% silt; over 50% clay and silt combined; 30–40% sand
Clay Loam	30% or more clay; 20% or more silt; 50% or less sand
Clay	30% or more clay; 21% or more silt; very little sand
Silt	20% or less clay; 30% or less sand; 50% or more silt
Peat	65% or more organic matter
Muck	25–65% organic matter; 35–75% silt and clay; very little sand

FIXING SOIL TEXTURE

A soil's texture is determined by the relative amounts of silt, clay, and sand in it. So, logically, it would seem that to change a soil's texture all you have to do is change the amount of sand, silt, or clay. You will soon find, however, that to alter the texture of even a small amount of soil would require the addition of large amounts of material, sometimes enough to double the soil volume.

Fortunately, there is one substance that will improve almost any soil: organic matter. Whether in the form of compost, peat moss, or manure, organic matter improves whatever soils it is added to. It helps hold nutrients and water in sandy soils; it aids in the drainage and aeration of clay and silty soils. The bottom line is that however it is added, organic matter makes almost any soil healthier.

Soil Structure

As bacteria and other microorganisms process the organic matter in soil, they produce a strange sort of glue. This adhesive binds tiny particles of minerals and organic matter together into granules, or *aggregates*. The number and size of the aggregates determine a soil's structure.

Soil aggregates contain nutrients that plants need to grow well. They sit in the soil like pellets of slow-release fertilizer waiting to be used. Particles of silt and clay form the nuclei for small, very fertile aggregates. These small aggregates in turn form *micropores* (also called capillaries) in the soil, which are nearly always filled with water. Sand, on the other hand, is the seed for the formation of larger, less fertile aggregates that create *macropores*. Macropores are filled with a combination of water and air, or air alone.

The best soil structure is a network of micropores surrounding aggregates of silt, clay, and organic matter, plus one of macropores surrounding aggregates of sand and organic matter.

Soil Drainage

How well a soil drains determines how much oxygen reaches plant roots and soil organisms, as well as how much water is available to growing plants. Soils that drain too efficiently have excellent air exchange but poor water retention. Soils that drain poorly, however, hold vast stores of water but often have low oxygen levels. For garden plants to grow at their best, they need a balance between *soil air* and *soil water*.

SOIL AIR

Plants and other organisms that live in the soil metabolize oxygen and discharge carbon dioxide. For these plants and organisms to survive there must be a constant, uninterrupted movement of oxygen from the air to the soil, and carbon dioxide from the soil to the air. These gases diffuse through the soil via the network of passages called macropores that form around aggregates of sand and organic matter, as well as through the tunnels made by worms and other subterranean creatures. Soils high in silts and clays have poor macropore networks; this can inhibit good root growth. You can increase aeration in such soils by adding organic matter. Soils high in sand, on the other hand, tend to have excellent macropore networks.

Adding organic matter to the garden is a sure-fire way to improve your soil.

SOIL WATER

During a rainstorm water soaks into the earth, moving through the macropores and micropores, or capillaries, of the soil. As the earth dries out, the columns of capillary water break up and the movement of water stops. When this happens (just after the surface of the soil looks dry) the soil holds the ideal balance of moisture and air for plant growth.

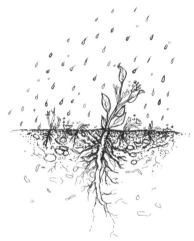

Good garden soil holds moisture for days or weeks after it rains.

The longer this charge of water remains in the soil, the more vigorous plant growth can be. At maximum charge clay soils hold twice as much water as silty soils and four times as much as sandy soils.

Sandy soils, which often do not hold enough water, can be made more retentive by amending them with organic matter; this will increase the proportion of micropores, which increases water retention while simultaneously slowing water loss through evaporation. Clay soils hold so much moisture that they may not contain enough air to ensure vigorous plant growth. Adding organic matter to clay soils increases the proportion of macropores, which aids in drainage. Silty soils have a good balance of soil moisture and air.

But even the best soil can lose too much water during periods of drought, when evaporation quickly steals moisture from the soil. To conserve as much soil moisture as possible during droughts, farmers routinely cultivate their fields, scuffing just the top few inches of soil. This very light cultivation breaks up the capillaries in the soil, which traps moisture below. This technique can be used in the garden by lightly hoeing along your rows and between your plants on hot summer days.

Maintaining Good Soil Structure	
Action	**Reaction**
Add organic matter regularly.	Organic matter is used by microorganisms to create soil aggregates; helps retain water and nutrients in soil; helps create macropores that aerate the soil; encourages healthy populations of beneficial soil organisms; and reduces the incidence of soilborne diseases, especially in high-clay soils.
Cultivate soil when moist.	Cultivation of soil when it's too wet or too dry destroys air spaces and breaks up soil aggregates, which hinders aeration and drainage and causes compaction.
Cover bare soil with mulch.	Mulch protects the soil from compaction via heavy rains or foot traffic.
Switch from till to no-till practices.	Gardens maintained under no-till practices have consistently better soil aggregates, drainage, and aeration, plus higher populations of worms and other soil organisms.

Tilling in organic matter helps create more fertile, well-drained soil.

Some plants grow best in specific soil conditions, such as dry or wet. These plants, called indicator plants, can convey the type of drainage a soil has simply by being there. For example, if bayberry grows in your yard it is a good bet you have dry, sandy soil. Cattails, on the other hand, reveal poorly drained, wet soil.

PLANTS THAT GROW IN DRY SOILS

Bayberry *(Myrica pensylvanica)*
Cinquefoil *(Potentilla* spp.)
Eastern red cedar *(Juniperus virginiana)*
Flannel mullein *(Verbascum thapsus)*
Indian paintbrush *(Castilleja coccinea)*
Mother-of-thyme *(Thymus serpyllum)*
Mouse-ear chickweed *(Cerastium vulgatum)*
Prickly pear *(Opuntia* spp.)
Sweet fern *(Comptonia peregrina)*
Yucca *(Yucca* spp.)

PLANTS THAT GROW IN WET SOILS

Alders *(Alnus* spp.)
Blue flag *(Iris versicolor)*
Cattail *(Typha* spp.)
Coltsfoot *(Tussilago farfara)*
Joe-pye weed *(Eupatorium* spp.)
Leatherleaf *(Chamaedaphne calyculata)*
Ragged-robin *(Lychnis flos-cuculi)*
Summer-sweet *(Clethra alnifolia)*
Sweet gale *(Myrica gale)*
Willow *(Salix* spp.)
Winterberry *(Ilex verticillata)*
Yellow flag *(Iris pseudacorus)*

PLANTS THAT GROW IN WET AND DRY SOILS

Horsetail *(Equisetum* spp.)
Meadowsweet *(Spiraea* spp.)
Poplar *(Populus* spp.)
Sumac *(Rhus* spp.)
Tawny daylily *(Hemerocallis fulva)*
White pine *(Pinus strobus)*
Yarrow *(Achillea millefolium)*

A Gallery of Organic Matter

There are many kinds of organic matter, from compost to peat moss to manure. They all improve the soil they are added to, but they are not all the same.

COMPOST

Compost is the champagne of organic matter. Well-made compost provides ideal conditions for beneficial soil organisms, buffers both acidic and alkaline soils, helps retain vital plant nutrients, aids soil aeration and drainage, increases moisture retention, and improves soil texture and structure. Chapter 2 tells you all you need to know about compost.

MANURE

There are as many types of manure as there are animals in the world. In the United States the most popular come from farm animals — everything from horses to chickens. Some fresh manure contains high amounts of nitrogen in a form that can damage plant roots, has high amounts of soluble nutrients that often leach away before plants can use them, and can contain such undesirable substances as antibiotics. Composted manure has none of these problems and is great for the garden.

Ruminant manures. Such animals as cattle, sheep, and goats have complex digestive systems that produce moist manures rich in microorganisms. Cattle manure can have abundant weed seeds that can be killed by hot composting or by covering the manure with a thick layer of mulch. Manures from sheep and goats have many devoted followers.

Horse manure. This manure has a low moisture content and is best used once it has been composted, preferably with the stable bedding. It usually contains a few weed seeds here and there, but not nearly as many as in cattle manure. The texture of horse manure is coarse and lends body to the soil.

Poultry manure. Poultry manure is extremely high in urea and ammonia — forms of soluble nitrogen that can damage plant roots. Once composted, however, poultry manure is an excellent source of organic matter for the soil.

Cover crops contribute valuable nutrients to the soil.

COVER CROPS

Many types of cover crops, or *green manures,* are grown by gardeners throughout the country. Cover crops include alfalfa, beans, clover, cowpeas, hairy indigo, buckwheat, millet, lupine, vetch, barley, rye, and wheat. Growing cover crops that are then turned into the soil benefits the garden in a number of ways:

- **Free fertilizer.** Legume crops, such as alfalfa, vetch, and beans, have the ability to fix nitrogen from the air and deposit it in the soil, enriching the earth with this valuable nutrient. Other cover crops, such as buckwheat and sweet clover, accumulate phosphorus, which is added to the soil when the crop is turned under.
- **Weed control.** Fast-growing cover crops, such as buckwheat and rye, can choke out weeds.
- **Improved soil health.** Once cover crops are turned into the soil, they decompose into rich compost that enhances soil structure, encourages microorganisms, retains moisture and nutrients, and increases aeration.

PEAT

Peat, the remains of bog or aquatic vegetation, can come from various species of moss or from reeds and sedges. It is harvested from bogs in Canada, Europe, and the northern United States, packaged into bales, and shipped throughout the world. It enhances soil structure, aeration, and water retention. Its pH of between 3.8 and 4.5 is quite acidic and makes it useful for growing acid-loving plants.

Reed-sedge peat, the remains of swamp plants, is common in the South. It lends the same advantages to the soil as peat moss but is not as acidic — its pH is between 4.5 and 7.0.

Soil Chemistry

Improving soil texture and structure enhances the matrix through which air and water flow. Soil nutrients dissolve in the water and are transported along this underground highway to the roots of plants, where they are absorbed. To pass into the plant, these mineral nutrients must be in solution. Soil chemistry is what regulates whether they are able to dissolve or not, and hence whether they can be used by plants growing in the soil.

PLANT NUTRITION

The minerals that plants need for proper nutrition are most frequently grouped according to how much of each plants require to maintain good health. Using this criterion, the most critical plant nutrients are nitrogen, phosphorus, potassium, sulfur, calcium, magnesium, iron, zinc, manganese, boron, and molybdenum.

Once absorbed, these elements move through a plant's tissues to wherever they are needed. After this initial movement some nutrients, such as calcium and zinc, stay put, while others, including nitrogen and phosphorus, can flow from one part of the plant to another, as needed. This ability or inability to move, or *translocate,* within the plant is critical to diagnosing nutrient deficiencies in plants. Deficiencies of minerals that do not translocate will first be apparent on young, emerging leaves and stems. Deficiencies of minerals that do translocate show up on older, mature leaves.

The Essential Plant Nutrients

Boron

ROLE IN PLANTS: Proper growth

DEFICIENCY SYMPTOMS: Deformation and/or death of terminal tip; chlorosis (yellowing or blanching) of young leaves

INDICATOR PLANTS: Apple (corky lesions on fruit); root crops (black and brown heart), celery (cracked stems); lettuce (dead growing point); rose (black leaf margins)

TRANSLOCATES: No

NOTES: Excess calcium in the soil can produce boron deficiencies. Correct by adding borax. Beans are sensitive to boron and shouldn't be planted in soil where borax has been added.

Calcium

ROLE IN PLANTS: Constituent of cell walls; maintains balance between magnesium and potassium

DEFICIENCY SYMPTOMS: Lack of growth in terminal tips; short, stubby roots, often with dieback of tips

INDICATOR PLANTS: Corn and legumes (stubby roots)

TRANSLOCATES: No

NOTES: Excess calcium can produce boron deficiencies. Calcium deficiencies can occur in acid soils and can be caused by continuous use of high-phosphorus fertilizers. Correct deficiencies by adding limestone or dolomite (will raise soil pH) or gypsum (does not alter soil pH). Soils formed from limestone, dolomite, or marble are rich in calcium.

Iron

ROLE IN PLANTS: Formation of chlorophyll

DEFICIENCY SYMPTOMS: Chlorosis of young leaves with yellowing of interveinal areas (areas along veins remain green)

INDICATOR PLANTS: Azalea, rhododendron, citrus (chlorosis of leaves at growing tip)

TRANSLOCATES: No

NOTES: Continuous use of high-phosphorus fertilizers can induce iron deficiencies. Iron is much more available in soils with a pH below 5.5. Chelated iron can correct problems even in alkaline soils. Before applying chelated iron read the instructions carefully as improper application can damage plants.

Magnesium

ROLE IN PLANTS: Formation of chlorophyll

DEFICIENCY SYMPTOMS: Interveinal chlorosis of lower, mature leaves with yellowing of interveinal areas (areas along veins remain green); reduced growth rate

INDICATOR PLANTS: Tomatoes (interveinal chlorosis of lower, mature leaves); cabbage (lower leaves puckered, turning white along margin)

TRANSLOCATES: Yes

NOTES: Many soils along Atlantic and Gulf Coasts are naturally deficient. Continuous use of high-phosphorus fertilizers can induce magnesium deficiencies. Correct by adding dolomite (will raise soil pH) or Epsom salts (does not alter pH).

Manganese

ROLE IN PLANTS: Activates essential plant enzymes and is used to produce oxygen during photosynthesis.

DEFICIENCY SYMPTOMS: Chlorosis and freckle-like dead spots of young leaves with yellowing of interveinal areas (areas along veins remain green, giving leaf a netted appearance); in apple the middle of new stems has a herringbone appearance; English Walnut shows leaf scorch.

INDICATOR PLANTS: Tomatoes, Apple, Cherry, English Walnut

TRANSLOCATES: No

NOTES: Manganese, like iron, is more available to plants in acid soils. Reduce soil pH to below 7.0. Some sphagnum peat moss is high in manganese.

Molybdenum

ROLE IN PLANTS: Needed in minute amounts for proper growth.

DEFICIENCY SYMPTOMS: Yellowing of younger leaves and sometimes browning of leaf edges. Plants produce fewer flowers.

INDICATOR PLANTS: Cabbage, Broccoli (whiptail-shaped leaves); Grapes, Citrus, Apple (yellowing of leaves)

TRANSLOCATES: Some

NOTES: Unlike iron and manganese, molybdenum becomes less available in acid soils and deficiencies can usually be corrected by increasing soil pH. Deficiencies are rare.

Nitrogen

ROLE IN PLANTS: Synthesis of proteins

DEFICIENCY SYMPTOMS: Uniform yellowing of all leaves; younger mature leaves smaller than older mature leaves; sometimes red pigmentation along veins.

INDICATOR PLANTS: Azalea (pale green leaves with reddish tone); poinsettia (all leaves uniformly light green); snapdragon (leaves bend down); apple (reduced fruit yield and small fruit size); pansy (easily damaged by *excess* nitrogen)

TRANSLOCATES: Yes

NOTES: Growing plants need some nitrogen at all times. Correct deficiencies with applications of high-nitrogen fertilizers. Prevent deficiencies by using green manures, especially legumes, and compost.

Phosphorus

ROLE IN PLANTS: Aids cell division, flower and fruit development, formation of starches.

DEFICIENCY SYMPTOMS: Young leaves dark green, while mature leaves have bronze cast; purplish stems and leaf stalks; poor root growth; slow overall growth.

INDICATOR PLANTS: Tomatoes (purple color in leaf stalks and leaves)

TRANSLOCATES: Yes

NOTES: Too much phosphorus can cause an aluminum deficit in hydrangeas, inhibiting blue flower color. It can also cause deficiencies of iron, calcium, and magnesium.

Potassium

ROLE IN PLANTS: Photosynthesis, respiration, enzyme activation, and disease resistance

DEFICIENCY SYMPTOMS: Brown leaf edges and bronze, rust-like cast to entire leaf; symptoms on older, lower leaves first, advancing up stem. Growth very slow resulting in plant appearing stunted. Leaves crinkled and curled at edges. Weak stems and leaf stalks.

INDICATOR PLANTS: Hydrangea (progressive browning of leaf); sweet pea (young flower buds drop); celery and rhubarb (weak leaf stalks); potato, (bronze color of leaf with marginal browning); squash and pumpkin (deformed fruit and bronze color of leaf)

TRANSLOCATES: Yes

NOTES: Correct by adding wood ashes (will also raise the pH of the soil) or fertilizers with at least 5% potassium content. Soils formed from granite are high in potassium.

Sulfur

ROLE IN PLANTS: Formation of proteins and vitamins

DEFICIENCY SYMPTOMS: Light green foliage similar in appearance to nitrogen deficiency but affecting youngest leaves first

INDICATOR PLANTS: Hydrangea (new growth light green, leaves more susceptible to mildew); onions, cucumber, squash, pumpkin, melon (young leaves pale green)

TRANSLOCATES: Variable

NOTES: Deficiency more common in manufactured soil mixes. Correct by adding sulfur to the soil (will lower pH). Powdered sulfur is the oldest known fungicide and has been used for thousands of years. Though proper soil levels are needed for proper growth of cucumbers, squash, pumpkins and melons, do not apply powdered sulfur to the foliage of these plants as it can reduce the yield of the crop.

Zinc

ROLE IN PLANTS: Synthesis of plant hormones, reproduction

DEFICIENCY SYMPTOMS: Very short internode growth, young leaves are small, chlorotic, and crinkled. Growth is slow with leaves occurring in rosettes.

INDICATOR PLANTS: Almond, apricot, citrus, grape, peach, plum (small, crinkled narrow leaves); pecan, walnut (no nuts produced in trees)

TRANSLOCATES: No

NOTES: Severe deficiencies are accompanied by defoliation. Soils with high amounts of phosphorus and/or calcium are often deficient in zinc. Correct deficiencies in tree crops with sprays of zinc sulphate applied to trees when they are dormant. For herbaceous plants, including vegetables, apply zinc sulphate to soil.

Soil pH

A water molecule comprises two atoms of hydrogen plus one of oxygen and is electrically neutral. When the molecule breaks apart it forms one hydrogen ion (H+), with a positive charge, and one hydroxyl ion (OH-), with a negative charge. The pH scale measures the concentration of these ions in water. Solutions with high concentrations of hydrogen ions are acids, while those with high concentrations of hydroxyl ions are bases.

On the pH scale, neutral solutions are represented by 7.0. All solutions with values of below 7.0 are acids; those with values of between 7.0 and 14.0 are bases. Most plants grow best when the soil pH is between 6.0 and 7.0. Plants that prefer more acid soils usually prefer those with a pH value of from 4.5 to 6.0; those that prefer more alkaline conditions grow best in soils with a pH between 7.0 and 8.0. To grow the best plants it is essential not only to have great soil, but also to have soil with the proper pH for the particular plant.

Certain plant nutrients dissolve better in acid solutions, while others dissolve better in alkaline solutions. Many plants can only obtain the balance of nutrients they need when growing in a soil with an appropriate pH.

Soil Tests

Soil tests evaluate the pH of the soil as well as the concentrations of many essential nutrients. Do-it-yourself kits usually determine values for pH, nitrogen, potassium, phosphorus, calcium, and magnesium. Some professional laboratories will do all of that plus give you values for trace nutrients, directions on what to add to the soil to best grow the plants you want, and values for organic matter content. Professional soil tests are available through your state's Cooperative Extension Service as well as through private testing companies. To get the most accurate assessment for the plants you wish to grow, collect separate soil samples for different plant groups. For example, get a soil evaluation for the area where you grow acid-loving plants, such as rhododendrons, and a separate evaluation for your vegetable garden or lawn.

COLLECTING THE SOIL SAMPLE

To collect a soil sample, push the blade of a trowel into the soil so it penetrates at least 6 inches. Rock the blade back and forth a little and pull it from the ground. Turn the blade and reinsert the trowel into the soil until a plug of earth is cut from the ground. Lift the plug from the ground and lay it on a sheet of newspaper. A professional lab will send instructions on how to mix and dry the sample

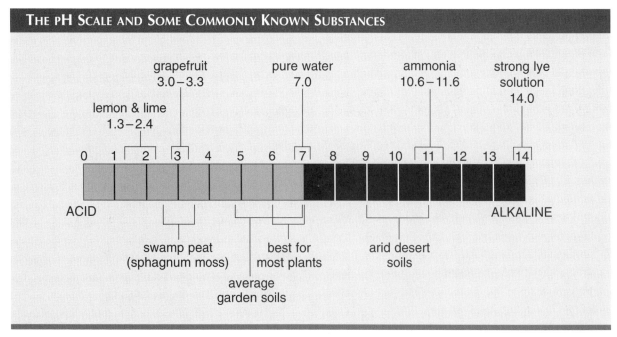

THE pH SCALE AND SOME COMMONLY KNOWN SUBSTANCES

lemon & lime
1.3–2.4

grapefruit
3.0–3.3

pure water
7.0

ammonia
10.6–11.6

strong lye
solution
14.0

0 1 2 3 4 5 6 7 8 9 10 11 12 13 14

ACID   ALKALINE

swamp peat
(sphagnum moss)

best for
most plants

arid desert
soils

average
garden soils

Follow simple directions for obtaining and preparing a soil sample for an at-home or professional lab test.

before mailing; at-home kits always include directions for sample preparation. If you perform your own soil test, note that using distilled water (which is pH neutral) will provide much more accurate results than using tap water.

AN EXCEPTION TO THE RULE

The soil gathered for most soil tests is collected from the top few inches of earth. When this is analyzed for pH and nutrient levels, it accurately relates the conditions for vegetables, annuals, perennials, and some woody plants with shallow root systems. Large shrubs and trees, however, have roots that penetrate many feet below the topsoil layer into mineral soils. These deep roots gather minerals more shallow rooted plants can't reach. As a general rule do not treat healthy-looking trees for deficiency symptoms reported from a shallow soil test. If a tree shows symptoms, however, amend the soil according to the test results.

ORGANIC MATTER AND SOIL pH

Not all soils are created equal, especially when it comes to changing the pH. Organic matter and clay in a soil act as buffers, neutralizing the effect of whatever substances you add in order to raise or lower pH. This means that soils high in organic matter or clay will require more limestone per square foot to raise the pH value by 0.1 than would be needed to raise it in comparable soils with little organic matter or clay.

Soil Ecology

The rain forests of Amazonia, Africa, and Asia contain some of the most diverse ecosystems on earth. One square mile of forest can contain hundreds of different species of trees, birds, and insects. And while such fascinating diversity may seem far removed from your backyard cabbage patch or flower garden, it isn't. In fact, the earth beneath your feet is just as diverse as a rain forest. One small handful of soil can contain thousands of different species of bacteria and other organisms; a single pound can hold over 120 billion microbes.

What these organisms can do is even more impressive. When sprayed with certain herbicides, a soil rich in microbes can degrade most of the chemicals in about two months, while one with few microorganisms will still contain large quantities of the herbicide up to three years later.

The organisms that live in the soil not only purify their environment of toxins, but they also enrich and restore it as they process organic matter, breaking complex nutrient molecules into simple forms that are then stored in the crumbs of soil called aggregates. These aggregates are held together with sticky substances, again produced by microorganisms. The tunnels of worms and moles conduct air and water through the soil to a depth of as much as 25 feet.

CARING FOR SOIL CREATURES

A healthy soil is a complex ecosystem of plants and animals, predators and prey. If left to itself a healthy soil is a balanced, self-sustaining system. But many soils are not left to themselves — they are modified when we humans grow crops and gardens. The secret to beautiful gardens thus lies not only in viewing the soil as an ecosystem, but also in seeing ourselves as an intricate part of that system.

Soil naturally contains a balance of beneficial and harmful creatures. One secret to keeping it healthy is to keep this balance intact; another is to remember that every action you take produces a reaction in the soil environment.

Studies have compared farms with plowed fields to those maintained under no-till methods.

The plowed fields suffered more wind and water erosion than the no-till fields, but that was no shocker. What did catch scientists by surprise, however, was the difference in the health of the organisms in the soils. Earthworms are often used as indicators of healthy soil: the more worms, the better the soil. And the study found that the plowed fields had very few worms. After only a couple of years under no-till methods, though, populations of earthworms had substantially increased. The longer the fields were cultivated under no-till techniques, the greater the number of worms. Researchers concluded that no-till farming could increase yields while decreasing the need for fertilizers and pesticides.

Resting Rototillers

Rototillers are mechanical worms: They turn the organic matter resting on the soil surface into the earth, just as worms do, only a lot faster. But tilling also destroys worm burrows. Do it too much and the worms will leave for a quieter neighborhood. The health of your soil will then decline, period. Tilling also breaks apart soil aggregates and capillaries and makes the earth more prone to compaction, all of which can adversely affect soil organisms. It isn't necessary to retire your tiller, but for the healthiest soil, use that mechanical worm as little as possible.

Mycorrhizae

Roots of plants absorb moisture and nutrients through growths called root hairs. These single-celled filaments, which grow at the very tips of roots, are produced in incredible numbers: The roots of a single clump of grass can have billions. Root hairs weave around soil aggregates and particles, absorbing the dissolved nutrients in the soil solution. It's a very efficient system, but even the billions of root hairs produced by a typical plant cannot supply all of the nutrients it needs. Enter *mycorrhizae*. This is the name of a group of fungi that live in virtually every soil on earth. One end of each long, very slender fungal filament penetrates the epidermis of a root hair, absorbing carbohydrates and other nutrients from the cell's fluid cytoplasm; the other end wraps around a microscopic soil particle. The fungus absorbs nutrients directly from the rock particle, a neat trick. It then translocates the nutrients to the root hair, where the plant absorbs them.

Mycorrhizae are important to almost all plants, but extremely so to those growing in wet areas or in acid soils whose nutrients are not all readily available. In such soils mycorrhizae often supply the nutrition that makes the difference between healthy and unhealthy plants.

Mycorrhizae are not easy to see, for they most often exist as a thin, nearly colorless film covering a plant's roots. Maintaining a few permanent plants in a seasonal garden — by keeping some perennials in your vegetable garden, for instance — is a way to keep these beneficial fungi close by.

Feed Your Friends

As good hosts always feed their guests well, so a good gardener properly feeds the critters that live in the soil. In fact, nourishing your subterranean buddies is even easier than pleasing your human guests because your earthbound guests want just one thing: organic matter. Though you have heard this refrain before, it is worth repeating one more time. Organic matter in the form of compost, rotted manure, mulch, or cover crops is as close to a guarantee of healthy soil as there is. Adding it annually attracts healthful organisms like ringing the lunch bell in a mess hall brings hungry soldiers. The beneficial creatures that thrive in rich garden soil do so in large part because of the organic matter it contains. It is that simple.

2

Making Compost: Gardener's Gold

We humans like to think that we invented composting, but — humbling as this may be — we didn't. The art of composting was actually practiced eons before people ever walked the earth.

In the monsoon-swept islands of the Indonesian archipelago lives a bird called the orange-footed megapode. The male of this species spends the better part of the year building a compost pile of fallen leaves and sand. When he is done, the mound measures from 3 to 10 feet deep and up to 20 feet around. The female then excavates a hole in the middle of the mound and lays a clutch of eggs, which she buries beneath the compost. The male then takes over the care of the eggs. As the compost decomposes, the heat it gives off incubates the eggs. The male checks the temperature of the mound every few hours by sticking his head in the compost, and adds or subtracts material to keep the mound at an even 92°F. In about two months the chicks hatch, climb out of the pile, and fly away.

When people discovered composting it was not as a revolutionary system of day care or a way to keep men productively occupied. Instead, they saw the art of composting as a method of increasing the fertility of farmlands, which allowed for the production of more food per acre of tilled land. For much of the twentieth century, though, this age-old practice was replaced by applications of synthetic fertilizer. Composting became quaint and old-fashioned until it became increasingly obvious that the use of synthetic fertilizer alone was decreasing the fertility of thousands of acres. Little by little people began to rediscover the value and art of composting. New methods were invented and old ones rediscovered. As scientists investigated the once-lowly compost, they discovered that this simple substance was vital to the creation and maintenance of healthy soil — something old-timers knew all along.

This Indonesian bird builds a compost pile that it uses to incubate its eggs.

Why Is Compost So Valuable?

Compost improves soil by adding both major and minor nutrients in forms that make them available to plants a little at a time over a long period. The organic matter in compost binds to existing soil particles, which augments the earth's ability to retain moisture while also increasing the amount of oxygen in the soil. The improved soil structure allows capillaries to form, which improves both drainage and aeration. The microorganisms naturally present in compost can aid plants in the uptake of nutrients, buffer the populations of any pathogenic organisms, and beneficially modify the pH of the soil. All that, *and* it incubates little orange-footed megapodes. What more could you ask for?

TYPES OF MICROORGANISMS

Psychrophiles. These are cool-weather bacteria that grow between 32 and 85°F but are most active when temperatures are between 50 and 70°F. These are the beasties that commonly survive well in refrigerators, turning milk sour and spoiling food. They metabolize food by oxidation. A by-product of this is heat, which warms the compost to a temperature suitable for the growth of other types of bacteria.

Mesophiles. When the temperature of the compost reaches about 70°F, mesophilic bacteria begin to grow rapidly. Most bacteria are mesophiles and thrive at between 70 and 105°F. As temperatures within the compost climb past 100°F, the cool-temperature psychrophiles decline in number and the compost pile becomes dominated by mesophiles.

Thermophiles. As the mesophilic bacteria heat the compost pile past the 100°F mark another type of bacteria, called thermophiles for their love of heat, takes over. Thermophiles continue to metabolize the organic matter in the pile, sending the internal temperatures of the mound to as high as 160°F. This high temperature usually lasts for only a short time — sometimes as little as three days.

How to Decompose

Decomposition is the engine that drives the creation of compost — and the fuel that runs that engine is microorganisms. There are many different kinds of microorganisms, from bacteria (in their myriad forms) to fungi, but all play similar roles in the creation of compost: They simplify the complex. They take large molecules that growing plants can't use and break them into smaller ones that plants can use. It's a rotting job, but somebody's got to do it.

MICROORGANISMS

A microorganism is a living thing that is too small to be seen with the unaided eye. There are thousands of kinds, from viruses so small they can only be observed with an electron microscope, to bacteria and fungi that can form large, slimy colonies. To grow and multiply, microorganisms need four principal things:

- A source of carbon
- A source of nitrogen
- Adequate moisture
- Oxygen to help metabolize it all

Carbon. The molecule at the heart of all life on earth, carbon is a principal ingredient in carbohydrates and the main source of energy for microorganisms. As plants grow, they photosynthesize carbon dioxide and water into carbohydrates. When those same plants are added to the compost pile, they provide a rich source of carbon for microorganisms.

Nitrogen. Nitrogen is used by microorganisms to produce substances called enzymes, which in turn break down complex carbon compounds into smaller, more digestible bits. While an enzyme breaks apart complex carbon molecules, the enzyme itself remains intact. In other words, a little nitrogen goes a long way in a compost pile. Too little nitrogen and the microorganisms can't manufacture enough enzymes to properly decompose the plant material; too much, and lots of smelly ammonia is produced.

Moisture. Water is essential for microorganisms to do their work, but that water needs to be in balance with everything else. Too little, and the decomposition process slows dramatically; too much expels oxygen from the compost pile, suffocating the aerobic bacteria. The optimal moisture content is 45 to 50 percent.

Oxygen. Most of the microorganisms working in a compost pile use oxygen to metabolize the goodies they are decomposing. Bacteria that use oxygen are called aerobes, while those that do not are termed anaerobes. Aerobic bacteria work much faster and more efficiently. The microorganisms break down carbon compounds into carbon dioxide and water, and release important nutrients, including nitrogen, phosphorous, potassium, and magnesium.

ACTINOMYCETES AND FUNGI

Actinomycetes are the gray, threadlike filaments you commonly see as you turn over the cool sections of nearly finished compost piles. Fungi, like their near relatives the actinomycetes, also work in the cooler sections of the compost pile after the bacteria have done their jobs.

Commonly called mold bacteria, actinomycetes seem to be part bacterium and part fungus. Among other things, actinomycetes produce some of the most important antibiotics used to control diseases. In the compost pile they sweep up after the bacteria, consuming the tidbits left

---

ENZYMES

Enzymes are nitrogen-based substances produced by most living things, including bacteria and fungi, and are essential to the healthy production of compost. Different enzymes assist in the digestion of different substances, including starch, cellulose, lignin, and plant oils. Enzymes break these complex compounds into simpler substances that are then more easily metabolized. An interesting aspect of enzymes is that they continue to work long after the creature that produced them has itself become part of the compost pile.

---

behind. As they work they give off the compounds that give compost and soil a sweet, earthy smell.

Fungi are primitive plants that break down cellulose and lignin, substances that provide support for plant cells and are indigestible to just about everything else. Newspaper, a favorite target for decomposition by fungi, is loaded with lignins and cellulose. This explains why newspapers are some of the last things to completely decay.

WONDERFUL WORMS

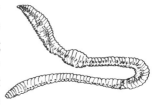

Earthworms and their relatives are never going to win any prizes for being photogenic or aesthetically pleasing. This doesn't matter, of course, because worms have a very high self-image. They know how important they are to the health of both soil and compost.

Worms like to do two things: eat and make more worms. As worms slide through the compost pile they munch on whatever gets in their way, ingesting partly decayed organic matter and bacteria. As this slurry makes its way through each worm's gut tiny stones grind it into finer particles, and digestive enzymes break down the complex organic molecules into easily absorbed ones. Worms absorb some of the freed nutrients while expelling others in the dark, fertile, granular "castings" left behind. These castings are concentrated sources of many nutrients, including nitrogen, phosphorous, potassium, and magnesium.

A single worm can efficiently digest and recycle its own weight in compost every day. Thousands of them can literally turn over a large compost pile in just days. Each worm produces about twenty new worms every week or so. These mature in as little as six weeks and begin producing more offspring. Over the course of a year thousands of worms can become part of an active compost pile.

Worms thrive in places that are moist, dark, and warm, with adequate levels of oxygen. Because microorganisms make up a large portion of what a worm digests, plentiful worm populations are indicative of good microbial activity.

Great Compost from the Right Ingredients

Some folks say that great compost can be made from just about anything that was once alive. But it isn't quite that simple. While it's true that everything eventually goes from "ashes to ashes and dust to dust," some things really stink along the way. Great compost should be easy to make, easy to manage, and inoffensive. To do this the ingredient list becomes as important as the method. The best ingredients for great compost that doesn't offend the more delicate senses have one thing in common; they all come from vegetative sources.

ASHES

Those of us who still routinely use fireplaces and woodstoves generate a good supply of wood ashes over the course of a year. Wood ashes contain many different nutrients used by plants, especially potassium, and the burning process makes them easily absorbed into the matrix of the compost pile. In addition to firewood, some gardeners toss the rinds of such fruits as oranges, grapefruit, and bananas into the fire, along with used tea bags. These add even more phosphorous and potassium to the bed of ashes. Ashes from commercially produced charcoal or municipal incinerators should not be used.

Before adding ashes to your compost pile, sift them through a screen to remove any large pieces of unburned wood or inorganic items. Sprinkle a fine layer atop each 12- to 18-inch-thick layer of organic matter as you construct your pile.

GRASS CLIPPINGS

Many folks today have mulching lawn mowers that chop grass clippings into fine pieces and redeposit them over the lawn. This effectively recycles the nutrients back into the environment. If you still rake, bag, or otherwise collect your grass clippings, they can be effective additions to the compost pile — although clippings gathered from lawns treated with pesticides should not be used.

Remember, however, that fresh, green grass clippings tend to form mats that seal out oxygen from sections of the compost pile, producing unwanted odors. To avoid this, allow the clippings to dry in the sun before you rake the lawn. If drying on the lawn is impractical, the fresh clippings can be mixed with organic material that is already dry, such as dead leaves. Finally, fresh clippings can be added in thin layers as the compost pile is built up. This works even better if the clippings are covered with a sprinkling of wood ashes.

PINE NEEDLES

Because they have very thick cuticles, pine needles break down very slowly in the compost pile, even with the aid of a activator. They should be considered a good texturizer, for they keep the compost light and fluffy, but should not make up the majority of any pile. Pine needles, as well as the leaves of beech and oak, also contain high amounts of water soluble acids, such as tannic acid, and compost made from them tends to have a low pH — perfect stuff for growing evergreens such as rhododendrons, pines, spruces and hollies.

KITCHEN SCRAPS

The kitchen yields a lot of garbage, some of which can be turned into great compost. The wrapper leaves of cabbage and lettuce, stalks of broccoli and cauliflower and celery, pea pods, and corn husks are just some of things from the grocery store that never make it to the table. A benefit of these vegetable scraps is micronutrients. Generations ago, people ate food grown from just their local area. If the region was deficient in a trace mineral, such as molybdenum, then so was the food. Today a garden salad can be made from vegetables grown in California, Florida, and a host of other places. Each region contributes its unique blend of micronutrients to the salad — as well as to the garbage that lands on the compost pile.

To add kitchen scraps to a compost pile, first chop them into fine pieces, then distribute them over the pile. To speed the process of decomposition, some folks give everything a brief spin through a food processor before adding it to the pile.

Don't add garbage from animal sources, however, as this is very slow to break down, often produces foul odors, violates many local ordinances, and attracts unwelcome animals. One well-known conservation group in New England adds animal as well as vegetable scraps to its compost pile each summer. The pile has to be closed down periodically when black bears camp out there awaiting dinner. At least they turn the pile free of charge.

NEWSPAPERS

Instead of hauling them to a recycling center, consider adding newspapers to your compost pile. Some folks don't, because the ink used to print them contains polycyclic aromatic hydrocarbons (PAH), and some people question whether food grown from compost that includes newspapers is safe.

To avoid this debate entirely, use the newspapers only as a mulch around ornamental plantings. Spread sections a few pages thick on freshly raked ground, water until the papers are soaked, then add a layer of organic mulch. The wet papers form a barrier to weeds and slowly decompose without troubling anyone. Newspapers printed from soy-based inks can be added straight to the compost pile after being chopped, diced, or sliced.

LEAVES

For many people leaves can provide a large portion of any compost pile. Even a small yard yields bags and bags in autumn. One thing that should be noted up front, though, is that leaves are not all created equal. Some decompose quickly and easily, while others take their own sweet time. The speed at which a leaf decomposes is often related to the thickness of a leaf structure called the cuticle. Leaf cuticles are thin films that inhibit the loss of moisture from the surface of the leaf. They also inhibit decomposition. Some trees, such as maples and deciduous magnolias, along with many plants that grow in wet soils, have thin leaves with almost no cuticles. These leaves break down quickly in the compost pile. Other leaves, such as those from deciduous oaks and beeches, have a shiny gloss that signals the presence of thick cuticles. These break down much more slowly than thin-cuticled leaves. As for evergreen plants, their leaves almost always have very thick cuticles; they can take years to decompose completely.

To add leaves to your compost pile, make sure they are first chopped up; mix thin-cuticle leaves with those having medium and thick cuticles. A good way to chop leaves is to mow the lawn instead of raking it. The mower will chop the leaves while also blending fresh grass clippings into the mix. Rake it all up and add it to your pile. The grass clippings will speed microbial activity and the leaves will keep the clippings from forming mats. A leaf shredder is also excellent for chopping leaves.

SEAWEED

If you garden by the sea, you'll find a ready supply of excellent compost material washing up on the beach twice a day. Seaweed is high in potassium and micronutrients, including boron, iodine, calcium, and magnesium, that such crops as potatoes need to thrive. When adding seaweed to the compost pile, be sure to mix it thoroughly with other ingredients to help prevent it from concentrating into a thick mat. Seaweed contains considerable sodium, but that can be kept to acceptable levels if the bulk of the pile is other than seaweed.

Coal ash. Ashes from coal contain sulfur and iron in amounts high enough to damage plants.

Charcoal. Almost pure carbon and thus very stable, charcoal added to the compost pile will probably just sit there, never to decay. Charcoal that is ground into a powder can be added if sprinkled over the pile.

Colored paper. Papers with colored inks should not be added to compost piles because some of the ink ingredients may be toxic.

Diseased plants. Some plant diseases can survive even hot composting if the conditions are right. If diseased plants are added to the compost pile the compost should be sterilized, not just pasteurized, before use.

Pet litter. Pregnant women and children should not handle pet litter, because cat droppings can sometimes contain parasites that can infect humans. *Toxoplasma gondii,* a parasite transmittable to unborn children, can cause brain and eye disease. *Toxocara cati* is a parasitic nematode that can cause eye infections.

Pet droppings. Manures from omnivores and carnivores should not be added to the compost pile, but manures from most herbavores are essentially processed plant material and make excellent additions. Bird droppings, however, can also transmit diseases.

Pesticides. Some people have been known to spray their compost piles with pesticides to keep insects and pests away. In addition to contaminating the entire pile with toxic chemicals, pesticides often kill the very microorganisms needed to make the compost in the first place.

Animal products. Meats, oils, bones: If it comes from an animal, don't use it in the compost pile. Bits and pieces of animals decompose very slowly compared to plant material, and they're often much more, ahem, aromatic.

Seeds and pits. Besides attracting rodents, which like to nibble on them, seeds and pits are slow to decompose.

Carbon and Nitrogen

Organic matter contains carbon and nitrogen compounds. Both of these elements are continually recycled through plants by two processes, the carbon cycle and the nitrogen cycle. But not all plants contain the same ratios of these elements. As microorganisms decompose organic material they produce ammonia (NH_3), which is then metabolized into nitrates (NO_3). If the plant material being decomposed contains high amounts of nitrogen compared to carbon, the microorganisms cannot metabolize all the ammonia they produce, and the compost pile begins to smell like household cleanser. If the plant material being decomposed contains low amounts of nitrogen compared to carbon, the microorganisms metabolize not only all of the ammonia they produce but also any other available nitrogen in the soil. This slows the decomposition process to a crawl and often leads to a nitrogen deficiency in the compost as well.

To produce fertile, sweet smelling compost, a compost pile's ingredients should have an average carbon to nitrogen ratio of about 25 or 30 to 1. Nobody expects you to be absolutely precise. This isn't rocket science; educated guesses are permitted. With a little practice most veteran composters find their favorite recipes and stick to them. Some like their compost to have a little ammonia smell so they know that enough nitrogen remains in the pile to guarantee speedy decomposition. Others walk on the wild side and try to achieve a exact carbon-nitrogen balance in their search for the perfect compost. Either way the end result is good stuff for the garden.

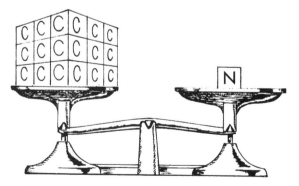

The carbon-to-nitrogen ratio of your compost pile should be about 25 or 30 to 1.

Alfalfa	12:1
Ash, alder leaves	25:1
Manure with stall bedding	25:1
Manure, rotted	20:1
Oak leaves	50:1
Pine needles	60:1 to 100:1
Vegetable trimmings	25:1
Grass clippings	20:1
Clover	20:1
Sugarcane	50:1
Cornstalks	60:1
Paper	170:1
Sawdust	500:1
Straw	80:1 to 150:1
Timothy hay	25:1
Weeds	30:1

Compost Activators

Lists and charts of carbon-to-nitrogen ratios offer excellent ingredient guidelines for mixing the perfect compost pile. In truth, however, backyard compost piles consist less of ideal recipes and more of what is handy. Because of this, new compost often has too much carbon and too few microorganisms. To remedy these imbalances, activators are added to the pile. A compost activator contributes either high nitrogen, microorganisms, or both, and provides a quick boost to the decomposition process.

MANURE

Many manures are potent compost activators and contain abundant quantities of beneficial microorganisms and nitrogen as well as potassium and phosphorous. Aged or rotted manures are best, because they have lower urea levels than fresh manure, are easier to handle, and are much less smelly.

It seems that everybody who uses manure as an activator has a favorite kind. Horse and cow manures are widely available and probably used more than any other kinds. Some gardeners swear by sheep and goat manures. Poultry has a large following, with the highest ratings given to chicken, duck, turkey, and goose manure. Its adherents testify that poultry manure gets compost off to a faster start than anything else. In recent years, however, processed cricket manure has become a very popular activator. It is now widely available in garden centers.

COMPOST

In a way, making compost is like baking good sourdough bread, where the activator for one batch comes from the preceding. Once you have made a batch of great compost, just save some of it to add to the new pile. The old compost has the correct carbon-to-nitrogen ratio and is full of beneficial organisms. You can add old compost by mixing it directly into the new pile or by making a batch of compost tea (see page 20).

SOIL

All soils teem with life, but some are better for activating the compost pile than others. The best soil to add is rich, sandy loam. Soil should be added in 2- to 3-inch layers every 6 inches throughout the pile. Do not take soil from areas that have been sprayed with pesticides. If sandy loam isn't available, any good topsoil will do, including forest soil and muck soil.

MEALS

Whether derived from animal or vegetable sources, meals are excellent sources of nitrogen. The most common animal meals include blood meal, horn meal, bonemeal, and hoof meal. Many folks don't like adding powdered livestock to their compost pile and instead sprinkle on cottonseed or alfalfa meal. Whatever meal you choose, simply supplement with a heavy sprinkling every 6 inches or so and add water; within forty-eight hours the pile will already be warming up.

♦ Compost Activators

Alfalfa meal	Cottonseed meal
Blood meal	Fish meal
Bonemeal	Manure
Compost	Soil

Compost slowly and reliably adds nutrients to the garden. But sometimes it is nice to speed things up a bit, as when the summer veggies need a little boost. Enter compost tea. Place about a bushel of fresh, finished compost in a waterproof garbage can and add water to within about a foot of the top. Cover and allow to brew for a few days in a cool, shady place. Decant into a watering can and pour over the garden for a safe, natural, easily absorbed fertilizer.

Ethics and Aesthetics

For one reason or another, having a big pile of stuff decomposing in the backyard makes some people's neighbors nervous. They complain that the pile is unsightly, that it smells bad, or that it attracts nasty vermin to the neighborhood. Once compost is in the garden, of course, you're home free: Nobody complains about the finished product. It's the process that gets to them. Or more correctly, what some folks believe the process to be. Of course compost made from the correct ingredients and in the proper way has none of these negative qualities. However, it remains a fact that to make compost in many areas of the country, a good gardener has to be a good diplomat in addition to being a good gardener.

LOCATION AND APPEARANCE
Compost piles should be located close to a water source and within easy distance of the garden. In northern regions the pile is often located in a sunny spot with retaining walls on the east, north, and west sides, to maximize exposure to the sun. To increase the warming effect of a southern exposure drape black plastic over the compost pile in cold weather. This not only keeps the compost warm and toasty, but makes it look more presentable to any neighbors sneaking a peek over the backyard fence. Be sure to place the pile on well-drained soil, for a pile with a soggy bottom will be much more inefficient. During cold winters cover the compost pile with a foot or two of hay to insulate the pile, and make the compost more decorative. Sort of a barnyard motif. In warm areas compost is often made in the shade to help retain moisture. Many people design their compost systems to be out of their neighbors' line of sight, either below a fence line or behind a hedge. In addition, more permanent compost structures are often incorporated into the garden, with the walls used as homes to flowering vines (such as morning glory or wisteria) or vining vegetables (including melons and indeterminate tomatoes).

SIZE
A compost pile must be at least 1 cubic yard to heat up to the ideal temperature. Small piles are affected by outdoor conditions, often cooling off too quickly in cold weather. Piles that are too large, on the other hand, often have poor air circulation at the center, which can overheat the pile and kill off beneficial microorganisms. A compost pile of 1 cubic yard measures 3 feet by 3 feet by 3 feet.

LAYERS

Just about every recipe for compost calls for the pile to be built in layers. Traditional compost piles were made of tiers constructed by alternating layers of three or more materials, including manure, vegetable matter, sand, and soil. After the first set of layers was built, another was built on top of the first. More and more tiers were added atop each other until the pile reached the desired height. Many people still construct their compost piles this traditional way. Layering is an easy way to gauge the approximate amounts of each ingredient in the pile. What layering also does, which is undesirable, is concentrate individual ingredients in different parts of the pile.

Another method of building a compost pile, and one that is easier for many people, is to use turned tiers. This method produces a uniform compost from the start, with none of the pockets of concentrated material common in new, layered piles. Make the base tier of layers, including an activator, following the traditional method. When the first tier is finished, use a garden fork to lightly mix the layers. Construct the next tier atop the first, turning it lightly as well. Continue until the pile has reached the desired height. Piles made this way heat up quickly, are more uniform from the start, and produce a high quality compost.

DRAINAGE

A compost pile should drain as well as good garden soil. Just as you wouldn't put a garden on top of hardpan, compost piles shouldn't be placed in depressions that collect standing water, on areas of compacted soil, on slabs of asphalt or concrete, or atop sheets of plastic. Piles built on such features drain poorly and have poor aeration. Compost from these piles is often smelly and of poor quality. To avoid these problems construct a raised compost pile. Raised piles are built on bases, such as wooden pallets, that allow easy drainage of excess moisture and improved aeration. Be sure the platform is no more than 6 inches high, however, or the air beneath the pile will stay so cool that it will slow the decomposition process.

Simple compost bins are often all you need. This system uses six wooden stakes to support a wrap of chicken wire. The wire provides good aeration but allows the edges of the pile to dry out during warm weather. In summer be sure to sprinkle the sides and top frequently to keep the compost pile moist.

BEAUTIFYING THE COMPOST PILE

People who make their compost in bins have proved quite inventive when it comes to beautifying their compost piles. One plan consists of smoothing the top of the pile and planting vining types of cherry tomatoes or cucumbers on the flat space. As the plants grow larger, train them to cascade over the sides of the bin. If you mix in a few squash seeds as well the resulting avalanche of foliage will also be decorated with plentiful, showy squash blossoms. Some people insist that cherry tomatoes grown this way taste even better than those grown in the garden. After harvest the plants are easy to uproot and add to the compost pile.

A second way to beautify the compost bin is to plant the bin as you would a strawberry jar. Insert flowering-size plugs of bedding plants, such as petunias or impatiens, into the sides of the bin. They will grow and cascade down, providing color and camouflage all summer long.

Sunflowers can also be used to provide camouflage for compost piles. Plant tall varieties of sunflowers such as 'Russian Giant' or 'Giant Sungold' around the perimeter of the pile. In short order they will grow into a beautiful green screen that in summer is topped with huge golden yellow blooms.

The Best Compost Makers

As we have seen, the best makers of compost in the world are not agricultural researchers, farmers, or master gardeners, but birds, the megapodes of Australia and Indonesia, and worms. When the composting systems of megapodes and worms are carefully examined, they reveal three factors common to the making of great compost: inclusion of sand and soil, turning the pile, and appropriate particle size.

The compost piles of megapodes are templates for hot composting. They include a combination of leaves and sandy soil. The sandy soil contributes microorganisms that break down the organic matter, while its high sand content provides excellent drainage. The birds turn the pile daily, which maximizes aeration and regulates temperatures.

Nightcrawlers and other worms have perfected cold composting. Nightcrawlers leave their burrows at night in search of pieces of dead leaves. When they find one they grab it and withdraw back into the earth to eat it. The plant parts are digested by the worm, which breaks them into smaller pieces that are just the right size for smaller worms, called nematodes, to break into even smaller pieces. Fungi and bacteria then reduce the particles to a size that allows many of the plant's nutrients to be released into the soil, where other plants can use them. The keys to a worm's cold composting are movement and reduction of small amounts of plant material.

Using the principles employed by these natural composters, two excellent recipes have been developed — one hot and one cold.

THE CALIFORNIA MEGAPODE SYSTEM (HOT)

Combining some of the principles used by megapodes with formulas developed at the University of California, the California Megapode System uses an easily constructed portable bin.

Making the Bin: From 2 x 4 lumber make four frames, each 3 feet high and 4 feet wide. Reinforce the corners with angled braces. Cover each frame with chicken wire. (You can use the larger mesh illustrated here, and it's less expensive. The half-inch mesh, however, will hold its shape better than larger meshes.) Stretch the chicken wire tightly across the frame and staple into place. Join two frames together by installing a pair of hinges set so the frames can easily open into an **L** shape. Repeat with the second pair of frames. Install screen-door hooks on the frames so that when the frames are placed into an **L** shape, they can be locked together, forming a closed bin.

Making the Compost: Whatever plant material you choose, be sure to shred it, chop it, or mow it before putting it in the pile. The smaller the pieces, the more efficient the decomposition will be. A rotary mower that makes a few passes over a lawn covered with dry autumn leaves produces bountiful amounts of raw organic matter chopped to perfection. Spread a 6-inch layer of shredded, chopped or otherwise processed plant material in the bottom of the assembled bin, then sprinkle on a generous amount of an activator, such as alfalfa meal or manure. Top with an inch or 2 of clean sand or sandy soil, and water well. Continue to add layers until the bin is full. Every three days or so unhook the frames, reassemble them next to the pile, and fork the compost into the empty bin. In two weeks to one month, depending on the season, the compost will be ready to use. Spread on the garden immediately, or cover with a waterproof tarp and store until ready to use.

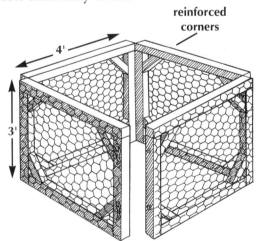

Bin for "hot" composting consists of four simple frames, reinforced at the corners and covered with chicken wire. Frames are attached at two corners with pairs of hinges.

THE SHEET METHOD (COLD)

Sheet composting uses some of the same principles employed by worms when they compost plant refuse from farm fields. Instead of constructing a compost pile, with sheet composting you return plant material directly to the soil that is to be enriched. Sheet composting involves mixing organic material with the soil itself, usually with the help of a spade or rototiller. It's an excellent way to improve heavy soils high in clay, or alluvial soils with abundant sand or gravel.

Sheet composting is a cold, and therefore slower, system and is done either in fall, after the garden has been harvested, or in areas that can lay fallow for several months. Whatever organic matter you gather will work, including leaves, grass clippings, and manure. To retain as much fertility in the soil as possible, do not chop the plant material into extremely small pieces. Small pieces decompose quickly, releasing nutrients into the soil before plants can use them.

Making the Compost: Before collecting the plant material, rototill the garden to a depth of at least 6 inches. Spread a 6- to 12-inch layer of plant material, such as leaves or grass clippings, over the soil.

Sprinkle a layer of activator, such as manure, over the plant material and rototill everything into the soil. The rototiller does the job of the worm, dragging plant material to where bacteria and fungi can incorporate it into the soil.

COMPOST AND GUNPOWDER

In times past the people of Europe found uses for compost that had nothing to do with gardening. One such use took advantage of the fact that as compost piles made of plant and animal remains decomposed, potassium nitrate formed. After these piles sat around for about two years, potassium nitrate was at its highest level, and it was extracted from the compost pile. The chemical was then mixed with sulfur and charcoal to produce gunpowder, which, in turn, was used in weaponry. Not the most peaceful use of compost perhaps, but interesting nonetheless.

To sheet compost, spread 6 to 8 inches of plant material on the soil, sprinkle with manure, and rototill the soil.

THE INDOOR WORM METHOD

In winter, when outdoor composting becomes impractical in many regions, a small indoor system can be used to recycle food scraps from the kitchen. The system is easy to construct and use — worms are the only moving parts. The best place for a worm compost box is a cool, dimly lit place that stays above 40°F but below 80°F. Popular places include the basement or a heated garage.

To determine how many worms your system will need, estimate the weight of compostable kitchen scraps your family produces each day. You will need twice as many worms as the average daily amount of compostable garbage. (If your daily scraps weigh 1 pound, for instance, you will need 2 pounds of worms.) You can purchase specially bred compost worms from many garden centers and mail-order garden supply companies.

Making the Box: For a typical family (2 adults and 1.3 kids producing a pound of kitchen scraps per day), build a box that measures about 2 feet wide and 3 feet long, with sides about 1 foot high. Prepare the worm bed by mixing equal parts of at least two of the following: shredded newspaper, rotted manure, compost, leaf mold, and potting soil. Moisten the ingredients lightly but thoroughly. Spread the bedding mix over half of the box, leaving the other portion empty, and add the worms to the bedding. Cover with a sturdy screen of hardware cloth to keep unwanted visitors, such as cats or mice, away from the bedding.

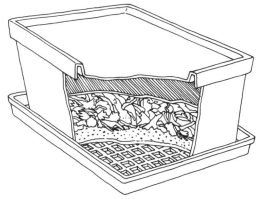

Worm-casting compost is richer and more fertile than any other type. It makes a wonderful addition to seed-starting mix or a fine ingredient in mixes for container plants.

Making the Compost: At the end of the day reduce your kitchen scraps with a blender, using only enough water to process, and add them to the bedding. To collect the finished compost mix up another batch of bedding, fill the other side of the box, and add the daily scraps to the new bedding. After the worms have migrated to the new bedding, collect the castings from the old side.

Troubleshooting Tips

People who compost tend to be an independent bunch and often like to tweak established recipes and systems in attempts to improve them. Here are some points to keep in mind as you experiment in your search for the perfect compost system.

WATERING

Good compost should have a moisture content resembling that of good garden soil. This ensures that the microorganisms responsible for decomposition have enough air and water. To add water after the pile is built, make a shallow well or dish-shaped impression in the top of the pile to collect rainwater. Then poke holes into the bottom of the depression periodically with a crowbar.

TURNING

Turning the compost pile may be a ritual, but people do it to increase the compost's uniformity and shorten the time needed to produce it. If you never turn the pile, compost will still happen, but on *its* time schedule, not yours. Most compost piles should be turned every four to seven days while they are hot (over 100°F). After that time they can be turned every six to ten weeks until the compost is ready.

CHOPPING

The smaller the particles, the faster they decompose. Chunks of plant material, such as brush, cabbage stems, and matted leaves, should be chopped into smaller pieces before being put in the compost pile. Chopping breaks down the cell walls of plant tissues, allows places for microorganisms to enter the material, reduces the size of the pile, and increases the surface area of the plant material — all of which speed the decomposition process.

AERATION

Compost systems the size of the California megapode system or smaller usually have no problem with oxygen content within the pile. Large piles, however, often do. To increase the aeration of large piles, try building them around ventilating stacks made of perforated pipe or rolls of wire mesh. The pipes can be placed either horizontally or vertically, with the top portion extending above the pile. Some people add coarse materials, such as cornstalks or brush. This does increase aeration, but the coarse material decomposes so much more slowly than the rest of the pile that the quality of the finished compost is often compromised. A simpler aeration technique is to use a crowbar and poke deep holes into the pile. This imitates wormholes, which are responsible for the natural aeration of garden soil.

VENTILATING STACKS

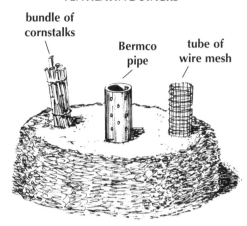

bundle of cornstalks

Bermco pipe

tube of wire mesh

Many different types of materials can be used to conduct fresh air into the heart of the compost pile. Regardless of the material used it is much easier to build the pile around the aerator, rather than attempt to add it later.

TROUBLESHOOTING YOUR COMPOST PILE

SYMPTOM	POSSIBLE CAUSE	SOLUTION
Unpleasant odor; pile is not excessively wet; no ammonia smell	Not enough oxygen reaching the center of the pile	Improve aeration.
Unpleasant odor; pile very wet	Excess water depleting the oxygen in the pile	Improve drainage by aerating the pile or turning it onto a raised platform.
Unpleasant ammonia odor	Too much nitrogen in the pile	Add high-carbon materials, turn, and aerate.
Pile not heating up	Too much carbon in the pile	Add high-nitrogen materials, turn, and aerate.
Pile not heating up	Not enough moisure throughout the pile	Poke deep, vertical holes into the pile with a rod or crowbar and pour water into them.
Pile not heating up	Turning needed	Turn the pile.
Pile not heating up	Heating cycle completed	Examine the compost for dark, crumbly texture and earthy smell, which means it's ready for the garden.
Compost warm only in the center of the pile	Pile too small	Collect more materials and turn them into the existing pile.
Weeds on the pile	Seeds at surface of cold compost pile germinate	Pull up the weeds as they appear so they don't rob the compost of moisture and nutrients.
Maggots in the pile	Some species of flies lay eggs on decomposing plant material	Add a layer of hay to the pile and cover with screening or cover pile with 2 inches of sandy soil.

Plant material that is completely chopped makes more uniform compost in less time.

WOOD ASHES AS ODOR CONTROL

Many of the large commercial facilities that produce compost sewage sludge and other materials use wood ashes to control the often-offensive odors. Other producers cover the fresh piles with ash to insulate and retain heat while also controlling any odors. Though the exact mechanism by which wood ash absorbs odor is not known, many people suspect that ashes work much like activated charcoal.

Backyard composters can control odors by adding wood ashes to the pile as it is built or by sprinkling ashes over the surface of the pile periodically. This is most effective right after the pile has been turned. The use of wood ashes commonly raises the pH of finished compost to between 7.0 and 9.0.

COMPARISON OF TRADITIONAL COMPOSTING METHODS

TYPE	ADVANTAGES	DISADVANTAGES
Slow outdoor pile	low maintenance	takes up to two years to produce compost; often loses nutrients to leaching before the compost is usable; can be large and untidy
Hot outdoor pile	produces compost quickly; destroys many pathogens and weed seeds; retains fertility; does not attract insects or animal pests	can be large and unsightly; needs to be turned often and is therefore time- and labor-intensive
California megapode bin	neat appearance; portable; produces compost quickly and destroys many pathogens and weed seeds; does not attract insect pests; not susceptible to disease; holds heat and provides better aeration than pile systems; retains fertility	requires time and labor to build the bin and turn the compost
Other bins or boxes	neat appearance; holds heat and provides better aeration than pile systems; faster than some pile systems	requires time and labor to build the container
Tumblers	neat appearance; some very easy to use; can produce compost quickly with no loss of nutients through leaching	often expensive; produce only small amounts of compost
Sheet composting	can compost large amounts of material at a time; improves the quality of the soil; needs no piles or containers	requires many months to produce compost; requires time and labor to turn the material into the soil
Garbage can composting	easy; can be done in small spaces; not labor-intensive	often smells bad; can attract flies; requires proper carbon to nitrogen ratio to avoid a slimy, smelly mess
Worm composting	easy; can be done indoors in a small space; no odor; can be added to continuously; produces very fertile compost; recycles food waste	can attract fruitflies; requires time and labor to build the worm box

The Finished Product

Compost is much more valuable than the time and effort it takes to make it, but good compost is most valuable right after it is "done." Compost that lies around unused for months on end loses much of its nutrient value and structure. So how can you tell when a compost pile is ready to use? Fortunately, finished compost has certain characteristics distinct from raw compost. Once you're familiar with them, determining the finishing point of compost is easy.

TEXTURE AND FEEL

Finished compost looks crumbly. Crumbly, of course, is one of those great words that can mean a host of things. When describing compost, though, it means that large clumps of compost easily fall apart into many smaller clumps. These clumps, which are held together with the by-product of microbial activity, indicate that the compost is fertile. You may still recognize some bits of plant material, such as straw fibers, but even these should easily fall apart into smaller pieces.

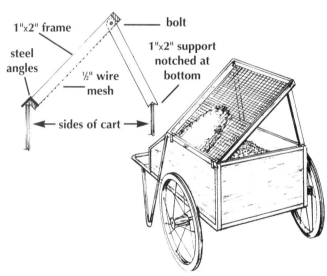

To make compost ready for use in container growing it should be screened first. Set a wood-framed, ½-inch mesh screen on a garden cart. Sift the compost through the screen. Large bits can be discarded and the uniform compost that remains added to soil mixes or used as a side dressing in the garden.

COLOR

Finished compost has a dark, rich color that ranges from deep brown to nearly black. Truly black material that has a greasy texture is usually the product of anaerobic decomposition and an excessively wet environment. Sometimes descriptively called "black butter," it is inferior compost.

SMELL

There are many words to describe how finished, high-grade compost smells, including sweet, earthy, and rich. The odor of compost is difficult to describe because its fragrance derives from many different aromatic compounds produced by thousands of different species of aerobic bacteria. No two batches of compost smell exactly alike, but all smell like earthy, fertile soil. Compost that smells moldy, rotten, or musty has large populations of anaerobic bacteria.

WHEN TO ADD COMPOST TO SOIL

To get the maximum benefit from your compost, spread a layer over the garden (at least half an inch deep) in fall and let it just sit there over winter. In spring till in the compost as you prepare the garden for planting. (In warmer regions spread the compost in winter, about one month before planting time, and till it into the soil.) Throughout the growing season — but especially during the months after the summer solstice — side-dress your plants with compost and mix it into the soil with a hoe.

Compost not only improves soil texture and structure, but also makes it more fertile. These fertile nutrients are held within tiny clumps, or aggregates. When you till the soil the tines break up these aggregates, releasing the nutrients. Nutrients released at times when plants are not growing, such as fall and winter, are wasted.

Improving the Soil

Compost can improve almost any type of soil. Soils consist of mineral particles (either clay, silt, or sand) and organic matter. The organic matter in compost improves soil by enhancing its structure and texture, increasing nutrient availability to plants, encouraging healthy populations of soil organisms, and reducing soilborne pests and diseases.

Compost is very powerful stuff; the addition of even small amounts can make a large difference in your soil. For example, a soil with less than 2 percent organic matter content has very low populations of microorganisms and earthworms, suffers from poor drainage and/or water-holding capacity, and is often deficient in available nutrients. Increasing the organic matter content to at least 5 percent dramatically changes the soil. Microorganisms and earthworms multiply, which markedly increases the fertility of the soil. Drainage, aeration, and moisture-holding also improve. These changes result in more vigorous plant growth, less plant stress in droughts, and less incidence of disease.

To build up soil that has very little organic matter, evenly spread between 200 and 400 pounds of compost for each 100 square feet of earth and till to a depth of 4 to 6 inches. Apply in spring and again in fall for two to three years. After this, the organic matter content of the soil should be between 5 and 10 percent. Your plants will thank you.

USING COMPOST ON ANNUALS AND VEGETABLES

If you're using compost on vegetable or flower beds, it should first be screened through half-inch hardware cloth. This will separate out the larger pieces of decomposed material, which can be returned to the compost pile. When you're planting seeds, dibble the furrow and layer the bottom with a lining of screened compost and soil. Set the seeds in the furrow, cover with soil, and water. When you're transplanting, dig a hole larger than the rootball and refill partway with a mixture of three parts garden soil and one part compost. Set the plant in the hole and cover with either soil or a mixture of compost and soil. Side-dress plants with compost throughout the growing season. Mix the applied compost into the soil with a hoe.

USING COMPOST ON PERENNIALS

When you're planting a bed of perennials, dig a trench about 1 to 1½ feet deep and at least 8 inches wide. Mix the soil from the trench with compost at a ratio of 3 parts garden soil to 1 part compost. Refill the trench and water well. After the water has drained, dig a hole and transplant the perennials. To add compost to existing beds of perennials, put a layer about 1 to 1½ inches deep around the base of the plant; apply only a trace amount adjacent to the stem.

USING COMPOST ON SHRUBS AND TREES

When you're planting shrubs or trees, mix the soil from the planting hole with compost at a ratio of 3 parts garden soil to 1 part compost. Acid-loving plants, such as broad- and narrow-leafed evergreens, prefer an acid compost. This can be made by using plenty of pine needles, oak leaves, and beech leaves; do not add wood ashes. After planting and for mature shrubs and trees, apply compost as a thin layer of mulch during the growing season.

NOT ENOUGH COMPOST

What do you do when you have too much garden and not enough compost to go around? There are two schools of thought. The first is to spread the compost in a layer one to two inches deep until it runs out. The second is to cover the entire garden with at least a little compost. The third, and best, approach is to use the compost you have in the furrows when you're planting seeds, in the planting holes when you're transplanting, and as sidedressing during the growing season. This puts the most compost in the places where it will do the most good.

3

New Plants from Old

The civilizations that arose around the world in ancient times took root in part as a response to the growing sophistication of agriculture. The more food could be produced in one place, the less need there was to wander from here to there in search of sustenance. Yet agriculture itself could not evolve until people learned how to propagate the plants they grew. At first all they needed to know was how to collect, store, and sow seeds. But seeds did not always produce uniform crops; so in response, ancient peoples learned the more complex art of asexual, or vegetative, plant propagation.

The end result of asexual propagation is an exact duplicate of the parent plant. This in itself is magical. In an age where headlines are reserved for the next species of mammal to be cloned by scientists, we don't think twice about going to the garden and layering a rhododendron or dividing a daylily. Yet in the end the wonders of science and the skills of the gardener are exactly the same: Both produce clones of living creatures.

THE EFFECT OF ENVIRONMENT ON CLONES

A clone is an exact duplicate of the original plant, but sometimes, as it grows, a clone looks different from the original plant. How can an exact copy not be exactly the same?

Clones share the genetic makeup of the original plant, but genetics is only one component of appearance. The other is environment. For example, all Delicious apple trees are clones, or identical copies, of the original tree found by Jesse Hiatt in his orchard in Iowa in 1870. Because they are identical to each other, all Delicious apple trees should produce fruit that looks exactly alike, but they don't. Trees in Washington or New England bear long, conical fruit, while those in the Carolinas produce round fruit. The trees are the same but the long, warm seasons of the South cause the apples to grow differently from those in the North. Similarly, clones grown in shade often look different from those grown in sun.

Methods of
Asexual Propagation

Propagating plants is a partnership between person and plant, gardener and garden. It can be as complex as grafting or as simple as dividing, but regardless of the technique, the partnership remains.

The trick is in knowing what technique to use. A skill that works well for irises may not be effective for viburnums. Over the years horticulturists have discovered which techniques work best on which plants, and we now have easy methods of propagation for many of the most widely grown and beloved of garden plants. Of these many ways to asexually propagate plants, the easiest and most effective include cuttings, layering, and division.

Cuttings are pieces of stems, leaves, roots, or buds that are used to produce more plants. They can be used to propagate an immense variety of plants, including deciduous shrubs and trees, evergreen shrubs and trees, fruits, greenhouse crops, and perennials. Such propagation produces a large number of plants in a limited space, is inexpensive, requires no specialized techniques, and is both quick and easy.

In *layering,* roots are encouraged to form along a stem while still attached to the parent plant. Even easier than cuttings, this method is often used to propagate plants that do not root easily by other methods. Most layering is done outside, in the garden, though some houseplants can be layered effectively indoors. Plants that respond well to layering include many deciduous shrubs and trees, evergreen shrubs and trees, fruits, vines, and, of course, houseplants.

Some plants possess specialized stems and roots whose functions are food storage and natural vegetative reproduction. These stems or roots can be separated by various methods summarily called *division.* Because the plant does so much of the work, division is often seen as the easiest of all asexual propagation methods. Plants commonly propagated by division include lilies, irises, daylilies, and lily-of-the-valley.

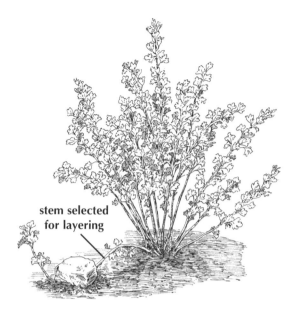

stem selected for layering

Layering is just one of many easy ways of propagating garden plants. Here, new roots will form on the stem at the left where it is pressed to the ground.

CLONING DOLLY AT HOME

In 1997 scientists in Scotland announced that they had successfully cloned an adult sheep. They named the ewe Dolly. News reports called the procedure extremely complicated, involving intricate techniques only replicable in modern laboratories. In response horticulturists countered that they have been cloning adult plants by a simple propagation method known as division for years. Here is a quick and easy method for making your own Dolly at home. Sort of.

Sheep Sorrel (*Rumex acetosella*) is a common plant that grows on dry hillsides all over the country. To make your own Dolly, simply dig up a small plant of sheep sorrel and put it in a pot. Water and fertilize it faithfully until little plants begin to show at the base of the crown. When these get large enough to have a few leaves, gently separate them from the original plant. Plant the small sheep sorrel into another pot, name it Dolly, and enjoy. Cloning is an everyday event in the garden, but that shouldn't diminish the value of your own sheep sorrel clone.

Propagation by Cuttings

Plants are really made up of three parts: roots, stems, and leaves. If these parts were people, a psychologist would say that they all had strong self-identities. A root is a root and would be deeply offended if it were called a stem. Yet in a crisis — such as getting your stem tip cut off by some fanatic with garden shears — these parts can change their minds about who they are. This ability is the basis for successful propagation by cuttings.

HOW IT WORKS

The process of changing a stem into a root begins when the stem is cut to gather the cutting. At the beginning of the healing process the cells around the wound *dedifferentiate*. Like a person suffering an identity crisis, they go from knowing who they are to not knowing who they are. These cells are collectively called *callus*. The plant then sends chemical messengers called hormones to these confused cells, telling them that they are now going to be roots. Some cells ignore this message but others join to create a little group that takes the form of a small root, a *root initial*. Pretty soon, through a kind of group therapy, they convince each other that they have always been roots, look around to see that they are surrounded by aimless callus cells and bits of stem, and begin to grow.

When the root initial finally emerges from the callus and stem tissue, it is officially a *new root* and gets down the job of absorbing moisture and nutrients and feeling good about itself again.

HOW TO USE ROOTING PREPARATIONS

Rooting preparations are generally available as powders or liquid concentrates. Powders are composed of small amounts of IBA (indolebutyric acid) and sometimes NAA (naphthaleneacetic acid) dispersed in a powdered inert ingredient, such as talc. IBA is used more than NAA because it is nontoxic to the plant over a wider range of concentrations. (See the box on page 32 for more information.)

Powders

Powder preparations are usually available in concentrations of 1,000, 3,000, and 10,000 parts per million (ppm) of active ingredients. Each preparation comes with directions and a long list of plants that respond best to its particular dose. It cannot be overstated that the dosage recommendations should be carefully followed. The promotion of root formation in plant cuttings is a delicate balancing act of compounds. Too much of this or too little of that can easily produce tissue damage or root inhibition.

Using powders. Place a small amount of powder in a disposable container, such as a paper cup. Do not dip cuttings into the main container, for moisture, bacteria, or fungal contamination can ruin the remaining product. Make a fresh cut at the base of the cutting and dip it into the powder. Tap gently to remove any excess. With a dibble, make a hole in the rooting medium and insert the cutting.

Advantages and disadvantages. Powders are generally more readily available and are easier and faster to use than liquid products. There are sometimes problems, however, with uniform transference of chemicals from powder to plant.

JUVENILITY AND THE ROOTING OF CUTTINGS

Plants have childhoods, just as people do, and, like people, juvenile plants look a bit different from their adult counterparts. In many plants, leaves from adult stems look different from those produced on juvenile stems. Some juvenile stems have thorns, for example, while the adult stems do not. Yet the difference between juvenile and adult, young and old, extends beyond mere appearance. Studies with many different species of plants have shown that the ability of a plant to form *adventitious roots* (the type of roots produced by cuttings) decreases with age. As a general rule cuttings taken from juvenile plants root more easily than those from adult plants.

Concentrated Liquids

Years ago it was common for cuttings to be soaked in a dilute rooting solution for up to twenty-four hours before being placed in the rooting medium. It was a tiresome procedure that was nevertheless frequently used in commercial nurseries because it ensured that the plants absorbed a uniform amount of chemicals, and even absorption resulted in uniform root production. Another advantage was that the concentration of chemicals could be more finely tailored to the type of plant. Today, however, solution concentrates have replaced the old dilute method and can be made in concentrations varying from 500 to 10,000 ppm.

Using liquid concentrates. Chemical crystals are dissolved in a solution of 50 percent isopropyl alcohol to the desired concentration. An easy formula to remember is $100 + 100 = 1,000$. Using this formula, 100 mg of chemical dissolved in 100 ml of alcohol solution equals 1,000 ppm. Put the prepared solution in a container to a depth of half an inch. Make a fresh cut at the base of the cutting. Put the basal end of the cutting in the solution for five seconds, then remove it and stick it in the rooting medium. Use the solution as soon as possible, because evaporation will change the concentration of the solution.

Advantages and disadvantages. Concentrated liquids are not as widely available as powders, though the amount of chemical absorbed by the plants tends to be more uniform than with powders.

ROOTING MEDIA

Good growing mixes and good propagation mixes have a lot in common. Both should have enough body to provide some support to the plants or cuttings; retain enough moisture so that frequent watering is not needed; allow excess moisture to drain easily, thus maintaining proper aeration; and be free of harmful pathogens and pests.

These conditions are best obtained by mixing equal amounts of three ingredients: perlite, vermiculite, and peat moss.

- Perlite is sterile with a neutral pH and serves to increase aeration; it can hold four times its weight in water.
- Vermiculite is also sterile with a neutral pH, but it holds even more water than perlite. It also has the ability to retain nutrients that cuttings will need once roots are produced.
- Peat moss is relatively sterile with small amounts of nutrients and a decidedly acid pH.

Together, these three ingredients make up a propagation medium that meets the conditions of a wide range of plants.

WHY DO ROOTING PREPARATIONS WORK?

Hormones are chemical compounds, other than nutrients, that in small amounts influence the growth of plants. There are many different plant hormones and each type of plant has its own unique blend — a hormonal cocktail, if you will — that individually regulates the plant's growth in the best way. When it comes to plant propagation some of these combinations stimulate root initiation and growth, while others inhibit it. The most powerful of these root-promoting compounds are called *auxins*.

In the 1930s scientists began to learn how auxins worked. They discovered that these chemicals could promote root development in cuttings from difficult-to-root plants. Two chemicals — indolebutyric acid (IBA) and naphthaleneacetic acid (NAA) — were found to have very strong auxin properties and soon came into wide use in research labs, because many difficult-to-root plants would root if IBA and/or NAA was applied to the base of the cutting.

Eventually this research led to the creation of commercial rooting preparations, which have now been widely available for many years. Most consist of small amounts of IBA mixed with talc or another inert powder. Some also contain a fungicide to inhibit fungal infection of the cutting during rooting. The base of the cutting is dipped into the powder and then stuck in the rooting bed.

BASIC PROPAGATION TOOLS

The two basic propagation tools to use are hand pruning shears and grafting knives.

Pruning shears are used to gather woody cuttings. They come in either anvil or shear models: Anvil pruners have a sharpened blade that descends atop a flattened one, while shear pruners have two blades that scissor past each other. Both types do a good job if kept sharp. Recently, hand pruners have been made easier to use with the introduction of ergonomic handles that reduce hand fatigue.

Grafting knives, also called horticultural *knives,* are most commonly used to trim cuttings just before sticking them in the propagation medium. They come in either folding- or fixed-blade models and usually have a uniquely shaped blade called a sheepsfoot, which gives them long, straight cutting edges. The best blades are made of high-carbon stainless steel. The cutting edge of the knife blade can be beveled on one or two sides, but a blade beveled on just one side is much easier to sharpen and maintain.

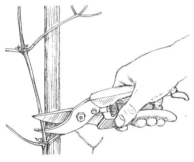

A good pair of pruning shears should have a molded handle to reduce hand strain.

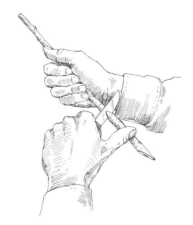

Sharp, clean cuts are essential to good propagation, and no tool makes them better than a grafting knife.

The multiflat is the workhorse of propagation containers.

PROPAGATION CONTAINERS

There are many types of containers, from clay pots to wooden windowboxes, that work perfectly well for growing plants. But most of these same containers just aren't adequate for propagating plants. The best container for propagating the widest range of plants is inexpensive, reusable many times, easily cleaned and disinfected, big enough to hold a large number of cuttings while isolating diseased plants, and easy to move when full of cuttings. These are exacting standards, but one product comes close to meeting them all while another does meets them all.

In Europe the favorite home propagating container is the 7 centimeter (2 inch) square plastic pot. In the United States the 3-inch round plastic pot is most often used. These containers are inexpensive and easy to use and clean. If many plants are propagated at once, however, moving a horde of these little guys around gets awkward.

An improvement on the small, round plastic pot is the multiflat. Multiflats go by many names, but all are made of individual round pots molded into a single sheet of heavy-gauge plastic. The most popular sizes are the 72- and 96-hole models which roughly correspond to 2-inch and 1.5-inch containers. The multiflat provides each cutting with just the right amount of soil to minimize wet and dry spots. Also, because the cuttings do not share soil, diseased plants are less likely to infect nearby cuttings. And once rooted, cuttings propagated in multiflats can be easily popped out of the container with their rootballs intact, which makes transplanting much easier.

Creating a Propagation Unit for Cuttings

Water is essential for plants to survive, and the stems, leaves, and roots combine to form a very efficient pathway for that water. The roots absorb water from the soil, the stem conducts that water to the leaves, and the leaves expel it into the air.

When we snip a cutting from a plant we interrupt a part of the water pathway, but the rest of it continues to function. In a stem cutting, for instance, the stem continues to move water to the leaves, and the leaves continue to expel it into the air. The problem is that there are no roots to replace the water lost through the leaves. If the leaves dry out they die, and dead leaves cannot manufacture the carbohydrates needed to fuel root initiation and growth. Therefore, the trick to good propagation is to keep the leaves, and thereby the cutting, alive long enough for that cutting to grow new roots and reestablish the water pathway. This is the key to keeping a cutting alive: Stop the evaporation of water from its leaves.

The inside of a leaf is a very moist place — the humidity is always about 100 percent. Naturally, however, the air just outside the leaf is much drier. One of the rules of nature is that things always flow from an area of high concentration to an area of low concentration; moisture always tries to pass from the leaf to the outside air. To stop this evaporation, the humidity of the air outside the leaf must match that inside.

Some commercial nurseries accomplish this with mist systems that expel a fine fog over the cuttings until the leaf surfaces are covered with little droplets. As these droplets evaporate, they raise the humidity of the air adjoining the leaf surface to about 100 percent. Because these systems are not practical for most home use, small-scale propagators use a device called the plastic tent.

A plastic tent is a simple device that raises the humidity of the air in the propagation area in order to greatly reduce or stop evaporation from the leaves of cuttings. A vapor barrier of plastic film creates a humid environment that completely surrounds the cuttings.

Larger tents can be made by using old tables. Cover the table with a sheet of 4-mil clear or white plastic. Fill some large pots with gravel or small stones and insert wooden stakes, each about 1½ feet long, into them. Place the pots, complete with stakes, at the corners of the table. Stick cuttings into flats filled with propagation medium, water well, and put the flats onto the table. Drape a second sheet of 4-mil clear plastic over the supporting stakes so that it hangs down beyond the tabletop. The more airtight you can make the tent, the better it will be for the cuttings. Be sure to keep the medium moist and supply adequate indirect light. The air temperature inside the tent should be about 70 to 85°F during the day. Do not allow the temperature to exceed 90°F.

Propagation of plants by cuttings has become very popular in recent years, which has prompted some garden supply companies to market small, inexpensive tabletop-size propagation systems. These devices are usually called little greenhouses, but they utilize the principles of the plastic tent.

HOW TO MAKE A SMALL PLASTIC TENT

For a small plastic tent, use a large, clear polyethylene bag. Fill a clean container (6 inches wide or larger) with moist propagation mix, stick the cuttings into the mix, and water. Bend two metal coat hangers into arches and place the ends into the soil. Put the bag over the pot, fastening the loose end with a twist tie. Keep the pot out of direct light so that cuttings don't overheat.

Types of Cuttings

Four types of cuttings are commonly used to propagate plants: stem cuttings, including hardwood (deciduous and evergreen), softwood, and herbaceous; leaf cuttings; leaf-bud cuttings; and root cuttings. Many plants can be successfully propagated via different types of cuttings but are most easily propagated with just one. For example, a few species of viburnums can be propagated from hardwood cuttings, but many more species root successfully from softwood cuttings.

Old gardening books overflow with lists of plants that our gardening ancestors labeled easy to propagate but that we now view as difficult. Often this change is due to a virus infection that has been passed on through nurseries and gardens for decades. Many virus infections produce no visible symptoms of illness in the plant but can make cuttings very difficult to root. Stress, caused by drought, poor nutrient availability, or insect infestation, can also make an easy-to-root plant difficult. Good propagation begins with healthy plants. Starting with anything less is really just a waste of time.

In some species of trees, such as beech, maple, and oak, the juvenile parts retain their leaves longer into fall than adult portions of the same tree. Juvenile parts are usually found on branches close to the trunk in the middle of the tree. Juvenility can also be induced in some species by shearing the plant back and taking cuttings from the shoots that sprout below the cut. This is effective in many types of evergreens.

CUTTINGS WITH LEAVES ARE BETTER

For years it has been known that stem cuttings with leaves rooted better than leafless cuttings. The difference can be amazing. Leafy cuttings routinely have two to four times as many roots as their leafless counterparts in the same amount of time. Leaves contribute to more rapid rooting by producing carbohydrates that then travel down the stem and are used in root initiation. Leaves also produce substances called auxins that stimulate root formation.

STEM CUTTINGS — HARDWOOD (DECIDUOUS)

Hardwood cuttings are pieces of stem ranging from 4 to 8 inches in length. They are most often used to propagate woody ornamentals and, because they are dormant and leafless, require almost no attention once placed in the propagation bed. The cuttings are gathered while the plants are dormant, usually in late fall or winter; stored until early spring; and then set into outdoor planting beds. To ensure the best rooting, take cuttings from the previous year's growth and from stems between ¼ inch and 1 inch in diameter.

Make your cuttings all the same length. Collect them into a bundle, right-side up, and secure with a rubber band. Bury the bundle upside down in a bucket of clean sand or sawdust and place outdoors until spring. This cold treatment concentrates root-promoting compounds at the base of the cuttings while inhibiting bud development. In spring, treat the base ends with powdered rooting compound. Plant in garden rows 2 to 3 inches apart, and with only the top 2 inches of each cutting poking above the soil. Leave the plants in place for at least one growing season. You can then transplant them to your desired locations.

◆ **The Best Deciduous Plants to Propagate from Hardwood Cuttings**
    Burning bush *(Euonymus alata)*
    Forsythia *(Forsythia* spp.)
    Mock orange *(Philadelphus* spp.)
    Privet *(Ligustrum* spp.)
    Rugosa Rose *(Rosa rugosa)*
    Spirea *(Spiraea vanhouttei)*

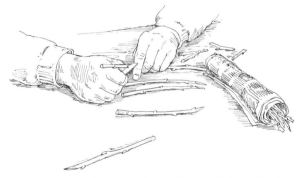

Make hardwood cuttings from pieces of stem 4 to 8 inches long. Keep them damp during preparation by covering them with moist newspaper.

STEM CUTTINGS — HARDWOOD AND SEMIHARDWOOD (EVERGREEN)

Evergreen cuttings have needles (hemlock, juniper) or leaves (rhododendron) that must be protected from drying out; thus they are best propagated in plastic tents. In midwinter, gather tip cuttings (about 6 inches long) of needled evergreens grown in full sun. Strip all needles from the lower third of each cutting and dip into powdered rooting compound with a concentration of 3,000 ppm. Then stick the cuttings into a moistened rooting medium made of equal parts perlite and peat moss or into clean, washed sand. Needled evergreen cuttings need bright light, high humidity, and temperatures of about 70°F to root well.

Not all needled evergreens are created equal, and some types root much more easily than others. The easiest types to root include spreading junipers (*Juniperus* spp.), false cypress (*Chamaecyparis* spp.), and arborvitae (*Thuja* spp.). Difficult-to-root evergreens include pine (*Pinus* spp.), spruce (*Picea* spp.), hemlock (*Tsuga* spp.), and fir (*Abies* spp.).

Semihardwood cuttings are used to propagate broad-leafed evergreens, including rhododendron (*Rhododendren* spp.), camellia (*Camellia* spp.), pittosporum (*P. tobira*), holly (*Ilex* spp.), and ever-green euonymous (*Euonymous* spp.). The cuttings are gathered in early summer from stems of the present season's growth, in the early hours of a cool morning, and from plants that have been grown in full sun.

After the leaves have fully expanded but before the wood has completely stiffened, collect the cuttings in a moistened plastic bag. Once indoors, trim to between 3 and 5 inches long, with the lower third of the stem bare of leaves. Dip the base of each stem in rooting compound with a concentration of 10,000 ppm, stick it in a moistened rooting medium made of equal parts of perlite and peat moss, and place in a plastic tent. Semihardwood broad-leafed evergreen cuttings prefer moderate light in the tent, with no direct sunlight and a temperature of about 70°F. Most species root in about three months and should be potted as soon as the roots are large enough.

◆ **The Best Broad-Leafed Evergreens to Root from Cuttings**

Bougainvillea (*Bougainvillea* spp.)
Camellia (*Camellia japonica; C. sasanqua*)
Confederate Jasmine (*Trachelospermum jasminoides*)
Firethorn (*Pyracantha* spp.)
Gardenia (*Gardenia jasminoides*)
Holly (*Ilex* spp.)
Pittosporum (*Pittosporum tobira*)
Podocarpus (*Podocarpus* spp.)
Rhododendron (*Rhododendron* spp.)

◆ **The Best Narrow-Leafed Evergreens to Root from Cuttings**

Arborvitae (*Thuja* spp.)
False Cypress (*Chamaecyparis* spp.)
Cryptomeria (*Cryptomeria japonica*)
Leyland Cypress (x *Cupressocyparis leylandii*)
Hemlock (*Tsuga* spp.)
Juniper (*Juniperus* spp.)
Mugo Pine (*Pinus mugo*)
Yew (*Taxus* spp.)

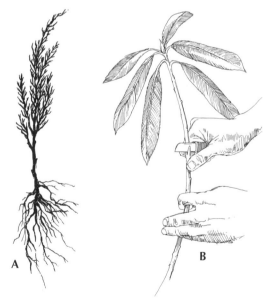

(A) Juniper cuttings taken from prostrate form root more easily than those from upright types.
(B) Rhododendrons are best propagated from terminal stem cuttings taken in summer.

STEM CUTTINGS — SOFTWOOD

The pliant stems of softwood cuttings root more readily than most other types of cuttings, but their young, tender leaves also lose moisture faster. The cut stems are also more prone to infection by disease, and the leaves are easily damaged by strong light. Consequently, the successful rooting of softwood cuttings is a delicate balancing act that sometimes works — and sometimes doesn't.

Collect softwood cuttings from woody plants in spring or early summer when the stems of the new growth snap cleanly when bent. The best cuttings come from the outer branches of plants grown in full sun, and are neither very thin nor overly thick. Gather them in the cool of the morning, drop them into a moistened plastic bag, and keep away from direct sunlight. Some folks drop cuttings in a bucket of cool water, but this actually damages the cuttings more than helps them.

Trim each cutting to between 4 and 5 inches long and strip the lower two nodes of their leaves. Make a fresh basal cut just below the lowest node. Large leaves should be trimmed in half to reduce moisture loss. Stick the cuttings in a moistened propagation mix made of equal parts peat moss, perlite, and vermiculite, and place them in a plastic tent. The cuttings will root best in moderate, indirect light at a temperature of 70 to 75°F.

◆ Plants Easily Rooted from Softwood Cuttings
Hydrangea (*Hydrangea* spp.)
Smoke tree (*Cotinus coggygria*)
Trumpet creeper (*Campsis radicans*)
Weigela (*Weigela* spp.)

STEM CUTTINGS — HERBACEOUS

Herbaceous cuttings are made from the succulent growth of nonwoody plants, such as annuals, biennials, and some perennials. They can be made from either leafy stems or leafless stem pieces. The typical herbaceous cutting is 3 to 5 inches long; keep the leaves at the top but remove them from the two basal nodes. This is the type of cutting most folks first experiment with, because many herbaceous plants, such as the zonal geranium, root so easily that a glass of water is an acceptable propagation medium.

For best results with the widest range of plants, treat herbaceous cuttings as you would softwood cuttings. When making them from plants that exude a thick, sticky sap, allow the basal end of each cutting to dry out a little before sticking it into the propagating medium. This inhibits infection by fungal and bacterial organisms.

◆ Some Easy-to-Root Herbaceous Plants
Ageratum (*Ageratum houstonianum*)
Aloe (*Aloe* spp.)
Begonia (*Begonia* spp.)
Candytuft (*Iberis* spp.)
Chrysanthemum (*Chrysanthemum* spp.)
Dieffenbachia (*Dieffenbachia* spp.)
Impatiens (*Impatiens* spp.)
Jade plant (*Crassula argentea*)
Philodendron (*Philodendron* spp.)
Pink (*Dianthus* spp.)
Rockcress (*Arabis* spp.)
Snapdragon (*Antirrhinum majus*)
Zonal geranium (*Pelargonium* x *hortorum*)

HOW TO ROOT A CUTTING

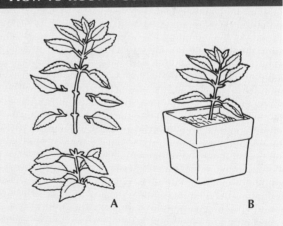

A   B

Stem cuttings are made from healthy, terminal shoots and contain several nodes and internodes with multiple sets of leaves. Remove the leaves from the basal portion of the cutting (A), apply the rooting chemical and then stick the cutting into the propagation medium (B).

LEAF CUTTINGS

A simple leaf consists of a stalk, called the petiole, and the leaf blade. Connecting the petiole and the leaf blade are veins, which are often embedded in the petiole and appear as ridges on either the lower or upper surface of the leaf blade. These three structures — petiole, leaf blade, and veins — all have a role in propagation via leaf cuttings.

It should be noted that most plants cannot be propagated by leaf cuttings. For those that can, however, this is often the easiest method of propagation. Treat leaf cuttings in the same way as softwood or herbaceous cuttings.

In some species, new plants arise directly from the leaf blade. For example, the walking fern (a small plant that clings to limestone boulders) has slender fronds, the tips of which produce new plants when they come into contact with damp soil. Many begonias (*Begonia* spp.), sedums (*Sedum* spp.), and African violets (*Saintpaulia* spp.) are propagated by cutting the veins on the underside of the leaf, then laying the leaf flat on a propagation medium inside a plastic tent. New plants arise at the site where the vein was cut. You can propagate African violets and peperomia (*Peperomia* spp.) by sticking the petiole of an entire leaf in the propagation medium inside a plastic tent. New plants then arise from the base of the petiole. Another common

African violets are easy to root from leaf cuttings. Simply stick the leaf petiole into some soil mix leaving the leaf blade exposed.

houseplant, sansevieria (*Sansevieria* spp.), can be propagated by slicing the long, tough leaves into 4-inch sections and inserting them into the propagation medium inside a plastic tent. New plants form at the base of the cutting.

Although a large number of plants propagated by leaf cuttings happen to be tropical houseplants, this method also proves useful in the garden. Many flowering bulbs, including grape hyacinth (*Muscari* spp.), blood lily (*Haemanthus* spp.), cape cowslip (*Lachenalia* spp.), and hyancinth (*Hyacinthus* spp.), can be propagated via leaf cuttings. Gather healthy green leaves before they begin to yellow and slice them into sections about 4 inches long. Stick the basal ends into the propagation medium so that half the cutting is buried, and place in a plastic tent. Bulbets form at the base of the cutting in about a month; plant them outdoors to continue their growth.

◆ Plants Easily Propagated from Leaf Cuttings
African violet (*Saintpaulia* spp.)
Gloxinia *(Sinningia speciosa)*
Kalanchoe (*Kalanchoe* spp.)
Peperomia (*Peperomia* spp.)
Sansevieria (*Sansevieria* spp.)
Sedum (*Sedum* spp.)

CUT FLOWERS DON'T MAKE GOOD CUTTINGS

When some plants flower, they have a one-track mind. Nothing else matters but popping out those flowerbuds.

People don't notice anything different about a plant in bloom compared to one not in bloom other than that one has flowers and the other doesn't. What they can't see are the chemical changes that a flowering plant undergoes. In many plants, flowers produce chemicals that then inhibit the ability of cuttings taken from that plant to root. The effect is temporary, however, for cuttings taken before or after flowerbuds develop root normally.

LEAF-BUD CUTTINGS

A leaf-bud cutting includes the leaf blade, petiole, and small piece of stem at the base of the leaf. This stem section contains a small bud, called an axillary bud, that is crucial to the rooting of the cutting. Gather leaf-bud cuttings from healthy plants with well-developed, actively growing leaves, because these plants also tend to have strong buds. Cut the stem about ¼ inch above and below the base of the leaf, or node. Dip the stem portion into a powdered rooting preparation of 1,000 ppm for succulent plants or 3,000 ppm for woodier plants. Stick the cutting in washed sand so that the stem and bud are below the surface. Place in a warm plastic tent.

Leaf-bud cuttings can be used to root many of the plants that also take well to stem cuttings. The advantage of using the leaf-bud method is that you can make three or four cuttings from the same material you would need to make just one stem cutting. Many types of berries, including black raspberry *(Rubus occidentalis)* and boysenberry *(Rubus ursinus* var. *loganobaccus* 'Boysen'), can be propagated by leaf-bud cuttings; so, too, can such shrubs as evergreen rhododendrons *(Rhododendron* spp.), tropical hibiscus *(Hibiscus rosa-sinensis)*, and camellias *(Camellia* spp.)

Some plants, such as jade plant *(Crassula argentea)*, have the peculiar ability to produce roots but no shoots from leaf cuttings. These rooted leaves make good conversation pieces, for they can live a long time and require little attention. Of course, they don't do anything but just sit there, and some folks consider this a big drawback. Other people pot the little guys up and keep them on the windowsill calling the diminutive bits of foliage pet leaves. If having a pet leaf isn't quite fulfilling you can make an entire plant with a leaf-bud cuting. Take the cutting from a healthy specimen, preferably one that has been grown in enough sun to give its leaves a reddish edge. Stick the cutting into a propagation medium so that the stem and bud are about ¼ inch below the surface, and place in a warm plastic tent. The bud will sprout as the cutting roots, and the new plant will be ready to pot up in one or two months.

◆ **Plants Easily Propagated from Leaf-Bud Cuttings**

    Black raspberry *(Rubus occidentalis)*
    Jade plant *(Crassula argentea)*
    Lemon *(Citrus limon)*
    Rhododendron *(Rhododendron* spp.)
    Tropical hibiscus *(Hibiscus rosa-sinensis)*

ROOTING CUTTINGS IN WATER: THE FOUR-INCH FORMULA

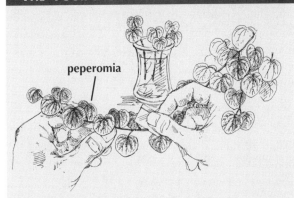

peperomia

For easy-to-root species, perhaps the most economical propagation medium is clean tap water. For the best results, take a clean glass container, measure 4 inches up from the bottom, and mark the spot with a magic marker. Put a few freshly gathered cuttings into the container and add water to the 4-inch mark. Replace the water every other day.

For any cutting (even the easy-to-root kind) to root well it needs a continuous and adequate supply of oxygen in the rooting medium. The plant uses this oxygen to develop new roots. Standing water absorbs oxygen from the air, but because the water is static the oxygen doesn't penetrate very far beneath its surface. In fact, only the top 4 inches of standing water contains enough oxygen to stimulate fast and abundant root growth. The higher oxygen content also inhibits some types of microbial infection.

ROOT CUTTINGS

Roots and stems are remarkably similar in structure and growth, with only a few minor differences. This similarity unfortunately leads some gardeners to treat root cuttings in the same way as stem cuttings. There is, however, a major difference between roots and stems that must be respected: polarity. *Polarity* simply means that the top of a plant is always noticeably different from the bottom. In stem cuttings new shoots arise from the top, or distal, end, while new roots develop from the bottom, or proximal, end — that is, the portion of the cutting that was originally closest to the plant's crown. In roots this polarity is reversed: New shoots arise from the proximal end, new roots from the distal.

The polarity of a cutting cannot be reversed. Root cuttings planted upside down will produce deformed plants with stems rising from beneath the roots. To avoid this, make a straight cut at the proximal end of the root and a slanted cut at the distal end. Stick the cutting vertically into the propagation medium so that the proximal end (the straight cut) is closest to the surface but still covered by about ½ inch of medium. (See the box for more information on polarity.)

The best root cuttings are gathered just after the plants go dormant in fall; at this point their roots are full of the carbohydrates produced over the summer. It's easy to trim the roots of perennials, shrubs, and trees that you lift from the soil to divide or transplant. Plants with slender roots, such as garden phlox *(Phlox paniculata)*, should be cut into 2- to 3-inch sections. Fill a flat ⅔ full of washed sand or vermiculite and lay the cuttings flat against the surface.

When cutting large roots remember that the cut must be clean, and each portion should contain at least two strong buds, or eyes.

CUTTINGS AND POLARITY

Among the most interesting aspects of plants is the phenomenon known as polarity. In horticulture, the word *polar* simply means that the top of a plant differs noticeably from the bottom; that is, the top has leaves and shoots, while the bottom has roots.

In the 1870s scientists discovered that when a stem was sliced into cuttings, the top, or distal, end developed new shoots, and the base, or proximal, end grew new roots. No surprise there. However, when they stuck stem cuttings upside down, shoots still grew from the morphologic top of the cutting — even though it was upside down. This remained true no matter how small the researchers made the cuttings: Each piece stayed true to its polarity.

When propagating plants polarity is thus important to keep in mind, because its effects are not altered by gravity or light. If cuttings are accidentally stuck upside down, the results will be bizarre and disappointing.

Cover with 1 inch of the sand or vermiculite, and water. Keep in a plastic tent until shoots appear. For plants with fleshy roots, such as oriental poppy *(Papaver orientale)*, cut the roots into sections about 3 inches long and stick them vertically into the propagation medium, leaving about the top ¼ inch of the cutting above soil level. Water well and place in a plastic tent until shoots develop.

The root-cutting method is fun to experiment with because a large number of plants respond to it, and the cuttings are easy to maintain. The only possible drawback is that root cuttings usually take longer to root than many other types.

◆ **Some Plants Easily Propagated from Root Cuttings**

Bee balm *(Monarda* spp.)
Bleeding-heart *(Dicentra spectabilis)*
Garden peony *(Paeonia lactiflora)*
Garden phlox *(Phlox paniculata)*
Oriental poppy *(Papaver orientale)*
Yarrow *(Achillea* spp.)

Caring for Cuttings

A cutting-propagation device resembles the intensive care unit in a hospital. The cuttings in it have all suffered potentially fatal injuries and are on life support until they can regenerate the organs they need to survive on their own. This life support takes the form of light, moisture, warmth, and media. Each ingredient must be just right, and stay just right, or the cutting could perish.

Be sure to remove fallen leaves promptly, as well as any dead or dying cuttings. Do not allow the temperature to drop below 60°F or rise above 90°F. Some rooting powders also contain a fungicide that will further inhibit disease.

CHECKING FOR ROOTS

Like kids waiting to unwrap gifts at Christmas, gardeners sometimes find it very hard not to poke around the base of cuttings looking for tiny roots. Of course, the more disruption a cutting endures, the greater the chance that those new roots will be damaged. There are two ways to gauge when it's time to look beneath the soil for roots. First, watch the progress of emerging shoots; cuttings without well-formed roots generally do not grow as fast as those with roots. Second, examine the base of the container. If any roots appear near the drainage holes, the cutting is sufficiently rooted to be repotted.

Once cuttings are well rooted they should be potted into individual pots.

AFTERCARE

In a hospital, patients are moved from the intensive care unit to another room where they can continue their recuperation before going home. Newly rooted cuttings must be treated the same way or they will quickly whither and die. Once cuttings have rooted, the first step is to raise the flaps of the plastic tent. This allows the plants to adjust to a less humid environment with greater temperature fluctuations. After a few days — at least during warmer seasons — they can be moved to a shady spot outdoors. After they have adjusted to life on the outside, transplant them into growing pots and treat them just like any other container-grown plant. After a few weeks in the pots they will probably be large enough to transfer to the garden.

TIMING

Some people can fail completely at rooting cuttings while their neighbors use the same equipment and methods and succeed. The difference may be as simple as timing. Precisely when during the year a cutting is taken can have a profound effect on whether it will root or not.

Lilacs, for instance, are very difficult to root from cuttings unless the cuttings are taken during a few days in spring when the new stems are 4 or 5 inches long and still growing. On the other hand, azaleas will root fairly well from tender cuttings taken just after the plants begin growing, but are next to impossible to root at any other time of year. Broad-leafed evergreens root best from cuttings taken from the new flush of spring growth; they root poorly when cuttings are taken from dormant stems. Narrow-leafed evergreens root poorly from cuttings taken from actively growing spring stems, but well from dormant ones. So if you're doing everything else right but your cuttings just aren't rooting, check the timing.

Propagation by Layering

Layering is a method of plant propagation in which roots form along a stem while it's still attached to the parent plant. Unlike cuttings that race to regenerate their entire root system before they perish, layered stems are kept constantly supplied with water and nutrients from the leaves and roots of the parent plant while they root. For many plants, layering is thus a much more successful method of propagation than cutting.

The art of layering has something for everybody. For those just beginning to propagate plants, layering is one of the first methods to learn. It's easy, has a high success rate, requires minimal equipment, and can result in very high-quality plants. And for the old-timer who can graft apple trees with surgical precision, layering can seem like a trusted friend who doesn't let you down. It produces plants from species and varieties that do not respond well to other methods of propagation, and it's also used to propagate plants that are naturally susceptible to reproduction by layering.

There are many different types of layering: tip layering, stem or simple layering, air layering, and mound layering. Gardeners can even take advantage of one of plants' own systems of propagation: natural layering. Each type, however, relies on the same four principles to induce root formation along the stem:

1. A stem exposed to continuously dark conditions undergoes changes that stimulates root initiation. Either bury the stem or wrap it with an opaque material.
2. An accumulation of carbohydrates and natural growth-regulators at the site where the roots will grow will initiate root production. This accumulation is accomplished by manipulating the stem through bending or cutting to interrupt the natural translocation of the root promoting substances.
3. New roots also need evenly moist, well-drained soil to supply proper amounts of oxygen and moisture.
4. For best growth, do not allow the soil to get too hot or cold.

NATURAL LAYERING

As creative as people have been in inventing ways to layer plants, they invariably drew their inspiration from observing the plants themselves. Many types of plants have been vegetatively duplicating themselves for millions of years. Over the eons a few ways have emerged as plant favorites — runners, stolons, and suckers. They are wonderfully effective and resourceful. All that is left for us to do is admire the ingenuity and pot up the plants.

Runners. In some plants an area of the stem near the soil line produces a long, pliant, aboveground stem called a runner. Because it is in reality a stem, a runner has all the parts of a typical stem, including *nodes* (places where leaves and buds emerge) and *internodes* (smooth, leafless sections). Instead of leaves rising from the nodes, however, runners produce little plants, called daughter plants, which take root and begin to grow while still attached to the mother. After a daughter has established itself, the long umbilical-like runner dies, separating the two. Plants that produce runners include strawberry (*Fragaria* spp.), strawberry begonia (*Saxifraga solonifera*), and carpet bugle (*Ajuga reptans*), along with many ground covers and grasses.

To propagate plants that produce runners, loosen the soil beneath a daughter plant and set it upright. Gently pin the runner on each side of the daughter to the ground with a weight or a small stake, and wait. The daughter will root in as little as a few weeks to several months.

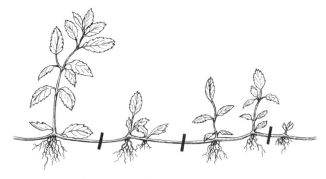

These daughter plants have established strong root systems and can be dug and transplanted: With a knife or shears, cut the runner stem an inch or so from the daughter plant. Plunge a trowel into the soil about 1½ inches from the plant, continuing around until a plug of soil is loosened. Lift the soil plug and transplant into well-worked soil. Water well and lightly mulch.

Suckers. These are daughter plants that rise from roots instead of stems; they can be treated the same as plants produced from stolons. Because suckers usually form on woody plants, many people prefer to cut the connecting root and transplant while the plants are dormant. Dig into the soil and examine the roots of the daughter plant near the spot where they join the sucker root. If the roots seem healthy, cut the connecting root and lift the plant from the earth with a shovel. Transplant into well-worked soil, water well, and mulch.

Stolons. A stolon can be defined as an underground runner. It emerges from the crown of the plant and grows through the soil. Along the way slender shoots form from some of the stolon's nodes and grow upward, emerging from the soil some distance from the mother plant. These new daughter plants eventually send out stolons of their own. Many ground covers and perennials produce stolons, including mint (*Mentha* spp.), betony (*Stachys* spp.), and red-osier dogwood (*Cornus sericea*).

To propagate plants from stolons, wait until the daughter is of good size. For herbaceous or lightly woody plants, such as mint, lift and transplant as for runners. The trowel blade will sever the stolon as you dig the plant. For woody shrubs or trees, such as dogwood, scrape away the soil between the daughter and mother plants until you uncover the horizontal stolon. Cut the stolon with shears. Lift the daughter from the earth with a shovel, along with as many roots and as much soil as possible. Transplant into well-worked soil, water well, and mulch.

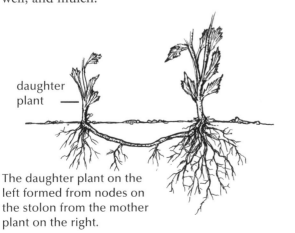

daughter plant —

The daughter plant on the left formed from nodes on the stolon from the mother plant on the right.

TIP LAYERING

In tip layering, roots are induced to form a few inches below the plant's growing tip. The method is most commonly used to propagate the bramble fruits, including raspberries, loganberries, blackberries, and boysenberries. Brambles have long stems called canes, which can grow over 6 feet per year. The first season's growth is entirely vegetative. During the second growing season, the cane produces berries. At the end of this fruitful year, prune out the old canes.

To produce the most tip layers from your bramble patch, allow the new canes to grow to about 24 inches tall in the spring, then snip off the top few inches of growth. Let the canes keep growing until about midsummer. As they get longer, they will bend toward the ground, and their succulent growing tips will turn sharply upward in a rattail shape. When about half the tips have assumed this rattail look, dig a hole about 6 inches long that slopes to a depth of about 6 inches. Lay the stem along the slope and cover completely with soil or compost. By fall the tips will have produced a large root system and a sturdy stem. For best results dig the young plants and transplant them the same day, preferably in early fall.

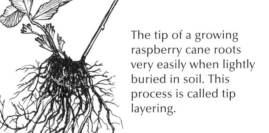

The tip of a growing raspberry cane roots very easily when lightly buried in soil. This process is called tip layering.

◆ **Plants Easily Propagated by Tip Layering**
Black raspberry (*Rubus occidentalis*)
Boysenberry (*Rubus ursinus* var. *loganobaccus* 'Boysen')
Loganberry (*Rubus ursinus* var. *loganobaccus* 'Logan')
Purple raspberry (*Rubus occidentalis* x *idaeus*)

SIMPLE LAYERING

Simple layering is usually done in early spring using one-year-old, dormant stems (½ inch to 1½ inches in diameter) from a bush or low-growing tree. Bend a branch into either a U or V shape without breaking the stem. Bury the bent section in rich compost to a depth of about 6 inches, allowing the leafy end of the branch to poke out above the soil.

Next, set a flat stake vertically in the ground and tie the upright, leafy portion of the stem to it for support. Apply a layer of mulch around the layered branch to keep the soil cool and moist.

The sharp bend in the branch inhibits the natural flow of root-inducing substances down the stem from the leaves and concentrates them, while the dark, moist soil helps stimulate root growth. Most species will produce a good root system by fall, though some plants take two growing seasons to root completely. Plants can be dug in fall or overwintered in place and moved the following spring.

You can also propagate many tropical houseplants this way: Bury the stems in individual pots using the same technique as for garden plants. One plant often propagated by layering is dieffenbachia.

Layering your favorite plants is a great way to add inexpensively to the garden.

◆ Plants That Respond Well to Simple Layering
Azalea, evergreen (*Rhododendron* spp.)
Camellia (*Camellia* spp.)
Clematis (*Clematis* spp.)
Dieffenbachia (*Dieffenbachia* spp.)
Lilac (*Syringa* spp.)
Magnolia (*Magnolia* spp.)
Rhododendron (*Rhododendron* spp.)
Viburnum (*Viburnum* spp.)

MODIFICATIONS TO SIMPLE LAYERING

Over the generations horticulturists have honed methods of simple layering, creating techniques that can improve root initiation and root growth.

Method 1. Bend the branch to be layered into a U or V shape, meanwhile working a small cut (about an inch long and ⅛ inch deep) on the underside of the branch at the deepest portion of the bend. Apply rooting powder to the cut, then bury, stake, and mulch the branch, as in simple layering.

Method 2. Make a slanting cut as above on the top, or dorsal, section of the stem angling away from the parent plant. Then twist the stem to bring the cut parallel to the ground. Bend the area near the cut into an upright L shape. Dust with rooting powder; bury, stake, and mulch the branch, as in simple layering.

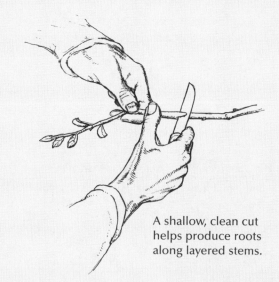

A shallow, clean cut helps produce roots along layered stems.

Method 3. After bending the stem into position wrap a copper wire around it. Bury, stake and mulch the stem as in simple layering. This method, called girdling, pools the natural root promoting substances more efficiently than bending alone.

AIR LAYERING

Air layering is simple layering taken to new heights. Some plants just do not produce branches that lend themselves to being bent to the ground and buried. In air layering this problem is solved by bringing the ground to the branch.

The evolution of air layering (also called Chinese layering or gootee) is a fascinating story in itself. The procedure originated in China. A pack of moist soil was molded around a branch and then secured with a bandage of bark or cloth. Roots would form along the covered section of stem and grow into the soil. Eventually the stem was severed below the soil ball and the plant was transplanted.

As this technique moved west it became pot layering. The bottom of a small clay pot was removed and the entire container slid over a branch to the point where the rooting was desired. The pot was then filled with peat moss and tied in place with a strip of cloth. A stake helped support the weighted branch as roots developed. When roots had penetrated the moss, the pot was shattered, the stem cut below the rootball, and the new plant potted in a fresh container. With the invention of plastic film, pot layering became air layering.

Air layers are best made in spring on stems one to two years old; in warm regions, they're best made in late summer with semihardwood stems. If done indoors (on rubber trees, for example) air layering can be done anytime, but it's most successful in spring and early summer.

◆ Plants Propagated by Air Layering

Azalea (*Rhododendron* spp.)
Dieffenbachia (*Dieffenbachia* spp.)
Holly (*Ilex* spp.)
Lilac (*Syringa* spp.)
Magnolia (*Magnolia* spp.)
Rubber tree (*Ficus elastica*)

HOW TO AIR LAYER

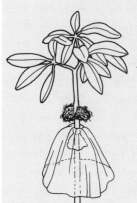

1. About 12 inches from the tip of the branch you intend to air layer, make a slanting cut about 1 inch long into the wood; insert a small piece of wooden matchstick to keep the wound open. Alternatively girdle the branch by completely removing a band of bark. In either case, dust the wound with rooting powder.

2. Soak a large handful of sphagnum moss in water and squeeze out the excess. Mold enough moss around the branch so that 2 to 3 inches surrounds the stem.

3. Wrap the moss with *clear* plastic film and tie the ends securely. Then wrap the moss again with *black* plastic film and tie securely.

4. Remove the layer from the parent plant when the moss ball shows an abundance of strong, healthy roots. In some plants this stage is reached in only three months while for others, such as holly, lilac, rhododendron, azalea, and magnolia, it may take two growing seasons.

The secret to successful air layering is the two different types of plastic.

Plastic film allows oxygen to pass through it, which enhances root growth, but does not allow water to pass, thus keeping the moss moist. Some people use only clear plastic so that they can see the root growth and gauge when to transplant the layer. Unfortunately, clear plastic allows light into the moss ball, which inhibits root growth. If only black plastic is used, on the other hand, the wrapping must be periodically removed to check on the growth of the roots — which allows the moss to dry out, killing the young roots.

With two types of plastic, however, the clear layer keeps the moss ball moist, while the black layer keeps out the light. You can then unwrap the black plastic to check on root growth without drying the moss or inhibiting root growth.

♦ **Plants to Mound Layer**

Azalea (*Rhododendron* spp.)
Euonymus (*Euonymus* spp.)
Forsythia (*Forsythia* spp.)
Rhododendron (*Rhododendron* spp.)
Species Rose (*Rosa* spp.)

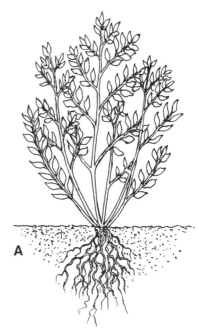

Mound layering is most effective for shrubs with multibranched crowns that produce many branches.

MOUND LAYERING

Mound layering employs the same principles as simple layering, but the entire plant is used. Its advantage is that it produces more plants; its disadvantage is that while being layered, the plant has no ornamental value.

Mound layering comes in handy when rejuvenating old landscaping. In late winter or early spring cut back the old shrubs, such as forsythia or rhododendron, to about 4 inches. In spring allow the shoots to grow to about 6 inches tall, then cover them with rich compost to about half their height. When the shoots reach 6 inches above the new soil level, again cover them to half their height. Add a layer of mulch and keep the mound moist throughout the summer.

In fall carefully remove the compost from the shoots; separate them from the parent plant, which you can then dispose of; and transplant the shoots immediately in the new landscape.

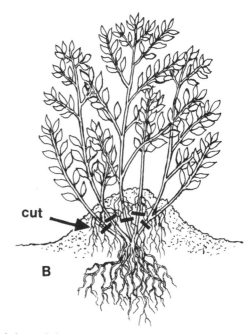

Each branch becomes a separate plant that can be transplanted after plentiful roots have formed.

THE EASIEST METHODS OF ASEXUAL PROPAGATION FOR SOME COMMON WOODY ORNAMENTALS

ORNAMENTAL	TECHNIQUE
Azalea, all types (*Rhododendron* spp.)	Simple layering
Broom (*Cytisus* spp.)	Midsummer cuttings, all-purpose medium, 10,000 ppm IBA rooting preparation
Butterfly bush (*Buddleia* spp.)	Summer cuttings, all-purpose medium
Clematis (*Clematis* spp.)	Simple layering
Cotoneaster (*Cotoneaster* spp.)	Summer cuttings, all-purpose medium, 3,000 ppm IBA rooting preparation
Cryptomeria, Japanese (*Cryptomeria japonica*)	Late-summer cuttings, all-purpose medium, 10,000 ppm IBA rooting preparation
Dawn redwood (*Metasequoia glyptostroboides*)	Summer cuttings, all-purpose medium, 10,000 ppm IBA rooting preparation
Forsythia (*Forsythia* spp.)	Hardwood cuttings taken in early spring
Heath (*Erica* spp.)	Early-summer cuttings, all-purpose medium, 1,000 ppm IBA rooting preparation
Heather (*Calluna* spp.)	Early-summer cuttings, all-purpose medium, 1,000 ppm IBA rooting preparation
Honeysuckle (*Lonicera* spp.)	Simple layering
Hydrangea (*Hydrangea* spp.)	*Late-spring cuttings:* all-purpose medium, 1,000 ppm rooting preparation; *softwood cuttings:* all-purpose medium, 3,000 ppm rooting preparation
Juniper (*Juniperus* spp.)	Winter cuttings, medium of ½ peat moss and ½ perlite, 3,000 ppm rooting preparation
Lilac, French hybrid (*Syringa vulgaris*)	Simple layering of one-year-old shoots
Magnolia (*Magnolia* spp.)	Simple layering of basal shoots; rooting may take two years
Mock orange (*Philadelphus* spp.)	Division of suckers, hardwood cuttings taken in winter and planted in spring
Privet (*Ligustrum* spp.)	Hardwood cuttings taken in winter and planted in spring
Rhododendron (*Rhododendron* spp.)	Simple layering, semihardwood cuttings, medium of ½ peat moss and ½ perlite, 10,000 ppm rooting preparation
Rose-of-sharon (*Hibiscus syriacus*)	Early-summer cuttings, all-purpose medium, 1,000 ppm rooting preparation
Rugosa Rose (*Rosa rugosa*)	Hardwood cuttings taken in winter and planted in spring
Smoke tree (*Cotinus coggygria*)	Softwood cuttings, all-purpose medium, 3,000 ppm rooting preparation
Spirea (*Spiraea vanhouttei*)	Hardwood cuttings taken in winter and planted in spring
Trumpet creeper (*Campsis radicans*)	Simple layering; *softwood cuttings:* all-purpose medium, 1,000 ppm rooting preparation
Viburnum (*Viburnum* spp.)	Simple layering
Weigela (*Weigela* spp.)	Softwood cuttings, all-purpose medium, 3,000 ppm rooting preparation
Willow (*Salix* spp.)	Hardwood cuttings taken in winter and planted in spring
Wisteria (*Wisteria* spp.)	Simple layering

EASIEST METHODS OF ASEXUAL PROPAGATION FOR SOME COMMON PERENNIALS

PERENNIAL	TECHNIQUE
Allium (*Allium* spp.)	Bulb offsets, spring-flowering in summer, summer-flowering in spring
Aster (*Aster* spp.)	Division in fall
Avens (*Geum* spp.)	Division in spring or fall
Baby's breath (*Gypsophila* spp.)	Division in spring or fall, single flowered varieties only
Balloon flower (*Platycodon grandiflorum*)	Terminal stem cuttings in summer
Basket-of-Gold (*Aurinia saxatile*)	Division in spring
Beardtongue (*Pentstemon* spp.)	Division of clumps in fall
Bellflower (*Campanula* spp.)	Division in spring
Blanket flower (*Gaillardia* spp.)	Root cuttings taken in fall
Bleeding-heart (*Dicentra spectabilis*)	Division in early spring or fall
Boltonia (*Boltonia* spp.)	Division in spring or fall
Catmint (*Nepeta mussinii*)	Division in spring; softwood cuttings of non-flowering shoots
Chrysanthemum (*Chrysanthemum* spp.)	Softwood cuttings of lateral shoots after flowering
Coralbells (*Heuchera* spp.)	Division in spring or fall; leaf cuttings in fall
Coreopsis (*Coreopsis* spp.)	Division in spring or fall
Crocus (*Crocus* spp.)	Division of cormels from corms in fall
Cupidsdart (*Catananche caerulea*)	Division in fall
Daffodil (*Narcissus* spp.)	Division of offsets of bulbs in fall
Daylily (*Hemerocallis* spp.)	Division of clumps into fans in spring or fall
Delphinium (*Delphinium* spp.)	Spring cuttings, all-purpose medium
Evening primrose (*Oenothera* spp.)	Division in spring or fall
False Indigo (*Baptisia* spp.)	Division in fall
Gayfeather (*Liatris* spp.)	Division of roots in spring
Geranium (*Geranium* spp.)	Stem cuttings taken from spring to fall
Globe thistle (*Echinops* spp.)	Root cuttings taken in fall or division in spring
Golden marguerite (*Anthemis tinctoria*)	Division in spring
Heliopsis (*Heliopsis* spp.)	Division in fall
Jacob's ladder (*Polemonium* spp.)	Stem cuttings in summer
Japanese Anemone (*Anemone japonica*)	Root cuttings in fall
Lavender (*Lavandula* spp.)	Division of clumps in fall
Leopard bane (*Doronicum* spp.)	Division in summer after plant is dormant
Lily (*Lilium* spp.)	Scaling of bulbs in summer or planting of aerial stem bulbils
Lily-of-the-valley (*Convallaria majalis*)	Division of pips in early fall
Monkshood (*Aconitum* spp.)	Division of tuberous roots in spring
Pasque flower (*Anemone pulsatilla*)	Division in spring or fall
Pampas grass (*Cortaderia selloana*)	Division in spring or fall
Peony (*Paeonia* spp.)	Division of clumps in fall, each piece having 3–5 eyes
Pink (*Dianthus* spp.)	Simple layering
Phlox (*Phlox* spp.)	Division of clumps in fall
Poppy Anemone (*Anemone coronaria*)	Division of tuberous roots in fall
Rockcress (*Arabis* spp.)	Division in spring or fall; Softwood cuttings taken after flowers fade
Sage (*Salvia* spp.)	Late-spring cuttings, all-purpose medium
Snowdrop (*Galanthus* spp.)	Division of offsets from bulbs
Snow-in-summer (*Cerastium tomentosum*)	Division in fall or softwood cuttings taken in summer
Thrift (*Armeria* spp.)	Division in spring or fall
Yarrow (*Achillea* spp.)	Division of clumps in fall

Divide and Conquer

Propagation of plants is a wonderful pastime, but some people don't have the time to build plastic tents and prepare cuttings. They need a method in which the plants do the work and they supervise. Well, believe it or not, here is just that method.

The *crown* of a plant is that area near the surface of the ground from which new shoots grow. In woody plants, the crown refers to the part of the stem that forms the transition between the trunk and the roots. In herbaceous plants, however, the crown is where new shoots arise each spring. Many plants, especially perennials and woody shrubs, produce numerous new shoots from their crowns each year. Many of these shoots also have roots. To propagate them, just separate and transplant the plants, a technique called crown division.

CROWN DIVISION

Crown division is not only a very easy method of propagation, but is also often essential for the healthy growth of many perennials. As the plants grow, more and more shoots crowd around the original crown. The plants become so packed together that none of them can glean adequate moisture and nutrients. If they aren't divided, they may become weak and spindly.

Plants that bloom in spring and early summer should be divided in fall at the end of the growing season. Plants that bloom in late summer or fall should be divided in spring at the start of the growing season.

SECRETS TO SUCCESS

There are two secrets to successful transplanting of bare root divisions:

- Water and loosen the earth around the plant and the new planting bed before you dig the plant.

- Work fast and never trim unbroken roots. The portion of the root that absorbs moisture is the root hairs. These minute structures at the very ends of the roots die quickly once exposed to air. The less time the plant is out of the soil, the better.

CROWN DIVISION OF SHRUBS

Many woody plants, such as spirea and mock orange, produce crowns with multiple stems that can be successfully divided.

1. Place the blade of a sharp shovel 6 to 12 inches from the crown. Plunge the blade into the soil, angling under the plant. Continue around the crown until you have freed the plant.

2. Determine where the plant should naturally be divided. Each division should have a good number of stems and roots. Small clumps can be separated by cutting the crown with a shovel blade; thick clumps may need a hatchet. Most of the soil will probably fall off the roots.

3. Transplant the clumps into a hole that is larger than the sprawling roots. Spread the roots evenly and fill with loose soil. Water well and mulch.

Crown Division of Perennials

As with shrubs, prepare the new planting bed before you dig the clump to be divided. Loosen the soil around the perimeter of the clump with a garden fork and lever the plant out of the soil. Small crowns can be pulled apart with your hands. Separate large crowns by working in from the edges of the clump. Insert the tines of a hand fork into the clump and pry three to four small stem clumps from the main crown. This method is a little slower than chopping the plant up with a knife or shovel blade, but it causes much less plant damage.

Once the clumps are separated, transplant into a hole that is larger than the sprawling roots. Spread the roots evenly over the hole and fill with loose soil. Water well and mulch.

◆ **Shrubs and Perennials for Division**
Daylilies (*Hemerocallis* spp.)
Forsythia (*Forsythia* spp.)
Mock orange (*Philadelphus* spp.)
Mint (*Mentha* spp.)
Red-osier dogwood *(Cornus sericea)*
Spirea (*Spiraea* spp.)
Yarrow (*Achillea* spp.)

DIVIDING FLOWERING BULBS

In some plants the crown is structurally more specialized than in others. These modified stems and roots include bulbs, corms, tubers, rhizomes, and tuberous roots and stems. In commerce as well as the garden, these structures are often lumped together and called flowering bulbs. In practice, flowering bulbs serve as repositories for food reserves as well as the sites for bud formation and vegetative reproduction. Plants that produce bulbs are herbaceous plants that die back to the ground at at the end of each growing season; they are adaptations that enable the plants to survive the seasons of inclement weather present in temperate and semi-arid regions of the world.

DIVIDING CORMS

A *corm* is a compact stem wrapped in a sheath of dried leaves. Corms reproduce by producing little corms, or *cormels,* at the base of the mother corm. During the growing season the mother corm whithers away as it sends its energy to the flower shoots. The food produced by the leaves travels to the cormels, which grow into new corms.

The best time to divide corms is about two to three months after they have finished flowering, or when fall frosts have browned the leaves. Dig the corms from the ground and separate the new corms and cormels. Discard any diseased plants. New corms and cormels of hardy plants can be replanted immediately; those of tender plants should be dusted with a fungicide and dried in a warm, shady spot for about a week. Place the corms in a paper bag and store in a dark, dry place at about 40 to 45°F until spring. Large corms will flower the next year, while it may take cormels two growing seasons to blossom.

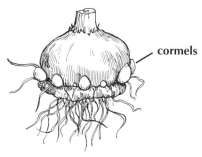
cormels

This gladiolus corm has produced small corms, or cormels, at its base. In the fall, dig the corm, gently remove the cormels, dust them with a fungicide and dry them before storing them in a paper bag until spring planting.

◆ **Some Plants Grown from Corms**
Autumn crocus *(Colchicum autumnale)*
Crocus (*Crocus* spp.)
Freesia (*Freesia* x *hybrida*)
Gladiolus (*Gladiolus* spp.)
Tritonia (*Tritonia* spp.)
Winter daffodil (*Sternbergia lutea*)

DIVIDING TUBERS

A *tuber* consists of an underground stem swollen with the accumulation of food materials and sprinkled with buds called eyes. Some common garden plants that produce tubers include the potato *(Solanum tuberosum),* Jerusalem artichoke *(Helianthus tuberosus),* and caladium *(Caladium* spp.). Tubers mature in just one growing season, but they do not begin to form until the days begin to shorten after the summer solstice. At this time the plant produces hormones that initiate flowering, slow vegetative growth, and begin tuber enlargement. Tubers grow best during warm days followed by cool nights.

Dig tubers in fall, gently cleaning them of excess soil. Then store the tubers intact in a dark, cool place in fresh sawdust or vermiculite (50–60°F for a week, then 40–45°F). A few days before planting time, move them to a warm, humid environment. Division consists of cutting the tuber into 2-ounce sections, each piece having at least two eyes. Place the cut sections in a warm, humid environment for two to three days so the cut portions can heal, and then plant them.

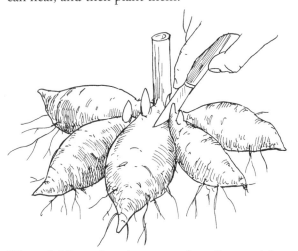

When dividing tubers be sure each section contains healthy buds.

♦ **Some Plants Grown from Tubers**
  Caladium *(Caladium* spp.)
  Jerusalem artichoke *(Helianthus tuberosus)*
  Potato *(Solanum tuberosum)*

Dividing Tuberous Roots

A *tuberous root* differs from a tuber in that one is a root and the other a stem. This may seem like a trivial distinction, but it's not. Divisions of most tuberous roots must include a portion of the crown with the root if the plant is to grow successfully. To accomplish this, most plants bearing tuberous roots are propagated by dividing the crown so that each tuberous section also contains a bud. Some common plants producing tuberous roots include tuberous begonia *(Begonia* x *tuberhybrida),* dahlia *(Dahlia* spp.), lily-of-the-Nile *(Agapanthus africanus),* and gloxinia *(Sinningia speciosa).*

The plants are lifted in fall, dried for a few days, and then stored in vermiculite at about 45°F through the winter. At planting time each is divided, dusted with a fungicide, and dried for about three days so the cut portions can heal.

♦ **Some Plants Grown from Tuberous Roots**
  Black calla *(Arum palaestinum)*
  Dahlia *(Dahlia* spp.)
  Florists cyclamen *(Cyclamen persicum)*
  Gloxinia *(Sinningia speciosa)*
  Lily-of-the-Nile *(Agapanthus africanthus)*
  Tuberous Begonia *(Begonia* x *tuberhybrida)*

Dividing Rhizomes

A *rhizome* is a segmented stem that grows horizontally just underground. Some plants that grow from rhizomes include lily-of-the-valley *(Convallaria majalis),* iris *(Iris* spp.), canna *(Canna* x *generalis),* and achimenes *(Achimenes* spp.). Rhizomes come in two types, which have Latin-sounding names that confuse the heck out of most folks, so in my mind I think of them as the Laurels and Hardys of the plant world: One type is long and thin, the other short and stout.

Plants with long, thin rhizomes, such as the lily-of-the-valley, have a bud above a rooted stem. Simply separate the stem below the roots and plant.

Plants with short, stout rhizomes, such as the iris, are a bit more complicated. These thick stems have an old central section and many new secondary stems growing perpendicular to it. After you lift the rhizome from the soil, separate the new, firm sections from the old, spongy one. Each section should have an attached fan of leaves. Dust with a fungicide, if you like, and leave in a shady spot for a few hours so the cut sections can heal. Replant in fertile ground with the rhizome covered by half an inch to an inch of soil. Divide these plants in late summer to early fall.

♦ **Some Plants Grown from Rhizomes**
    Achimenes (*Achimenes* spp.)
    Canna *(Canna* **x** *generalis)*
    Iris (*Iris* spp.)
    Lily-of-the-valley (*Convallaria majalis)*

AERIAL BULBILS

Some lilies, notably the bulbil lily *(Lilium bulbiferum),* Sargent lily *(Lilium sargentiae),* sulphur lily *(Lilium sulphureum),* and tiger lily *(Lilium tigrinum),* produce small bulbs called bulbils in the axils of the leaves. These begin to form in summer and grow to the size of a pea just before falling from the plant in early autumn. The bulbils may begin to grow roots while still on the parent plant.

Harvest bulbils in late summer when they can be picked easily from the axils. Fill a flat with moist growing mix and firm gently. Dibble holes into the mix 1 inch apart; plant one bulbil in each hole. Fill the holes with soil and place the flat in a sealed plastic bag. Store the flat in a warm spot out of direct light for two months. The bulbils will use this time to grow roots. Move the flat into the refrigerator for another three months so the plants can complete their seasonal chill requirement. In spring, plant them in the garden.

The first year they will produce just one leaf or a slender stem of leaves. Some can reach flowering size the following year. Some species that do not ordinarily produce bulbils will do so if the flower buds are pinched off and one week later the stem is cut back to half its height.

♦ **Lilies Propagated by Bulbils**
    Bulbil lily (*Lilium bulbiferum)*
    Canada lily (*Lilium canadense)*
    Chalcedonian lily *(Lilium chalcedonicum)*
    Nankeen lily (*Lilium* **x** *testaceum)*
    Sargent lily (*Lilium sargentiae)*
    Sulphur lily (*Lilium sulphureum)*
    Tiger lily (*Lilium tigrinum)*
    Umbel lily (*Lilium* **x** *hollandicum)*

DIVIDING TRUE BULBS

True bulbs are best described as big underground buds surrounded by modified leaf bases called scales. The scales to the outside of the bulb are used to store food, while those deep in the bulb are thinner and more leaflike. At the center of the bulb there is usually a flower bud. There are two types of bulbs: *Scaly* bulbs include lilies; *laminate* bulbs include daffodils, tulips, and onions. Both types can be propagated by division.

Propagating Bulbs by Offsets

Different bulbs grow in different ways. In bulbous irises and tulips, the mother bulb sends up a flower shoot in spring. After flowering the mother bulb withers, to be replaced by a cluster of new bulbs. These new bulbs need very fertile conditions in order to grow to flowering size in one year. Daffodil bulbs, however, do not wither, but continue to grow for years.

Tulips. To keep tulips blooming year after year, plant the bulbs in fertile, well-drained soil well amended with organic matter. After the flowers have shattered in spring, cut off the old flower head but leave the foliage intact. Water and fertilize plants throughout the growing season, keep-

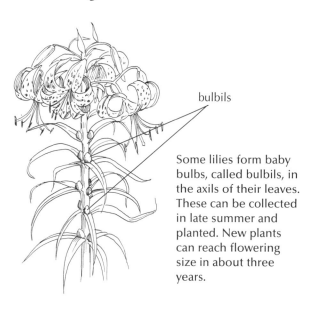

bulbils

Some lilies form baby bulbs, called bulbils, in the axils of their leaves. These can be collected in late summer and planted. New plants can reach flowering size in about three years.

ing them vigorous for as long as possible into summer.

Unfortunately, the weather has a great influence on tulips. Cool springs followed by hot summers will force dormancy before the new daughter bulbs reach flowering size. Areas with long cool springs and summers (such as the Pacific Northwest) produce the best offset bulbs.

After the foliage has turned brown in late summer, lift the plants from the soil. Separate the new offset bulbs from the remains of the mother bulb. If you wish, dust the new bulbs with fungicide and replant. If you prefer to force the bulbs during winter, first shake off all loose soil. Place the bulbs on screens in a warm (65–70°F), dark place to dry. After about three weeks pack the bulbs in fresh sawdust and store at between 40 and 50°F for two months, after which the bulbs will be ready for planting.

Daffodils. With daffodils, it takes about five years for a small offset bulb to become a large mother bulb. When an offset first splits from the mother, it is called a spoon. Spoons can be gathered and replanted but are not yet of flowering size. After a spoon grows for an additional season, a flower bud develops at its center; the bulb is now called a

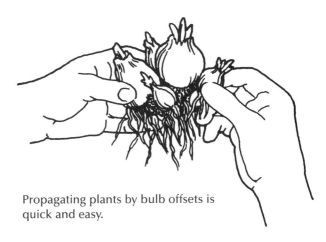

Propagating plants by bulb offsets is quick and easy.

SCALING

Scaling is used to propagate many cultivated lily varieties. The best time to scale lilies is just after they have completed flowering. Carefully lift the lily from the earth with a garden fork, shaking off any clinging soil. Remove the outer two rows of scales from the plant and store them between the folds of a moist towel. Lightly dust the parent plant with fungicide, or dip it in a fungicide solution, and replant. Snip off the old flower heads but leave the leaves intact.

To prepare the scales, fill a pot with moist growing mix — for example, one made of equal parts peat moss, vermiculite, and perlite — and firm gently. Dibble holes into the mix 1 inch apart; plant one scale in each hole. Fill the holes with soil and place the pot in a sealed plastic bag. Store the pot in a warm spot out of direct light for two months. During this time the scales will grow little bulbs at their bases. Move the pot into the refrigerator for another three months so the plants can complete their seasonal chill requirement. In spring plant the little guys in the garden and watch them grow.

Scaling of lilies is done just after flowering in summer, leaving plenty of time for the foliage to replenish the mother bulb before winter sets in.

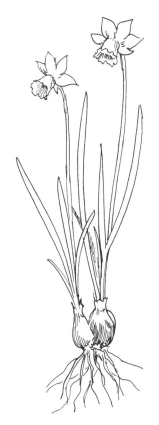

If an offset is not separated from the mother bulb it will become large enough to produce a flower stem. These bulbs are called double-nosed and represent the highest grade of daffodil bulb.

round or single-nose. Another season of growth produces a pair of flower buds and the bulb becomes a double-nose. Double-nose bulbs begin to produce offsets the following year and are hence called mother bulbs.

Lift daffodils after the foliage has browned in late summer. Gently separate the offsets from the mother bulbs and remove any excess soil. Offsets can be replanted immediately, if you wish. To keep the larger bulbs for forcing during winter, store them in a container of fresh sawdust at a temperature of 45 to 50°F for two months, after which the bulbs will be ready for planting.

◆ **Plants That Can Be Propagated from Offsets**
 Daffodil (*Narcissus* spp.)
 Hyacinth (*Hyancinthus* spp.)
 Tuberose (*Polianthes tuberosa*)
 Tulip (*Tulipa* spp.)

Leaf Cuttings from Bulbous Plants

One of the more fascinating ways to propagate some plants that grow from bulbs is by leaf cuttings. This is a proven method of reproducing such plants as the blood lily (*Haemanthus* spp.), grape hyacinth (*Muscari* spp.) and cape cowslip (*Lachenalia* spp.).

When the leaves are actively growing in spring, cut them from the bulb. Then cut each leaf into two or three pieces, being careful to note up from down. Place each cutting into an all-purpose propagation medium with the base of the cutting several inches beneath the surface. Place in a plastic tent for about one month during which small bulblets will form at the base of each cutting. You can then plant the bulblets in the garden.

◆ **Bulbous Plants That Can Be Propagated from Leaf Cuttings**
 Blood lily (*Haemanthus* spp.)
 Cape cowslip (*Lachenalia* spp.)
 Grape hyacinth (*Muscari* spp.)

Bulb Cuttings

Some bulbous plants can be propagated by a technique known as bulb cuttings. Cut a pre-chilled, dormant bulb of flowering size into four pieces, using two vertical/perpendicular cuts. All cuttings should have a portion of the bulb's basal plate attached. These sections can be further divided by cutting each piece along the center of the concentric scales so that each resulting piece has a section of basal plate and three to four bulb scales. Plant the cuttings in a moist, all-purpose propagation medium, and then cover with a plastic tent. After six to eight weeks remove the flat from the tent and place it in a shaded cold frame for the rest of the growing season. In early fall remove the cuttings from the flat and plant them in the garden.

◆ **Plants to Propagate from Bulb Cuttings**
 Albuca (*Albuca* spp.)
 Blood lily (*Haemanthus* spp.)
 Chasmanthe (*Chasmanthe* spp.)
 Daffodil (*Narcissus* spp.)
 Magic lily (*Lycoris squamigera*)
 Spider lily (*Hymenocallis* spp.)
 Squill (*Scilla* spp.)

In This Chapter

- *Seed Viability*
- *Some Basic Growing Concepts*
- *Preparing the Soil*
- *Growing Information*
- *The Top 10 Pests and Diseases of Cool-Weather Vegetables*
- *Beneficial Insects: Pollinators*
- *Beneficial Insects: Predators*
- *Longer Growing Seasons*
- *The BIGGEST Root Crops*
- *Catalog of Cool-Weather Vegetables*

4

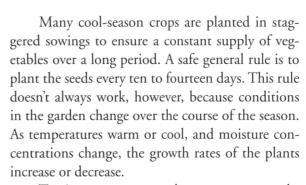

Cool-Season Vegetables

The cool season is that time of year when night temperatures stay above about 25°F but below 60°F. The length of time the cool weather lingers will differ every year, but the typical cool season ranges from less than sixty days in the Far North and Deep South, to more than one hundred days elsewhere. In some locations in the southern Appalachians and southwestern mountains the season can even last longer. The cool season comes in winter in the Deep South and much of California, in spring and fall through most of the United States and southern Canada, and in summer in far northern areas.

There are ways to gauge the approximate times of year your area has cool seasons. In spring the season lasts from about thirty-five to forty-five days before the last frost to thirty-five to forty-five days after. In fall the season extends from thirty-five to forty-five days before the first frost to thirty-five to forty-five days after. In many temperate areas the spring cool season begins about the time such trees as maples and birch blossom. In fall the season begins when the cicadas, those large, red-eyed bugs, begin to sing from the treetops.

Many cool-season crops are planted in staggered sowings to ensure a constant supply of vegetables over a long period. A safe general rule is to plant the seeds every ten to fourteen days. This rule doesn't always work, however, because conditions in the garden change over the course of the season. As temperatures warm or cool, and moisture concentrations change, the growth rates of the plants increase or decrease.

To time your staggered crops more exactly, sow your second plantings of root crops and greens, such as radishes and spinach, when the seedlings show their first set of true leaves. For other crops, such as peas, make successive plantings when the seedlings from the previous sowing are as tall as your index finger is long.

Another old-time gardening secret can tell you when to begin harvesting brussels sprouts and parsnips. When transplants of brussels sprouts or seeds of parsnips were planted in the garden back then, the farmer would cut a small notch at the base of his or her thumbnail. When the notch reached the end of the thumbnail, it was time to begin the harvest.

Seed Viability

Not all seeds are created equal. Seeds of some plants can be stored for years and still germinate while others survive for only days after they ripen. Most vegetable plants produce seed that remains viable for at least one year and often more.

Seed packets have a date stamped on them so folks know what growing season they have been packed for. Unfortunately, this gives the impression that the seeds in the packet are viable only for that season. So each year lots of perfectly good seeds get thrown out. The truth is that many vegetable seeds can be stored for many years without losing their vitality. The trick is in the storage of the seeds.

To maximize the longevity of your seeds make sure that the seeds are dry. Place the seeds in a clean, dry, opaque container and seal. Place the container in a cool to cold location. Cool to cold are pretty general guidelines but generally the seeds will keep better at temperatures just above freezing.

The map below shows average last-frost dates in spring throughout the United States and southern Canada. Use these guidelines to plan your optimal seed planting schedule. Many cool-weather vegetables can be sown a couple of weeks before the expected date of the last spring frost.

STORAGE LIFE (IN YEARS)		
NAME	OPTIMUM	MAXIMUM
Asparagus	1–3	4–8
Beans	1–3	4–8
Beets	1–4	5–10
Broccoli	1–4	5–10
Cabbage	1–2	3–4
Carrots	1–3	4–9
Celery	1–5	6–15
Corn	1	2
Cucumbers	1–5	6–10
Eggplants	1–5	6–10
Lettuce	1–5	6–9
Melons	1–5	6–9
Okra	1–2	3–10
Onions	1	2–4
Parsnips	1–2	3–4
Peas	1–3	4–7
Peppers	1–3	4–12
Pumpkins	1–4	5–8
Radishes	1–3	4–10
Spinach	1–4	5–7
Squash	1–2	3–4
Tomatoes	1–3	4–12
Turnips	1–4	5–10

AVERAGE DATES OF LAST SPRING FROST

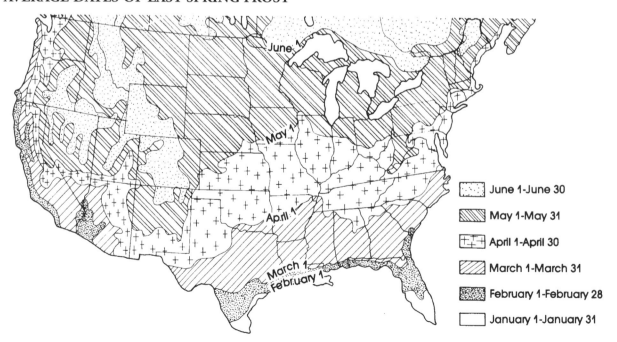

June 1-June 30

May 1-May 31

April 1-April 30

March 1-March 31

February 1-February 28

January 1-January 31

Some Basic Growing Concepts

Many people grow very nice gardens by simply following directions on seed packets or doing what they have seen others do over the years. Often their gardens mix crops that do very well, with others that are just okay. In an effort to create a more uniform garden they try the latest varieties and fads — but still get mixed results.

In the end, improving your skills as a gardener comes down to understanding concepts that almost everyone skips over in the race to plant the vegetable patch. Here are some of those concepts; once understood and put into practice, they will improve your garden.

PLANTING AND GERMINATION

Most seeds are like little vehicles that come with a full tank of gas as standard equipment. The energy stored in the seed is designed to last until the seedling pokes into the sunlight and begins to produce energy from photosynthesis. If the emerging seedling has to travel through too much soil before it reaches the light, or if temperature or moisture conditions slow its growth, it becomes stressed. The chemistry of stressed plants is much different from unstressed ones: One focuses on mere survival, the other on continued active growth.

Whether you're starting seeds indoors or out, be sure that the seedbed is well worked, loose, and smooth. Temperatures and moisture should be near the optimum for that crop. Each seed should be planted and covered with fine soil or, better yet,

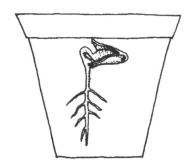

Most emerging seedlings have a curved stem that helps push away soil as the stem grows.

vermiculite to a depth equal to twice its diameter. Once broad-leaved vegetables, such as beans, germinate, they push their arch-shaped stem through the soil while continuing to absorb moisture and nutrients from the remains of the seed. When light contacts the stem, it straightens up, and the seed leaves can unfold. If the seed has been planted too deep the seedling may weaken before it reaches the soil surface, or be in a state of stress when it does. Seeds planted too shallow may emerge before the young plants have had time to absorb enough nutrients from them, and the plants will die.

These guidelines apply to those seeds that require darkness to germinate. Other plants produce seeds that need light to germinate and must be planted uncovered on the soil surface. The key to the successful germination of these seeds is plenty of indirect light and an even supply of moisture.

PHOTOSYNTHESIS

Photosynthesis is the process by which plants convert sunlight into energy. As plants grow and the foliage expands, the uppermost leaves receive plenty of sunlight. These same leaves, however, shade other leaves or plants, decreasing photosynthesis there. For the highest-quality yields, plants that produce fruits (tomatoes, eggplants, peas) or storage parts (potatoes and turnips) need large amounts of sunlight throughout the growing season. Crops grown for their leaves, such as spinach or Swiss chard, do not need as much sunlight to produce great yields. Site and space the former for maximum sunlight.

Plants need much more than just light to accomplish photosynthesis, however. And if the other things are missing, then photosynthesis won't happen. Certain minerals are essential to the process: magnesium, iron, phosphorus, and chlorine. In addition, other minerals, including sulfur, calcium, boron, zinc, copper, and manganese, are important. Soil with a good supply of major and minor elements, bathed with sunlight, is the best bet to produce great gardens.

WATER SUPPLY

Many vegetable crops contain up to 95 percent water and need ample soil moisture to maintain even growth and produce high-quality crops. If the moisture supply is restricted, such as during the hottest hours of a bright, sunny day, physiologic changes occur within the plant that can affect crop quality. When a plant is water-stressed, it begins to conserve moisture by closing the stomates in the leaf. These tiny pores not only allow moisture to transpire from the leaf, but also allow carbon dioxide (CO_2), a compound needed for photosynthesis, to enter. As the stomates close to conserve moisture, they block intake of CO_2 and photosynthesis slows, which interrupts growth and ultimately affects the quality of the crop. Maintaining soil moisture at all times is critical to uniform and consistent growth of vegetables.

Preparing the Soil

Site your garden on nearly level ground with an open southern exposure in northern regions, and an open northern exposure in southern regions. If your garden is on a slope, be sure to follow the contour of the land when tilling.

In fall till the garden well, incorporating compost, leaves, or rotted manure into the soil. North of Zone 7, where the ground freezes for long periods in the winter, the loosened soil can then be hilled into raised beds. The tops of the raised beds will dry out and warm up earlier in the spring than

Raking the garden in spring helps warm the soil while improving drainage.

soil left flat, allowing for earlier planting. In spring loosen the soil lightly before planting, raking and smoothing the seedbed.

From Zone 7 south, plant a cover crop, such as alfalfa, in the loosened soil, to inhibit leaching of soil nutrients during winter. In spring till the cover crop into the garden a few weeks before sowing dates. Lightly rake the ground before planting to produce a smooth seedbed.

Most vegetables require fertile soil, because they have root systems that are small for the size of the plant and so are not very efficient collectors of nutrients. Preparing the soil by amending it with organic matter and protecting soil nutrients from leaching during winter provide the best foundation for a successful garden season. Addition of organic matter improves soil fertility and water absorption, inhibits erosion and runoff, improves aeration, encourages beneficial bacterial growth, and even helps the soil warm more quickly in spring. Soils amended with well-rotted livestock manure, especially horse manure, are said to produce better-tasting vegetables than any others.

All vegetables grow well in soils with a pH range of from 6.0 to 6.5. Some, such as asparagus, beets, squash, and melons, can thrive in more alkaline soils, while others, including parsnips, peppers, and eggplants, can grow well in more acid soils. Pumpkins, tomatoes, beans, carrots, and cucumbers are very versatile, producing good harvests in soils ranging from moderately acid to moderately alkaline.

Soil pH can also be used to control certain vegetable diseases. Potatoes grown in soil with a pH of 5.0 to 5.5 are less likely to suffer from scab, and cabbage grown in soil with a pH of 7.5 to 8.0 is less likely to have club root.

ADDING GROUND LIMESTONE

MOST VEGETABLES PREFER A SOIL pH OF ABOUT 6.5. THE CHART BELOW GIVES APPROXIMATE AMOUNTS OF LIMESTONE NEEDED TO RAISE THE pH TO THE OPTIMUM RANGE FOR VARIOUS SOILS.

pH VALUE	POUNDS PER 100 SQ. FT.		
	SANDY SOILS	SILT LOAMS	CLAY LOAMS
6.5 and above	0	0	0
6.2–6.4	22	44	44
5.8–6.1	44	66	66
5.4–5.7	66	88	110
4.8–5.3	88	132	154

Growing Information

A few tips that nobody ever told you can make the difference between a great cool-weather garden and disappointment. Root crops, such as turnips and radishes, are most tender and flavorful if they grow at a steady pace from germination to harvest. If their growth is interrupted by drought or by hot or cold temperatures, though, the cells in the roots begin to toughen, changing the flavor and texture of the plant. Transplanting also interrupts growth, stimulates root formation, and toughens the leaves. Because of this transplanted crops, such as lettuce, don't produce their best-flavored leaves until three to four weeks after transplanting.

Hardening slows a plant's growth rate, helps it better absorb moisture, and stimulates storage of carbohydrates; all of which help the plant thrive in the garden.

For cool-season crops that can be started indoors, sow seeds about four to eight weeks before your expected planting date. Use a fine seed-starter mix and the type of containers — plastic flats, cell packs, or pots — that you prefer.

Scatter very small seeds atop the mix and cover lightly. Small seeds, such as cabbage, can be planted in drills 1/4 inch deep and covered. Plant larger seeds, such as beet, in 1/2-inch-deep drills and cover. Keep the soil moist while the seeds are germinating.

To thin seedlings without damaging roots, snip unwanted plants at soil level with a pair of manicure scissors.

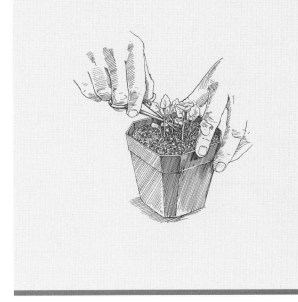

HARDENING PLANTS

Hardening is any process that acclimates plants to new environments. This acclimatization produces changes in the internal aspects of the plant that manifest as a toughening of plant tissues, literally. As a seed germinates it uses stored food in the form of carbohydrates to emerge from the soil. As the leaves unfold above ground they begin to manufacture the sugars and starches needed for continued growth. At this stage in a plant's life there is little margin for error. Their vigorous rate of growth uses just about all of the energy that the young leaves produce with precious little left in reserve. If the plant is placed in an environment that disrupts the production of food by the leaves, the plant may just run out of gas before it adjusts to the new, harsher conditions.

Hardening allows the plant to adjust to a more challenging environment by slowing its metabolism. The process has two goals; to interrupt the fast rate of growth, and store food reserves for the future. Hardening involves reducing the amount of moisture available to the plant while exposing it to colder temperatures. This allows the plant to accumulate carbohydrates as well as effciently store moisture.

STARTING SEEDS OUTDOORS

After raking the seedbed smooth, mark the rows by placing a stake at each end and stretching a string down the row. Prepare a shallow trough or wide band along the row with a dibble stick, toll handle, or hoe blade. Drop the seeds into the trough, being sure to space them according to the guidelines on the seed packet. Label the beginning and end of the row, and cover the seeds with vermiculite: the light color of the vermiculite will mark the row until the seedlings emerge. Water well with a gentle spray of water.

ROTATING CROPS

After you have harvested the first crops from your garden, your next task is to fill the now-empty rows. Over countless generations of observation and experience, a list has emerged of succession crops: those that best use the empty space left after first crops are harvested. As a general rule, do not replant an empty row with a crop of the same family as the harvested plant. For example, as broccoli grows in the garden it will attract some pests that like broccoli. If the next crop in that row is another cole crop, then the bugs or diseases don't have far to go to find nirvana.

GOOD ROTATION

PLANT	FOLLOW WITH	DO NOT FOLLOW WITH
Beans	cauliflower, carrots, broccoli, cabbage, corn	onions, garlic
Beets	spinach	—
Cole crops	beans, onions	tomatoes
Carrots	lettuce, tomatoes	dill
Cucumbers	peas, radishes	potatoes
Kale	beans, peas	cole crops
Lettuce	carrots, cucumbers, radishes	—
Onions	radishes, lettuce, cole crops	beans
Peas	cole crops, carrots, beans, corn	—
Potatoes	beans, cabbage, corn, turnips	tomatoes, squash, pumpkins
Radishes	beans	cole crops
Tomatoes	carrots, onions	cole crops

TRANSPLANTING VS. DIRECT-SOWING

Here are some other factors to consider when deciding whether to transplant or direct-sow a particular vegetable crop:

Transplanting seedlings from flats or pots helps create great gardens in three ways. The first is correct spacing. It seems there's a natural tendency to transplant seedlings farther apart than those that are direct-sown. The resulting spacing favors the transplants. With more room to grow, they mature faster and produce higher-quality crops than their more closely spaced counterparts.

Second, the act of transplanting a seedling often snaps off the very tip of the roots. This induces the main roots to branch, creating a stronger root system.

Finally, transplanting acts to harden plants by checking their growth.

Some plants have such a small window of time in which they can be transplanted that they are almost always direct-sown. The secret to producing high-quality direct-sown crops is to space the seeds far enough apart that when the seedlings are thinned, the root systems of the remaining plants are not damaged.

An easy way to do this is to snip off the seedlings slated for thinning with a pair of scissors at the soil line, rather than uprooting them. Also, many crops, such as squash, can be direct-sown in hills without subsequent thinning.

BEST COOL-SEASON VEGETABLES TO TRANSPLANT	BEST COOL-SEASON VEGETABLES TO DIRECT-SOW
Broccoli	Beans
Cabbage	Mustard
Cauliflower	Peas
Lettuce	Radishes
Kohlrabi	Turnips
Brussels Sprouts	Spinach
	Parsnips
	Beets

The annual battle with Jack Frost has been waged by gardeners for generations. There are good ways and bad ways, popular methods and snake-oil tricks to extend the season a bit longer than nature had in mind. One of the most widely used products is the row cover, a lightweight blanket that you place around plants. Some row covers are semipermanent, with metal supports and plastic or fabric covers that turn the garden row into a little greenhouse. Floating row covers are sheets of light fabric that can be quickly deployed over plants. Row covers protect the plants beneath them from frost by slightly buffering the air temperature near the plant and providing a surface for the frost to form. Frost damages leaves by rupturing plant cells as ice crystals grow on the leaf surface. If the ice forms on the row cover it cannot damage the leaves beneath. It is therefore important to be sure no leaves are in contact with the row cover when it is placed over the plants.

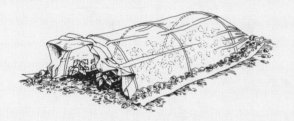

Row covers not only protect plants from frost, but can keep them warm on cool spring days.

Although row covers almost always take the form of tunnels, recent research has suggested that a horizontal blanket deployed 6 inches above and extending about 2 feet to the sides of the plants may be even more effective at protecting plants from frost. Just about any material will suffice for this frost blanket but the lightest and easiest to use are thin films made of spunbonded polypropylene. These are manufactured under a variety of trade names including Agrofabric. The most commonly used Agrofabric product is called Agrofabric 17 which offers frost protection to temperatures as low as 28°F.

You might also try water-filled plant protectors, which are designed to protect individual plants instead of rows or groups of plants. The most common water-filled device is the Wall-o-water. This product is made of double-walled plastic tubes arranged like a teepee to fit over plants. When filled with warm water the device can protect plants to an astounding 16°F. They are also used to warm small sections of the garden for earlier transplanting. A package of 3 usually can be purchased for under $10.00. Less expensive protectors can be made by folding a sheet of newspaper into the shape of a cone and placing it over small plants. Inverted flower pots also work. Seedlings can be protected remarkably well by covering them at dusk with styrofoam cups.

Don't forget that your best ally in fighting frost is water. As water freezes, it releases heat energy into the air. Thorough watering of the soil around plants the evening before an expected frost will help buffer air temperatures.

Protecting plants from frost is time-consuming, but today's methods are much better than those in the past. Years ago English gardens were protected from frosts by placing panes of glass supported by wire frames over the tops of the plants. I think I'll stick with row covers.

As water freezes it releases heat into the air. Thorough watering of the soil beneath a plant can help buffer air temperatures.

The Top 10 Pests and Diseases of Cool-Weather Vegetables

Aphids

AFFECTS: Cabbage, peas, cauliflower, broccoli, kale, lettuce, turnip

wingless adult

¹/₈"/3.2mm

Aphids are small, soft-bodied insects that feed on plant fluids. The bugs seek out soft, rapidly growing shoots, buds, and leaves, which are high in nitrogen and not yet hardened. Most species of garden aphids reproduce astonishingly fast because each bug is a female and can reproduce without mating. Populations can double literally overnight.

Control: Do not overfertilize or overwater plants. Harden plants thoroughly before setting out. Ladybugs and lacewings eat aphids. Direct controls include insecticidal soap, diatomaceous earth, garlic oil and water, and hot pepper wax.

Cabbage Worms

AFFECTS: Broccoli, cabbage, cauliflower, greens, brussels sprouts, collard, kohlrabi

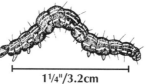

1¹/₄"/3.2cm

Cabbage worms are the soft-bodied larvae of many different butterflies, including the cabbage butterfly and cabbage looper. They all have a very large appetite and munch on the leaves, producing unsightly holes and mangled leaf margins. They can appear on the plants at any time, but they are most noticeable during late spring through summer.

Control: Crops grown under row covers are essentially made immune to attack by the physical barrier of the cover. As soon as you see damage, spray crops with Bt, a nontoxic bacterium. Commercial formulations are marketed under the names Dipel, Thuricide, and Biotrol.

Flea Beetles

AFFECTS: Beets, cabbage, broccoli, kale, cauliflower, turnips, brussels sprouts, Chinese cabbage, collard, arugula, kohlrabi

¹/₁₆"/1.6mm

Flea beetles are dark-colored, round-backed insects even smaller than the head of a pin. They are called flea beetles because they hop away from danger much as fleas do. Flea beetles chew small holes that can make leaves look like Lilliputian Swiss cheese.

Control: Row covers stop flea beetles from ever getting near the plants. Keep weeds out of the garden. Spray with garlic and water, or neem extracts.

Cutworms

AFFECTS: Beets, cabbage, broccoli, kale, cauliflower, lettuce

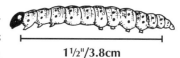

1¹/₂"/3.8cm

Cutworms are soft-bodied caterpillars that emerge from the soil at night and feed on young plants and seedlings, typically by cutting through the stem an inch or two above the soil line.

Control: Use plastic mulches instead of organic ones. Eliminate weeds from the garden: Place cardboard collars around the stems of plants. Spread bran mixed with Bt near plants and along the perimeter of the garden.

Leafminers

AFFECTS: Spinach, beets

¹/₈"/3.2mm

Leafminers, the soft-bodied larvae of flies, are so small they can tunnel between the upper and lower surfaces of leaves. The resulting damage produces whitish, winding mines over the leaf surface. There are many different species of leafminers, each producing its own particular pattern of tunnels.

Control: Start by using row covers. Use plastic instead of organic mulches. Yellow sticky traps can capture adults. Destroy infested leaves. Spray with neem oil extract.

Root Maggots

AFFECTS: Brussels sprouts, cabbage, cauliflower, radishes, turnips

Root maggots are the soft-bodied larvae of flies. The adult fly emerges in spring and then lays eggs on the ground near the stem; when the eggs hatch, the worms munch on the roots.

Control: Apply beneficial nematodes, under the commercial name Seek, to the soil. Place tar paper around stems. Use plastic mulches instead of organic. Use floating row covers, especially in cool weather.

Slugs

AFFECTS: Endive, lettuce, beans

Slugs are mollusks, like clams, and slide through the garden at night and on wet,  cloudy days. Slugs gnaw rather than cut, leaving rough edges. They also eat leaves before they uncurl, producing holes across the mature leaf.

Control: Slug traps can be as simple as a board laid in a shady place or an inverted pot on uneven soil. Low pans filled with beer also work. Spread diatomaceous earth around plants.

Damping Off

AFFECTS: Most plants

Damping off is a disease of seedlings that either rots the seed before it sprouts (pre-emergence) or kills the seedling shortly after it emerges from the soil (postemergence). Many organisms can cause the condition.

Control: Commercial fungicides can help prevent damping-off, but the best control is prevention. Clean and sterilize pots and flats with a 4:1 mixture of water and bleach, then rinse. Keep soil moist but not wet, and provide good air circulation. Dispose of infected plants as soon as they appear. Avoid overcrowding seedlings, and use well-drained soil mix.

Club Root

AFFECTS: Cabbage, broccoli, brussels sprouts, cauliflower, Chinese cabbage, kale, collard, kohlrabi, radishes, turnips

A disease of cole crops, club root migrated to North America from Europe over a century ago. The plants wilt on hot days but recover on cool days and overnight. Outer leaves turn yellow. Roots are distorted by swellings and rot.

Control: Inspect the roots of seedlings before you plant them, disposing of suspicious ones. The infection is at its worst in wet, cool soils. Rotate cole crops on a schedule of at least five years in infected soils. Plant resistant strains.

Leaf Spot

AFFECTS: Beets, spinach, Swiss chard

Leaf spot is a foliar disease that produces brown spots with purplish edges. The centers of the spots sometimes die, leaving little holes. The disease ruins the leaves and reduces the yield and quality of beets. Conditions that favor spread and infection include hot, humid weather; frequent rains; and contaminated garden tools.

Control: Leaf spot is not easily controlled. Rotation of crops on a three- to five-year schedule works best.

Beneficial Insects: Pollinators

Of course, not all insects are pests. In fact, if we think that we grow the tomatoes, melons, and beans in our gardens, in large part we're wrong. Yes, we grow the plants, but without pollinators we would have little to show for all the effort.

A *pollinator* is anything that transfers pollen from the anther of the male portion of a flower to the stigma of the female portion. In all but a few cases, pollination must occur for fruit to form. There are many different pollinators, ranging from the wind to tropical bats; in the vegetable garden, though, the most common and effective ones are insects, particularly honeybees, bumblebees, hover flies, and butterflies.

Honeybees

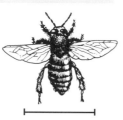

Honeybees are gentle, amber-colored insects that can polli-nate over 250 kinds of plants. Although not native to North America, they became natu-ralized soon after European colonists brought them here.

¾"/1.9cm

Honeybees live in a social group called a hive that consists of a queen, a few males, and thousands of sterile, female workers. About an inch long with clear wings and orange pollen sacs on their legs, the workers are the bees buzzing about the garden.

Honeybees are homebodies and don't like traveling too far from the hive. When flowers are plentiful they will stay within about four hundred yards of home, but when blossoms are harder to find, they will travel miles. Very sensitive to pesti-cides, they thrive best in areas where organic pest-contol techniques are practiced.

In the last few years hives across North America have been infested by two species of para-sitic mites. The mites weaken the bees, which then die from cold or hunger. Commercial apiaries have tried to control the epidemic via sprays, with some success. The wild, naturalized bees have no bene-factors, however, and in many places these extreme-ly beneficial insects have been wiped out.

Bumblebees

The dozens of species of bumblebees native to North America all look like big black and yellow balls of fluff buzzing through the air with a drone loud enough to do a small air-plane proud.

1"/2.5cm

Almost as gentle as honey-bees, bumblebees much prefer to forage among the flowers than to notice us. They live in hives that are started anew each spring when the queen seeks out an old mouse or vole run, a flower box, or a rotted tree, and lays a few eggs.

Unlike honeybees, each hive of bumbles has only a few hundred members. They are tough things, little fazed by bad weather. I have even seen them flying through spring snow flurries in search of nectar. They can endure the cold because they actually generate heat as they fly, keeping their big, fuzzy bodies much warmer than the sur-rounding air.

Hover Flies

Hover flies are truly excep-tional little creatures. Most species look like small, yel-low and black bees, but a moment's observation will quickly reveal that these flying insects are not bees.

½"/1.3cm

Wonderfully gentle, hover flies — unlike hon-eybees and bumblebees — zip around the garden completely unarmed. There are perhaps no better fliers in the insect world. They can hover in place or move backward, forward, and even side to side at will. Their oversize eyes can detect the slightest motion, but if you remain still they will often stop and rest on your hand.

Hover flies feed on nectar and pollinate the flowers as they forage. They enjoy marigolds, spearmint, cosmos, and coreopsis, among others. Planting a few of these among your vegetables will help ensure a bountiful harvest, with a little help from your neighborhood hover flies.

Butterflies

The most beautiful of
the insect pollinators,
butterflies encompass
many, many species,
all of which feed on
the nectar of flowers.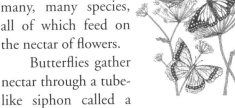

Butterflies gather
nectar through a tube-
like siphon called a
proboscis. They're notoriously nearsighted and can't
tell a colorful shirt from a flower until they're just
about on top of it. Many species have taste recep-
tors in their feet, which helps them determine if
they have landed on a flower or on Aunt Jane.

Butterflies are especially attracted to dark colors, such as deep reds, violets, and purples. A scat-
tering of asters, marigolds, petunias, phlox, and
yarrow in your vegetable garden will bring butterflies to visit as long as the flowers are in bloom.

Beneficial Insects: Predators

As the vegetables begin to grow you can be certain
that pests will find them. In times past people tried
to kill the pests by killing all bugs, good and bad.
Unfortunately, the nature of ecosystems is to produce many more herbivores (the bad guys, such as
aphids and caterpillars) than carnivores (the good
guys, including ladybugs and praying mantises).
The old strategy that employed broad-spectrum
insecticides killed most of the bad guys — but far
more of the good guys, which often made things
worse.

Today, with organic-based controls, the vegetable garden is again a working ecosystem, complete with predators, prey, and vegetables, but with
no pesticide residues.

Beneficial predators include ladybugs, praying
mantises, parasitic wasps, and green lacewings.

Ladybugs

Ladybugs are small beetles with rounded orange-red wing shields marked
with a sprinkling of black spots. The
adults can eat over two hundred aphids
a day. The adult beetles lay a mass of
bright yellow eggs that hatch into yel-

¼"/16mm

low and black larvae that immediately begin preying
on aphids. Ladybugs are attracted to such flowers as
single marigold varieties, yarrow, tansy, and butter-
flyweed. Plant a few of these in with your vegetables
and the ladybugs will patrol your garden for you. Be
aware, however, that some species of ants protect
aphids, which the ants farm for the honeydew they
produce. The ants will drive away the ladybugs
unless you lend a hand. Sprinkle boric acid on ant
trails.

Praying Mantis

A praying mantis sometimes reaches over 4 inches
in length. Unfortunately, the large size doesn't come
with an equivalent appetite. Mantises like to
ambush prey: Hiding motionless among the veggies, a mantis will wait until a caterpillar comes
within reach. In an instant its spine-covered fore-
arms reach out and grasp its prey. A quick bite at
the back of the head severs nerves and paralyzes the
caterpillar. The mantis can now dine at leisure.

An old myth states that, during mating, a
female mantis will kill and eat the smaller male.
The truth is that some years ago scientists who were
studying mating mantises didn't feed the insects
during the study, and soon the hungry females
devoured the males.

Females lay about a hundred eggs in a foamy
mass, which they attach to the branches of bushes.
You can gather these egg
masses, refrigerate them
over winter, and place
them in your garden in
spring. Three egg cases are
enough for about five thou-
sand square feet of garden.

2½"/6.4cm

Parasitic Wasps

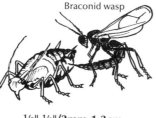

Braconid wasp

As predators, parasitic wasps are hard to beat. There are thousands of different kinds; the Trichogramma wasps are the best known of the group.

1/8"-1/2"/3mm-1.3cm

The wasps lay their eggs inside the eggs of pest species, such as hornworms. The infant wasp then eats the embryo of the pest, which is the best kind of control. Trichogramma wasps prey on over two hundred species of pests, including cabbageworms, corn earworms, cutworms, armyworms, loopers, and borers. The wasps are small and feed on the nectar of small wildflowers.

Braconid and chalcid wasps are small, dark-colored insects that prey on aphids, mealybugs, and beetle and butterfly larvae. The adults lay their eggs inside living, active insects. The eggs hatch, and the young wasp consumes the pest from the inside out. *Pediobius foveolatus* is a tiny, dark wasp that could easily be mistaken for a gnat. It attacks bean beetles, leaving nothing behind but a mummified shell.

Green Lacewings

Adult lacewings are delicate, fragile creatures about three-quarters of an inch long with misty, transparent wings and threadlike legs. Their bodies are

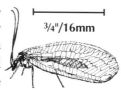

3/4"/16mm

pale green, and they have copper-colored eyes. This demure adult phase is a far cry from the ferocious larva, which devours countless aphids.

An adult female will fly during the night to a plant infested with aphids, where she lays her eggs. Within days the eggs hatch into larvae that look like small alligators with giant jaws. The larvae kill and eat up to two dozen aphids a day — not too bad for a beginner. Adults feed on the nectar of flowers, and having a few in the vegetable garden is always beneficial. They especially like Queen Anne's lace, cosmos, coreopsis, tansy, goldenrod, and angelica.

THE RADOCABBAGE

The story of the radocabbage is one that gets repeated from university classrooms to farm fields across the country. As it travels around the countryside and from generation to generation it changes a bit here and there, but the essence of the story remains the same. It has now become a piece of agricultural folklore that is entertaining while conveying a moral as true now as it was when the story of the radocabbage was first created decades ago.

Over a quarter century ago some agricultural researchers thought it would be a good idea to create a new vegetable from two old reliable ones. The scientists crossed a radish with a cabbage hoping to create a plant that had the best qualities of both; a root that produced a tasty radish and a top that grew a hearty head of cabbage. Radishes and cabbages are closely related plants but don't naturally hybridize, so a little scientific persuasion was needed to create a radocabbage seed. This was, however, accomplished, and the resulting seed was planted amid great anticipation. In a short while the seed germinated and was planted in a garden reserved for experimental plants. As the seedling rapidly grew into a mature plant the uniqueness of the radocabbage revealed itself.

As you know there are no radocabbage seeds for sale in catalogs and garden centers. And there are no radocabbage plants growing in gardens or fields across the country. The reason for the scarcity of this tribute to modern science is that the plant that grew in the experimental garden those many years ago had the roots of a cabbage, and the top of a radish.

Over the centuries there have been hundreds of vegetable varieties created by patient plant breeders across the world. Yet it is comforting to know that nature still has some secrets left for us to discover; such as how to create a real radocabbage.

DISORDER	AFFECTED PLANTS	CAUSE
Blossom drop	beans, peppers	combination of high air temperatures and low soil moisture
Blossom end rot	peppers, squash, pumpkins, tomatoes, melons	deficiency of calcium; low soil moisture; abrupt changes in soil moisture
Bronze leaf	beans	excessive soil salts (usually restricted to arid areas of the West)
	beets	deficiency of potassium
Black or brown heart	beets, cole crops, sweet potatoes, turnips	deficiency of boron, phosphorous
	celery	fluctuations of soil moisture
Chlorosis	beans	deficiency of copper, magnesium, manganese, zinc; low pH of soil; in the West, excessive soil salts
	beets	deficiency of iron, manganese
	cole crops	deficiency of magnesium, manganese
	carrots	deficiency of magnesium; low soil pH
	cucumbers	deficiency of nitrogen, potassium, manganese
	onions	deficiency of copper, manganese
	peas	deficiency of zinc, manganese
	potatoes	deficiency of boron
	squash, pumpkins	deficiency in manganese, nitrogen
Cracked stem	celery, rhubarb	deficiency of boron
Heart rot	parsnips	deficiency of boron
Leaf drop	potatoes	deficiency of magnesium
Leaf spot	melons	deficiency of magnesium
Tip burn	cole crops	deficiency of potassium

Longer Growing Seasons

The chief complaint of northern gardeners is that the growing season is just not long enough. Sometimes it seems too short to even qualify as a season at all. Up in Vermont, when tourists ask the locals what they do for fun in summer, they reply that they have a picnic that day.

Over the years many vegetable seed companies have tried to address the problem of short growing seasons by introducing a number of varieties specifically bred to mature earlier and in cooler conditions. Make no mistake about it, these new cultivars have added much-needed variety to the northern garden. Still you hear the complaint that if the season was just a week or two longer, every-thing would be better. As people wished for these few extra days, they probably held no hope that they would actually get them. If you have been one of those waiting for an early spring, the wait is actually over.

Recently completed studies using satellite measurements of vegetation growth have revealed that the growing season in northern areas of the globe is almost two weeks longer in 1997 than it was fifteen years earlier. Two separate studies, one tracing the carbon dioxide expelled by plants during photosynthesis and the other measuring actual vegetative growth, show that plants throughout the region begin to grow about eight days earlier in spring and continue to grow about four days later into fall than they did in the early 1980s.

The reasons for the longer growing season, which now occurs throughout much of Zones 2 through 4, remain undetermined. Some folks attribute it to global warming, while others consider it just a natural climatic variation that will soon reverse itself. Whatever the cause, there is no doubt that the annual winter snowpack across North America, Europe, and Asia is also melting earlier each year. (See Chapter 6 for secrets of extending the growing season even further.)

♦ **No-Pest Cool-Weather Crops**

> Corn salad
> Radicchio
> Red mustard
> Peas
> Parsnips

The BIGGEST Root Crops

Some people out there are not content to grow abundant crops of cherry-size radishes, baby carrots, or foot-long parsnips. Nope. These folks want BIG radishes, BIG carrots, and BIG parsnips. To them a 10-foot carrot is just a good start. And there are secret formulas galore for producing truly huge vegetables.

Most people don't want to grow parsnips the size of canoes: what they want is good-size crops that also taste good. For this, you don't need a secret formula, just some plain advice.

PREPARING THE SOIL

Getting the soil exactly right is most of the battle. Some people actually build raised beds and fill them with loamy soil and compost. This provides a great platform for root crops to grow in, but some of us have other things to do, so here's a shortcut. Take a crowbar — not a dinky pry bar, but a good five-foot-

THE COLORFUL, COOL VEGETABLE GARDEN

Some think that adding color to the cool-season vegetable garden means plunking a few pansies alongside the lettuce. Flowers are always welcome, but the vegetables themselves can accent the garden with a rainbow of colors and hues.

VEGETABLE	COLORFUL CULTIVAR	DESCRIPTION
Brussels sprouts	'Rubine'	Bears beautiful red sprouts in fall
Cauliflower	'Violet Queen'	A hybrid with large, deep purple heads
	'Orange Bouquet'	Produces heads of antique orange
Cabbage	'Roxy'	A deep red cabbage with burgundy heads
	'Super Red'	Early, flavorful, and attractive, with dark red heads
Kale	'Red Russian'	Has blue-green leaves and violet-red stems
Flowering kale	'Red Peacock'	Stunning black-red edges frame a scarlet center
Kohlrabi	'Kolibri'	Bears beautiful, deep purple stems
Lettuce	'Impuls'	Gorgeous heads of glossy burgundy red
	'Sesam'	Beautiful as 'Impuls'
	'Redina'	Bears leafy heads of burnt burgundy
	'New Red Fire'	Has wavy leaves of green deeply edged with dark red
	'Cerise'	An iceberg type with greenish red leaves
	'Sangria'	A butterhead with greenish burgundy leaves
Mustard	'Red Giant'	Has large purple-green leaves
	'Osaka Purple'	Bears abundant green leaves stained with dark purple
Orach	'Red Orach'	A spinach-like plant with beautiful powder red leaves
Radicchio	'Medusa'	Bears glossy red and white heads

long crowbar — and go out to the garden. Plunge the bar into the soil, then swirl it in a circular motion to make a cone-shaped hole. Keep doing this until the cone is about two or three feet deep. Then select a spot down the row and about a foot away, and repeat the process. Do this until it isn't fun any more.

Take a break by passing peat moss, sand, and compost through a screen with a one-quarter-inch grid. Make separate piles of each, then blend them all together in equal parts. Make sure the mix is dry enough to flow, then pour it into the holes, filling them to the top. Water well until the mix settles. Top off each hole with mix and water again. Select the crop and seed you wish to grow and direct-sow into the moist mix, being sure to plant each seed in the center of the area of mix. To hasten germination cover each planting hole with a Wall-o-water teepee or similar device to keep the soil warm.

PRESSURE-TREATED LUMBER AND GARDEN BEDS

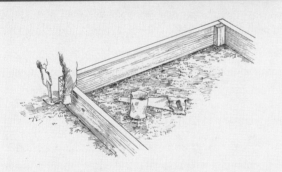

Many people like the neat appearance and convenience of building raised garden beds from timbers. And as a practical matter, timbers preserved with chromated copper arsenate (CCA) last much longer than those left untreated. The obvious question is whether the arsenic in the timbers stays there or migrates into nearby soil and vegetables.

The matter is far from settled, but some studies have shown that soil in raised beds constructed of CCA-treated timbers contained a little less than half the average, or natural, background levels of water-soluble arsenic. Whether or not to use treated timbers in the garden is a matter of personal choice, but at least there is a choice to make.

AVOIDING NITRATES

Nitrates can harm us when eaten in large amounts. When we do so, the digestive process helps turn the nitrates into nitrosamines, substances that have been linked to cancer. To limit your exposure to nitrosamines, eat foods high in vitamin C along with any rich in nitrates, to inhibit nitrosamine formation.

Here are some other tips:

- Eat tender, inner leaves. In many types of salad greens, the outer leaves have more nitrates than the inner ones.
- Add only as much nitrogen fertilizer to your soil as the plants need. The more nitrogen that is available, the more nitrates that find their way into the plants.
- Pick root crops late in the day. Plants have fewer nitrates in their tissues in the late afternoon than at other times.
- Remember that some plants have more nitrates than others. Beets, lettuce, radishes, and spinach have higher nitrate levels than many other crops.

GROWING AND FERTILIZING

Once the seeds germinate and the plants are a few inches high, you can begin to fertilize. One of the keys to growing giant veggies is to keep an optimum level of nutrients available to the plant for the entire growing season. Organic fertilizers are best for this purpose because their lower analysis (level of nutrients) is low enough not to damage most plants if you happen to get too zealous with the application. Use fish emulsion or a similar type of fertilizer. Mix up a batch that is only one-quarter strength and use this to water the plants. Every time the plants are watered use this diluted formula but do not exceed three applications per week. Then simply let the plants grow — be they radishes, turnips, carrots, or parsnips — just as you do everything else in the garden. When it's time to dig these beauties from the ground, you'll be amazed.

Catalog of Cool-Weather Vegetables

Arugula, Roquette
Eruca vesicaria spp. *sativa*

LIGHT: Full sun to partial shade
SOIL: Evenly moist, pH 6.0–7.0
PARTS USED: Leaves
WHEN TO PLANT: Early spring, late summer to fall (Zones 2–8); winter (Zones 9–10)
DAYS TO MATURITY: 40 from seed

Arugula is a half-hardy annual native to the Mediterranean, where it is a favorite addition to spring and fall salads. The plant produces large, medium green leaves that combine the texture and consistency of spinach with a pungent, peppery taste. The foliage is arranged  in a loose rosette around a central stem that quickly bolts into a 2-foot-tall flower stalk with the arrival of hot weather. One of the easiest vegetables to grow, arugula provides tasty salad greens about a month after sowing.

How to Grow: Direct-sow as soon as the soil can be worked in spring. In the Deep South sow in early winter. Arugula will grow best in the cooler spots of the garden. Plant seeds 1 inch apart in single rows or band rows spaced 3 inches apart. Do not thin. Sow every three weeks while the weather is cool. Use a fabric row cover to keep flea beetles and other pests from the leaves.

Harvest and Use: Harvest individual leaves as needed when they are 2 to 3 inches long, or harvest entire plants. Arugula is often used with other greens, including red mustard and escarole, to create salads with a decidedly European accent. Leaves get bitter once flower buds form. Pull plants when they begin to bolt, or wait until the buds blossom and add the flowers to salads. The fresh leaves will keep in the refrigerator for up to two weeks. Do not freeze.

Beans, Broad
Vicia faba

LIGHT: Full sun
SOIL: Well drained, pH 6.0–7.5
PARTS USED: Seeds
WHEN TO PLANT: Spring (Zones 3–7); fall (Zones 7–10)
DAYS TO MATURITY: 75 from seed

In areas where the growing season is too short to grow lima beans, the fava, or English broad bean, is an excellent stand-in. The long, cool summers of the British Isles are perfect for fava  beans, but summers in most of North America were once just too warm. However, new varieties selected for flavor, yield, and heat tolerance make the fava bean a must for the garden. Its broad, medium green pods grow from 6 to 10 inches long and hang in pairs from attractive plants that can reach over 4 feet tall. The pods yield large, meaty, flavorful seeds perfect for hearty soups and stews or when served hot with butter, salt, and pepper.

How to Grow: In the North plant in spring at the same time as garden peas. In the South plant in September. Direct-sow 1 inch deep and 6 inches apart in single rows spaced every 2 feet. When seedlings emerge, set stakes or brush supports to protect the plants from winds. Corn rows can also be used as windbreaks. The plants will tolerate light frosts, but in far northern areas a mulch of pine needles or straw will further protect them from colder temperatures. Fertilize with regular applications of fish emulsion or compost tea.

Harvest and Use: When beans are still small — 3 or 4 inches long — they can be harvested and prepared like snap beans. When the pods have filled out and appear plump, the beans can be picked and the green seeds shelled and prepared like lima beans.

Cultivar: 'Loretta'

Beet
Beta vulgaris

LIGHT: Full sun
SOIL: Well drained, evenly moist, fertile, pH 6.0–7.0
PARTS USED: Leaves, roots
WHEN TO PLANT: Spring to early summer (Zones 3–7); fall to late winter (Zones 9–10)
DAYS TO MATURITY: Leaves 30–45 from seed; roots 45–60 from seed

Beets are native to the Mediterranean region, where they were first cultivated in the third century. For hundreds of years this tasty vegetable was the Rodney Dangerfield of garden plants, getting no respect. At the beginning of the nineteenth century, though, northern Europeans began selecting new varieties, and the popularity of beets has been growing ever since.

How to Grow: Beets are most vigorous and flavorful when grown in soil amended with well-rotted manure. In some areas of the Northeast, Midwest, and Northwest, boron must be added to the soil to prevent black heart, a discoloring of the root that can also result from insufficient phosphorus. High temperatures during root development often lead to poor color formation in roots. Plant the seed balls in band rows 1 inch deep and 6 inches apart, each band consisting of from three to six rows, and thin as needed. Use a fabric row cover to keep flea beetles, leafminers, and other pests away.

Harvest and Use: Gather the greens when they are small and tender. Harvest when roots reach 1¼ to 1½ inches in diameter. The flesh of beets is less flavorful and more pithy the longer they remain in the ground. Store roots in the refrigerator or root cellar, or slice them and dry in a dehydrator.

Cultivars: *Hybrids:* 'Red Ace', 'Warrior'; *Standard:* 'Early Wonder'

Broccoli
Brassica oleracea Botrytis Group

LIGHT: Full sun
SOIL: Well drained, evenly moist, fertile, pH 6.5–7.5
PARTS USED: Flower heads
WHEN TO PLANT: Spring (Zones 3–4); spring, late summer (Zones 5–7); winter (Zones 8–10)
DAYS TO MATURITY: 50–70 from transplanting

Today broccoli is so ubiquitous it seems strange to think that just a few decades ago it was nearly unknown in American gardens. The plants produce a rosette of large blue-green leaves with a central head of densely packed flower buds. The heads may be green or purple, depending on the variety.

How to Grow: All cole crops prefer soil that is well drained, fertile, and evenly moist. Insufficient stores of boron can result in a browning of the heads. Other nutrient problems include leaf chlorosis, from too little magnesium or manganese; tip burn of leaves, from insufficient potassium; and failure to produce heads, from soil that is too acidic. Set hardened transplants in the garden about the time of the last spring frost. Space plants 1 to 2 feet apart in single rows 2 feet apart. Use a fabric row cover to keep flea beetles, cabbage worms, root maggots, and other pests from plants.

Harvest and Use: Harvest broccoli heads when the flower buds are still small and tightly packed in the head. After the central head is harvested, small sideshoots often develop, especially in fall- and winter-grown crops, though the yield per plant is small. Broccoli keeps for up to a month in the refrigerator and also freezes well.

Cultivars: *Hybrids:* 'Packman', 'Emperor', 'Saga', 'Marathon'; *Standard:* 'De Cicco'

Broccoli Raab
Brassica rapa Ruvo Group

LIGHT:	Full sun
SOIL:	Well drained, evenly moist, fertile, pH 6.5–7.5
PARTS USED:	Leaves, flower buds
WHEN TO PLANT:	Fall (Zones 3–8); winter (Zones 8–10)
DAYS TO MATURITY:	30–35 from transplanting

Broccoli raab has been grown for generations in Italy, where the small florets are prepared with olive oil and garlic. It has been grown in North America for over a century. The plant resembles common broccoli, with its upright habit and blue-green leaves, but instead of forming a large central head, the small florets appear at the tips of slender shoots. The florets are nicely flavored and yield well right up to frost.

How to Grow: Broccoli raab bolts quickly in warm weather and is best planted as a fall crop, especially in northern areas, where it can extend the broccoli season considerably. Set transplants in the coolest spot of the garden four to six weeks before the first frost. Use fabric row covers to keep insect pests from the plants and extend your harvest into the colder months. Fertilize the same way as common broccoli, making sure that the soil has adequate supplies of boron, magnesium, manganese, calcium, and potassium.

Harvest and Use: Harvest the florets when the buds are still small and tight, because their quality deteriorates rapidly once the flower buds begin to open. Cut the shoots just below the florets, leaving enough stem for more florets to form. Prepare the small leaves that embrace the floret right along with the flower buds; they are both delicious. Broccoli raab is excellent steamed, sautéed, or as an ingredient in soups and stews.

Cultivars: 'Spring Raab', 'Sessantina Grossa'

Brussels Sprouts
Brassica oleracea Gemmifera Group

LIGHT:	Full sun
SOIL:	Well drained, evenly moist, fertile, pH 6.5–7.5
PARTS USED:	Buds
WHEN TO PLANT:	Spring (Zones 3–7); winter (Zone 8)
DAYS TO MATURITY:	90–120 from transplanting

Brussels sprouts, like cauliflower and broccoli, derive from the wild cabbage. The plants produce leaves with long petioles and large blue-green leaf blades. The thick stem elongates throughout the growing season, reaching up to 3 feet in height. As the plant grows, the small buds tucked into the axils of the leaves swell into small, cabbage-like sprouts that enlarge from the ground up and completely obscure the stem by harvest time.

How to Grow: Sow seed indoors about four weeks before setting out. North of Zone 7 plant hardened transplants in the garden with other spring crops. In Zone 8 set transplants in the garden in winter. Fertilize the same way as other cole crops, devoting careful attention to calcium, magnesium, boron, and potassium levels. Keep the soil evenly moist. Aphids, caterpillars, and harlequin bugs can be controlled with sprays of insecticidal soap. Avoid club root, by rotating cole crops with other vegetables on a three-year schedule.

Harvest and Use: The best-tasting sprouts are harvested from plants that have been grown in soil amended with well-rotted manure and that have matured after a frost. Harvest the sprouts when they are about 1½ inches across. In many areas sprouts can be gathered from the plants into early winter. These scrumptious vegetables are sweet and mellow; they're delicious steamed and topped with a little butter.

Cultivars: *Hybrids:* 'Oliver', 'Igor', 'Valiant'

Cabbage

Brassica oleracea Capitata Group

LIGHT: Full sun
SOIL: Well drained, evenly moist, fertile, pH 6.0–7.5
PARTS USED: Heads
WHEN TO PLANT: Late fall, early winter (Zones 7–8); winter (Zones 8–10); early spring (Zones 3–6); early summer (Zones 3–6)
DAYS TO MATURITY: 65–95 from transplanting

The wild cabbage is a biennial plant native to Europe, where it has been eaten for thousands of years. There are many types of cabbages, including Savoy, red, pointed head, and green. Cabbage plants produce a rosette of large leaves with a massive  bud, or head, at the center. As the plant matures the head eventually splits, and a flower stalk bolts from the base of the plant. Cultivate carefully: The roots are shallow and easily damaged.

How to Grow: Cabbage tolerates a wide range of conditions. Transplant hardened seedlings into rich soil that has ample supplies of boron, calcium, potassium, magnesium, and manganese. Young, hardened plants can withstand some frosts, while mature plants can tolerate temperatures of from 25 to 30°F. The 'Wakefield' varieties can withstand temperatures as low as 15°F. Fertilize with fish emulsion regularly, keeping the soil evenly moist. Abrupt changes in soil moisture can produce a condition called oedema, which causes the heads to split.

Harvest and Use: Harvest early cabbage as heads size up. Pick late cabbage before the first hard frost.

Cultivars: *Green Hybrids:* 'Grenadier', 'Columbia'; *Standard:* 'Early Jersey Wakefield', *Red Hybrid:* 'Ruby Perfection'; *Standard:* 'Lasso'; *Savoy Hybrids:* 'Julius', 'Savoy Ace'

Cabbage, Chinese

Brassica rapa Pekinensis Group

LIGHT: Full sun
SOIL: Well drained, fertile, pH 6.0–7.0
PARTS USED: Leaves
WHEN TO PLANT: Spring (Zones 6–10); late spring to early summer (Zones 2–5)
DAYS TO MATURITY: 45–55 from transplanting

Chinese cabbage is a staple of Oriental cuisines — the tasty leaves and juicy petioles are used in stir-fries, salads, and other dishes. Various types feature thick green leaves that resemble leaf lettuce, while others form a head  that resembles a cross between romaine lettuce and Savoy cabbage. The leaves have a juicy texture with a mild, lightly sweet flavor.

How to Grow: Growing Chinese cabbage can be tricky if the weather goes against you. If the seedlings are exposed to more than about a week of nights below 50°F, or if a hot spell arrives, the plants may bolt no matter how bolt-resistant your variety. Set the plants after danger of frost has past, or in late summer in northern areas. Fertilize with fish emulsion and mulch the soil in warmer regions. Water evenly. Cultivate carefully, because the plants are easily damaged.

Harvest and Use: Harvest head-type cabbage by cutting the entire plant at the base. Discard the outer leaves. Use fresh or store in the refrigerator. Leaf-type cabbage should be harvested as needed for recipes and salads; the best, most flavorful leaves are the more tender inner ones. Cover plants with a fabric row cover to keep insect pests away.

Cultivars: *Heading Napa Hybrids:* 'Summer Top', 'Blues'; *Open Head Napa Standard:* 'Lettucy Type'; *Heading Michihli Hybrid:* 'Jade Pagoda'

Cauliflower
Brassica oleracea Botrytis Group

LIGHT: Full sun
SOIL: Well drained, evenly moist, fertile, pH 6.5–7.5
PARTS USED: Flower heads
WHEN TO PLANT: Early spring or fall (Zones 6–8); late spring (Zones 3–5); late September to February (Zones 9–10)
DAYS TO MATURITY: 50–75 from transplanting

Cauliflower descended from the wild cabbage but differs from it in that it produces a swollen flower cluster rather than a head. The plants resemble broccoli in appearance, with large blue-green leaves emanating from a central stem. The large flower head may be white, purple, or green, depending on the variety.

How to Grow: Of all the cole crops, cauliflower is the most finicky — not difficult, mind you, just finicky. The plant needs a soil well amended with organic matter. Nutrients, especially phosphorus, potassium, magnesium, manganese, calcium, and boron, must be available. The soil should have a pH near neutral and always be evenly moist. Cauliflower will set *buttons* (small, prematurely set flower buds) if seedlings are exposed to freezing temperatures, moisture changes, or excessive warmth. Set one-month-old, hardened seedlings in the garden about 2 feet apart. When a flower head is about the size of an egg, tie a few wrapper leaves over it and secure with a clothespin.

Harvest and Use: Harvest when the head is full size but before the tight pattern of the curd loosens. Early cauliflower is grown across the country, while the late varieties are popular in the West.

Cultivars: *White Hybrids:* 'Snow Crown', 'Cumberland', 'Fremont'; *White Standard:* 'Amazing'; *Purple Hybrids:* 'Violet Queen', 'Burgundy Queen'; *Green Standard:* 'Alverda'

Collard, Georgia Collard
Brassica oleracea Acephala Group

LIGHT: Full sun
SOIL: Well drained, evenly moist, fertile, pH 6.5–7.0
PARTS USED: Leaves
WHEN TO PLANT: Spring (Zones 3–6); late summer through fall (Zones 3–10)
DAYS TO MATURITY: Sixty from seed

A hardy relative of the wild cabbage, collard resembles a headless cabbage, with large, white-veined, blue-green leaves. Although grown everywhere, it is a signature vegetable in the South. The leaves are very nutritious, with large amounts of vitamins A and C. The flavor is distinct but pleasant, though the smell when it's cooking can clear the room.

How to Grow: Collard will grow well in soil that other members of the cabbage family won't tolerate. Add dolomitic limestone to raise soil pH, and fertilize with fish emulsion regularly. Direct-sow in early spring or in late summer through fall and thin to 18 inches apart. The plants will grow to between 2 and 4 feet tall. They tolerate heat and drought well enough to produce through summer. Mulch your soil to keep the roots cool, and use fabric row covers to protect small plants from insects.

Harvest and Use: For best flavor gather the small, young leaves a few inches below the terminal growing point of the plant in the cool of the morning. Leaves harvested in the spring are full flavored, while those gathered in fall and winter are sweet and very tasty. Cut out the terminal growing point before the first hard freeze in fall for a real high-quality taste. Store the leaves in plastic bags; they keep in the refrigerator for a few days.

Cultivar: 'Champion'

Corn Salad, Mâche
Valerianella locusta

LIGHT: Full sun to partial shade
SOIL: Well drained, dry to evenly moist, pH 6.0–7.0
PARTS USED: Leaves9
WHEN TO PLANT: Spring, fall (Zones 2–10); overwinters (Zones 7–10)
DAYS TO MATURITY: 50 from seed

Corn salad, also called mâche or lamb's lettuce, is an Old World annual grown as a salad green. The plant produces a rosette of deep green, sorrel-shaped leaves with a mild, faintly sweet flavor. Corn salad goes to flower when the weather warms. After it bolts, the leaves of most varieties become bitter. Corn salad is so easy to grow that in much of Europe it is grown also as a forage crop.

How to Grow: Direct-sow in late winter or early spring two weeks before the last frost. Seeds may be sown in single rows at 1-inch intervals, with seedlings thinned to about 2 inches apart; in hills of four to six plants each; or in wide band rows set 4 inches apart. To over-winter, cover fall crops with a mulch of straw or pine needles. Plants usually do not need winter protection farther south. In Zones 2 and 3 plants can be sown in cold frames in fall and covered with mulch. Corn salad adapts well to a variety of soils and usually needs no fertilizing. Provide a location with good air circulation, and grow in well-drained soil for fall and winter plantings. Corn salad has no serious problems with pests or diseases.

Harvest and Use: Gather entire rosettes by pinching off the stem when plants are about 2 inches tall. Store in plastic bags in the refrigerator until ready to use, and rinse under cold water before eating. Corn salad keeps for about three weeks.

Cultivars: 'Vit', 'Piedmont'

Endive, Escarole
Cichorium endivia

LIGHT: Full sun (Zones 4–6); partial shade (Zones 7–10)
SOIL: Well drained, evenly moist, fertile, pH 5.5–7.0
PARTS USED: Leaves
WHEN TO PLANT: Spring to summer (Zones 4–6); summer to fall (Zones 7–10)
DAYS TO MATURITY: 50–70 from seed

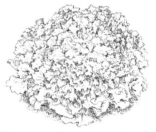

Sometimes called European lettuce, this plant looks much like leaf lettuce, with masses of light green, curled, wavy leaves. The outer leaves have a mild, piquant flavor with a touch of bitterness, while the blanched inner leaves are sweet and crunchy.

How to Grow: In the North start plants indoors two months before the last frost. Set hardened transplants 1 foot apart one week before the last frost. For later crops, direct-sow. In Zones 7 through 10 direct-sow every three weeks from late summer through fall. Blanch plants by placing an inverted *clay* pot atop for about three weeks. After rainfalls, remove the pot and allow the leaves to dry. Excessive humidity and moisture can promote damping off and gray mold in seedlings. Tip burn of the leaves is caused by high temperatures and uneven soil moisture. In some northeastern states, brown heart results from a boron deficiency.

Harvest and Use: Harvest the outer leaves when they have fully expanded but before any browning or tip burn. Or cut the entire planting. Rinse it with cool water, and refrigerate for at least two hours.

Cultivars: *Très Fine Maraîchère Type:* 'Rhodos'; *Frisée Type:* 'Neos'; *Wallone Type:* 'Salad King'

Fennel, Florence
Foeniculum vulgare var. *azoricum*

LIGHT: Full sun
SOIL: Well drained, evenly moist, fertile, pH 6.5-7.0
PARTS USED: Stem bases
WHEN TO PLANT: Spring (Zones 4–6); fall (Zones 6–10)
DAYS TO MATURITY: 80 from seed

Florence fennel is the vegetable version of the popular anise-flavored herb. It produces large, celerylike leaf petioles topped with ferny foliage that resembles dill. The leaves arise from thickened stem layers arranged tightly into a bulb, or apple, the most commonly eaten part. In cool weather Florence fennel forms a rosette of long-stemmed leaves; in warm weather it bolts, producing a tall flower stalk. The plant has been grown in Europe for generations. Though not nearly as popular here, it is avidly grown by those who like a gourmet-quality vegetable that is also a bit unusual.

How to Grow: Florence fennel grows best in cool weather. Direct-sow in single rows in spring through early summer, setting the seeds a little more than 1 inch apart, and the rows 18 to 24 inches apart. Thin the seedlings to 6 inches apart. Florence fennel will bolt if its roots are disturbed, so direct-sow rather than transplant, and practice shallow cultivation. Plants grown in soil well amended with rotted manure and kept evenly moist produce the best-flavored, most uniform bulbs.

Harvest and Use: Traditionally, soil is mounded up around the base of a plant a couple of weeks before harvest to blanch the bulb. After it grows for a total of about three months, pull the entire plant. Trim the stalks to about 1 inch from the bulb.

Cultivars: *Hybrid:* 'Rudy'; *Standard:* 'Zefa Fino'

Kale
Brassica oleracea Acephala Group

LIGHT: Full sun
SOIL: Well drained, evenly moist, fertile, pH 6.5–7.0
PARTS USED: Leaves
WHEN TO PLANT: Late summer (Zones 2–5); fall (Zones 6–10)
DAYS TO MATURITY: 60 from seed

Kale, like collard, is a headless cabbagelike vegetable whose nutritious leaves are eaten as cooked greens. Though not as popular today as in times past, kale is still a favorite fall vegetable in many regions, especially coastal Virginia, which produces much of the nation's commercial crop. Kale is an attractive plant, with deeply lobed, sometimes curly-edged leaves that have a blue-green sheen. Ornamental varieties have lacy leaves and a central patch richly colored in shades of white or red.

How to Grow: Direct-sow about three weeks before the first fall frost, spacing the seeds 1 inch apart. Thin the seedlings to 6 to 10 inches apart. Plants sown in rich, evenly moist soil well amended with organic matter will grow quickly and produce leaves that are tender and tasty. Slow-growing plants yield tougher leaves with many stringy veins. As with other cole crops, keep the soil pH near neutral, and have proper amounts of calcium, magnesium, manganese, phosphorus, and boron in the soil. A light mulch will help keep the soil cool.

Harvest and Use: Fast-growing kale can be harvested by picking the entire plant, because even the older leaves will be tender. Slower-growing plants should have only the small, tender leaves gathered. Leaves produced in cool weather, especially after a frost, are more flavorful.

Cultivars: *Hybrids:* 'Winterbor', 'Verdura'; *Standard:* 'Konserva'

Kohlrabi
Brassica oleracea Gongylodes Group

LIGHT: Full sun
SOIL: Well drained, evenly moist, fertile, pH 6.0–7.0
PARTS USED: Stems
WHEN TO PLANT: Spring, late summer (Zones 3–8); winter (Zones 9–10)
DAYS TO MATURITY: 35–60 from seed

One more strange variation of the wild cabbage, kohlrabi grows quickly from seed, producing a bulbous, enlarged stem that sits just above the ground like a turnip that has lost its way. From the stem, long-stalked blue-green leaves poke out in all directions.

How to Grow: Direct-sow seeds about 1 inch apart in rows spaced 12 inches apart. In the most regions sow two weeks before the last frost and again six to eight weeks before the first fall frost. In the Deep South sow in midwinter. Thin plants to 4 to 5 inches. Fertile, evenly moist soil encourages rapid, uninterrupted growth, which produces mild, tender vegetables. Kohlrabi does not do well during hot or dry periods. Cover the plants with fabric row covers to keep insect pests away.

Harvest and Use: Plants are ready for harvest when the bulbous stem is 2 to 3 inches in diameter. Bigger is not better: Large stems have an unpleasantly strong flavor and a tough, pithy texture. The small stems, on the other hand, are very flavorful. Pull the entire plant, removing the leaves and roots. Kohlrabi is excellent cut into cubes and steamed, or thinly sliced and added raw to salads. Cultivars have either greenish white or purple skin, but all are white inside, and their sweet flesh has an apple-like consistency.

Cultivars: *White Hybrids:* 'Eder', 'Winner'; *Purple Hybrid:* 'Kolibri'

Lettuce
Lactuca sativa

LIGHT: Full sun to partial shade
SOIL: Well drained, evenly moist, fertile, pH 5.5–7.0
PARTS USED: Leaves
WHEN TO PLANT: Spring (Zones 4–8); summer (Zones 2–3, northwestern coast); winter (Zones 7–10)
DAYS TO MATURITY: 40–60 from seed

Lettuce has been cultivated for at least 2,500 years. Four types are commonly grown: leaf, which has loose, open heads of broad, green leaves; romaine, with long heads of thick-veined leaves; bibb or butterhead, with broad, loose wrapper leaves around a small central head; and crisphead or iceberg, with large heads of tightly packed leaves.

How to Grow: Lettuce needs fertile soil because its root system is so small. Hardened transplants can be set a few weeks before the last frost and spaced 8 inches apart for leaf, romaine, and butterhead types; 12 inches apart for crisphead types. Mulch between rows to keep the soil cool and moist. Fertilize with fish emulsion. A browning of the leaf tips, called tip burn, appears with dry soil and warm temperatures. Overly wet soil encourages lettuce drop, a disease characterized by the wilting of the outer leaves. Remove leaves that touch the soil, because they can infect the plant with bottom rot.

Harvest and Use: Harvest lettuce as soon as the leaves are large enough to use or when the heads have formed but are still soft.

Cultivars: *Green Leaf Types:* 'Black Seeded Simpson', 'Two Star', 'Oakleaf'; *Red Leaf Types:* 'Redina', 'Impuls', 'Red Oakleaf'; *Romaine Types:* 'Rouge d'Hiver', 'Jericho', 'Romulus'; *Butterhead Types:* 'Mantilia', 'Sangria', 'Juliet'

Mustard, Red
Brassica juncea var. *foliosa*

Light:	Full sun
Soil:	Well-drained, sandy loam; pH 5.5–6.5
Parts Used:	Leaves
When to Plant:	Spring, fall (Zones 2–8); winter (Zones 9–10)
Days to Maturity:	40–50 from seed

The yellow stuff in the jar is made by blending the seeds of black mustard with vinegar. Red mustard, in contrast, is grown for its delicious leaves, which give fresh salads and vegetable dishes a delightful zing. Red mustard has broad, slightly wrinkled, greenish purple leaves in a loose rosette.

How to Grow: Direct-sow the seeds 1 inch apart in shallow rows in early spring and late summer, or in winter in the deep South. Thin to about 6 inches apart, with rows 18 to 24 inches apart. Sow every ten days to ensure a constant supply. Cover plants with fabric row covers to keep flea beetles and other pests from the leaves. Mustard will produce good crops in many types of soil, but the most flavorful leaves are grown in light, sandy loams amended with rotted manure or compost. Keep moisture levels even to ensure uniform flavor.

Harvest and Use: Gather the leaves from the outer part of the rosette after they reach edible size. Leaves from 3 to about 5 inches long are best for salads; use those 5 to 8 inches long for steaming. Use fresh leaves soon after harvesting, because they wilt quickly and do not store well. Gather the leaves in the cool of the morning, rinse them lightly with cold water, and store them in plastic bags in the refrigerator until you are ready to use them. Mustard attracts cabbage looper butterflies, so plants should be pulled as they go to flower.

Cultivars: 'Red Giant', 'Osaka Purple'

Parsley, Root
Petroselinum crispum var. *tuberosum*

Light:	Full sun
Soil:	Well drained, light, pH 6.0–7.0
Parts Used:	Roots
When to Plant:	Spring (Zones 4–10)
Days to Maturity:	90–100 from seed

Root parsley is not grown for its leaves, like common parsley, but for its tasty taproot. A relative of celery and parsnips, it looks a little like both. The plant has a rosette of long, slender leaves that resemble celery. Beneath the soil is a long, pale white taproot that looks very much like a parsnip. Root parsley has been grown for centuries in Europe, where it is used in winter soups and stews. Although it nearly disappeared from North American gardens after 1900, in recent years this very tasty vegetable has made a well-deserved comeback.

How to Grow: Soak the seeds in warm (80°F) water for twelve to twenty-four hours before sowing. Direct-sow in early spring, about one month before the last frost, in a deeply worked, raked seedbed. Evenly moisten the soil and cover it with a sheet of wet burlap, which you should remove promptly when seedlings appear. Mulch to retain soil moisture and keep weeds down.

Harvest and Use: Dig the roots as needed, harvesting them after the first few frosts of fall but before the ground freezes hard. They can be stored in fresh sawdust in a cool cellar for months. If you prefer, leave some plants in the ground, add a layer of mulch, then dig the roots in spring before new leaves appear. The sliced roots can be used like parsnips: steamed, added to soups and stews, or sautéed with garlic, onions, and butter.

Cultivar: 'Bartowich Long'

Parsnip
Pastinaca sativa

LIGHT: Full sun
SOIL: Well drained, light, pH 6.0–7.0
PARTS USED: Roots
WHEN TO PLANT: Spring (Zones 2–10)
DAYS TO MATURITY: 110–120 from seed

Grown in vegetable gardens since ancient times, the parsnip found its way to North America during the early colonial period. Historically, the plant was very popular, being one of the few fresh vegetables available during the winter. Today, the parsnip has been nearly, and unjustly, forgotten. Parsnips have rosettes  of long, finely cut, spreading leaves above footlong, pale white roots. Properly grown and harvested, parsnips are sweet and tender, with a distinctive, pleasant aftertaste.

How to Grow: Direct-sow about the time of the last spring frost in deeply worked, loose soil. Set the seeds about 1 inch apart in shallow rows. Then drop in seeds of small, round radishes every few inches along the row. (Parsnip seeds can take weeks to germinate, while radishes pop up quickly and serve as row markers. The parsnips emerge at about the same time the radishes are ready to pull.) Mulch the plants as they grow, to retain soil moisture and reduce weeds. Two or three applications of fish emulsion over a summer is plenty.

Harvest and Use: The best-tasting parsnips are harvested in fall after a good frost. Before the ground freezes hard, store the roots in fresh sawdust in a cool cellar. The flavor gets sweeter with storage. You can also leave roots in the ground if you cover them with mulch. Dig in spring before the leaves appear. Use the sliced roots in stews or soups, or sauté them.

Cultivars: 'All America', 'Lancer', 'Andover'

Pea
Pisum sativum var. *sativum*

LIGHT: Full sun
SOIL: Well drained, evenly moist, fertile, pH 5.5–6.5
PARTS USED: Fruits
WHEN TO PLANT: Spring, fall (Zones 2–8); winter (Zones 9–10)
DAYS TO MATURITY: 50–70 from seed

Freshly picked, steamed peas are something that I rarely eat: Try as I might, the peas I pick just don't make it as far as my  kitchen. People have been eating peas since ancient Greece. Cool-weather peas are divided into edible podded types and shell, or English, peas. Both are vining annuals that cling to supports by means of twining tendrils.

How to Grow: Direct-sow in spring as soon as the soil can be worked, or in fall about eight weeks before the first frost. In warm regions sow in December. Plant the seeds 2 inches apart in rows 3 inches apart. In dry areas soak the seeds overnight before sowing. Treat your seedbed with a bacterial inoculum, to increase growth rate and yield. Set stakes, pea netting, or tree branches so that seedlings have immediate support. Peas grown on sandy loam underlain with a clay subsoil ripen fastest. Peas do not need large amounts of fertilizer, but they do need adequate calcium, magnesium, iron, zinc, and manganese. They are susceptible to bacterial blight, so plant only disease-free, disease-resistant seed.

Harvest and Use: Harvest edible podded peas anytime after the pods begin to form. Shell peas can be picked when the pod is full but before it begins to bulge. Peas can be used fresh in salads, steamed, added to soups and stews, or frozen.

Cultivars: *Shell Peas:* 'Knight', 'Daybreak', 'Lincoln', 'Multistar'; *Snap Peas:* 'Sugarsnap', 'Sugar Ann', 'Super Sugar Mel'

Radicchio
Cichorium intybus

LIGHT: Full sun
SOIL: Well drained, pH 6.0–6.5
PARTS USED: Leaves
WHEN TO PLANT: Summer (Zones 2–3); spring, fall (Zones 4–8); winter (Zones 9–10)
DAYS TO MATURITY: 60–70 from transplanting

Radicchio is a head-forming chicory with wine-red leaves accented by thick, snow-white veins. The small, attractive heads — usually about the size of a tennis ball — add a distinctive color and crisp, somewhat bitter taste when cut into garden salads.

How to Grow: Radicchio used to be a difficult thing to grow. Each plant had to be cut back at a certain time for heads to form, and even then the heads were often irregular — if they formed at all. Today there are self-healing varieties for warm-weather regions ('Alto'), northern areas ('Augusto'), and uniform heads ('Medusa'). Set two- to three-week-old transplants about a week or so before the last frost in spring, or eight weeks before the first frost of fall. Space the plants 10 inches apart. Mulch soil and water regularly to inhibit bolting. Common problems include interior browning of the head, caused by either insufficient moisture or, especially in the Northeast, boron deficiency. High temperatures and low moisture together cause browning along leaf edges. Fertilize with fish emulsion every other week for uniform growth. In warm regions, shade the plants for the hottest hours.

Harvest and Use: Cut the heads from the plants as needed after the heads become firm to the touch. They will keep in the refrigerator for about a week.

Cultivars: *Hybrids:* 'Rossana', 'Medusa'; *Standards:* 'Alto', 'Augusto'

Radish
Raphanus sativus

LIGHT: Full sun
SOIL: Moist, sandy loam (spring types); well-drained, moist silt and clay loam (Daikon types); pH 5.5–7.0
PARTS USED: Roots
WHEN TO PLANT: Spring, fall (Zones 2–8); winter (Zones 9–10)
DAYS TO MATURITY: Spring types 25–30 from seed; Daikon, 50–60 from seed

Radishes have been cultivated since the time of the Pharaohs. The plants are either annual or biennial, depending on the cultivar, and produce a rosette of long, deeply lobed leaves above a spicy-tasting root.

How to Grow: The most flavorful radishes are grown in light, fertile, moist soil. This permits fast, uninterrupted growth and crisp, mild-tasting roots. Direct-sow spring types about a month before the last frost, and Daikon types in either spring or late summer, depending on the variety. Set the seeds 2 inches apart in rows placed 1 to 2 feet apart. Thin the plants to 4 inches. Heavy soils are more prone to root maggots. Radishes are also subject to many diseases, but harvesting the plants as quickly as they mature is usually the only control you need.

Harvest and Use: Pull spring types as soon as they reach 1 to 1½ inches in diameter. Harvest Daikon types after about two months. The extra can be stored in fresh sawdust over winter. Radishes are delicious sliced into salads or served with dip.

Cultivars: *Spring Types:* 'Easter Egg', 'Marabelle', 'Red King', 'Cherry Belle'; *Daikon Hybrid (Spring):* 'Spring Leader'; *Daikon Hybrid (Late Summer):* 'Summer Cross'

Spinach
Spinacia olearacea

LIGHT: Full sun to partial shade
SOIL: Well drained, evenly moist, fertile, pH 6.0–7.0
PARTS USED: Leaves
WHEN TO PLANT: Spring, fall (Zones 2–10)
DAYS TO MATURITY: 40 from seed

Native to Asia, spinach migrated to our gardens the long way round the barn, wandering to Africa before arriving in Europe. The plants form a very loose rosette of heart-shaped, emerald-green leaves. High in vitamins and minerals, spinach is one of the most nutritious of vegetables.

How to Grow: A hardy plant, spinach should be direct-sown about one month before the last spring frost; direct-sow fall crops about one month before the first autumn frost. Set the seeds about 2 inches apart in spring, 1 inch apart in fall, in shallow rows spaced about 18 inches apart. Thin seedlings to about 4 inches apart. Repeat sowings every ten to fourteen days to ensure a continual supply. Use blight-resistant varieties for fall plantings. Grow plants beneath fabric row covers to protect the plants from leafminers and other insects. Spinach responds well to fertilizers; try regular applications of fish emulsion. Excellent air circulation is needed to inhibit mildew, also known as blue mold, especially in fall. Mulch the soil to keep the leaves clean.

Harvest and Use: Pick the outer leaves as needed or cut the entire plant. Harvest in the cool of the morning. Store spinach in the refrigerator until you're ready to use it, then rinse it in cold water and pat it dry. Spinach is excellent in fresh garden salads or when lightly sautéed.

Cultivars: *Hybrids:* 'Tyee', 'Space', 'Wolter', 'Indian Summer', 'Melody'; *Standard:* 'Winter Bloomsdale'

Turnip
Brassica rapa Rapifera Group

LIGHT: Full sun
SOIL: Well drained, rich, evenly moist, pH 5.5–6.5
PARTS USED: Leaves, roots
WHEN TO PLANT: Spring (Zones 2–4); spring, fall (Zones 4–8); winter (Zones 9–10)
DAYS TO MATURITY: 35–50 from seed

The turnip originated in Siberia and northern Europe. In the sixteenth century the plant wandered to western Europe; a century later it hopped a ride to North America. Once here the turnip developed a split personality — northern and southern. Northerners grew turnips mostly for their mild-tasting roots, while southerners ate the plant's leafy greens and fed the bottoms to livestock.

How to Grow: Turnips, beets, and carrots have similar requirements. Direct-sow the seeds about 1 inch apart in single rows spaced 12 to 15 inches apart. Thin to 4 inches when seedlings emerge. Fertilize with fish emulsion and water regularly. Cover with fabric row covers to inhibit flea beetles and other pests. Keep the foliage dry and grow in an area with good air circulation to inhibit foliar diseases. Have your soil tested to ensure proper amounts of calcium, magnesium, manganese, boron, potassium, and phosphorus.

Harvest and Use: Begin to harvest the greens and bottoms when the roots are about 1½ inches across. Pull the entire plant and snip off the top. For best flavor the roots should be gathered before they exceed 3 inches in diameter. Prepare the greens by lightly cooking them with a good pepper sauce. The roots can be stored in fresh sawdust in a cool cellar.

Cultivars: *For Greens:* 'Japanese Shogoin', 'Just Right', 'All Top'; *For Bottoms:* 'Hakurei', 'Market Express', 'De Milan', 'Purple Top', 'White Globe'

COMPANION CROPS FOR SOME COOL-WEATHER VEGETABLES

VEGETABLE	GOOD COMPANIONS	COMPANIONS TO AVOID
Beans, broad	potatoes, marigolds, summer savory	onions, fennel
Beet	onions, cole crops, lettuce, bush beans	mustard
Broccoli	beets, onions, herbs such as sage, thyme, and rosemary	tomatoes, strawberries
Broccoli, Raab	beets, onions, herbs such as sage, thyme, and rosemary	tomatoes, strawberries
Brussels Sprouts	beets, onions, sage, thyme, rosemary	tomatoes, strawberries
Cabbage	beets, onions, thyme, sage, rosemary	other cole crops, tomatoes, strawberries
Chinese Cabbage	aromatic herbs (including mint, thyme, sage, rosemary, lemon balm), beets, onions	strawberries, tomatoes
Cauliflower	celery, borage, thyme, sage	tomatoes, strawberries
Florence fennel	none	cole crops, coriander, caraway, strawberries, tomatoes, beans
Kale	onions	tomatoes
Kohlrabi	onions, beets, herbs (including thyme, sage, rosemary)	tomatoes, strawberries, peppers
Lettuce	carrots, tomatoes, cucumbers, radishes	
Mustard	Traditionally, mustard has been planted to repel harmful species of nematodes, but the validity of this is questionable.	cole crops such as cabbage, broccoli, cauliflower
Parsley	tomatoes, carrots	
Peas	almost everything	alliums
Radish	Alternate rows of radishes with rows of lettuce to give a nice flavor to both.	
Spinach	strawberries, peas, celery, parsley	
Turnips	peas, other legumes, beets, lettuce, spinach, carrots	

5

Warm-Season Vegetables

Planting the warm-season vegetable garden marks the end of the long transition between winter and summer, indoor and outdoor gardening. The soil is warm enough to foster the growth of tender seeds, and the corn, tomatoes, and pepper plants explode with life. The houseplants and potted herbs migrate to the deck and patio, while marigolds and petunias are planted between the vegetables to attract beneficial insects. It is a time when lunch consists of multiple servings of tomato sandwiches made with thick slices of big red tomatoes, gobs of mayonnaise, and tasty white bread; dinner is stacks of freshly picked sweet corn slow-roasted in their husks over a smoldering fire.

Some of the plants of the warm-season garden are holdovers from spring. Carrots, potatoes, and Swiss chard all can stand cool weather, but unlike other cool-season plants they can also tolerate or even thrive in the warm days of summer. Other warm-season crops, such as tomatoes, corn, and snap beans, evolved in the semitropical regions of the world, where cool nights alternate with warm days for most of the year. This is still the best environment for their cultivated relatives; the best crops are grown where the summer nights are at least 15°F cooler than the days. The final group in the warm-season garden are the very tender plants descended from relatives acclimatized to the steady warmth of the Tropics. Cucumbers, melons, lima beans, squash, and sweet potatoes all fall into this group. These plants require long periods of warmth to produce their most bountiful yields.

Keeping so many plants with such different likes and dislikes happy in one garden is a bit of a challenge. It doesn't need to be daunting though, for even though these plants are a varied group, they still have much in common. All of them thrive in evenly moist soil rich in organic matter bathed in sunshine. There are some subtleties to master here and there, but they make the resulting accomplishments that much sweeter. The warm season garden can be amazingly productive, bestowing a bounty of nutritious food as well as fond memories.

Knowing When to Plant

Trying to guess the exact date of the last spring frost or the first fall freeze is like trying to pick winning lottery numbers. The information gleaned from charts, zone maps, and local experts may be accurate one year but totally off the mark the next. The reason for this is really quite simple: The information gardeners get reflects the average conditions of a large region gathered over many years, not the specific conditions of your yard that particular year. There is, however, a way to obtain specific information on the microclimate of your backyard that is correct every single year. And it's not even difficult to do.

PHENOLOGY

Phenology is the science of using indicator plants to determine when certain weather conditions will prevail and certain insect pests will be active. Aphids, for instance, need consistently warm weather to be active — weather that coincidentally matches the conditions needed by black locust trees to flower. So each spring when you see black locusts bloom, you can also be sure that aphids will soon appear. Cole crops, such as cabbage and broccoli, can be planted in early spring, but if you wait a bit longer, until the flowering dogwoods have dropped their petals, the plants will have much less chance of being damaged by root maggots.

This neat science, which has been practiced by observant gardeners for generations, can also tell you just when to plant certain vegetables. Plant Swiss chard, spinach, beets, and onions when your daffodils bloom, for instance. Plant peas when the maple trees flower, and potatoes when the emerging leaves of white oaks are the size of a cat's ear. When the petals are dropping from the apple trees, sow bush and pole beans and cucumbers. When black locust and peonies flower, transplant tomatoes, melons, eggplant, and other warm-weather crops. One other little secret: Transplanting should be done when you see swallows swooping close to the ground over the fields. The insects they eat fly closer to the ground before it rains. When they fly higher, the coming weather will be dry.

TO START OR NOT TO START

Any vegetable plant can be transplanted, but the window of time you have to accomplish this without damaging the seedling differs from crop to crop. This window is determined by the rate of root growth as compared to the rate of top growth. Plants with rapid root growth and slower top growth, such as tomatoes and eggplants, can be easily transplanted over many weeks. Those with slow root growth and rapid top growth, such as corn and beans, can be successfully transplanted only for a few days when the seedlings are very small.

A garden myth states that transplanted crops have stronger root systems and higher yield than direct-sown plants. This is actually only partially true. Transplanting anything at any stage of development checks the growth of the plant. If the plant is transplanted when it's small, the check in growth is slight and stimulates the branching of roots. This increased root area can ultimately lead to higher yields. If the plants are transplanted after the roots have filled the growing container, however, the results can be completely different. These plants often have their growth checked for many days, resulting in delayed maturity, smaller yields, and poorer-quality crops. Remember the golden rule of higher yields; uninterrupted early season growth results in heavier crops later on.

Vegetable plants started indoors should be transplanted to the garden before they become potbound.

♦ **Best Warm-Season Crops to Transplant**

Tomatoes	Peppers
Eggplant	Celery

♦ **Best Warm-Season Crops to Direct-Sow**

Beans	Melons
Corn	Squash
Cucumbers	Pumpkins

A GARDEN SECRET — BRUSHING TOMATOES

Tomatoes started indoors can look pretty weird by transplanting time. After growing in dim light for weeks the plants are tall and weak, with thin stems and small leaves. The problem could be solved by growing the seedlings under lights. But what do folks who can't afford the expense of artificial lighting do? One solution is to let the local garden center grow them.

But if you want to grow transplants indoors, there is a wonderful secret to use — and it doesn't cost a thing.

Tomato plants stretch out due to low light, which stimulates particular hormones to elongate the cells in the plant stems. A different hormone, called cytokinin, can counteract this effect. Cytokinins induce cell walls in plant stems to thicken and become stronger.

To stimulate cytokinin formation simply brush your hand lightly over the tops of the seedlings twice a day. The back-and-forth movement of the stem helps promote cytokinin, which in turn helps create plants with thicker, stronger stems. Remember to give the plants as much light as possible, and stroke them gently in the morning and the evening. The results will amaze you.

INTO THE OUTDOORS

Vegetable gardeners are often fans of the story of the turtle and the hare, because they see themselves as one or the other. Hares are those folks who want to get their warm-season plants in the ground as soon as possible every year. The turtles take a more relaxed perspective, waiting until nature has made it quite obvious that warm weather really has arrived. The debate that results, of course, concerns which style produces the better harvest.

Here are the facts: Many plants harvested for their fruit, such as melons and tomatoes, need warm weather and soil to produce rapid vegetative growth. The crop should be timed so that the fruit begins to enlarge and ripen when the days and nights are growing cooler. This cool weather slows cell division, which helps to accumulate sugars in the fruits, making them more flavorful and tender than those ripening in hot weather. The bottom line is that rabbit gardeners who put their plants in early often have earlier crops while turtle gardeners wait a bit longer for their harvest but have tastier yields.

Cantaloupes are one of many crops that grow better when direct sown in the garden after the soil has warmed in the spring.

Getting the Best Flavor

Many factors influence the flavor of vegetables. In a nutshell, the flavor of any vegetable results from the blend of sugars, minerals, and other substances that collect in the fruit, leaves, stem and roots as the plant grows and matures. Some soils, such as sandy loams, produce vegetables with a full rich flavor, while muck soils can sometimes yield veggies with a more earthy taste. Plants grown in drought conditions with inadequate irrigation often are less sweet and in some cases can even taste more sour than well-watered crops. Over-watering also affects flavor by diluting the concentration of sugar, producing a watery, bland-tasting harvest. Finally, the amount and type of fertilizer used on the garden can also affect flavor. Organic fertilizers that contain some trace minerals seem to add a fullness to the taste of vegetables and fruits, while those low in nitrogen can produce crops that are low in sugar with a strong, unpleasant aftertaste.

THE COLORFUL WARM-SEASON GARDEN

The warm-weather vegetable garden can be as colorful as many flower gardens, if you plant the right varieties. Unlike the colorful cool-season garden, where much of the color comes from attractive foliage, the warm-weather garden relies more on fruit. There are brilliant peppers, eggplants, and okra, as well as the beautiful blossoms of runner beans that attract hummingbirds all season long. Here are a few choices to lend a splash of color to the omnipresent backdrop of green.

VEGETABLE	COLORFUL CULTIVAR	DESCRIPTION
Beans	'Trionfo'	A robust pole bean from Europe with violet-black beans
	'Royal Burgundy'	A bush bean that yields lots of deep purple beans
	'Sequoia'	A Romano type that bears plentiful deep purple beans
	'Royalty Purple'	A bush bean with purple pods and attractive red flowers
	'Scarlet Emperor'	A scarlet runner bean with beautiful red flowers
Eggplants	'Italian White'	Has very tasty, creamy-white early fruits
	'Turkish Orange'	Yields a plentiful supply of bright orange fruit
	'Purple Blush'	A hybrid that yields light violet fruit
	'Neon'	Produces slender, very tasty fruit, colored a bright purple-pink
Melons	'Golden Beauty'	Has skin of soft yellow with pale green flesh
	'Swan Lake'	Produces flavorful melons with golden skins
	'Sweet Thing'	Bears golden-orange fruit with white flesh
Okra	'Burgundy'	An attractive plant with deep red pods
Peppers	'Islander'	Bears lots of dark lavender fruit
	'Corona'	A sweet pepper with bright orange fruit
	'Sweet Chocolate'	Bears green peppers that ripen to a deep-chocolate brown
	'Pretty In Purple'	Has dark purple leaves and cherry-shaped red fruit
	'Orange Belle'	Bears an orange sweet pepper
Squash	'Hopi Orange'	A traditional plant with orange-red skin
	'Red Kuri'	A Japanese squash with orange skin
	'Table Gold'	An acorn type with bright yellow skin
Tomato	'Gold Nugget'	A cherry type with bright yellow fruit
	'Yellow Perfection'	An heirloom bearing tasty fruit of clear yellow

Some gardening problems are easy to diagnose. For instance, it's pretty tough to miss a tomato hornworm the size of the Loch Ness monster as it munches through the tomato patch. But some problems pop up that give greater pause. Here are some of the common but less obvious problems that might appear in your warm-season vegetables. (Also consult the "Nutrient and Climate Disorders" chart on page 67.)

PLANT	PROBLEM	CAUSE
Melon	leaf spots	magnesium deficiency
Onions and garlic	shattered flower	periods of sunny weather alternating with cloudy times; most common in areas with frequent air pollution
	leaf scorch	high air temperatures coupled with erratic watering
	yellowing of leaves	copper or manganese deficiency
Peanuts	yellowing of leaves	deficiency of iron, magnesium, or manganese due to high soil pH
Peppers	fruit beginning to rot from the base	insufficient soil moisture and/or deficiency of calcium
	sunscald of fruit	inadequate shading of fruit by leaves, often noticed after defoliation of plant during hot, dry weather
Potatoes	tips of leaves turning brown	weather change from cool and moist to hot and dry
	black discoloration after cooking	hot, dry weather during tuber formation, or potassium deficiency
	hollow center of tuber cracked or knobby tuber	too much soil moisture and/or overfertilizing changes in soil moisture during late tuber formation
	tipburn of leaves	cool, moist weather followed by hot and dry
Squash and pumpkins	fruit beginning to rot from the base	change from cool, moist weather to hot and dry conditions
	yellowing of leaves	deficiency of nitrogen
	misshapen fruit and/or leaf	
	margins that brown and die	potassium deficiency
Sweet potatoes	potato mushy inside	cold spell before harvest
Swiss chard	cracked stem	boron deficiency
Tomatoes	fruit rotting from the base	changes in soil moisture and/or calcium deficiency
	leaf edges that roll	soil too moist
	wilting when plants grown near walnut trees	reaction to excretions from walnut trees
	uneven ripening	nutrient deficiency
	fruit with cloudy colored spots	injury from tarnished plant bugs
	leaf edges curled	excessive soil moisture
	fruits that don't turn red	temperatures that remain above about 80°F, or inadequate air circulation

Common Pests and Diseases of Warm-Weather Vegetables

Potato Beetle

AFFECTS: Tomatoes, potatoes, eggplants, peppers

Adult potato beetles look like little Volkswagens striped yellow and black, while larvae are dull orange with black dots along their sides. Both adults and larvae feed on the foliage of plants in  ⅜"/10mm the Solanaceae family. Adults overwinter in the soil, emerging in spring. Overwintered beetles do not have enough energy to fly and must walk to susceptible plants. Up to three generations can appear during one growing season.

Control: Plant resistant cultivars and cover rows with a rough textured mulch, such as straw, to impede the travel of emerging beetles. Grow susceptible crops under row covers through spring. Handpick adults from plants in the cool of the morning and drop them into a container of soapy liquid. Spray plants with neem or BTSD to control larvae.

Cucumber Beetle, Striped and Spotted

AFFECTS: Corn, cucumbers, peanuts, potatoes, melons, pumpkins, squash

Both types of cucumber beetles are small, narrow beetles with either black stripes or spots on a yellow background. The larvae, called corn rootworms, are thin, white worms that ¼"/6mm tunnel into the stems of plants. The larvae of the striped cucumber beetle are also thin and white but feed on the leaves, stems, and fruit. The insects are thought to infect plants with viral and bacterial diseases as they feed. Up to four generations can be produced during one growing season, and the best way to control them is to destroy as much of the first generation as possible.

Control: Plant disease-resistant cultivars and grow them within floating row covers. Spray insecticidal

soap on exposed larvae, or use parasitic soil nematodes. Control heavy infestations by spraying pyrethrins. Remove annual vegetables from the garden in fall.

Japanese Beetle

AFFECTS: Almost everything

Adult Japanese beetles are heavy-bodied with brown wing shields and metallic blue-green bodies. They congregate in great numbers on plants warmed by the sun, where they chew flowers  ½"/1.3cm and leaves. The adults burrow into the ground in late summer and lay eggs. The larvae then feed on the roots of lawn grasses, overwinter, and emerge as adults in early summer.

Control: Handpick adults in the cool of the morning and drop them into a container of soapy water. Spray lawn areas with neem or milky spore. Protect crops with floating row covers when adults appear.

Corn Earworm, Tomato Fruitworm

AFFECTS: Corn, tomatoes, peppers, okra, beans, squash

The larva of the corn earworm, or tomato fruitworm, is a green- 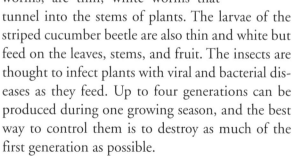 **larva 1¼"/3.2cm** ish brown, 1½-inch-long caterpillar with a yellow head and black legs. It feeds on corn ears, burrows into tomatoes, and eats the leaves of many other crops. Adults emerge from the soil in early spring in the South and migrate north as the weather warms.

Control: Planting flowers in the vegetable garden attracts beneficial insects that prey on the larvae. Spray with neem or BTK.

Whitefly

AFFECTS: Tomatoes, squash, potatoes, melons, pumpkins, eggplants, peppers

Adult whiteflies are very small insects with white wings that cluster on the undersides of leaves.

When the plant is disturbed a little cloud of insects hovers around its leaves. The nymphs are even smaller; they look like yellowish translucent dots on the undersides of the leaves. Both adults and nymphs suck plant juices, much as aphids do.

¹⁄₁₀"/2.5mm

Control: Whiteflies are common in warm regions and in the North are often introduced into the garden via plants purchased from infested greenhouses. Keep weeds under control and plant resistant flower species to attract beneficial insects. Spray plants with neem or insecticidal soap. Inspect purchased plants very carefully.

Bacterial Rot, Wilt

Affects: Many crops

Bacterial rot and wilt are primarily caused by a bacteria called *Erwinia*. The disease first appears as a water-soaked spot, which enlarges rapidly. As the bacteria expands it gives off a distinctive stink. Infected tissues become soft and brown, then fall apart into a slimy mush. The disease can infect plants in the garden or in storage.

Control: The disease does best in humid weather, when moisture remains on the leaves and stems for extended periods. Water the soil and not the plants whenever possible. Do not water late in the day. Space plants for good air circulation. Practice good sanitation procedures.

Early Blight

Affects: Plants of Solanaceae Family

A fungal disease, early blight first appears on older, shaded leaves as sunken brown spots marked with concentric rings. The spots expand, sometimes covering most of each leaf. Early blight enters tomato fruits from the stem ends, producing dark spots on the skins and a dark rot inside the fruits. Potatoes are infected as they flower; leaf symptoms are similar to those of tomatoes. The tubers also have spots of dry rot.

Control: The disease is spread by rain, overhead watering, wind, garden tools, and flea beetles. It overwinters in the soil and thrives in humid weather above 85°F. Remove weeds and clean the garden of all plant material each year. Space plants for maximum air circulation. Water the soil and not the plants. Rotate plants on a three-year schedule.

Late Blight

Affects: Potatoes, tomatoes

Late blight is a disease that has literally altered the course of history. It caused the potato famine in Ireland in 1845 that killed over one million people. A century later, in 1946, the same disease devastated the tomato crop in America. The fungus, though extremely virulent, is only epidemic when weather conditions are just right. A cool, wet period in early summer followed by a hot, humid period almost always results in outbreaks of blight.

The disease usually begins when infected tubers are planted in spring; the fungus then travels up the emerging stems and infects the leaves. Next, spores are produced and splashed from plant to plant during rainstorms or irrigation. Extensive blight soon follows, with entire fields dying in a matter of days. Potatoes are usually infected first, followed by tomatoes. In potatoes dark spots appear on the lower leaves following wet weather. The spots enlarge, and a white growth appears on the undersides of the leaves. As the top of the plant rots, a strong odor is released. Tubers have a sunken spot on the skin and a brown dry rot within. Symptoms are the same on tomato leaves; tomato fruits develop large brown spots on the skin that enlarge into watery rots.

Control: So-called resistant cultivars can resist some strains of the fungus, but not the newer, emerging ones. Thus, clean your garden of all plant debris each fall. Dig potatoes at least two weeks after the tops have been killed by frost. Bordeaux mix, which can inhibit fruit set and stunt tomatoes, should be used only on adult plants.

A Catalog of Warm-Season Vegetables

Artichoke, Globe
Cynara scolymus

LIGHT:	Full sun
SOIL:	Well drained, evenly moist, fertile, pH 6.5–7.5
PARTS USED:	Flower heads
WHEN TO PLANT:	After last frost
DAYS TO MATURITY:	100 from transplant

Perennial artichokes were traditionally treated as biennials. Their involved culture limited their growth to California, the Southwest, and the Deep South. Recently, though, new short-season cultivars have allowed many more gardeners to enjoy growing these delicacies.

How to Grow: Sow seeds indoors in late winter or early spring. Transplant to the garden when the soil has warmed and the danger of frost is past. Space the plants about 2 feet apart in single rows, with 3 feet between rows. The plants will grow about 3 feet tall. Keep the soil moist, and mulch. Fertilize from spring to midsummer with fish emulsion or another organic fertilizer. Cut the plant back in mid to late fall. In Zones 4 through 7, cover the plant with an inverted bushel basket, and mound leaves or pine needles over the basket. Plants in Zones 8 through 10 usually need no winter protection. If plants overwinter they will produce well the following year. After a second harvest, uproot the plants and discard. Artichokes have few insect pests but are sometimes troubled by root rot organisms, which like wet soil. Grow in raised beds with good drainage and excellent air circulation.

Harvest and Use: Flower buds begin to form in late summer through fall. Cut the stem about 2 inches below the flower bud with pruning shears.

Cultivars: 'Imperial Star' (best short-season variety)

Asparagus
Asparagus officinalis

LIGHT:	Full sun to light shade
SOIL:	Well drained, loose, fertile, pH 6.5–7.5
PARTS USED:	Shoots
WHEN TO PLANT:	Spring (Zones 3–7); late fall or winter (Zones 8–10)
DAYS TO MATURITY:	Light harvest in one year

Of all the wonderful aspects to spring, none can compare to a meal of fresh asparagus right from the garden. It is included in the warm weather crops because summer is the season that determines just how good the following spring's crop will be.

How to Grow: Work the soil well the fall before planting. In spring, after the soil has dried out a bit, dig a furrow about 10 inches deep and 10 inches wide. Mix compost, rotted manure, or peat moss equally with the soil and cover the bottom of the furrow with a 4-inch-thick layer. Place the crowns 15 inches apart and cover with 2 inches of the mix. Water well. In warm regions with heavy soils, shallow-plant by filling the furrow with 6 inches of mix; plant the crowns and cover. Space rows 5 feet apart. As the plants grow, gradually fill in the furrow, until by late spring or early summer the bed is level. Keep the soil evenly moist. Mulch each fall with a 2-inch layer of compost. Asparagus beds should yield well for at least fifteen years.

Harvest and Use: Gather no more than one or two spears per crown from one-year beds, and up to 50 percent of the spears from established ones. Harvest by grasping the spear near the soil line and bending the shoot until it snaps. "When you harvest early peas, let the asparagus go to seed." Keep asparagus fresh in the refrigerator by storing in a jar with the base of the spears standing in about an inch of water.

Cultivars: 'Jersey Knight', 'Jersey King'

Beans, Bush
Phaseolus vulgaris

LIGHT: Full sun
SOIL: Evenly moist, well drained, pH 6.0–7.5
PARTS USED: Fruits
WHEN TO PLANT: Late winter to early spring, fall (Zones 7–10); mid-spring to early summer (Zones 3–6)
DAYS TO MATURITY: 45–55 from seed

When it comes to saving space in the garden as well as producing early crops, there are no better beans than bush beans. If space is really limited, they can even be grown in containers.

How to Grow: Bush beans achieve their best growth when the soil temperature is above 65°F. Plant seeds 2 inch deep and 2 to 3 inches apart in rows spaced 2 to 3 feet apart. Cover with soil or vermiculite and water well. Add an inoculant of nitrogen-fixing bacteria if legumes have not been grown in the soil in the previous three years. Water often and mulch between the rows. Fertilize lightly when the flowers appear.

Harvest and Use: Bush beans can be harvested at any size but taste the best when they're between 3 and 5 inches long. Pick them before the pods begin to get bulgy. Harvest often to encourage heavier yields. For best flavor water them well the day before you pick, and harvest them in the cool of the morning. A favorite treat is pickled beans. A variation on the standard recipe calls for the generous addition of minced garlic to the brine.

Cultivars: *Green:* 'Provider', 'Narbonne', 'Tenderpod'; *Yellow Wax:* 'Brittle Wax', 'Goldcrop', 'Goldkist'

Beans, Pole
Phaseolus vulgaris

LIGHT: Full sun
SOIL: Well drained, evenly moist, pH 6.0–7.0
PARTS USED: Fruits
WHEN TO PLANT: Midspring (Zones 7–10); late spring through early summer (Zones 3–6)
DAYS TO MATURITY: 55–65 from seed

Pole beans are traditional favorites for children's gardens, where their leafy tepees provide unique summertime hideouts. The fast-growing plants yield abundant, long-season crops that have better flavor than even the best bush bean. The extra effort of providing support for the plants is well worth the rewards of their superb flavor.

How to Grow: Set trellises, poles, or mesh netting along rows. For tepees, arrange three or four poles and secure the top with twine. Plant five to seven seeds at the base of each pole. Be sure to site pole beans where their growth will not shade other plants that need full sun. Leaf crops, such as Swiss chard, do well in the shade of pole beans. When the soil temperature is about 60°F, sow seed about 1 one inch deep and 4 inches apart. Cover with soil or vermiculite and water well. If legumes have not been grown in the soil in the last three years, use an inoculant to introduce nitrogen-fixing bacteria. Water often and apply a mulch. Fertilize lightly when the plants begin to set flowers.

Harvest and Use: Begin to harvest beans when they reach from 4 to 6 inches in length. Great fresh, they are also good for freezing. Avoid the older cultivars that must be picked before they turn stringy.

Cultivars: *Green:* 'Northeaster', 'Fortex', 'Kentucky Wonder'; *Yellow Wax:* 'Goldmarie'; *Purple:* 'Trionfo', 'Dow Purple Podded'

Carrots

Daucus carota var. *sativus*

LIGHT: Full sun
SOIL: Well worked, loose, well drained, pH 5.5–6.5
PARTS USED: Roots
WHEN TO PLANT: Early spring, fall (Zones 8–10); spring (Zones 3–7)
DAYS TO MATURITY: 55–75 from seed

Initially used in the Middle East as a medicine and did not become a popular food item until the early 1900s. The roots have an outer core, where most of the sugars are stored, and an inner core that is pithy and bland. The highest-quality carrots are those with large outer cores and small inner ones. Older roots have larger amounts of carotene than younger ones.

How to Grow: The shape of a carrot's root is largely determined by the cultivar grown but also by the temperature of the soil. Between 45 and 60°F the roots are thin and long, with poor color. At soil temperatures above 70°F the roots are shorter. Normal size and growth occur between 60 and 70°F. Planting too early can lead to summer bolting. Use pelleted seeds to ensure proper spacing of carrots.

Sow seeds in shallow rows and cover with a thin layer of vermiculite. Water well and cover with black plastic for three weeks. Then remove the mulch and keep the rows watered and weeded. Manure that is not well rotted can cause deformed and branched roots. Lightly fertilize with fish emulsion after plants are established.

Harvest and Use: Pull or dig carrots anytime after they show good color. Be careful not to bruise them, which can cause rot during storage.

Cultivars: *Hybrids:* 'Nelson', 'Artist', 'Blaze', 'Navajo'; *Standards:* 'Scarlet Nantes', 'Thumbelina', 'Red Core Chatenay'

Celery

Apium graveolens var. *dulce*

LIGHT: Full sun
SOIL: Well drained, evenly moist, very fertile, pH 5.5–6.5
PARTS USED: Leaf petioles
WHEN TO PLANT: Mid to late spring (Zones 4–7); late summer to fall (Zones 8–9); winter (Zone 10)
DAYS TO MATURITY: 80–130 days from transplanting

Celery is one of the more difficult crops to grow well because it demands so much of your time. Commercially, the best celery is grown on dark muck soils or very fertile sandy loams that are regularly irrigated.

How to Grow: Amend soil with compost or other organic matter at least six months before planting. Loosen the soil again before planting and warm with black plastic mulch. Sow indoors eight to ten weeks before planting time. Soak the seeds in warm water for twenty-four hours before planting. Immediately sow flats, keeping temperatures above 60°F. Plant in the garden when temperatures average above 55°F and the plants are about 4 inches tall. Space the plants from 6 to 10 inches apart. Water the row a few hours before transplanting and again afterward. Keep the soil evenly moist, and fertilize twice a week with fish emulsion. Keep the row well weeded and practice only shallow cultivation. Mulch to increase yields. Black heart, a disorder caused by a calcium deficiency, is exacerbated by high levels of sodium in irrigation water.

Harvest and Use: Celery can be harvested anytime after the plants reach the desired size. Gather individual stalks from the outside of the plant, or cut the entire clump at the soil line. Irrigate the day before harvesting.

Cultivars: 'Ventura', 'Utah Tall', 'Pascal Giant'

Corn, Sweet
Zea mays var. *rugosa*

LIGHT:	Full sun
SOIL:	Well drained, fertile, pH 6.0–7.0
PARTS USED:	Seeds
WHEN TO PLANT:	Winter to spring (Zones 7–10); spring to summer (Zones 3–6)
DAYS TO MATURITY:	65–90 from seed

There are few things on earth as flavorful as fresh sweet corn, although even this seemingly undebatable fact can get you into trouble in the company of real corn connoisseurs. These gourmets will tell you that fresh is measured in mere seconds; that as soon as the ear leaves the stalk, the flavor of the corn begins to change. From then on, minutes matter. The folks who claim to enjoy the best corn have the water already boiling on the stove, and a companion holding the kitchen door open as they advance toward the garden. They pick the corn, husk it on the run, and drop it into the pot before a minute has elapsed. No joke — they say it makes a difference. Regardless of the consequences, I still prepare my corn on a more leisurely schedule.

How to Grow: Sow corn about 1 inch deep and 8 inches apart, in rows spaced 30 to 36 inches apart. Plant in blocks of at least four rows. The most important determinants of corn growth are moisture and temperature. Even moisture is required throughout the season. The warmer the summer, the faster corn will grow and mature. Corn grown in cool summers can ripen up to two weeks later than that grown in warm summers. Fertilize every other week with fish emulsion. Practice shallow-cultivation until the corn is waist high.

Harvest and Use: Knowing when to harvest corn is an art in itself. As the kernels grow the juice inside is clear. During this stage, called the premilk phase, the kernels are still enlarging and beginning to store sugars. Corn at this stage of growth has kernels that look small, do not fill out the row, and lack plumpness. As the kernels ripen the juice becomes white and milky. This phase, called the milk phase, marks the best time to harvest. Kernels in the milk phase have the maximum sugar content with a minimum amount of starch. The corn has kernels that are plump and full and that fill out the rows, but do not appear crowded. Following the milk phase, the kernels quickly turn their accumulated sugars into starch. This phase is called the dough stage. The kernels begin to lose their juiciness and become chewy, with a pasty taste. The ears appear overcrowded, with their kernels tightly packed.

It would be easy to pick the best corn if you could partially husk each ear and take a peek inside. No doubt you have seen people do this at the farmers' market. There is no leeway here: Opening the husk to gauge the ripeness of corn is a sure sign of the amateur. It not only makes the ear unsalable to others, but it's also not even necessary. There is a way to tell the stage of growth each ear is in without peeking: When corn is in the premilk phase, the silk is mostly green and the tip of the ear feels narrow and pointed. When the ear is ripe and has entered the milk phase, the silk is entirely brown and the tip of the ear feels plump and rounded. When corn is overripe, the silk is also brown, but the tip of the ear is quite blunt, with almost no rounding. It does take a little practice to get this skill down just right, but once you have it mastered you will have learned one of the true secrets of the old-time farmers.

One more little tidbit. Once the ear is picked, regardless of what stage it is in, its sugars immediately begin to change into starch. Corn picked and stored at about 80°F for only one day will lose half of its entire sugar content. Pick corn in the cool of the morning and store unhusked in the refrigerator. The sugar loss will be less than 15 percent after twenty-four hours.

Cultivars: *Yellow Hybrids:* 'Earlivee', 'Tuxedo', 'Breeder's Choice', 'Early Choice'; *Bicolor Hybrids:* 'Delectable', 'Quickie'; *White Hybrids:* 'Silver Queen', 'Argent', 'Pristine'; *Super-Sweet Hybrids:* 'Fantasy', 'Honey 'n Pearl'

Popcorn
Zea mays var. *praecox*

LIGHT: Full sun
SOIL: Well drained, fertile, 6.0–7.0
PARTS USED: Seeds
WHEN TO PLANT: Winter to spring (Zones 7–10); spring to summer (Zones 3–6)
DAYS TO MATURITY: 85–120 from seed

Popcorn was a staple winter food of many Native American tribes centuries before Europeans arrived on the continent. It was used to supplement many dishes, adding nutrition and fiber to the diet. Today it has become a favorite of the children's vegetable garden, but often the harvested corn doesn't pop as well as the store-bought kind. This isn't the fault of the corn, but rather of kernels that haven't been properly cured or stored.

How to Grow: Plant popcorn at the other end of the garden from sweet corn. Sow seeds about 1 inch deep and 8 inches apart, in rows spaced 30–36 inches apart. Plant in blocks of at least four rows. The most important determinants of corn growth are moisture and temperature. Even moisture is required throughout the season. Fertilize every other week with fish emulsion. Practice shallow cultivation until the corn is waist high. Allow the ears to fully mature and partially dry while on the stalk.

Harvest and Use: Harvest the ears when the husks are tan and dry. The kernels should be shiny, plump, and slightly pointed at the tips. Some people recommend removing the husks; others just pull the sheaths back and leave them attached to the base of the cob. Allow the corn to cure in a well-ventilated, dim, cool place for about four weeks. At this time, twist the kernels from the cob and store in a sealed jar in the refrigerator for at least a day or so before popping. The corn can be kept in the refrigerator for many, many months.

Cultivars: *Hybrid:* 'M-212'; *Standard:* 'Tom Thumb'

Cucumber
Cucumis sativus

LIGHT: Full sun
SOIL: Well drained, fertile, pH 6.0–7.0
PARTS USED: Fruits
WHEN TO PLANT: Late winter, fall (Zones 8–10); spring to early summer (Zones 4–7)
DAYS TO MATURITY: 50–60 from seed

Cucumbers are truly warm-weather plants but can be grown even in the far North because they mature rapidly. Open-pollinated varieties yield less and mature later than hybrid types.  Gynoecious types produce nearly all female flowers; they combine the heaviest yields with early ripening.

How to Grow: Cucumbers may be started indoors, but don't disturb the roots during transplanting. To direct-sow, plant seeds ½ inch deep and 2 inches apart in shallow rows. The soil should be at about 70°F. In northern areas use black plastic mulch and row covers to warm the soil as well as to deter pests and weeds. Thin the plants to 6 to 8 inches apart. Plant flowers nearby to attract pollinating insects. Once cucumbers begin to set fruit, keep the soil moist. Dry periods will lower yields and quality.

Harvest and Use: Cucumbers taste best when they are 4–8 inches long and entirely green. Yellow blossom ends indicate overmaturity. Pick daily to encourage heaviest yields. Pickling cucumbers mature slightly earlier than slicing cukes.

Cultivars: *Hybrids:* 'Aria', 'Jazzer', 'Fanfare', 'Early Pride'; *Standards:* 'Marketmore', 'Lemon', 'Ashley', 'Poinsett'; *Gynoecious Hybrids:* 'Supersett', 'Cherokee', 'Gemini'

Eggplant
Solanum melongena var. *esculentum*

LIGHT: Full sun
SOIL: Well drained, fertile, pH 5.5–7.0
PARTS USED: Fruits
WHEN TO PLANT: Late winter to midspring (Zones 7–10); mid to late spring (Zones 4–6)
DAYS TO MATURITY: 55–65 from transplanting

It is thought that the Arabs brought the eggplant to Spain, and from there it found its way across the rest of Europe. It comes in different shapes and colors, ranging from large, pear-shaped, dark purple forms to slender, magenta-pink varieties.

How to Grow: Sow seeds indoors about eight weeks before the last frost. Keep the soil medium warm, about 80°F, until germination. Grow the seedlings at about 70°F and brush them twice a day (see page 89). Transplant to the garden when they're about 4 inches tall, spacing them 18 to 24 inches apart. Eggplant is very susceptible to transplant shock: Be sure not to damage the roots, water thoroughly, and shelter them from north and northwest breezes. Fertilize with fish emulsion about once a month, and keep soil evenly moist. Rotate plants on a three- to five-year schedule to lessen the risk of blight and wilt diseases.

Harvest and Use: Eggplants can be harvested anytime from when they are half size to full ripeness. The earlier and more often you pick, the heavier your yield. To harvest, clip the stem, leaving the green cap attached to the fruit. Handle gingerly, because the fruit is easily bruised.

Cultivars: *Hybrids:* 'Orient Express', 'Black Belle', 'Purple Blush', 'Neon'

Garlic
Allium sativum

LIGHT: Full sun to light shade
SOIL: Well drained, fertile, pH 6.0–7.0
PARTS USED: Bulbs
WHEN TO PLANT: Beginning about the time of the first frost, and continuing for about four weeks. In frost-free areas plant from November through January.

Garlic is related to the onion but has a compound bulb composed of individual cloves instead of one large bulb. It has historically been used to repel vampires — which it must do, because I have yet to see a vampire anywhere near a garlic patch. Recent research suggests that consuming garlic has many health benefits. There are three types commonly grown: white, or softneck; pink, or stiffneck; and elephant.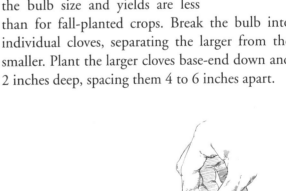

How to Grow: Garlic can be grown in spring and summer, but the bulb size and yields are less than for fall-planted crops. Break the bulb into individual cloves, separating the larger from the smaller. Plant the larger cloves base-end down and 2 inches deep, spacing them 4 to 6 inches apart.

Fall-planted garlic gives higher yields than spring-planted garlic.

Harvested garlic should be cured on a screen for several days before storing.

Cover with soil, and mulch with a thick layer of straw to prevent heaving. The smaller cloves can be planted in a shallow row about 1 inch deep and 2 inches apart. In spring snip off the emerging tops to use like chives.

Harvest and Use: The bulbs are ready to harvest when the green tops begin to yellow up and wilt. Loosen the soil with a fork and lift the bulbs. Shake off the soil, and place the bulbs on screens to dry for several days.

After curing, cut off roots and tops, and store in a cool, dry place. White garlic is often braided and stored, but research has shown that bulbs prepared this way have a shorter storage life than topped bulbs.

Cultivars: *Softneck types:* 'New York White', 'California Early', 'Inchelium Red'; *Stiffneck types:* 'German White', 'Pioneer', 'Spanish Roja', 'Chesnok Red'

Leek
Allium ampeloprasum, Porrum Group

LIGHT:	Full sun
SOIL:	Well drained, fertile, well worked, pH 6.0–7.0
PARTS USED:	Stems
WHEN TO PLANT:	Late winter to early spring
DAYS TO MATURITY:	55–115 from transplanting

Leeks have not historically been popular in North America, but lately they have become quite fashionable. They resemble onions, but instead of forming a bulb they produce a long, cylindrical stem.

How to Grow: Start leeks indoors in late winter or early spring, placing the seeds in flats about ¼ inch apart and ¼ inch deep. Transplant them to cell packs when they're about 2 inches tall. Plant outdoors about a week after the last frost; transplants should be 6 to 12 inches tall. Plant by either of two methods. *To dibble,* dig a hole that is 2 to 3 inches shallower than the plant is tall. Place the transplant in the hole and loosely fill in around it with soil. *To trench,* set the plants in a furrow. As the leeks grow, gradually fill in the trench. Both methods produce long, tender stems, but dibbling requires less labor. Keep the soil evenly moist, and fertilize with fish emulsion once a month during the growing season.

Harvest and Use: Harvest leeks when plants are large enough to use. Lift them carefully from the growing bed by loosening the ground with a fork. To keep soil pliable well into winter, mulch the row heavily with straw or salt hay just before the first hard freezes of fall. Dig mulched leeks as needed, but harvest all before growth renews in spring. Leeks can be used like onions to impart a mild oniony flavor to soups, stews and side dishes. My personal favorite is leek and potato soup.

Cultivars: 'Varna', 'King Richard', 'Laura', 'Titan', 'Winter Giant', 'Falltime', 'Scotland'

Melon

Cucumis melo

LIGHT:	Full sun
SOIL:	Well drained, evenly moist, fertile, pH 6.0–7.0
PARTS USED:	Fruits
WHEN TO PLANT:	Late winter to midspring (Zones 6–10); late spring (Zones 4–5)
DAYS TO MATURITY:	70–80 from transplanting

All melons belong to the same species, *Cucumis melo*, but are divided into separate groups and types. The Reticulatus Group includes the galia and muskmelon, (cantaloupe in the United States). Muskmelons have a light-tan-colored rind, richly netted with raised ridges. The flesh is deep orange with a sweet, aromatic flavor. Galia melons resemble muskmelon, with lightly netted rinds. The whitish-green flesh is renowned for its rich, tropical flavor. The Inodorus Group includes honeydews, casabas, and crenshaws. Honeydew melons have a smooth, butter-white rind and light-colored flesh that tastes sweet and airy. Casaba melons bear large fruit with smooth, bright yellow to greenish-yellow rinds. The sweet flesh is greenish-white and coarse. Crenshaw melons have slightly oblong or pear-shaped fruits with smooth, dusky yellow rinds. The flesh is salmon pink with a light but complex flavor. The Cantalupensis Group are the true cantaloupes, including the Charentais types. They have smooth rinds ranging in color from tan to metallic gray; the flesh is orange and aromatic with a zesty sweet flavor.

How to Grow: Warm the garden soil by laying black plastic mulch over it (after working it well) in spring. Melons can be direct-sown or transplanted. To direct-seed, sow in shallow rows or hills; if you're using rows, sow the seeds from ½ to 1 inch deep in groups of three spaced every 18 inches. Thin to about 2½ feet by cutting the stems at the soil line with scissors. Melon seeds don't germinate well in cold soil, so don't plant until your soil reaches daytime temperatures of 65 to 70°F (about two weeks after the last frost).

To transplant, start seeds indoors in cell packs about three weeks before your expected last frost. Keep the soil warm (80°F) and evenly moist until the seeds germinate. As the plants emerge, drop the temperature to 70°F. Transplant as soon as seedlings show their first set of true leaves. Avoid transplant shock with melons: Damaging the roots can severely set the plants back and reduce yields. To transplant safely, carefully cut away the plastic cell pack and gently place in the garden. Space the plants 2½ feet apart, in rows 5 feet apart.

Grow inside floating row covers to add warmth and protect the young plants from insects. Fertilize every ten days with fish emulsion, and keep the soil evenly watered. Remove the row covers when the plants begin to flower. If you can train melons up fences or other sturdy supports, place fruits in an old onion bag that is secured to the fence.

Harvest and Use: Just to make life difficult, different types of melons are harvested in different ways. As they ripen muskmelons become completely netted and their color changes from green to buff. They are fully ripe when the stem slips cleanly from the melon under firm but gentle pressure. If the stem slips but a portion of it remains attached, the fruit is not quite ripe. Allow it to ripen in a warm kitchen for two to four days before eating. Other melons should be harvested by cutting the stem about 1 inch above the fruit when the melon has changed color and the small leaf closest to the fruit begins to yellow.

Cultivars: *Muskmelon:* 'Ambrosia', 'Sweet 'n Early', 'Earligold', 'Athena'; *Galia:* 'So Sweet', 'Passport', 'Sweet Dream'; *Honeydew:* 'Honey Orange', 'Honey Ice', 'Earli-Dew'; *Casaba:* 'Sungold'; *Crenshaw:* 'Burpee Early Hybrid'

Okra
Abelmoschus esculentus

LIGHT:	Full sun
SOIL:	Well drained, fertile, pH 6.5–7.5
PARTS USED:	Fruits
WHEN TO PLANT:	Late spring to early summer
DAYS TO MATURITY:	90–140 from seed

Okra is most strongly identified with the southern United States. There is nothing quite like pickled okra, or sliced okra dipped in light batter and fried to a light brown. And without okra Louisiana gumbo just wouldn't exist. In addition to the edible pods, okra bears beautiful yellow, hibiscus-like flowers throughout the summer.

How to Grow: Okra likes it hot. In the South, plant when the summer heat is just getting going in early June. Direct-sow in raised beds to aid drainage. In the North, select a place with a strong southern exposure and grow in raised beds mulched with black plastic. Soak the seeds overnight in warm water, then direct-sow 2 inches apart in shallow rows. Transplanting is not encouraged, because even slight root disruption can substantially lengthen the time needed to produce a crop. With scissors, thin plants to 12 inches apart for dwarf forms, 20 inches apart for others.

Harvest and Use: The most tender pods are gathered when 2 to 3 inches long. Cut the stem, leaving the cap attached to the pod. Prepare immediately. The pods are eaten as a side dish or used to thicken hearty soups and gumbos. At the end of the growing season the remaining pods can be dried and used in indoor arrangements.

Cultivars: 'Annie Oakley', 'Burgundy', 'North and South', 'Cajun Delight', 'Star of David', 'Red Velvet', 'Clemson Spineless'

Onion, Bulb
Allium cepa

LIGHT:	Full sun
SOIL:	Well worked, fertile, well drained, pH 6.0–7.5
PARTS USED:	Bulbs
WHEN TO PLANT:	From seeds, fall to early spring (Zones 8–10) or spring (Zones 4–7); from sets, fall *or* spring (Zones 8–10) or late winter to spring (Zones 3–7)
DAYS TO MATURITY:	125–150 from seed, 100 from sets

The most popular onions are the American, Spanish, and Bermuda. The American and Spanish types produce bulbs only during long days (when day length is longer than night length). Bermuda types need short days to form bulbs and are best grown in the Deep South, California, and the Southwest, where they are harvested in late winter and early spring. Long-day onions should be grown in the North, where they will bulb up in the warm days of late summer.

How to Grow: Onions are grown from plants, sets, or seeds. Avoid buying bulbs from companies that claim to produce big bulbs quickly unless you live where growing seasons are very short. Usually these have been grown to the size at which bulbs just begin to form, then pulled, sorted, and shipped to you. This interrupts the plant's growth and has a negative effect on eventual bulb size and yield. Small, dormant onion sets are planted in the ground like seeds and often produce good crops of large bulbs. Onions from seeds take the longest to grow but, because of their long period of uninterrupted growth, produce the highest-quality crops.

Onions have small root systems and need a loose, fertile soil with abundant available nutrients and plentiful organic matter to grow well. Muck soils, especially in northern regions, produce slightly better-quality bulbs than clay or sandy loams. Mucks (dark-colored soils, usually found near wet places with abundant quantities of fine organic matter) should be tested for pH and nutrient content before planting, because some are deficient in potassium and (to a lesser degree) phosphorus, manganese, and copper.

For American or Spanish types plant sets or seeds as soon as the ground can be worked in spring. Plant sets 3 inches apart and cover so that the tips barely emerge above the soil. Sow seeds ½ inch apart, in shallow rows spaced 12 inches apart. Thin to 3 inches apart to produce average-size bulbs; spacing of about 4 inches encourages larger bulbs that take a few more days to mature, while spacing of 2 inches or less will produce bulbless green bunching onions quickly. Onions grown from plants or sets should not be grown near those produced from seed.

Onions tend to grow more slowly than many other vegetables and are very sensitive to competition from weeds. Shallow cultivation each week, followed by watering (if needed), promotes strong growth. When the bulbs begin to mature, watering should stop to allow the soil to dry.

Harvest and Use: Harvest green bunching onions when the leaves are about the diameter of a pencil. Mature bulbs are harvested at different stages of growth, depending on the region. In the South and warmer regions of the Southwest and West, begin to harvest when a quarter of the leafy tops have flopped over. In most other areas, harvest begins when half of the tops have flopped over, although in the East, harvest doesn't begin until almost all the tops have flopped over.

In areas with dry, heavy soil, water deeply one day before harvest to help loosen the ground. Then follow the three simple steps at the right.

Cultivars: *American Types:* 'Early Yellow Globe', 'New York Early', 'Empire'; *Spanish Types:* 'Craig Exhibition', 'Spanish Yellow Hybrid'; *Bermuda Types:* 'Granex' ('Vidalia'), 'Stockton Red'

1. To harvest onions for storage, loosen the soil with a fork and lift the bulbs from the ground.

2. Shake off excess soil and cure the onions with their tops attached on screens in a dry, sunny place for one week.

3. When dry, clip off the tops and store the bulbs in onion bags.

Peanut
Arachis hypogaea

LIGHT: Full sun
SOIL: Well drained, well worked, pH 6.5–7.0
PARTS USED: Nuts
WHEN TO PLANT: Spring (Zones 7–10); late spring (Zones 4–6)
DAYS TO MATURITY: 120 from seed

The peanut is a major food crop in the Tropics. In North America it is most often grown in the South, where it has become imbedded in the culture, along with okra, pecans, and sweet potatoes. In cooler areas yields are small, and the plant is grown primarily as a novelty. The plant has cloverlike leaves and two types of yellow flowers, one sterile and the other fertile. After the fertile flowers have been pollinated, the stalk bends over and grows into the ground. Fruit then develops underground.

How to Grow: Gently remove the seed nuts from the shell. In the North plant the nuts indoors in individual pots six weeks before the last frost. In the South direct-sow pairs of nuts every 6 inches. Thin with scissors to 12 inches apart. Raised beds grow excellent peanuts. Warm the soil with black plastic mulch before and after planting, but *remove the mulch when first flowers appear.* Do not water during the last weeks of growth.

Harvest and Use: Peanuts form continually from the time the flowers first appear. This means that at harvest, some peanuts will be overmature, others undermature, and some just right. Dig the plants when frost has killed the foliage. Place them in an airy location until the pods dry, then soak the pods and in salt water for several hours. Place in a 300°F degree oven for an hour or until dry.

Cultivars: 'Jumbo Virginia', 'Tennesse Red'

Pepper, Sweet
Capsicum annuum

LIGHT: Full sun
SOIL: Well drained, pH 6.0–7.0
PARTS USED: Fruits
WHEN TO PLANT: Early spring (Zones 7–10); late spring, early summer (Zones 3–6)
DAYS TO MATURITY: 70–100 from transplanting

Peppers are native to South America, where they have been grown for thousands of years. Like cole crops and melons, peppers belong to one species that is divided into many different groups. The Cerasiforme Group contains the very hot cherry peppers. The Grossum Group includes pimentoes, sweet bell, and sweet frying peppers. Cayenne, paprika, jalapeño, and chili peppers are members of the Longum Group. All peppers contain various amounts of capsicum, the compound that gives them their zesty flavor. Research has shown that capsicum, particularly from cayenne peppers, is useful in treating a number of ailments, ranging from migraine headaches to sore muscles.

How to Grow: Even though all peppers have similar growth requirements, the quality of the fruit can differ greatly in different climates. For example, pimentoes grow best along the southeastern coastal plain from South Carolina to Georgia. The highest-quality chili peppers are produced in the warm, arid climate that extends from southern California through Arizona to New Mexico. This area also grows excellent paprika. Peppers require the same growing conditions as tomatoes, with one critical difference: The best-flavored peppers grow in soil that has a bit more nitrogen and potassium than tomatoes require. The soil moisture level is tricky but important to good pepper growing. During blossoming and fruit set, the soil should be kept evenly moist. Dry conditions at this time result in buds, flowers, and small fruits dropping from the plants. After the fruit has sized up but before it ripens, let the soil dry out a bit. This concentrates the flavors, either hot or sweet, in the peppers.

Sow seeds indoors in flats or pots about two months (northern areas) to one month (southern regions) before the last frost. Keep the soil at about 80°F to encourage rapid, even germination. When the seedlings show the first set of true leaves, transplant them into individual pots. Transplant to the garden one to two weeks after the last frost, when the soil is warm. In the North, plants should be about 6 inches tall at this time; in the South, 3 to 4 inches. Space plants from 15 to 18 inches apart, in rows that are 20 to 24 inches apart. Remove any flower buds that form before transplanting to the garden. Water the transplants with a cup or so of compost tea or fish emulsion. For earlier harvest use black plastic mulch and ventilated row covers. Practice shallow-cultivation to keep weeds under control. Peppers achieve the best color in light, sandy loam soils amended with well-rotted animal manure.

Harvest and Use: Peppers can be harvested anytime after they reach full size, but they have much richer flavor when they're allowed to turn color. Peppers do not last long in storage and should be used quickly. Like tomatoes, peppers are damaged when stored at temperatures below 45°F and therefore should not be kept in the refrigerator. They can be pickled, frozen, or preserved in vinegars or oils.

Cultivars: *Sweet Bell:* 'Ace', 'King Arthur', 'Great Stuff', 'Big Dipper'; *Orange Bell:* 'Orange Belle', 'Valencia', 'Golden Giant'; *Yellow Bell:* 'Orobelle', 'Lemon Belle'; *Lavender Bell:* 'Islander', 'Secret'; *Brown Bell:* 'Sweet Chocolate', 'Chocolate Beauty'; *Sweet Frying:* 'Sweet Banana', 'Lipstick', 'Italia', 'Biscayne'; *Chili:* 'Numex', 'Ortega', 'Ancho', 'Superchili', 'Serrano', 'Thai Dragon'; *Jalapeño:* 'Delicias', 'Early Jalapeño'; *Cayenne:* 'Salsa Delight', 'Yellow Cayenne'; *Paprika:* 'Paprika Supreme; *Pimento:* 'Figaro', 'Apple'

Potato
Solanum tuberosum

LIGHT:	Full sun
SOIL:	Well worked, well drained, pH 5.5–6.5
PARTS USED:	Tubers
WHEN TO PLANT:	Early spring, fall (Zones 7–10); spring (Zones 3–6)
DAYS TO MATURITY:	60–80

The most valuable vegetable crop in the world, the potato is grown from the Tropics to the Far North. The plant is native to South America, where its wild relatives still grow in the Peruvian Andes. The foliage resembles tomatoes in appearance, producing purple, lilac, or white flowers. The starchy tubers form below the ground, but above the main roots.

How to Grow: Potatoes are grown from budded pieces of tuber called seed potatoes. The pieces should always have at least two buds, or eyes. It is wise to plant only certified seed potatoes to ensure that disease, especially late blight, does not become part of your garden. In the Deep South, plant in late fall or early winter for a main crop. If potatoes are planted too late in the South, the hot weather later in the season will inhibit tuber formation. To plant, follow these three illustrated steps:

Step 1. If you need to cut the tubers into smaller pieces, sterilize your knife between cuts and allow the pieces to air-dry for twenty-four hours before planting.

Step 2. Prepare for planting about four weeks before the last frost. Plant 3 inches deep in shallow trenches. Space pieces 12 inches apart.

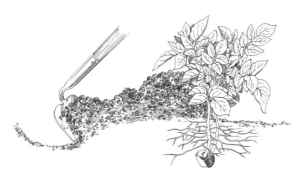

Step 3. When the plants are between 8 and 12 inches tall, hill them with loosened soil until only the top 2 or 3 inches remains above the soil. Hill again when the plants are once more about 12 inches above the soil.

THE USED-TIRE TECHNIQUE

Instead of hilling potatoes, place an automobile tire around each plant and fill it with soil. As the plant gets taller, add another tire atop the first one, and fill that with soil or compost. This method is very handy at harvest time, because all you need to do is remove the tires; the potatoes then just about fall into your hands.

Hilling not only produces excellent crops of potatoes but also protects the plants from potato tuberworm. Potatoes attract some nasty pests, including potato beetles. Control these by growing the crop under row covers. Water often enough to keep the soil evenly moist, especially once tubers begin to form. Even a short dry period at this time can result in small, knobby, cracked tubers. Fertilize with fish emulsion every two weeks.

Harvest and Use: Tubers begin to form about the time the plant begins to blossom. New potatoes can be harvested about two months after planting. Gently scrape away some soil from the edges of the hills and select a few tubers. Take only a few. Harvest the main crop after the foliage has died back. This allows the skin of the tuber to thicken, or set. Harvest potatoes as needed; when freezing weather threatens, harvest the remainder of your crop. Store the tubers unwashed in a dry, relatively humid location that stays at 55 to 60°F for two weeks; a cellar is a good spot. Then store tubers at about 40°F through the winter. Most potatoes will be naturally dormant for about three months following harvest. After that, the cold temperatures will help inhibit sprouting. Potatoes are used for everything from soup to stews. It seems that everyone has a favorite potato recipe as well as a favorite potato. A relative of mine is sure that potato salad is always better made with baby red potatoes prepared with the skins left on. The best potato I have ever had, however, was freshly dug from a garden in northern Maine, cleaned, peeled, and boiled in fresh spring water until tender, then blatantly smothered in fresh butter. Simple and wonderfully satisfying.

Cultivars: *Fingerling Types:* 'Russian Banana', 'Swedish Peanut', 'Rose Fin Apple'; *Red Types:* 'Dark Red Norland', 'Red Pontiac', 'Red Cloud', 'Desiree'; *Yellow types:* 'Yukon Gold', 'Rose Gold', 'Island Sunshine', 'Yellow Finn'; *Blue Types:* 'All-Blue', 'Purple Viking', 'Caribe'; *White Types:* 'Kennebec', 'White Cobbler', 'Chipeta', 'Mainstay'; *Russet Types:* 'Frontier', 'Acadia', 'Nugget'

Pumpkin

Cucurbita spp.

LIGHT: Full sun
SOIL: Well drained, fertile, pH 6.0–7.0
PARTS USED: Fruits
WHEN TO PLANT: Before last spring frost
DAYS TO MATURITY: 90–120 from sowing

Pumpkins are much easier to grow than to classify. At least three different species are called pumpkins, and all can also correctly be called squash. Pumpkins are not even all the classic orange color: They come in green, blue-green, and even white. There are four types commonly grown. *Miniatures* are used for centerpieces and indoor decorations. *Pie pumpkins* make flavorful baked goods, while *field types* are favored for jack-o'-lanterns and outdoor decorations. *Giants* indulge our American appetites for big stuff.

How to Grow: Pumpkins dislike being transplanted, so it's best to direct-sow in hills one to two weeks before the last frost. Plant three seeds per hill, leaving about 4 feet between hills. Keep the area well weeded until plants begin to vine.

Harvest and Use: When your thumbnail doesn't easily cut the skin, cut the vine a few inches from the fruit, leaving a good handle. The fruit must now be cured, which allows the skin to harden. Field-curing is done by leaving the pumpkins in a bright, sunny, dry spot in the garden for seven to ten days. Cover pumpkins if frost threatens because it weakens the skin, allowing rot to set in. Store indoors until ready to use.

Cultivars: *Miniatures:* 'Baby Boo', 'Jack Be Little', 'Baby Bear'; *Pie Types:* 'New England Pie', 'Small Sugar', 'Long Island Cheese'; *Field Types:* 'Howden', 'Rocket', 'Ghost Rider'; *Giants:* 'Atlantic Giant', 'Prizewinner'

Rhubarb

Rheum x *cultorum*

LIGHT: Full sun to light shade
SOIL: Well drained, fertile, pH 5.0–6.5
PARTS USED: Leaf petioles
WHEN TO PLANT: Spring or fall (Zones 3–7)
DAYS TO MATURITY: 1 year from planting

Garden rhubarb is an ancient hybrid plant cultivated around the world. It grows best in the North, where its slightly sour leaf stalks are made into pies whose zesty taste builds character as well as any New England winter. It does not grow well in the South.

How to Grow: This perennial vegetable really does live forever. An old gardener friend dug up one plant each spring, roots and all, to give away. And each summer it came back, having regenerated itself from its deep taproot. Plant rhubarb from crowns or nursery-grown plants set along the edge of the garden. Allow the plants to grow for two full seasons before harvesting. Divide the crowns every five to ten years to revitalize the plants. One or two plants will be all you will ever need to supply your family.

Harvest and Use: For best yields cut off the flower stalks as they form in spring. Gather the leaf stalks by snapping the petiole as close to the soil line as possible. Stalks gathered in spring are more tender than those picked in summer or fall. Trim off the leaves, which are poisonous. Pies made from just rhubarb are very good, but few desserts taste better than a strawberry-rhubarb pie.

Cultivars: 'Valentine', 'MacDonald', 'Cherry Red', 'Victoria'

Squash, Summer
Cucurbita pepo

LIGHT: Full sun
SOIL: Well drained, evenly moist, fertile, pH 6.0–6.5
PARTS USED: Fruits
WHEN TO PLANT: Late winter, early spring, fall (Zones 7–10); mid to late spring, midsummer (Zones 3–6)
DAYS TO MATURITY: 50–60 from seed

Cultivated in the Americas ten thousand years ago, summer squash is one of the world's most important food crops. Types include yellow, crookneck, patty pan, and zucchini, each with a distinctive flavor. Harvest fruits from bushy or vining plants long before maturity.

How to Grow: Squash grows best in raised beds warmed with black plastic mulch for a few weeks before planting. Seeds germinate best when soil temperatures are above 65°F. Direct-sow one to two weeks after the last frost, planting seeds about 4 inches apart and 1 inch deep in rows about 3 to 4 feet apart. The best-tasting squash comes from soil that contains composted manure. Keep the soil evenly moist throughout the growing period.

Harvest and Use: Harvest summer, crookneck, and zucchini squash when the fruit is from 3–5 inches long. Pick patty pan when it's 3–4 inches in diameter. Snip the vine with scissors, and handle the fruit carefully to avoid bruising. Squash will keep for up to two weeks in the refrigerator and can be pickled or frozen. The flowers are delicious when dipped in tempura batter and fried.

Cultivars: *Summer:* 'Seneca Prolific', 'Butterstick', 'Saffron Prolific'; *Crookneck:* 'Supersett', 'Pik-n-Pik', 'Yellow Crookneck'; *Zucchini:* 'Fiorentino', 'Golden Bush', 'Goldrush', 'Condor'; *Patty Pan:* 'Sunburst', 'Peter Pan', 'Bennings Green Tint'

Squash, Winter
Cucurbita spp.

LIGHT: Full sun
SOIL: Well drained, evenly moist, fertile, pH 6.0–6.5
PARTS USED: Fruits
WHEN TO PLANT: Late winter, early spring (Zones 7–10); mid to late spring (Zones 4–6)
DAYS TO MATURITY: 90–110 from seed

A brief rundown of popular winter squashes includes acorn, buttercup, butternut, spaghetti, delicata, and hubbard.

How to Grow: Winter squash grows best in raised beds in soils amended with well-rotted manure. Direct-sow pairs of seeds about 1 inch deep, spacing them every 18 inches. Thin when the seedlings emerge. Grow under floating row covers until blossoms appear. Keep evenly moist, especially after the fruit has begun to set. Mulch around the plants, and fertilize every month with fish emulsion.

Harvest and Use: When your thumbnail doesn't easily cut the skin, the fruit is ripe. Cut the vine a few inches from the fruit, then let the fruit cure, which allows the skin to harden. To field-cure, leave the squash in a sunny, dry spot for seven to ten days. Cover if frost threatens, because frost weakens the skin, allowing rot to set in. Winter squash stores well, often all winter long. It's delicious baked in the oven, and butternut makes a pie that rivals any pumpkin.

Cultivars: *Acorn:* 'Tuffy', 'Ebony', 'Heart of Gold'; *Buttercup:* 'Emerald Bush', 'Ambercup'; *Butternut:* 'Early Butternut', 'Butterboy', 'Waltham Butternut'; *Spaghetti:* 'Hasta la Pasta'; *Delicata:* 'Sweet Dumpling', 'Sugarloaf'; *Hubbard:* 'Blue Ballet', 'Blue Hubbard'

Sweet Potato
Ipomea batatas

LIGHT: Full sun
SOIL: Well drained, well worked,
pH 5.5–6.5
PARTS USED: Tubers
WHEN TO PLANT: Spring (Zones 5–10)
DAYS TO MATURITY: 90–100 from transplanting

Native to the tropical regions of Central and South America, where they have been grown for thousands of years, the sweet potato is a vigorous vine that produces swollen tubers along the rootstock. A staple garden plant in the southern United States, it can also be easily grown as far north as New Jersey, and is cultivated commercially from Maryland to California.

How to Grow: Sweet potatoes are grown from shoots called slips. In the North, they are planted after danger of frost has past; in the Deep South, in late winter to early spring. Rake a hilled row about 6 inches high and level off the top. With a dibble make holes deep enough to accommodate the roots of the slips, spacing them 12 to 18 inches apart; the closer spacing produces heavy yields of average-size potatoes, while the farther spacing produces lower yields of larger potatoes. Water the holes before and after planting the slips. Keep well watered until the plants are established.

Harvest and Use: In much of the South the crop is harvested in early October, after the vines have been killed by frost. Farther north the harvest occurs a few weeks earlier. The roots are dug when the soil is dry; lift the tubers very carefully to avoid bruising. Cure the roots in a warm room (about 80°F) for ten to fourteen days. This allows any cuts to heal and also thickens the skin. Sweet potatoes should be stored at temperatures between 50 and 65°F.

Cultivars: 'Bush Porto Rico', 'Centennial', 'Georgia Jet', 'Vardaman'

Swiss Chard
Beta vulgaris Cicla Group

LIGHT: Full sun to light shade
SOIL: Well drained, fertile
pH 6.0–6.8
PARTS USED: Leaves
WHEN TO PLANT: winter (Zones 9–10);
spring or fall (Zones 3–8)
DAYS TO MATURITY: 50–60 from seed

It would be nice to have more vegetables like Swiss chard. It's easy to grow and produces bountiful yields all season long, even in partial shade. Its leaves are nicely curled, like spinach, and are sweet and meaty. Unlike spinach, Swiss chard stays tasty all summer and usually doesn't fall prey to insects or diseases.

How to Grow: Direct-sow seeds in early to late spring in shallow rows. Plant them about ½ inch deep and 2 inches apart. Thin to 6 inches when the seedlings are a few inches tall. Keep evenly watered to encourage tenderness in the leaves. If flea beetles are a problem, grow under floating row covers. Slugs sometimes find the shady stems of chard a nice place to rest — which can come as a surprise while harvesting. Swiss chard is very ornamental; there are varieties with bright red stems as well as creamy white ones. It is often used as an edging plant in flower gardens or interspersed with marigolds.

Harvest and Use: Gather the outer leaves by twisting the base of the leaf stem. In the kitchen, cut the stem and midrib from the leaf blade. Steam the leaves lightly and serve with butter and garlic. Cook the stems like asparagus and serve with butter. Swiss chard also freezes well. It's used in soups, stews, omelets, and baked pasta dishes.

Cultivars: 'Fordhook Giant', 'Ruby Red', 'Vulcan', 'Paros', 'Argentata'

Tomato
Lycopersicon lycopersicum

LIGHT: Full sun

SOIL: Well drained, evenly moist, fertile, pH 6.0–7.0

PARTS USED: Fruits

WHEN TO PLANT: Fall, spring (Zones 9–10); spring (Zones 4–8)

DAYS TO MATURITY: 55–80 from transplanting

Native to South America, tomatoes were introduced to Europe by Spanish explorers, but they weren't listed in an American seed catalog until 1817. Many of the old cultivars have been lost, but a few, such as Brandywine, can still be found. Tomatoes are classified by growth habit into two large categories: determinate and indeterminate. *Determinate* or *bush tomatoes* produce shoots that end in a flower cluster, and stop growing while they're still fairly short. *Indeterminate* or *vining tomatoes* produce shoots that continue to grow after fruit set.

These groups are then subdivided based on use or size. *Main-crop tomatoes* include varieties that range in size from 4 to over 14 ounces. *Patio* and *cherry types* bear smaller and sweeter fruit, but produce very heavy yields. Most of these have fruits that are about 1 inch in diameter and weigh from ½ to 2 ounces. *Pasta* or *paste tomatoes* were developed for cooking and are less juicy and sweet than fresh varieties. The fruits average from 3 to 4 ounces and are more lemon shaped than round. *Currant tomatoes* are even smaller than cherry types. Fairly new to gardeners, these are little changed from the wild tomatoes that still grow through the Andes. *Heirloom types* are open-pollinated varieties generally more than a hundred years old, with superior flavor. Dropped from catalogs when traits facilitating commercial production became important earlier this century, they are often very well suited for the home garden.

How to Grow: Start tomatoes indoors six to eight weeks before the last frost. The seedlings have the nasty habit of succumbing to a number of diseases soon after germinating; thus you should always use pasteurized soil soilless mixes when starting seeds. Sow seeds in sterilized flats and cover with a thin layer of vermiculite. Keep the flats at about 80°F until the seedlings have their first set of true leaves. Transplant into individual pots and grow in bright light at 65 to 70°F. Brush the seedlings twice a day to encourage the growth of stout stems (see page 85). Transplant when the seedlings are from 6 to 8 inches tall. Space the plants 18 to 24 inches apart, and the rows 3 feet apart. Transplant by digging a hole a few inches shallower than the height of the plant, but not more than 6 inches deep. Set the plant in the hole so that its top 4 inches remains above the soil. Backfill the hole, removing any leaves that would be covered with soil. Indeterminate tomatoes benefit from transplanting, while determinate types can be set back. Transplant determinate varieties very carefully, being sure not to damage the root system.

If night temperatures drop below 45°F, protect the plants with row covers or water-filled cones. Growing under floating row covers until blossoming lessens many pest problems. Determinate types are best for hot, arid regions of the Southwest; indeterminate types are best for hot, humid areas, such as the Southeast and East, where training to stakes or trellises decreases the incidence of rot and blight. Wire cages are excellent devices to support determinate types. Indeterminate types should be tied to individual wooden stakes or trained to a string or bamboo trellis mounted between steel fence stakes. Prune away the nonflowering shoots that arise from the main stem. In late summer remove all flowers and fruit that will not ripen before the first frost.

Fertilize every two to three weeks throughout the season with fish emulsion. Tomatoes are very sensitive to nutrient levels in the soil as well as to airborne chemicals. A white margin around the leaves can indicate a deficiency of potassium. Purple leaf stalks are a sign of phosphorus deficiency. Thin stems and few flowers come insufficient nitrogen. These nitrogen deficiencies are often caused by dry soil, and watering the plants more faithfully corrects the problem. Tomatoes do not grow in temperatures above about 90°F or below about 45°F. If temperatures consistently stay above 85°F, flower buds drop and the fruit does not color up well.

Harvest and Use: Tomatoes ripen best when the average daily temperature (the mean of the daily high and low) stays below 75°F. In these conditions red color of the fruit indicates ripeness. When daily mean temperatures exceed 75°F, however, the fruit colors inconsistently and becomes soft before reaching full ripeness. Thus, in hot weather pick the fruit while it's still firm and pink, and ripen it in the cool indoors. Tomatoes will ripen off the vine when they're picked after reaching the stage of development called *mature green*. Tomatoes in this stage are green with a slight yellowing of the shoulder near the stem. To ripen tomatoes off the vine, keep them at room temperature in a place with good air circulation. Storing tomatoes in the refrigerator inhibits ripening and damages the fruit.

Cultivars: *Indeterminate Main-Crop Hybrids:* 'Early Cascade', 'Early Girl', 'Better Boy', 'Delicious', 'Dona'; *Determinate Main-Crop Hybrids:* 'Celebrity', 'Daybreak', 'Red Sun'; *Indeterminate Cherry Hybrids:* 'Super Sweet 100', 'Sun Cherry', 'Yellow Pear', 'Sun Gold'; *Determinate Cherry Hybrids:* 'Whippersnapper'; *Heirloom Cherry Varieties:* 'Gardeners Delight', 'Washington', 'Chadwicks Fox'; *Pasta Varieties:* 'San Remo', 'Bellstar', 'Sheriff', 'Artela', 'San Marzano', 'Chico'; *Heirloom Main-Crop Varieties:* 'Brandywine', 'Striped German', 'Cherokee Purple', 'Old Flame'; *Currant Tomatoes:* 'Red Currant', 'Yellow Currant', 'Matts Wild Cherry'

Watermelon
Citrullus lanatus

LIGHT:	Full sun
SOIL:	Well drained, evenly moist, pH 6.0–7.0
PARTS USED:	Fruits
WHEN TO PLANT:	Late winter to midspring (Zones 6–10); late spring (Zones 4–5)
DAYS TO MATURITY:	70–85 from transplanting

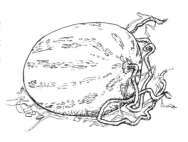

Native to Africa, the watermelon was not cultivated in Europe until the 1500s. A popular summertime treat, it's most often grown in Zones 6 through 10.

How to Grow: Watermelons can be direct-sown or transplanted. For direct-seeding sow in shallow rows or hills. For rows, sow the seeds from ½ to 1 inch deep in groups of three spaced every 18 inches. Thin to about 2½ feet by cutting the stems at the soil line with scissors. Do not plant until soil temperatures reach 65 to 70°F. For transplants, start the seeds indoors in cell packs about three weeks before the expected last frost. Keep the soil warm (80°F) and evenly moist until the seeds germinate. As plants emerge, drop the temperature to 70°F. Transplant as soon as the seedlings show their first set of true leaves, but take care to avoid damaging the roots or yields will be severely reduced. To transplant, carefully cut away the plastic cell pack and gently space plants 2½ feet apart, in rows 5 feet apart. Grow inside floating row covers to add warmth and deter insects. Fertilize every ten days with fish emulsion and keep the soil evenly watered. Remove the row covers when plants begin to flower.

Harvest and Use: Pick watermelons when the tendril closest to the fruit begins to brown or when the underside of the fruit turns from white to creamy yellow.

Cultivars: 'Sugar Baby', 'Carolina Cross', 'New Orchid', 'Redball Seedless'

It is much easier to tell you the optimum conditions for plants than to describe the limits of their endurance. Yet for most gardeners both criteria come into play when growing a successful vegetable patch. The *hardy* vegetables are those whose seeds germinate well in the cold, moist soils of early spring, and whose seedlings or emerging shoots can tolerate light frosts. The seeds of *half-hardy* plants germinate best when the soil has slightly warmed and the danger of frost is diminishing. *Tender* plants require warm soil and cool but frostless nights. *Very tender* plants prefer warm nights and hot days.

HARDY	*HALF-HARDY*	*TENDER*	*VERY TENDER*
Asparagus	Beets	New Zealand spinach	Cucumbers
Broccoli	Carrots	Snap beans	Eggplants
Brussels sprouts	Cauliflower	Sweet corn	Lima beans
Cabbage	Celery	Tomatoes	Melons
Collard	Swiss chard		Okra
Kale	Chinese cabbage		Peppers
Kohlrabi	Artichokes		Pumpkins
Mustard	Endive		Squash
Onion	Lettuce		Sweet potatoes
Root parsley	Parsnips		
Peas	Potatoes		
Radishes			
Spinach			
Turnips			

COMPANION CROPS FOR SOME WARM-WEATHER VEGETABLES

VEGETABLE	*GOOD COMPANIONS*	*COMPANIONS TO AVOID*
Bush beans	celery, cucumbers, strawberries, summer savory, marigolds	fennel, onions, garlic, or chives
Pole beans	corn, marigolds, radishes	kohlrabi, onions, garlic, fennel
Carrots	tomatoes, lettuce	dill
Celery	beans, tomatoes, onions	
Sweet corn	beans, peas, cucumbers, squash, potatoes	tomatoes (share the same susceptibility to damage from the corn ear worm, a.k.a. tomato fruitworm
Popcorn	same as sweet corn	
Cucumbers	radishes, peas, beans	potatoes
Eggplant	bush beans, use pole beans as a windscreen on its north side	tomatoes, potatoes, or raspberries
Garlic	tomatoes	
Leeks	carrots, onions, celery, tomatoes, beets	beans or peas
Melons	corn	potatoes, tomatoes, eggplants
Onions	tomatoes, beets	not legumes such as peas
Peppers	basil	
Potatoes	marigolds, cabbage, corn, beans, and peas	tomatoes, cucumbers, melons, pumpkins, or squash
Rhubarb	cabbage, broccoli, cauliflower, kale	
Squash	tomatoes	
Swiss chard	lettuce, cabbage, beans, and peas	

6

Longer Seasons and Higher Yields

A walk through a typical supermarket in the dead of winter is an extraordinary thing. There in the produce section, arranged in neat rows, are fresh tomatoes from Mexico, grapes from Chile, apples from Australia, and peppers from Holland. This worldwide garden makes fresh vegetables and fruits available to many people year-round, providing a ubiquitous bounty that was unknown a generation ago. This easy access to out-of-season produce has turned the supermarket into a community garden, where people come and harvest what others have already picked. It is easy to see how the modern marketplace benefits those who use it. It is less simple to see what is being lost.

Generations ago, when "out-of-season" meant "not available," the ingenuity of gardeners rose to the surface. Through a blend of ingenious self-sufficiency and stubborn independence many people learned age-old techniques that put fresh food on their plates in every season of the year. There were methods to start seeds earlier than the season would normally permit, or to grow warm-weather melons side by side with cool-weather peas. Cold frames and hotbeds allowed fresh, homegrown salads to be gathered and eaten even on days when snow fell outside, and everything from potatoes to brussels sprouts, cabbage, and turnips was stored and eaten all winter long. There were old-fashioned ways of planting and growing, from wide rows to catch cropping, that made heavy yields a common thing. With these techniques even small gardens could feed the family every day for months on end.

But in an era where every season is supermarket summer, some of these skills and techniques of self-sufficiency are being lost. Many, from making a hot bed that stays warm through cold weather without adding to the utility bill to methods of harvesting and storing crops that make them last longer, are generations old. Others, including ways to predict the exact day every crop will ripen year after year, and secrets of timing the harvest to gather the most nutritious crops, are products of more modern agriculture. These and many other techniques have been gathered into this chapter. The ways of the old-timers dove-tailed with the discoveries of the present to produce bountiful harvests. They offer you scores of diverse, ingenious secrets and methods to produce bigger, better-quality crops for more weeks of the year than you might have ever thought possible. There is nothing like a fresh spinach salad in winter harvested from the hotbed and not from the produce aisle.

High-Yield Horticulture

People who have acres and acres of corn usually don't worry about the straggly stalks that try to grow in the shade of the windrows, but those who have a twenty-foot-square garden care a great deal if their tomatoes don't ripen in the shade of the backyard maple tree. If a little space is all you've got, then that little space must be wisely used. It does not pay to plant tomatoes where they will be shaded, or spinach in the warm southern corner. Proper spacing, watering, and location of plants can make the difference between rows of onions good only for bunching, and bunches of large-bulb onions. Growing spinach in the light shade of deciduous trees can extend the harvest for days, while pruning a tomato can yield larger fruit. High-yield horticulture encompasses many different skills, from spacing to weeding, that are not difficult to learn and have a profound effect on garden yields. It also sets the foundation for the many skills still to come.

PROPER SPACING

Spacing — the distance one plant is set from another — is a primary factor in determining the eventual yield of a row of plants. Certain plants are less sensitive to close spacing than others. Root crops and plants whose leaves are harvested are the least sensitive to close spacing. Such root crops as carrots, radishes, and beets can be spaced just far enough apart that the mature roots nearly touch. The leaves of each plant will overlap with those of its neighbor, but this does not inhibit heavy yields. Leaf crops, such as spinach, celery, and lettuce, can also be more closely spaced, because they do not

Proper spacing allows plants to grow from seed to harvest without being disturbed.

need as much sunlight to mature as most fruit-bearing crops, such as peppers. These plants can be planted close enough so the leaves of the mature plants just overlap.

Fruit-bearing upright plants, such as peppers and tomatoes, give the highest total yields when the foliage of the mature plants almost overlaps. If the plants are spaced so that foliage of the mature plants is separated by three or four inches, the total yield declines but the size of the individual fruits increases. Vining crops, such as melons and pumpkins, need the most space as well as the most light. Increase the yields of small-fruited vining crops, such as cucumbers, by using the space offered by vertical supports.

LIGHT AND YIELDS

Light is the energy that plants use to produce the sugars and starches they need for their metabolic processes. The individual leaves of the plant are solar collectors, each one gathering the light energy that falls on it. Fruits, such as melons, and storage parts, such as potato tubers, are reservoirs that hold the accumulated energy gathered by all of the leaves. Those leaves that are in direct sunlight produce more of these metabolic substances than those that are shaded. To produce maximum yields nearly all of the leaves of such plants must remain in direct sunlight during most of the day. This includes the lower leaves of the plants, which are often shaded by those above. These plants yield best in locations where maximum light falls on the entire plant. These locations are sometimes in short supply in the garden, though, so it is nice to know that leaf crops do not need as much light as either fruit- or storage-type vegetables. Lettuce, Swiss chard, and other leaf crops can produce heavy yields in areas that do not receive direct sunlight all day.

PRUNING TO INCREASE YIELDS

The most commonly pruned vegetable plants are varieties of indeterminate tomato. (See page 117 for definitions of determinate and indeterminate tomatoes.) Indeterminate varieties do not stop growing but just keep on and on throughout the season. As each plant grows, branches — usually called suckers — arise from the axillary buds at the

Removing suckers from tomatoes increases yields by channeling energy to the developing fruit.

base of the leaves. These suckers can quickly turn a tomato plant into a tangled jungle. Pruning the suckers reduces the amount of vegetative growth and increases the quantity of fruit. To prune tomatoes for highest yields, snip off all suckers as soon as they appear. This allows a single stem to grow up along the stake, producing a tall, slender vine. The resulting plants are so thin that they can be set about a foot apart — two to three times closer than determinate types. The increased number of plants in combination with the weekly pruning results in very heavy yields of tomatoes.

One word of caution: Pruning markedly reduces the amount of foliage remaining on the plant, which in turn affects the moisture and light levels of the fruit. Pruned tomatoes are more sensitive to environmental changes than unpruned, determinate types. This sensitivity can result in increased cracking of the fruit.

WATERING AND HIGH YIELDS

Plants need different amounts of water at different stages of their lives. In the seedling stage, the roots are so small that even infrequent watering can provide enough moisture for all a plant's needs. But as the plant grows it expands its root system and collects more moisture from a greater area of soil. The ground dries out more quickly and must be watered to a greater depth to continue maximum growth of the plant. As the plant reaches maturity, its need for water again drops.

Insufficient water creates a domino effect that ripples throughout the plant. If the water stress lasts long enough, the tissues in the leaves and roots begin to harden, becoming tougher and more fibrous. The leaves can become bitter, while fruits

Gardens kept properly watered produce better-tasting crops that are often more nutritious as well.

become less sweet. Without adequate water the plant cannot manufacture enough food for itself, and its entire system begins to shut down.

To produce the best crops the plants should have uninterrupted growth — which translates, in part, to an even, constant supply of water. Under most conditions this means about an inch per week. This depends, however, on the stage of growth. Ripening strawberries that receive slightly less than an inch of water per week produce smaller but sweeter fruits; plants that get more than an inch produce large berries with a watery-sweet flavor. A little less water while fruits are ripening will reduce the yield but increase the quality.

Some plants, including potatoes and onions, need much less water just before harvest. The absence of water stops growth, which helps cure the crop by toughening the skin of the bulb or tuber. This change helps the crop last longer after harvest.

The best-quality yields result from plants that have even moisture and uninterrupted growth from the time of seeding to just before ripening of the fruit begins. Water should then be reduced slightly, to encourage the deposition of sugars in the fruit as it ripens. In some crops the moisture can then be further reduced, to encourage curing of the crop.

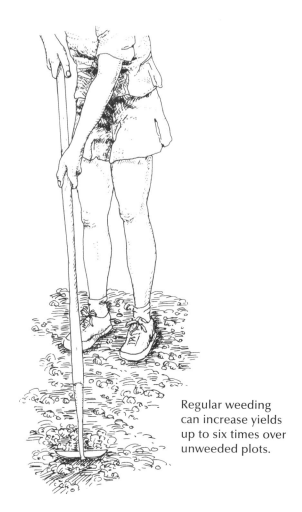

Regular weeding can increase yields up to six times over unweeded plots.

ALTITUDE AND WATERING

Gardens that are above about thirty-five hundred feet in elevation need more water than those at sea level. And folks growing vegetables and flowers near five thousand feet in elevation must give their plants about 25 percent more water as those at sea level.

WEEDS

It comes as no surprise that an unweeded garden produces much smaller yields than one regularly cultivated. What *is* a surprise is just how much a difference weeding makes in total yields. In experiments in New York, regularly weeded fields produced six times as many tomatoes as unweeded ones. Potato yields increased threefold, onions more than tenfold, and carrots more than fifteen-fold. Weeds diminish yields by competing for soil nutrients, moisture, and sunlight. Careful cultiva-

tion removes this competition and greatly increases the moisture available to the vegetables.

The timing of cultivation is also critical to increasing yields. Do not cultivate after a rain of less than half an inch. If you break the soil surface at this time you will actually lose soil moisture. Cultivate only when needed, and then just during dry times or after a heavy rain.

There is one more surprise concerning weeds and yields that can make the lives of many gardeners a lot easier. Vegetables are most susceptible to competition from weeds from the seedling stage through the time the fruit begins to enlarge and mature. After that time the plants can hold their own pretty well. What this means to the gardener is that total yields are almost identical in vegetable patches weeded throughout the season and those weeded only until fruit set. Do weed root and leaf crops right through to harvest; but for other plants, the hoe can be abandoned after the fruit begins to enlarge. Badminton, anyone?

SUPPORTS AND HIGH YIELDS

Training plants to grow on supports maximizes space, increases exposure to sunlight, enhances air circulation, and encourages better ripening of fruit. There are many types of supports, ranging from branches stuck in the ground, to nylon-mesh netting, to trellises. The plants most commonly trained to supports include peas, tomatoes, beans, cucumbers, melons, and squash.

Tomatoes and Eggplant

Both determinate and indeterminate tomato varieties benefit from growing on supports. Traditionally, tomatoes have been individually trained to wooden stakes about 4 to 6 feet tall. The stakes are set in the ground near the base of each plant within a few days of transplanting. As the plant grows the vine is loosely attached to the stake with ties. Tomatoes and eggplant produce numerous stems and some of these are routinely pruned when the vines are first trained. Some growers leave a single stem per plant, while others prefer two or three stems per stake. The more fertile the soil is, the more stems can be trained to a single stake. When deciding on which stems to keep, always select vigorous stems arising from the bottom of the plant.

A cane trellis supports an entire row of tomatoes, and is made by setting heavy-gauge steel fence posts every 10 feet along the row. Lengths of bamboo cane are then lashed horizontally to the posts, with about 12 inches between each course. The tomatoes are then tied to the canes as they grow. Tomato cages (which work beautifully for peonies as well) are round wire cylinders that support the vine as it grows. These work best for determinate types.

Training tomatoes is most beneficial in areas of the Northwest and east of the Mississippi River. In these humid regions training reduces the incidence of rot and other diseases. In arid areas training is helpful if windbreaks are placed near the crop to inhibit excessive loss of moisture from hot, dry breezes. Eggplants are trained in the same way as determinate tomatoes and perform very well when grown in tomato cages.

Tomatoes are classed as being either determinate or indeterminate. A determinate, or bush, variety (left) produces a terminal flower cluster and grows very little after fruit set. An indeterminate type (right) has no terminal flower cluster and continues to grow rapidly even after fruit set.

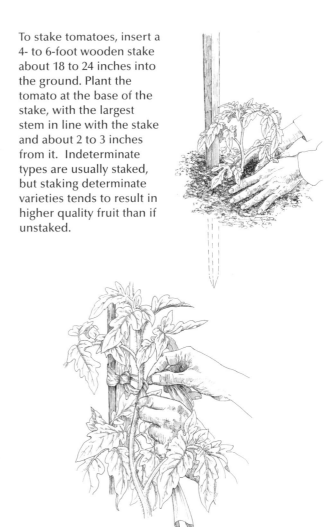

To stake tomatoes, insert a 4- to 6-foot wooden stake about 18 to 24 inches into the ground. Plant the tomato at the base of the stake, with the largest stem in line with the stake and about 2 to 3 inches from it. Indeterminate types are usually staked, but staking determinate varieties tends to result in higher quality fruit than if unstaked.

As the tomato grows, attach the primary stem to the stake by wrapping a bit of nylon stocking, twine, or twist ties around the stem, then around the stake. Be sure the tie is secure enough to give support, yet loose enough so the stem is not damaged.

Pole Beans

To many people, pole beans taste better than even the best bush bean, and they are definitely more productive. Their vining habit makes support essential but also reduces disease while making harvesting easier. The most popular support for pole beans is wooden poles. These are arranged in a triangle and tied at the top like a tepee. The beans are planted at the base of each pole and trained along it as they grow. A variation of this technique uses four poles measuring about 8 feet each. These are placed in a square shape and the tops lashed together. An alternate method consists of a string trellis made with heavy twine. The string is secured to the ground with tent stakes and angled to a wall support above. The plants grow along the twine, creating an awninglike cover. Some gardeners marry the pole support with the trellis support by tying rungs of twine around a three or four pole support. This allows beans to be planted in rows beneath the strings rather than just at the base of the poles. Pole beans interplanted with corn happily climb up the cornstalks. Finally it should be noted that all this effort can be completely avoided in the arid regions of California and other areas of the southwest. The dry climate there makes it possible to grow quality pole beans along the ground with no support at all.

Peas

Peas are not as heavy as many other climbing vegetables, and the most efficient support for them is a mesh trellis. In previous generations wire fencing was used as were thin bamboo stakes. Today's nylon mesh supports are both light, strong, and easy to use. The netting is usually 6 feet high, 15 feet long, and composed of squares measuring 7 inches to each side. String nylon mesh between poles set along the row; the tendrils of the plants will rapidly cling to the mesh as they grow. Mesh is more expensive than many other types of supports, however, and is time consuming to clean at the end of the season. An alternative method is to use a cane trellis to grow early peas, then plant tomatoes in their place once the harvest is done. The most inexpensive method of supporting peas is the twiggy trellis. Pruned tree branches with a base caliber of about 2 inches are set in the ground in the pea row every few feet. The plants then grow up the brush. After harvest the twiggy trellis is easily removed, old vines and all, chipped into bits, and added to the compost pile. Pea supports are usually placed along the sides of single rows, however the best yields are achieved when the supports are placed down the center of a double row.

Cucumbers

There is no doubt that cucumbers grown on supports are far superior to those left to crawl along the ground. The fruit is more uniform, is evenly colored, and often has better flavor. Most people do not make any special support for cucumbers but simply use structures normally found in most gardens. A favorite is the wire fence that often surrounds the vegetable patch. Cucumbers are planted in hills spaced about 6 feet apart at the base of the fence. As they grow the vines are trained in a fan pattern emanating from the hill. Harvest the fruit when the cucumbers are still small and lightweight — about 5 inches long — for the best flavor. Cucumbers can also be trained to the same pole frame teepee used for pole beans. Be careful when tying the stems to any support as the vines are more easily damaged than either peas or beans.

An easy-to-make, portable support can be made by securing a square of chicken wire fencing between a frame of 1- x 4-inch lumber. Props are then fastened to the back with wingnuts and the entire device set up in the cucumber patch.

Melons and Summer Squash

The garden fence need not just be used for cucumbers — it's also a great place to grow melons and squash. Melons, especially muskmelons, produce heavy yields of nicely shaped, flavorful fruit when trained to fence supports. Sow the plants in hills along the base of the fence in the manner of cucumbers, and train them to a fan pattern. As the fruit matures, place it in an onion bag, which you can in turn tie to the fence. The melon grows inside the bag, which takes the weight off the vine as well as supporting the melon during ripening. Larger melons, such as honeydew types, can also be grown in this way, but take extra care to make sure that the bag can support the weight of the melon. Fruit produced this way is always clean and suffers far less injury from pests and diseases. In recent years small varieties of watermelon have been introduced that also produce higher quality fruit when grown with support. These varieties are about the size of a muskmelon when ripe and can be supported in the same way.

Summer squash vines must be handled more gingerly than many other plants, with often twice as many ties used to secure them than cucumbers require. The fruit can be grown in onion bags in the manner of melons, but more often is allowed to grow on the vine. It is harvested when still small — about 4 to 5 inches long. Fence-grown summer squash is often higher quality and more flavorful than soil-grown crops.

Fruit grown in a sling made from a piece of stretchy cloth, such as a nylon stocking, can become very large without putting a strain on the fragile plant stem.

Saving Space

Will Rogers believed that people should invest in real estate, because it was the one thing that nobody is making more of. The backyard garden should be thought of in the same way. Space in the garden is a valuable commodity, and every effort should be made to utilize each inch to its best advantage. Over the years many systems have been developed to do this, including intercropping, succession planting, and container gardening. There are others as well, but they all have two goals in common: to produce as much as possible from the space provided, and to ensure that area's fertility for the next growing season.

Save Room for 'shrooms?

Sometimes high quality food can be grown in places a bit removed from the garden. It is doubtful anyone ever grew a great crop of broccoli in a closet, but that same space normally reserved for shirts and shoes can yield a nice supply of mushrooms anytime of year. There are four types of mushrooms commonly sold in kits for home use; white button, royal tan, portabella, and shitake. White, tan and portabella kits come in a cardboard box filled with a supply of compost inoculated with spawn. All you do is water the compost and place the box in a cool, dry place. Mushrooms can usually be harvested in about two to three weeks. The shitake mushrooms need indirect light to grow and need their medium soaked overnight before they begin to grow.

Growing mushrooms is fun but usually not the most economical way to stock the refrigerator. These grow-your-own mushroom kits commonly cost from under $20.00 for the white button and royal tan kits to $30.00 or more for the portabella and shitake kits. Bottom line is that mushrooms from the closet are fresher than store-bought, but often just as expensive. If you are as thrifty as I am, the closet mushrooms are just not economical. However, if one lands in your lap via a loved one's generosity you can enjoy lots of tasty mushrooms for weeks completely guilt-free.

WIDE-ROW PLANTING

Wide-row planting is best used for growing root and leaf crops, whose root systems can be spaced more closely together.

An example of a wide-row design combines a round root crop, such as radishes, with a leaf crop, such as lettuce, and a long-root crop, such as carrots. The traditional in-row spacing for these crops is 1 inch apart for radishes, about 8 inches apart for lettuce, and 2 inches apart for carrots. To grow this combination of plants in a wide row, plant the individual crops in staggered bands of three rows each. The first band row of radishes is planted 1 inch apart. The second row in the band is 1 inch from the first, with the first seed of the second row staggered ½ inch ahead of the first seed of the first row. The third row in the band reverts to the pattern of the first. This stagger pattern maintains the proper spacing for the plants but takes up less room.

The first row of lettuce is spaced 8 inches from the radishes and staggered the same way, but with 8 inches between plants, instead of just one. After three rows of lettuce have been planted, the carrots are set in rows 8 inches from the lettuce. The carrots follow the same stagger pattern, but are planted 2 inches apart. Plants in this arrangement must be fertilized more often than those in widely spaced rows but will yield many more vegetables. Weeds must be removed regularly for their competition is more keenly felt in wide-row situations.

Crops that do well planted in wide rows:
Round-root crops: beets, garlic, onions, turnips
Long-root crops: root parsley, parsnip, salsify
Leaf crops: arugula, chicory, corn salad, endive, mustard, spinach

SUCCESSION PLANTING

Succession planting, also called catch cropping, increases yields by replanting the space vacated by a harvested crop with another crop. Succession planting should be planned, and the crops used must complement each other in some way. For example, a crop that matures in a month or so can be matched with one that takes longer to mature. The first step in using this type of succession planting is to make a list of all the fast-maturing crops, usually defined as those that can be harvested within sixty days of planting and including radishes, leaf lettuce, bush beans, beets, minicarrots, cucumbers, mustard greens, kale, kohlrabi, spinach, summer squash, Swiss chard, and turnips. Next, divide the plants into a cool-season group, a warm-season group, and those that can grow equally well in cool and warm weather. Finally, match the plants to companions in other groups to create a sequential planting guide.

Another way to plan succession planting is by nutrient need. In this plan a crop that requires frequent fertilizing, such as broccoli, cucumbers, sweet corn, or cabbage is followed in the same space by crops that enrich the soil, such as peas, lima beans, and pole or bush beans.

First planting:

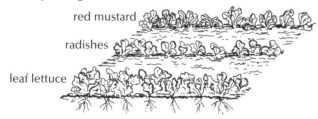

Second planting:

Third planting:

Succession planting keeps the garden productive by replanting rows from which crops have been harvested.

A Succession Garden

Row	Spring	Summer	Fall
Row 1	leaf lettuce	minicarrots	radishes
Row 2	radishes	cucumber	leaf lettuce
Row 3	red mustard	turnips	leaf lettuce
Row 4	kale	bush beans	kale
Row 5	spinach	Swiss chard	beets
Row 6	beets	kohlrabi	beets
Row 7	minicarrots	bush beans	lettuce
Row 8	kohlrabi	summer squash	red mustard
Row 9	turnips	bush beans	radishes
Row 10	leaf lettuce	summer squash	turnips

INTERCROPPING

Intercropping, the foundation of companion planting, works on the principle that certain plants respond synergistically to each other's company. Sometimes science has managed to discover just how these relationships work; other times the mystery remains. In general, though, intercroppping works by matching opposites. Fast-maturing crops, such as radishes, are intercropped with slow-growing plants, such as carrots. Corn, which takes large amounts of nutrients from the soil, is grown with pole beans, which put nutrients back into the soil. Lettuce, which has a shallow root system, is grown with carrots, which have a deep one. These types of relationships are easy to learn, in part because they are easy to visualize.

Still, when you're planning intercropping based on matching opposites, it's good to remember the two groups of plants that simply don't like each other. One side of the garden feud holds the Hatfields — onion and cabbage families. These include onions, garlic, leeks, chives, cabbage, kale, broccoli, cauliflower, and kohlrabi. The other side consists of the McCoys — the tomato family and the legumes, including tomatoes, potatoes, eggplant, peppers, beans, and peas. Gardeners have tried to negotiate a peace between these two groups for generations, but alas, nothing has worked. For a peaceful garden keep these crops separate.

Other intercropping relationships are equally mysterious. For example, many people plant aromatic herbs with their vegetables based on the belief that the aromatic oils of the herbs repel pests.

But some plants only like certain aromatic herbs and not others. Tomatoes seem to thrive near basil but do poorly when grown near fennel. Rosemary enhances the growth of carrots, while dill does just the opposite.

It takes some time and experimentation to discover all the intricacies of the relationships in the garden. In the meantime, however, there are some very amiable herbs and flowers that get along with just about every vegetable in the garden. These include basil, marigolds, thyme, oregano, and savory.

Intercropping blends companion planting with some of the principles of succession planting. For example, sweet corn stalks support pole bean vines, while the pole beans add nutrients to the soil that are used by the sweet corn.

Container Gardening

Many types of plants are grown in containers, from bedding plants produced in cell packs to dwarf fruit trees grown in large plastic pots. When nurseries grow plants in containers, they tailor the soil mix used to the needs of the plants as well as to the length of time each plant is expected to remain in the pot.

Bedding plants or other crops that are grown and sold in a matter of weeks are commonly grown in containers filled with commercial peat-based potting mixes — essentially the same stuff you buy from the garden center to pot your plants at home. Most of these mixes, designed for short-term use, are unsatisfactory when used to grow plants for months at a time.

To make these mixes more friendly to long-term container gardening, blend the potting mixture with screened garden soil and composted cow manure at the rate of 2:1:1. This modified soil mix is equally good for annuals, vegetables, herbs, and flowers, and contains nutrients, such as phosphorus, that are sometimes deficient in unamended commercial mixes.

TYPES OF CONTAINERS

Long-term container gardening demands pots and growing structures that promote healthy root and top growth for many months at a time. This is not easy to do, and no material really does an excellent job. The best containers, though, are made from clay, wood, and plastic.

Clay is naturally porous and allows air and moisture to be conducted through the pot, which enhances root growth. Traditionally, especially in Europe, clay pots have been made with one big drainage hole in the bottom, but this can inhibit proper drainage. Recently, pots with an array of smaller drainage holes have become available, and these should be used. Clay pots are heavy, a disadvantage that can be overcome by placing them on wheeled platforms. Also, in some growing situations clay pots can become encrusted with a white bloom of salts or a green covering of algae; this should be scrubbed off.

Wood has been used to make growing containers for many years. Although not as porous as clay, it's also not quite as heavy, though the difference can sometimes be slight. Redwood and cedar are often used because of their natural resistance to decay. For large plantings, recycled whiskey barrels have become quite popular. Be sure the container has enough holes in the bottom for proper drainage. Whiskey barrels have deposits of charcoal on their inside surfaces. The charcoal makes the container look a bit informal, but don't let appearances put you off. The charcoal can absorb certain toxins from the soil and aid plant growth.

Plastic containers are usually the least expensive to purchase, light in weight, and easy to clean and reuse. Air and moisture cannot pass through plastic, which can hinder soil aeration and drainage which in turn can restrict root vigor. Black plastic pots can become hot in the summer sun, heating the soil in the container to over 100°F. Some white-colored pots allow enough light to filter through the side of the container to inhibit root growth.

Containers not only come in many types and styles, they be used to complement different plant types. Cascading plants love a strawberry jar, edging plants thrive in a windowbox, and patio tomatoes can climb a trellis.

PORTABILITY

One of the advantages of container gardens is portability. Tropical plants, such as hibiscus, can be moved to the patio in summer and then back to the living room in fall. Though people like this flexibility, many plants get a little perturbed when asked to pack up and move. Some, such as schefflera, rubber trees, and Benjamin figs, will convey their displeasure by dropping some leaves in the few days following each move. Here are some tips to minimize your plants' moving-time blues:

- Water the plants the day before the move.
- Do not move plants into areas of extended direct sunlight, but to as shady a place as possible.
- Move to a sheltered spot away from strong breezes.
- Arrange containers into groups. This reduces evaporation and buffers temperature changes.
- Fertilize the plants lightly a day or so after the move.

CONTAINER VEGETABLES

Almost all vegetables can be grown in containers, and for the most part the techniques used in the backyard can be employed here as well. Use intercropping in large containers, such as whiskey

Clay pots can be heavy, but their porosity encourages excellent plant growth.

Containers come in all sorts of sizes and can be used to grow everything from flowers to vegetables.

barrels, where tomatoes can climb a trellis above clusters of parsley, carrots, and marigolds. Tomato varieties that do well in containers include 'Superb', 'Birdie', 'Red Robin', and 'Yellow Canary'. Succession planting can be used in the containers that have salad crops. Plant successive plantings of spinach, beets, lettuce, and other salad greens a week or two apart in a series of containers. Onions and garlic, plants sensitive to competition from weeds and other plants, can be easily monitored when grown in containers. A favorite summer pastime is growing cherry tomatoes in hanging baskets. A few varieties to try include 'Whippersnapper' that bears baskets of small, dark pink tomatoes in just over 50 days from transplant. For colorful container growing try yellow cherry tomatoes including 'Sun Cherry' with sweet, bright yellow fruit in long clusters; 'Gold Nugget' with tender fruit as bright as lemon drops; and 'Sun Gold' that bears very sweet, orange colored tomatoes sure to brighten up any salad. Some tomato varieties are better suited for hanging baskets than others; the best is 'Tumbler' that reliably produces large crops of tasty fruit. Other plants suited for container growing include eggplant, peppers, squash, cucumbers, and most greens such as lettuce, spinach, and kale.

PLANT	SUGGESTED VARIETIES	GROWING TIPS
Beans	*Bush:* 'Romano', 'Royal Burgundy', 'Venture'. *Pole:* 'Scarlet Runner'	Soak seeds in water overnight to improve germination. Use trellis or support for pole beans.
Beets	'Detroit Dark Red', 'Early Wonder', 'Burpee's Golden', 'Cylindra', 'Boltardy'	3–4 in. between plants if harvesting roots; 2 in. between plants if harvesting only tops. Plant any time indoors in sunny window. Avoid overcrowding.
Broccoli	'Spartan', 'Italian Green Sprouting', 'DiCicco'	1–3 plants per 5 gallon container. Continue fertilizing after first harvest to encourage secondary heads.
Brussels Sprouts	'Jade Cross Hybrid', 'Long Island Improved'	2–3 plants per 5 gallon container. Sprouts must mature during cool temperatures. Stake when plants are 10–15 in. tall. Remove tops of plants if necessary to force sprout development. Will produce year-round in southern states. Mild frost improves flavor. Grow indoors in sunny window.
Cabbage	'Earliana', 'Early Jersey Wakefield', 'Copenhagen Market', 'Red Ace', 'Ruby Ball Hybrid', 'Red Head Hybrid'	2–3 plants per 5 gallon container. Don't plant in same container as cauliflower, brussel sprouts, broccoli, kohlrabi, chinese cabbage, kale, or collards because of disease spread. Maintain uniform moisture.
Carrots	'Little Finger', 'Ox-Heart', 'Baby Finger', 'Royal Chantenay', 'Spartan Bonus', 'Nantes', 'Short N. Sweet', 'Gold Pak'	2 in. between plants. Use loose soil-less mix. Place plastic cover over container to improve germination. Grow indoors in sunny window.
Cauliflower	'Early Snowball', 'Snow Crown Hybrid', 'Purple Head'	1–2 plants per 5 gallon container. Avoid moisture stress during early growth or they'll form small heads. Tie large outer leaves together over developing head to prevent discoloration. Grow as winter crop if you have mild winters.
Cucumbers	'Burpee Hybrid', 'Bush Whopper', 'Salad Bush', 'Park's Burpless Bush', 'Pot Luck', 'Burpless Early Pik'.	2 plants per 5 gallon container. Support maturing fruit in a sling tied to support or suspend dwarf varieties in hanging basket. Plant vine varieties in long rectangular planter box with trellis.
Eggplant	'Slim Jim', 'Ichiban', 'Black Beauty', 'Small Ruffled Red', 'Thai Green', 'Bambino'	1 plant per 12–18 in. pot. Likes heat reflected from nearby wall or hang black plastic behind plant. Challenging to grow indoors but it will produce fruit under lights at 65–70°.
Endive	'Broadleaved Batavian', 'Salad King', 'Green Curled', 'White Curled'	To improve flavor before harvesting, gather outer leaves and tie loosely with string for 2 weeks. Grow indoors in sunny window.
Garlic	Most varieties	Need 8 in. deep container. Plant cloves 2 in. deep and 5 in. apart. Water well during warm weather. Lift bulbs when foliage shrivels in late summer. Tie in bunches and dry in sun.
Herbs	Most varieties	Annual herbs can be brought indoors during cold weather. Perennials should be placed in cold frame or cool basement for winter. Repot once a year. Grow indoors in sunny window.
Lettuce	'Oak Leaf', 'Buttercrunch', 'Salad Bowl', 'Dark Green Boston', 'Ruby', 'Bibb', 'Little Gem'	Can grow indoors year-round in sunny window. Leaf varieties are easiest. Fertilize weekly. Shield from intense sun.
Melons	Consult seed catalogs for best varieties.	6–8 plants in 1 ft. x 4 ft. box with trellis or support. Or 2 plants per 5 gallon container. Grow best against south facing wall. Make support out of galvanized, welded-wire, 2 in. x 4 in. screen. Support developing fruit with nylon sling attached to support. Reduce watering as melons near maturity.
Peas	'Sugar Snap', 'Snowbird', 'Alaska', 'Little Marvel', 'Frosty', 'Green Arrow', 'Burpee Sweet Pod'	3–6 plants per 5 gallon container. Edible pods are easiest. Plant in long planter boxes with trellis. Yields are reduced in containers so plant a large crop.
Peppers	*Bell:* 'Bell Boy', 'California Wonder', 'New Ace', 'Sweet Banana'. *Hot:* 'Red Cherry', 'Long Red Cayenne', 'Jalapeno', 'Thai Hot	1 plant per 8–10 in. pot. Stake the plants in windy areas. Bring the pots inside when the outside temperature goes below 60° or above 90°.

Potatoes	'Chippewa', 'Sable', 'White Cobbler'	Use a 30-gallon trash can with hole drilled in the bottom for drainage. Plant 3 seed potatoes in half soil/half compost in the bottom. When the potato sprouts are 6 in. high, cover them with soil/compost, leaving a few leaves showing. Continue to cover with more medium whenever the sprouts are 6 in. high until the medium reaches the top of the can. Water heavily and don't fertilize. At the end of the season, dump the can over or shovel out your harvest.
Radishes	'Cherry Belle', 'Scarlet Globe'	Plant weekly for continuous harvest all summer. When days shorten in fall, bring indoors under lights to extend harvest. Plant in any container at least 8 in. deep. Grows well with carrots, lettuce, and beets in large planter. Grow indoors in sunny window.
Shallots/Onions	*Bulbs:* 'White Sweet Spanish', 'Yellow Sweet Spanish', 'Southport White Globe', 'Southport Yellow Globe' *Bunching:* 'Evergreen', 'White Bunching', 'Kujo Green Multistalk'	Outside, plant onion sets 2 in. apart in spring. Plant mature shallot bulbs 2–3 in. deep, 4–6 in. apart in early fall. Overwinter plants, protecting from freezing. Mature shallots can be harvested in summer. Don't let either plant dry out. Grow indoors under lights for 12 hours/day at 60–70°.
Spinach	'Melody', 'Long Standing Bloomsdale', 'America', 'Avon Hybrid'	Best grown in spring and fall. Indoors, keep temperatures between 50–65°. Grow indoors in sunny window.
Squash	*Zucchini:* 'Green Magic', 'Burpee Golden Zucchini', 'Burpee Hybrid Zucchini' *Acorn:* 'Table King', 'Cream of the Crop Hybrid' *Butternut:* 'Early Butternut', 'Burpee Butterbush'	1–3 plants per 5 gallon container or 1 plant per 12 in. pot. Use trellis. Support fruit with nylon sling tied to trellis.
Swiss Chard	'Fordhook Giant', 'Burpee's Rhubarb Chard'	1 plant per 12 in. pot or 2–3 per 5 gallon container. Outside, plants will die back in winter and resume growth the following spring. Grow indoors year-round in sunny window.
Tomatoes	*Standard size:* 'Early Girl', 'Better Boy VFN' *Dwarf Determinates:* 'Patio', 'Pixie', 'Red Robin', 'Sugar Lump'	Dwarf determinates (patio or cherry types) grow 8 in. to 3 ft. tall. Dwarf indeterminates grow 3–5 ft. tall and produce larger, more standard size fruit. They are easily supported with a short stake. 1 plant of standard variety per 5 gallon container. Dwarf varieties can be planted in smaller pots or hanging baskets. Need consistent watering. Grow indoors under lights in warm location.
Fruit Trees	*Apple:* 'Garden Delicious', 'Starspur Compact Mac' *Apricot:* 'Stark Goldenglo', 'Goldcot' *Cherry:* 'Compact Lambert', 'North Star' *Nectarine:* 'Nectar Babe', 'Stark Honeyglo' *Peach:* 'Honey Babe', 'Stark Sensation'. *Naval orange:* 'Washington' *Grapefruit:* 'Oro Blanco' *Avocado:* 'Mexicola' *Banana:* 'Dwarf' *Fig:* 'Dwarf'	Plant early spring. Buy disease resistant varieties. Need at least 8 hours sun/day. Move to protected area during winter where tree can go dormant without soil freezing. If outdoors, mulch container with straw or newspapers and cover with large appliance box. Water well in early winter and not again until spring. Can train trees as espaliers, with branches growing flat against trellis.
Fruits, Small	*Blueberries:* 'Bluecrop', 'Blueray', 'Earliblue', 'Jersey' *Strawberries:* 'Alexandria', 'Blakemore', 'Surecrop', 'Solana', 'Tioga' *Raspberries:* 'Allen', 'Brandywine', 'Bristol', 'Latham' *Blackberries:* 'Darrow', 'Oregon Thornless', 'Thornfree'.	For strawberries, use strawberry pots or commercially available strawberry barrels. Some fruits, like blueberries, require 2 different varieties for pollination. Blueberries do especially well in containers because it's easy to keep soil acid enough. During the winter, move all fruits to an unheated garage or basement, mulch the soil, and cover with a protective cover such as GardenQuilt.

Adapted from *Just the Facts!* (Storey Publishing, 1993). Used with permission from Gardener's Supply, Burlington, Vermont.

Biointensive Farming

It has often been said that there are really no new ideas, just new ways to use old ones. Such is the case with biointensive farming, which originated in Europe many years ago. It has since evolved into a complex system of agriculture renowned for producing very high yields from very small areas. Because it uses organic methods and no power tools, it has become very popular in developing nations where farmers can feed their families as well as supply local farm markets, all on just a few acres of land.

Biointensive farming is a labor-intensive, full-time job. This, coupled with the very high efficiency of traditional American farms, has made it virtually unknown in the United States or Canada. This is unfortunate, because its principles can be readily adapted to the American garden. Biointensive gardening is still not an easy thing to embrace; it takes time and sometimes back-breaking labor. But it works.

Biointensive gardening uses the two basic tenets of biointensive farming: no power tools and double-dug raised beds. The lack of power tools, such as rototillers, may seem reactionary to some, but there is a method to the madness. Power tillers just cannot double dig a garden bed better than a person with a shovel. And double digging is the cornerstone of this very high-yield technique.

DOUBLE DIGGING

Double digging has been used around the world for generations, but its use declined rapidly after World War II, so that today most people are unaware of it. Double digging (also called trenching) creates a very deep bed of aerated, well-drained, very fertile soil that is nearly unrivaled for heavy production. The process consists of removing the topsoil from the bed and mixing it with finished compost or rotted manure. The subsoil is then turned and thoroughly mixed with finished compost or rotted manure. Finally, the amended topsoil is returned to the bed.

To make a raised, double-dug bed, build a frame of landscape timbers on the ground where the new bed is to be. Most raised beds are from 6 to 12 inches high, 2 to 4 feet wide, and 8 to 12 feet long. With a pointed shovel, remove all the soil in the bed to a depth of one shovel blade. Place the soil in a long mound adjacent to the bed. Dig another layer of soil, again one shovel blade deep, from half of the bed, and pile it at the opposite end of the bed. Layer finished compost or rotted manure onto the bottom of the trench to a depth equal to one-half the height of the timbers. Take the soil that was piled at the end of the raised bed and layer it atop the compost. Repeat these steps with the other half of the bed. Use a shovel or garden fork to mix the layers of soil and compost. Add another layer of compost or rotted manure equal to one-half the height of the timbers. Take the topsoil that was mounded beside the bed and layer it on top. Turn these last layers of compost and soil until they, too, are mixed. Raised beds created this way are so productive that many people use no fertilizer other than biannual additions of compost or rotted manure.

Though double-dug raised beds are extremely productive, they require so much work to create that most folks are content to make only one a year. In subsequent seasons you can add new beds while at the same time refreshing older ones. After building a new raised-bed frame from timbers, remove all the soil to a depth of two shovel blades from the bed. Mound this soil next to a pre-existing bed. Remove all the soil from the pre-existing bed and use it to fill the new bed. Fill the remaining empty bed with alternating layers of compost or rotted manure and soil.

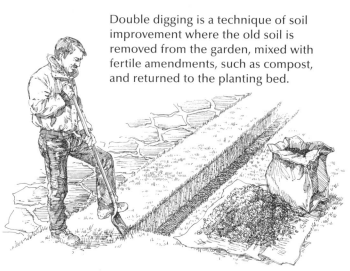

Double digging is a technique of soil improvement where the old soil is removed from the garden, mixed with fertile amendments, such as compost, and returned to the planting bed.

Extending the Season

I know a gardener who once lived up North and complained that there just wasn't enough time in the summer to grow as many tomatoes as he wanted. He tried everything he knew of to extend the season so he could have more tomatoes. Unfortunately, most of his techniques for extending the season relied more on guesses and hunches rather than sound advice. The first warm spell of spring would entice him to plant a bit too early, and a late frost would nip his dreams in the bud. He is a friendly soul, but a bit unaccepting of newfangled ways, so row covers and water-filled hotcaps never adorned his garden. He eventually retired and moved to Florida, where he has loads of tomatoes, but now he misses making real maple syrup.

Packing up the kids and pets and moving to a warm location is one way to extend the growing season, but there are less drastic methods. Extending the growing season really boils down to conserving resources. For example, black mulches act as solar collectors that warm the soil, and water-filled tepees conserve heat, keeping plants from cooling down too much. Growing plants at times when nature isn't entirely cooperative is a delicate dance of ingenuity and diligence. Over the years methods and materials have been invented that can make it possible to garden nearly year-round no matter where in the world your garden is.

LOCATION

Many properties, even small ones, do not have uniform growing seasons. The gardens near my cabin can be up to 6°F warmer than those at the base of the slope a few feet away. In my warm garden the snow melts away a month or more earlier than it does in the cold garden, about a hundred feet away.

In the North, the warmest spots are midway up open south-facing slopes. Steeper slopes, which are generally warmer than gentle slopes, are great locations for terrace gardens. These locations warm up earlier in the spring and often stay warmer in the early fall. While the sun is an ally to many plants grown on south-facing slopes, it is not friendly to all. Evergreens, such as rhododendrons, often suffer leaf scorch when planted on sunny southern slopes. In the Deep South the area midway up north-facing slopes stays cooler in the summer, extending a growing season often interrupted by hot weather. Many plants go dormant or have their growth interrupted by hot, dry weather and the cool conditions of northern slopes can keep plants actively growing when others around them stop. Windbreaks near the garden can help warm it faster in spring. In hot, arid areas of the Southwest, they can extend the growing season further into dry times by inhibiting wind-generated evaporation. Dark-colored walls and fences with sunny exposures serve as heat reflectors. When combined with a south slope these items can add weeks of growing time to small areas of northern gardens. Slopes drain water from the garden faster than flat places, a feature that also helps warm the garden earlier in spring. Just as the grade of the land helps drain water, it also encourages cold air to flow into the areas below.

MULCHES THAT COOL

Cool mulches are those that control weeds by blocking visible light from reaching the soil. Many of them differ from warming mulches in that, instead of absorbing most of the sun's energy, they reflect most of it. Cooling mulches include such materials as white plastic (which is used very rarely) as well as straw, pine needles, and black-and-white newspaper. The mulches inhibit weed germination and growth while allowing water to penetrate readily. Once it's on the soil, the mulch acts as a water conservator, allowing moisture to percolate down through the soil, but inhibiting it from evaporating. The slower rate of evaporation helps to cool the soil as well as the air near the soil even further. Temperatures beneath a cooling mulch such as straw can be several degrees lower than the ambient air temperature. Some plants, such as clematis and lilies, prefer full sun but also need cool soil to thrive. Adding a cool mulch around plants such as these is a secret that is easy to do and produces great results.

MULCHES THAT WARM

In early spring, when the sunlight is strengthening but the atmosphere is still cold, mulches can warm the soil much faster than nature alone. Mulches that warm are especially effective on sandy soils, where they not only help heat the ground but also significantly reduce the loss of nutrients through leaching. Three types of mulches have been designed to warm the ground as well as conserve soil moisture and control weeds by blocking out visible light.

Black poly mulch is made of 1.25-mil black plastic sheeting and is usually 3 or 4 feet wide. As the sunlight strikes the plastic, the dark color absorbs all of the wavelengths of light. This accumulated energy warms the plastic, which then warms the soil. Black poly mulch has been used for decades but has some significant disadvantages: The plastic is not biodegradable and is often difficult to remove from the garden and dispose of properly.

Black paper mulch works similarly. The black paper absorbs energy from the sun, which is then transferred to the ground. Black paper mulch does not warm the soil as efficiently as black poly, but the difference is slight. In contrast to black poly, black paper mulch allows water to seep through into the soil. Recently, a product called Planters Paper was introduced that does all the good things regular black paper mulch does and is also biodegradable.

IRT-100 is a new, dark-colored plastic mulch that warms the soil in a different way from traditional black plastic. IRT-100 absorbs energy from the sun, as black poly does, but allows a significant amount of energy to pass through to directly warm the soil. The plastic mulch then helps retain the accumulated warmth. IRT-100 is the most effective soil-warming mulch to date, though it, like regular black poly, is not biodegradable.

ROW COVERS

Row covers are lightweight blankets or semipermanent tunnels made of polypropylene, plastic, or sometimes even old storm windows. They provide a physical barrier to pests, damper drying breezes, and provide a warmer environment for plants to grow. Lightweight covers, most often called floating row covers, are made of very thin sheets of polypropylene fabric. They are set over a row of plants and supported by thin wire hoops. Polypropylene row covers allow water to penetrate, keep plants warmer during the day, and provide protection from light frosts at night. They allow between 80 and 90 percent of light to reach the plants, and on sunny days can warm the row from 5° to 30°F.

Some row covers are made of very thin clear plastic that has slits cut into it for ventilation. These often require delicate handling and often tear in bad weather. Water does not penetrate them. In northern regions white plastic row covers are used for an entirely different purpose: They are arranged over low hedges and other landscape plants to protect from winter damage.

Black plastic mulch increases yields by warming the soil, decreasing weeds, and conserving moisture. Before placing transplants, roll out black plastic over the planting area (A). You can use straw mulch to cover the edges and rocks to hold plastic down. Cut small holes in plastic and set plants in place (B).

Row covers can inhibit frost damage as well as hinder insects from attacking crops.

HOT CAPS

Generations ago gardeners used a device called the bell-glass to protect individual small plants from frost. It was also used to warm the environment immediately around the plant during the day to encourage faster growth.

In today's garden the bell-glass has been replaced with much less expensive options. One is the plastic milk container. Simply cut the bottom from a one-gallon container and set it over the plant. The cap can be left off for ventilation. Seedlings can be protected from frost by setting paper cups over individual plants. The best device for frost protection is the Wall-O-Water hot cap, which consists of several plastic cylinders joined into the shape of a tepee. The device is placed around the plant and the cylinders filled with water. In tests among paper cups, milk jugs, row covers, and Wall-O-Water tepees, the milk jugs were least effective in providing frost protection; Wall-O-Water tepees were most effective.

Here's a little secret to keep in mind when using hot caps to grow vegetables. Hot caps give the plants a head start on growth. If the plants are not weaned from them by blossom time, however, the resulting yield from those plants is smaller than that gathered from plants grown without hot caps.

Commercial
Wall-O-Water

Homemade milk-jug
hot cap

COLD FRAMES AND HOT BEDS

The cold frame is a small, easily built structure used to lengthen the growing season. When a source of heat is added, the cold frame becomes a hot bed.

Traditional cold frames are most often made of wood, typically redwood, white cedar, or cypress. The headboard is usually about 18 inches high, with the footboard 12 inches tall. Sloping, 6-foot-long boards connect the head- and footboards and serve as support structures for the window sash used as glazing. The entire structure is then set so that the footboard faces south.

The cold frame has come a long way in recent years. Today you can buy one made of pre-cut tubular polycarbonate sheets connected by aluminum joiners. Virtually indestructible, this type of glazing is almost as clear as glass.

Cold frames are used like small greenhouses. The glazing lets solar energy pass through to heat the ground, but traps the heat that the ground radiates back. Cold frames can allow northern gardeners to grow cool-season crops, such as lettuce, even during part of winter. For maximum heat retention, line the floor of the frame with black plastic. Keep a high–low thermometer in the frame to help you gauge when it's warm enough in spring to plant or hot enough to ventilate.

THE OLD-FASHIONED HOT BED

The old-fashioned hot bed is a wonderful invention that can keep fresh lettuce on the table just about all winter long. To build a hot bed, simply remove all the soil to a depth of 2 feet inside the cold frame. Line the earthen sides with 1- or 2-inch-thick panels of Styrofoam insulation. Add a wooden frame around the insulation to brace it, if desired. Add an 18-inch layer of fresh horse manure and firm well. Spread 6 inches of sand on top of the manure. Use a soil thermometer to track the temperature of the sand. As the manure composts it will heat the sand to over 100°F. Flats and pots of plants can be placed in the hot bed when the sand temperature drops below 90°F. The manure will heat the bed for many weeks. When the manure has composted, the hot bed can once again be used as a cold frame.

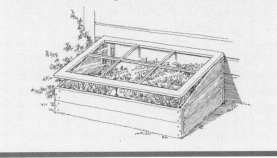

From the Ground Up

Many subtle things can affect the yield of the garden. Good soils can help strengthen plants, making them hardier. Temperatures that are too high can injure crops as much as those that are too low. And even something as apparently innocent as transplanting seedlings can impact the eventual yield of the garden. The highest yields and longest seasons result from a careful blending of many different conditions — some specific to one crop, others more generally applied to the entire garden. When viewed individually the techniques may not carry a great impact, but like many drops adding up to a large volume of water, so the combined effects of subtlety can be greater than the sum of the parts.

BUYING VEGETABLE PLANTS

Many gardeners start plants indoors in spring as a way to extend the practical length of their growing season. Garden centers and nurseries also routinely start vegetable plants from seed in late winter, grow them in the greenhouse, and sell them to gardeners to plant at home. A visit to a garden center in early spring reveals benches full of tomato, pepper, lettuce, cabbage, and other cole crops ready to transplant. No problem here. These plants all thrive after transplanting: Transplanted plants of these crops consistently yield more than those that are direct-sown.

Also on the benches, however, you will probably find flats of cucumbers, squash, melons, and believe it or not, even some beans and corn. The people who buy these plants, whether they know it or not, are purchasing stressed plants that ultimately give reduced yields. All the plants in this last group are very sensitive to transplanting shock and should only be direct-sown for highest yields. Once the plants are more than a couple of inches tall the time of safe transplanting has past.

Even the plants in the first group have their limits. Lower yields result from older, rootbound transplants, and from plants that have been transplanted into larger pots more than twice since leaving the seed flat. When buying vegetables, leftovers are not a bargain at any price.

CHANGING SOIL TEMPERATURE

Mulches are the most common way of changing soil temperatures and are generally used to warm the soil faster in spring or keep it cooler in summer. But just how does a mulch affect the soil temperature?

The temperature of the soil results from the balance among moisture, air, and solid particles. Each accumulates and loses heat at a different rate. Water heats and cools more slowly than solid particles, which in turn heat and cool more slowly than the air. Mulches that have a solid, compact surface, such as black plastic, heat faster than mulches with a broken surface, such as buckwheat hulls. A solid surface is a better conductor of heat than a broken one, in which the solid parts are separated by air or water.

Even if there is no mulch on the soil, a simple technique can alter the soil temperature. As soil dries it becomes more compact and more readily loses heat to the air. To keep the soil a bit cooler, cultivate it lightly, so that a thin, loose layer covers the surface. This loose layer is as not as effective a conductor of heat, and the soil beneath it will remain cooler.

FERTILIZING FOR GREATER YIELDS

Fertilizer needs vary from crop to crop; some plants need more fertilizer, especially nitrogen, than others. When using an organic fertilizer, such as fish emulsion, apply slightly more often to those plants that are heavy feeders. Follow label directions for the normal group. And give slightly less to those crops that need less to grow their best.

Fertilize more	Asparagus, cabbage, carrots, cauliflower, winter squash, potatoes, tomatoes
Fertilize normally	Beets, corn, lettuce, onions, peppers, spinach, turnips, parsnip
Fertilize less	Beans, cucumbers, eggplant, muskmelons, peas, summer squash, sweet potatoes, watermelon

---

Crop	Maximum pH Range	pH Range for Best Yield
Asparagus Beets Cabbage Melons	6.0–8.0	6.5–7.0
Peas Spinach Summer squash Celery	6.0–7.5	6.0–6.5
Lettuce Onions Radishes Cauliflower Corn	6.0–7.0	6.2–6.7
Pumpkins Tomatoes Beans Carrots Cucumbers	5.5–7.5	5.8–6.5
Parsnips Peppers Winter squash Eggplant	5.5–7.0	6.3–6.5
Watermelon	5.5–6.5	6.0–6.3
Potatoes	5.0–6.5	5.5–5.7

SOILS PLANTS PREFER

The ancestors of our modern vegetables, fruits, and flowers grew in all parts of the world and in various soils. Many of those original, evolutionary preferences for soil type are still valid today. For example, spinach evolved in the slightly acid to neutral silt and clay loams of southwest Asia. Current varieties of spinach taste better and yield more than their wild ancestors, yet still prefer to grow on clay and silt loams. Spinach yields earlier but smaller crops when grown on sandy loams. Although many plants will grow well in a wide range of soil types, to get the most from your garden it is helpful to match each crop to its favorite soil.

Asparagus is native to the coastal regions of Europe, Asia, and North Africa where it naturally thrives in the sandy and sometimes saline soils. Today's varieties are more vigorous and upright than the wild types but still grow best in sandy loams. Beans grow very well in many soils but harvest is often delayed on soils kept overly moist, again a trait left over from the climate of their native areas. Carrots like the same type of soil as asparagus, though with a slightly lower pH. The best celery and cucumbers are grown on sandy soils that have had liberal amounts of organic matter added. Melons prefer a soil very similar to that for celery and cucumbers, but with a finer texture. Peas produce heavy yields on many soils; moist silt and clay loams generate more pods, but they mature slightly later than those grown on sandy loams. Peppers also grow and produce well on a wide range of soils but develop earlier and brighter color on light soils. Potatoes yield heavy crops when planted in light sandy, silt, or clay loams that have lots of organic matter. Root crops in general prefer deep, fertile soils. Watermelons develop and ripen most quickly on warm, organic, rich sandy loams. Whatever crop you grow, it will do better in soil that is similar to the soils it's ancestors prefered.

SUCCESSION CROPS BY SEED SIZE

If you collect your own seeds or even sort through a packet of the purchased kind, you may notice that all seeds are not the same size. This is easiest to see in larger seeds, such as beans. Spread a bunch of beans on a table and try sorting the seeds into three categories: large, medium, and small. Put the large seeds in one container, the medium in another, and the small in a third. Come planting time, sow the large seeds in their own row. In the next row over, plant the medium seeds, followed in the last row by the small seeds.

Why all this fuss over the size of seeds? It seems that the largest seeds in a group will mature earlier and produce more uniform crop yields than either the medium or small ones. The medium seeds, likewise, will mature earlier than the smallest ones. By segregating the seeds and planting them at the same time, you get a crop of beans that ripens over a long period of time.

Tips for Tough Pests

In the era of synthetic pesticides, when millions of acres were sprayed with tons of chemicals, such as DDT, people didn't think too much about which chemical to use: Whatever they picked was sure to kill just about everything. Today's attitude is much more environmentally sensitive. People try to find the least-toxic, least-damaging way to protect their crops. There are no more easy solutions; there are, however, ingenious ones. Over the last few years a number of compounds have been isolated from natural sources, and inventive ways of using common things have produced a new, environmentally correct arsenal of pest control. Here are some that may interest you.

GARLIC

Garlic is one of the most purchased and consumed herbs in the United States. Some people use garlic to enhance their personal health, but some are using this beneficial plant to keep their garden free of pests. New Earth Resources is a company that offers a product called ENVIRepel, a garlic-based pesticide. It is claimed to control a wide range of pests including mites, whiteflies, aphids, ants, and many more. The product is nontoxic to wildlife and people; one application lasts for weeks.

In addition, other research has shown that garlic extracts may also be an effective means of controlling slugs and snails. To experiment on your own with garlic, mince an entire bulb of it in a bowl. Add enough warm water to cover, and mash well. Pour the mixture into a quart jar and fill with water. Cap the jar and place it in the refrigerator for a few days, shaking it every once in a while. When ready to use, strain the liquid into an atomizer or small hand sprayer. Experiment gingerly at first, testing the mix on different bugs here and there, and on single leaves to be sure no damage occurs. If you see a slug, give it a squirt, too. Garlic is supposed to kill them as well.

NATURAL HERBICIDE

It may seem strange that a plant would evolve a way to kill other plants — but then, after all, it *is* a jungle out there. The garden weed called lamb's-quar-

SUGAR SLUGS

For years it has been common belief that a saucer of beer left out in the garden would help control slugs. The slimy things would crawl into the beer seeking a good time, then drown in the abundance they found. And it works; the slugs really do like happy hour when it's offered. What just might work a little better, though, is beer with a little sugar added. It seems that slugs not only have a taste for beer but a sweet tooth (figurative, of course) as well. Add one teaspoon of sugar to a can of flat beer, stir well, and serve at dusk. Party hats and beer nuts are optional.

ter has a compound in its leaves and stem that inhibits the germination of seeds. It's logical enough: If the plant can stop seeds from growing near it, so much better for the lamb's-quarter. The compound is water-soluble, which makes concocting your own experiments that much easier. After weeding your garden of lamb's-quarters, put the plants in a bucket and fill it just enough to cover them. Then, using whatever happens to appeal to you, mash them so their juices blend with the water. Let the soup sit in the shade for a day or two — no longer — and strain into a sprayer. Use the solution to wet the soil around any recently cultivated soil to inhibit seed germination. Be careful not to use this mixture near rows you have recently seeded with new crops.

Like any new technique, this one is a work in progress, and it isn't yet known just how effective the homemade brew is on every species. Some have suggested leaving lamb's-quarters in the rows after weeding as a herbicidal mulch. It might be worth a try, though often natural plant substances quickly lose their potency when exposed to heat and sunlight.

Lamb's quarters contains substances that can be used to create an effective garden herbicide.

MURPHY'S OIL SOAP

This is wonderful stuff. It not only cleans the kitchen cabinets but dispatches bugs as well. What a bargain! To make an effective pesticide for white-flies, caterpillars, and other soft-bodied bugs, pour 1 gallon of warm water into a jug. Soft water is best, because hard water actually deactivates the soap. (Soap mixed in hard water appears milky, while that in soft water is clear.) Pour ¼ cup of Murphy's Oil Soap into the container. Stir until the mixture is uniform, but gently, so that it doesn't foam. One of the best ways to apply the solution is with the type of trigger sprayer that has a siphon tube attached.

As with any spraying, do not apply to plants in direct sunlight or when the leaves are wet. Test the solution on a small part of the plant before spraying the entire thing, just to make sure the soap doesn't harm it. And when spraying, be sure to cover all surfaces of the plant (along with any nasty bugs you happen on) until the solution runs off. Some plants, such as Japanese maples, are damaged by soap solutions and should not be sprayed.

HOT STUFF

One of the primary causes of reduced yields of cucumbers, melons, pumpkins, and squash is infection with mildew. This usually occurs well after fruit set and is worse during moist weather. As the mildew spreads over the plants they quickly weaken which in turn inhibits the ripening of the fruit and can even kill the plants. The tried and true method of mildew control is an easy-to-make solution of baking soda and water. When the first white splotch of mildew is noticed mix 1 teaspoon of baking soda with 1 quart of water. Spray the entire plant thoroughly in the cool of the day.

Another less perfected mildew treatment involves using row covers to raise the air temperature around the plants. Studies have shown that raising the air temperature to about 110°F for 2 hours twice a week can inhibit the effects of mildew and raise yields up to 40 percent over untreated controls. The technique requires careful monitoring of the temperature inside the row cover for extended high temperatures can injure the plants.

High-Yield Varieties

Since the beginning of civilization, the art of agriculture has involved learning how best to grow plants and how to grow the best plants. Almost all gardeners focus their attention on how best to grow plants. They learn how to plant seeds, amend the soil, fertilize, and water to produce the highest-quality crops. For thousands of years, however, a small percentage of gardeners have investigated the more mysterious aspects involved in actually improving plants. They have learned the art of how to grow the best plants.

We have all benefited from the curious nature of people who have bred and selected plants. Ancient Native American farmers produced improved varieties of corn, squash, and other vegetables over thousands of years of cultivation. Other cultures, from India to Africa, China, and Europe, did the same. From the stable, basic vegetables they passed down to us, further alterations have been made, and the modern gardener sees a plethora of choices adorning the pages of seed catalogs each winter. Sometimes these plants have undergone amazing changes as various breeders have worked with them over the years. An example is the garden carrot. This sweet, orange vegetable was derived from the wild carrot, a plant we know as Queen Anne's lace. If curiosity gets the best of you take a moment this summer and carefully uproot a plant of Queen Anne's lace. Beneath the crown of lacy leaves is a small, pale white taproot about three inches long. If you snap the root in half and give it a sniff the unmistakable aroma of carrots flows forth. The difference between the two plants is astounding and gives eloquent testimony to what can be accomplished through selection and hybridization.

For most of us the task of improving the garden harvest requires no more energy than picking the latest high-yield variety from the catalog. Others, however, take time to learn the basics of the art of selection and hybridization to create their own unique vegetables. Whether choosing the best from the latest catalog or choosing the best from the latest sowing of saved seeds, it is nearly certain that bountiful yields await.

One of the best ways to get higher yields is to grow a variety that produces a bit earlier than the standard forms do. An early cultivar coupled with a planting of a later variety can substantially increase the yield from the garden. In some short-season areas, the new, early cultivars can give bountiful yields when other varieties wouldn't even ripen.

VEGETABLE	VARIETY	DAYS TO MATURITY
Bush beans	'Earliserve'	48 from seed
	'Daisy'	48 from seed
	'Radar'	50 from seed
	'Triumph de Farcy'	48 from seed
Beets	'Early Wonder'	45 from seed
Cabbage	'Fast Ball'	45 from transplant
	'Primax'	60 from transplant
	'Earlianna'	60 from transplant
Carrots	'Nelson'	56 from seed
	'Ingot'	55 from seed
	'Suko'	55 from seed
	'Thumbelina'	50 from seed
	'Kinko'	52 from seed
Cauliflower	'Snow Crown'	50 from transplant
	'Early White Hybrid'	52 from transplant
Sweet corn	'Earlivee'	65 from seed
	'Early Choice'	66 from seed
	'Early Sunglow'	62 from seed
	'Champ'	64 from seed
	'Spring Rush'	59 from seed
Eggplant	'Millionaire Hybrid'	55 from transplant
	'Orient Express'	58 from transplant
	'Bambino'	45 from transplant
Muskmelon	'Earligold'	82 from seed
	'Earliqueen'	84 from seed
	'Sweet 'n Early'	75 from seed
Peppers	'King Arthur'	59 from transplant
	'Jingle Bells'	60 from transplant
	'Gypsy'	65 from transplant
	'Little Dipper'	66 from transplant
Tomatoes	'Kotlas'	55 from transplant
	'Siletz'	58 from transplant
	'Ruby Cluster'	58 from transplant
	'Early Pick'	62 from transplant
	'Early Girl'	54 from transplant
	'First Pik'	64 from transplant
Zucchini	'Gold Rush'	40 from transplant
	'Green Fingers'	20 from transplant

Creating Your Own Varieties

Many gardeners consider plant breeding too complicated to understand. Parts of the subject are indeed very complex, but the basics are pretty easy to learn. For backyard gardeners the method of plant improvement that is the most rewarding is selection, which is accompanied through keen observation and a bit of recordkeeping.

Selection is an ancient practice that involves growing a large number of the same type of plant, such as tomatoes, and choosing the best plants. Some seeds of the best plants are then saved and grown the following year; then the best of that group is again selected out. Using this method you can select the earliest-producing plants, or the plants that produce the best-tasting fruit, from the others of the group. Over the course of many seasons, selecting for these qualities strengthens them, and the desired traits become more reliable.

To begin to improve your own garden favorites through selection, be sure to choose varieties that are open-pollinated instead of hybrid varieties. Hybrid cultivars will be designated in seed catalogs by the word *hybrid* and sometimes also the designation *F1*. If you're still in doubt, choose a variety referred to as an *heirloom*, because these are all open-pollinated varieties. Many gardeners prefer to use heirloom cultivars, particularly the oldest ones, because they often have more variability than modern varieties. The more variability a cultivar possesses, the greater the chance that offspring will be noticeably different from parents.

Plant the seeds of your chosen variety in one area of your garden. As the plants grow try to treat them all alike: Give them all the same amount of fertilizer, water, and light. How a plant is grown affects what it looks like. Two plants of the same variety that are grown in different ways will look different. A well-fertilized plant will be better-looking than an unfertilized one, a difference called environmental variability.

As the plants grow keep an eye out for those that show the trait or traits you want. If earliness is what you seek, watch for the plant that bears the first ripe fruit. Save the seeds from it, and plant those seeds next year. As next year's plants grow, again select seeds from those that bear the first ripe fruit. Sometimes selection can result in rapid improvement of a variety; at other times the process brings out undesirable traits and the quality of the variety actually declines. Whatever happens, though, selecting plants adds a unique sense of anticipation to gardening. Each seed planted is potentially something special, something just different enough to be worthy of a name all its own.

OPEN-POLLINATED VARIETIES OF THE MOST POPULAR PLANTS FOR USE IN SELECTION

PLANT	VARIETY
Bush beans	'Blue Lake Bush', 'Bountiful', 'Earliserve', 'Provider', 'Tendercrop', 'Triomphe de Farcy', 'Topcrop'
Wax beans	'Brittle Wax', 'Cherokee Wax', 'Goldcrop Wax', 'Sunkist'
Sweet corn	'Golden Bantam', 'Black Aztec', 'Ashworth', 'Country Gentleman', 'Golden Jubilee', 'June White', 'Stowell's Evergreen', 'Double Standard'
Slicing cucumbers	'Ashley', 'Marketmore', 'Poinsett'
Eggplant	'Black Beauty', 'Florida Market'
Muskmelons	'Iroquois', 'Honey Rock', 'Jenny Lind', 'Minnesota Midget', 'Rocky Ford'
Garden peas	'Alaska', 'Alderman', 'Freezonian', 'Green Arrow', 'Knight', 'Laxton's Progress', 'Little Marvel', 'Novella', 'Wando', 'Tall Telephone'
Hot peppers	'Anaheim', 'Large Cherry', 'Hungarian Yellow Wax', 'Early Jalapeño', 'Long Slim Cayenne', 'Serrano'
Sweet peppers	'California Wonder', 'Purple Beauty', 'Sweet Chocolate'
Spinach	'Bloomsdale Long Standing', 'King of Denmark'
Tomatoes	'Beefsteak', 'Bonny Best', 'Delicious', 'Earliana', 'Fireball', 'Brandywine', 'Glamour', 'Kotlas', 'Marglobe', 'Rutgers', 'Ponderosa', 'Jubilee', 'Sunray'

Enjoying the Most Nutritious Vegetables

Over twenty-five years ago a number of institutions decided to breed vegetables that were more nutritious than those presently available. Scientists particularly focused on creating varieties with high concentrations of vitamins. People were becoming more conscious of the environment and their own health, so the time seemed right. A few varieties were developed and produced and entered the market in the 1970s. Among these more nutritious varieties was a tomato that had an unusually high concentration of vitamin C. It had so much vitamin C, in fact, that eating one of these tomatoes was more like eating an orange than a tomato. The plant was marketed for a few years but then quietly disappeared from the seed catalogs. There just weren't enough people looking for more nutritious vegetables.

Since then, public thinking has changed and nutrition has indeed become important to many more people. Gardeners relish fresh-picked food from the orchard and vegetable garden and berry patch. Many of these same people believe that home growing — particularly organic home growing — produces more nutritious fruits and vegetables. The question that remains is: Are they right?

SPINACH, ANYONE?

Spinach may turn Popeye into a superhero, but some people have cause to avoid this nutritious vegetable. Spinach leaves naturally contain high concentrations of oxalates. When eaten in high quantities, the oxalates in the leaves can inhibit proper absorption of calcium as well as aggravate some types of health problems. Research in Japan has shown that the oxalates accumulate as the leaves mature; the highest concentrations being in the oldest leaves. To enjoy spinach but avoid the higher concentrations of oxalates, harvest only young, very tender leaves from young, rapidly growing plants.

ORGANIC IS NUTRITIOUS

Recent studies comparing fresh organically and nonorganically produced fruits and vegetables have revealed that organically grown crops have substantially more nutrients than their nonorganic counterparts. Fresh organically produced crops consistently contain more calcium, iodine, iron, magnesium, potassium, phosphorous, and zinc than nonorganic crops, while levels of lead, mercury, and aluminum are lower.

HARVESTING AT THE PEAK OF NUTRITION

The production of vitamins in plants varies with the season and weather conditions. To harvest the most nutritious vegetables, it helps to know just when vitamins are at their peak. Vegetables that produce fruits, such as tomatoes, peppers, and eggplant, should be harvested when they reach maturity. Root crops, such as carrots and parsnips, are more nutritious when harvested after they reach full size. Baby carrots taste better but have fewer vitamins and minerals than more mature ones. Potatoes gathered from the largest plants have more vitamins than those harvested from smaller plants. For leaf crops, such as spinach and lettuce, harvest while leaves are actively growing. Cool-weather crops grown in spring have more vitamins than those grown in fall. Cherry tomatoes and wild types, such as currant tomatoes, are rich in vitamin C. Hot peppers have more vitamins than sweet peppers.

HARVESTING AT THE PEAK OF RIPENESS

Some large commercial growers can predict the exact day an entire field will be ripe enough to harvest. It's not that they have an extrasensory gift; they predict when to harvest by using the heat unit system.

The heat unit system, which is a way of calculating the amount of thermal energy a plant receives over a given amount of time, is much more accurate than a seed catalog's days-to-harvest listing. By keeping a careful record of crops, a grower can tell how many heat units each one requires to go from seed to harvest. Once that value is known, predicting the harvest is just a matter of keeping track of the daily temperature.

A modified heat unit system can be used in the garden. All that you need is a base temperature and a record of the average daily temperature in your garden. For cool-season crops use a base temperature of 40°F; for warm-weather crops, 55°F.

On the day you sow a crop, record the daily high temperature and the daily low, add them, and divide by two. Subtract the base temperature from this number to obtain the heat units for that day. For example, a day with a high of 70°F and a low of 60°F gives an average daily temperature of 65°F. Subtracting 55 (the base temperature) from 65 leaves 10, which is the number of heat units for that day. In this system cucumber seeds need about 100 heat units (HU) to germinate and about 1,000 until harvest.

By keeping track of each crop from the time of planting until harvest, you will know the HU number for each variety planted. That value will be unique to your garden. Each crop and each variety will have a different HU harvest number. It may take a few seasons to learn the HU requirements for each crop. After that, however, you will be able to predict when peak harvesttime is, and maybe even beat the raccoons to the corn.

Collected Tips for Better Yields

Asparagus. Plant varieties that produce predominantly male spears. These varieties, such as 'Jersey King', are longer lived and more productive than other cultivars. Fertilize the bed immediately after harvest season is over for a better yield next season. Harvested spears continue to grow and quality rapidly declines unless they are stored at temperatures below 40°F.

Beets. Beets are one of the few root crops that can be transplanted. Start in cool flats in spring and carefully set in the garden for an extra-early crop.

Broccoli. Eating lots of broccoli has been found to reduce the risk of certain cancers.

Brussels sprouts. For a more uniform harvest,

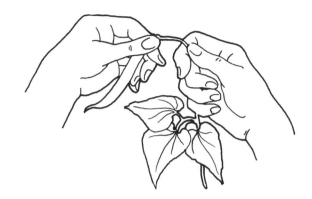

Some people believe that beans harvested in the late afternoon are more nutritious than those picked in the morning.

pinch the tops from the plants when lowest sprouts reach thumbnail size.

Bush beans. For earlier maturation, grow bush beans on sandy loams. Cultivating during pod set can reduce yields. Wet or dry weather can cause pods to drop.

Cabbage. 'Wakefield' types are the most cold-tolerant; when properly hardened off, they can withstand temperatures down to 20°F. If clubroot is a problem, use lime to raise soil pH to 7.0. Use small plants for spring planting to reduce bolting.

Carrots. Baby carrots taste better but are less nutritious than mature carrots. Even when the rest of the garden does not need water, carrots do, and will respond by producing larger roots.

Celery. Harden seedlings by slightly reducing watering. Hardening by exposure to cold temperatures will encourage plants to bolt.

Corn. For the best-tasting corn, plant supersweet varieties away from other types of corn. In rural areas do not plant sweet corn near fields of silage corn.

Cucumbers. Plant female, or gynoecious, varieties to increase yields.

Eggplant. Train slender varieties to stakes, as you would tomatoes, to encourage long, straight fruits.

Fava beans. In northern regions where lima beans won't grow, plant fava beans instead. They thrive in cool weather and produce meaty beans.

Lettuce. Too much water while heads are forming results in soft, loose heads.

Leeks. Unlike most vegetables, the larger the transplants, the better the yield.

Melons. Direct-sow rather than transplant. Do not overwater when fruit is ripening.

Peas. Although peas will grow in many different soils, they only produce heavy, tasty yields when grown in soil rich in organic matter.

Peppers. Cultivating while fruit is maturing can cause fruit drop. To increase yields, pick the first sweet peppers when they are full size but before they begin to change color.

Potatoes. If you store potatoes in cool cellars, they must be conditioned in spring before being used as seed potatoes. Store tubers at 65°F for ten to fourteen days before planting or cutting into seed pieces. Very warm soil can inhibit tuber formation.

Tomatoes. If early blight is a problem, plant potato-leaved varieties, such as 'Brandywine'. For more disease control, water plants only in the morning of clear days. Avoid wetting foliage when possible.

7

At Home with Herbs

Thousands of years ago, long before science began its attempt to provide rational explanations for everything, plants were seen as repositories of mysterious powers or conveyors of valuable gifts. The chamomile flower relaxed the sleepless mind, for instance, and the olive tree provided sustenance for the body. The ancient cultures of Egypt, China, India, Europe, and elsewhere did not cultivate plants for their beauty; they grew plants because they saw them as useful and spiritual additions to their lives.

Some herbs were considered gifts from the gods, their parts harvested, prepared, and used by priests for sacred ceremonies. Others held the power to cure sickness. At a time when illness was attributed to everything from bad vapors to demonic possession, a plant that could bring relief was powerful stuff. Ceremonies surrounded the growth, harvest, and use of many plants, and gardens were carefully planned and prepared to take into account the powers each plant possessed as well as its horticultural requirements.

Little by little the passing of the centuries has eroded these ancient traditions and taken the mystery from many herb plants. Science has told us the names of the chemicals in their leaves and roots that make pasta sauce spicy or ease our indigestion afterward. Worse, it has also declared that some of these herbs do nothing at all — that for thousands of years the herbalists from many cultures had just been fooled. By the middle of the twentieth century herbs had become anachronisms — snake oil, to the enlightened, or plants more easily gathered from the supermarket spice rack.

Over the last few decades, however, this narrow view has in turn fallen by the wayside. Suddenly we've found that some of the folklore of the ages is valid after all, and that fresh basil and thyme are so much better than the dried supermarket stuff as to seem to come from different plants entirely. And so we have gone back to the future, reserving space in our gardens for special plants that we can bring into our homes to enrich our lives.

Yes, there *is* always room for the lovely perennial that contributes beautiful flowers to a sunny summer day. But now we also save a place for the herbs that provide the warm seasoning in a winter meal or add a cooling touch to the lotion that eases our sore muscles at the end of the day.

Site and Soil

Herbs, like any other large group of plants, have a wide range of requirements for maximum growth. There are, however, some general rules that apply to most of those herbs commonly found in the garden.

SOIL

Most herbs will thrive in a well-drained loam soil generously amended with organic matter. This type of soil provides excellent aeration and retains both nutrients and moisture. Soil with a pH of between 6.0 and 7.0 — slightly acid to neutral — is best for the majority of herbs. A soil test will tell you the pH value of your soil as well as what and how much to add to bring that pH to the ideal level. Soil that is rich in organic matter is also more pH-stable than mineral soils. This stability provides a more predictable environment for the plants to grow in season after season.

SUNSHINE

Most herbs do best in a site that allows at least six hours of sunlight per day. Plants grown in full sun tend to produce more volatile oils than those grown in shade, and more volatile oils means more aromatic foliage. Some plants that prefer shade, such as bee balm, can also grow in full sun if the soil is moist. Many herbs, especially in the warm regions of the South and Southwest, benefit from a few hours of midday shade.

If your spot has only about six hours of sunshine, you can maximize that sunlight with a little ingenuity. Set your herb plants near a wall or fence that has been painted white. The white background reflects light, increasing the intensity of the sun during the time it shines. And because white

doesn't absorb light, it doesn't heat up, so your plants get more light without more heat.

NO COMPETITION

Trees, shrubs, and sometimes even lawns are the bullies on the block when it comes to competing for nutrients. These big boys and girls have wide-reaching root systems that tend to monopolize the nutrients and moisture in the top few inches of soil, spreading dendritic webs of feeder roots all over the place. As a consequence, the relatively small root systems of herbs must try to make do with the leftovers. When you can, site your herb garden away from such competition. If the garden has to be in a competitive environment, try putting the herbs in a raised bed.

◆ **Herbs That Like the Seaside**
Apothecary's Rose (*Rosa gallica* 'Officinalis')
Bay, sweet (*Laurus nobilis*)
Garden sage (*Salvia officinalis*)
Lavender cotton (*Santolina* spp.)
Rosemary (*Rosmarinus officinalis*)

Harvesting Herbs

Herb harvesting is easy: Simply snip what you need and you're done. The trick, however, is knowing when to harvest to be sure that you gather your crop at its peak. Many of the most treasured herbs produce heady aromas, such as lavender, basil, and rose. The fragrances come from the evaporation of the volatile oils that the plants produce. In many plants the amount of volatile oils varies during the growing season or even at different times of the same day. Knowing when the oils reach their peak is a good way to know when to harvest your crop for best flavor and aroma.

NUTRIENTS, WATER, AND SUN

The most potent herbs do not necessarily produce the most vigorous growth; abundant moisture and nutrients can dilute a plant's volatile oils instead of strengthening them. The most potent herbs are instead harvested from plants when nutrients, moisture, and sunlight have been balanced.

Few herbs require a regimen of fertilizer applications throughout the growing season to produce

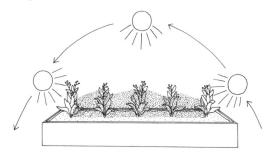

Plan your herb garden so it receives the most sun. Design it to run east to west with an open southern exposure.

a full-flavored crop. The biannual addition of rotted manure or compost fills their needs. In the few days or weeks before harvest, make sure you do not overwater your herb garden. Allow the soil to dry between waterings, but not so much that the plants are stressed or wilt. The more full-spectrum sunlight the plants receive, the more oils they produce. The light shade found beneath trees alters the spectrum of light as well as its intensity, which can lower the concentration of volatile oils.

Thus, the recipe for the best-flavored herbs is to limit fertilizing, reduce watering, and maximize sunlight in the days before harvest.

WHEN TO HARVEST

Many herbs harvested for their leaves achieve optimum flavor or potency after the flower buds appear but before they completely open. Even during this time, though, the flavor of the leaves can change. The best time of day to harvest is early in the morning, before the plants begin to receive direct sunlight. Make sure that the leaves are dry and that the morning temperature is 10 to 20°F cooler than the peak temperature of the previous day. When harvesting herb flowers for fresh use, follow the same guidelines but gather the flowers when they are about one-half to three-quarters open. Some plants, such as basil, can be harvested as needed throughout the season — though you may notice a subtle difference in flavor from day to day.

Harvesting herb roots, such as those of echinacea, is almost always done in fall. If a clump needs dividing, lift the plant from the soil and cut the roots from its crown. Then divide and replant the clump. If the clump doesn't need dividing, just lift it from the soil, gather no more than one-third of its roots, and replant.

For best flavor harvest herbs with aromatic leaves, such as thyme, when the flower buds just begin to open.

HOW TO HARVEST

If you need only a few leaves at a time, gather them individually from the plant. Tender, young leaves will taste different from older, mature ones. Try both until you discover the balance of flavors that best suits your palate. If you need a good amount of leaves, cut the entire stem from the plant and strip the inner leaves. For plants that grow from a central stem, such as parsley, harvest the outer leaves first, removing any damaged or yellow ones before you do so. If you cannot process the plants immediately, put the herbs, uncovered, in your refrigerator.

Preserving Herbs

Over the years people have tried to develop a process that preserves both the herb and its flavor. This isn't easy, because volatile oils, the substances that give each herb its distinctive flavor, are fragile stuff and easily destroyed. The most common preservation methods include drying, freezing, and making herbal vinegars.

DRYING HERBS

Drying involves the removal of moisture from the herb. This must be done quickly enough that molds and fungi cannot begin to grow and enzyme activity within the plant stops, but slowly enough that large amounts of volatile oils do not evaporate. To achieve this balance four methods have been developed: air-drying, microwave-drying, oven-drying, and — last but not least — fridge-drying.

Air-drying

Traditional air-drying involves hanging bunches of herbs by their stems until they're dry. The plants are hung upside down in a well-ventilated, shaded, warm place. Depending on the type of plant, the temperature of the air, and the air's circulation, the plants should be dry in from two to five days. If the leaves turn black or mold begins to grow on them, discard the batch. Don't leave herbs hanging for more than a few days before storing them in an airtight container; the longer they hang, the less flavorful they become. Spreading gathered herbs over a mesh screen also works well.

Air drying is quick and easy but can result in a noticeable loss of flavor. This method is best used for strong-scented herbs.

Advantages: This is a very good method for plants used in dried-flower arrangements and for some strong-scented herbs, such as sage and rosemary, that are dried on the stem. The plants are attractive and aromatic while drying and can lend a nostalgic ambience to the house. Air-drying is also good for saving large batches of herbs.

Disadvantages: Noticeable and sometimes unacceptably large amounts of volatile oils are lost during the process, leaving the herbs more weakly flavored. Humid or cool conditions can lead to moldy or discolored plants. The method is not good for mild-flavored herbs, such as lemon balm, as they often lose much of their flavor.

Microwave-Drying

A modern technique that genuinely improves on the old ways, microwave-drying is fast and easy, and it produces full-flavored herbs with excellent color. Gather herb sprigs, leaves, or flowers and gently wash them in cool water. Allow them to dry completely; herbs with surface moisture will cook instead of dry. Layer a microwave-safe pie plate with paper towels and then spread a single, even layer of herbs over the towels. Microwave on high for one to three minutes, checking the plants every 60 seconds. Herbs are done when they feel dry to the touch but have not lost any color. Allow them to cool, and place them in an airtight jar. This storage jar should not show any condensate; if droplets appear, briefly dry the herbs again.

Advantages: Microwave-drying is a fast and efficient way to dry small quantities of herbs. It produces excellent results — the plants retain both flavor and color.

Disadvantages: You can only dry small batches at a time. Pie plates heat up and must sit and cool every few minutes.

Oven-Drying

Oven-drying is not a good idea for leafy herbs, as the higher temperatures drive out as much flavor as they do moisture. The oven method is instead used primarily to dry roots. These should be cleaned and carefully sliced into thin strips. Spread the slices on a baking sheet and place it in an oven set on warm (about 140°F) for two to four hours. Test the slices often and remove them from the oven when they are dry, but before they become baked and brittle. Cool to room temperature and store in airtight containers.

Advantages: This is a good method for preparing roots of herbs.

Disadvantages: The high temperatures of oven-drying release an unacceptably large amount of volatile oils from leaves and flowers, leaving behind a weak-flavored, bland product.

Fridge-Drying

The best thing to happen to herb preparation in a long time, fridge-drying is both ingenious and simple. Frost-free refrigerators dehumidify as well as chill the air inside. This dry *and* cold air effectively dries herbs quickly with a minimal loss of flavor. It works best for preparing leaves and flower petals. To fridge-dry, gather sprigs, leaves, or flowers and gently wash them in cool water. Set them aside to allow their surface moisture to evaporate. If space permits, spread an even layer of herbs on a baking sheet covered with paper towels. If space in your fridge is at a premium, though — as it is for many folks — gather the dry herbs into a fine-mesh bag. Place a magnetic hook at the top of the fridge storage compartment, and hang the bag from the hook. Another option is to put the herbs in an

The low humidity and cool temperatures of refrigerators make them an ideal place to dry herbs.

uncovered bowl, but you must stir these at least once a day. Herbs that are drying in the fridge must be left uncovered. They can dry in as little as two days or take as long as a week. When they are dry to the touch, store them in airtight jars. Don't dry herbs in crisper bins. Fridge-drying can also be done in the freezer compartment, but expect only fair results.

Advantages: This is an excellent way to dry small batches of plants. The dried herbs retain the maximum amount of flavor and color. Fridge-drying works best for leafy herbs or flower petals.

Disadvantages: You can process only small amounts of herbs at a time. The method also takes up lots of refrigerator space.

FREEZING

Although a quick method of storing herbs, freezing doesn't work for all types. Gather herb sprigs, leaves, or flowers and wash them in cool water. Allow them to dry, and place them in clear plastic freezer bags. Seal the bags and place them in your freezer compartment. When you wish to use an herb, just open the bag and take out what you need.

Advantages: Freezing is quick and easy and retains the flavor and (usually) color of the herbs.

Disadvantages: This technique doesn't work for everything. For example, basil and lemon balm turn black and mushy when frozen. Dill, fennel,

marjoram, parsley, and most mints are good bets, though. Freezing damages the cell structure of herbs and will produce, at best, a limp, wilted product on thawing — at worst, a black, mushy mess.

VINEGARS

Vinegars preserve the flavor and character of herbs instead of the herbs themselves. The essential oils are drawn from the plant into the vinegar, imparting to the liquid the rich, full flavor of the herb. Unlike other preservation methods, vinegars concentrate the flavor of herbs, allowing you to create products ranging in taste from mild to very strong. The finished liquids can be used for cooking, as ingredients in marinades, and as salad dressings.

To make herbal vinegars, begin with a high-quality vinegar (such as red wine). Fill a clean glass container with washed, fresh herb. Pour in the vinegar until all of the herb is covered, and seal the container. Place the jar on a sunny windowsill for at least a few weeks so that the warm liquid can leach the flavors from the herb more efficiently. Strain the liquid into clean, sterilized jars and label. You may also wish to toss a bit of the fresh herb into the jars — this is decorative as well as practical, for it aids in identifying the product.

Advantages: Making herb vinegars is easy to do. You can also regulate the strength of the liquid and create blends of different herbs. The final product keeps longer than most other preserved herbs.

Disadvantages: It takes weeks to achieve maximum flavor.

For a great gift idea decant homemade herbal vinegars into attractive but inexpensive glass containers.

HERB SALTS

Creating salts, one of the most ancient methods of food preservation, is used for many different foods. Gather the fresh herbs and wash them carefully in cool water. Allow them to dry so that no surface moisture remains. Chop or finely cut them into very small pieces. Pour a one-inch layer of table salt into a clean glass container. Add a layer of herb, then cover with more salt. Repeat the process, ending with a one-inch layer of salt at the top. Use as much herb as salt. For example, if you have one cup of minced herbs, use one cup of salt to cure it. Allow the mixture to sit for a few weeks. Shake thoroughly to blend the mixture before using.

Advantages: Herb salts are fairly easy to make and lend a different taste to many meals. Moreover, they store well.

Disadvantages: The method is practical only for small amounts of herbs. It's not good for folks on salt-restricted diets.

The Medicinal Herb Garden

The medicinal herb garden had it beginnings in the distant past when certain plants were found to aid in healing, or at least in soothing the symptoms of illness or misadventure. At first the plants were gathered from fields and woodlands. Slowly, people grew more familiar with them and began to understand how to grow them, and one by one the medicinal herbs were collected into exclusive gardens where skilled healers could gather and prepare their medicines. The medicinal garden became as indispensable as the kitchen garden, orchard, or livestock pen. There were, of course, no drugstores back then, no pills in prescription bottles, no synthesized medicines. When someone fell ill, the cure was in the garden.

Those old gardens contained some plants that we would never think of using for home remedies today. Monkshood *(Aconitum napellus)* was once used as a sedative, even though just one flower can kill a person. Mandrake *(Mandragora officinarum)*, likewise used as a sedative, is also very poisonous. Autumn crocus *(Colchicum autumnale)* was used to treat gout but is, again, toxic. American hellebore *(Veratrum viride)*, an ancient treatment for hypertension, is now known to be a toxic narcotic.

As modern medicine evolved, the backyard medicine garden withered into disuse; the plants became parts of the perennial border or the kitchen garden or were left to return to the wild.

Today's medicinal garden resembles its ancient prototype in some ways but differs in others. The dangerous and questionable plants have been wisely replaced with effective but much safer herbs. And the garden itself has become attractive as well as functional. There are many, many herbs that can be chosen for the medicinal garden, but the following are some of the safest and most useful when used wisely and in small amounts.

♦ **Plants for the Medicinal Herb Garden**
    Apothecary's Rose *(Rosa gallica* 'Officinalis')
    Basil *(Ocimum basilicum)*
    Chamomile *(Chamaemelum nobile)*
    Echinacea *(Echinacea* spp.)
    Garden sage *(Salvia officinalis)*
    Garlic *(Allium sativum)*
    Hyssop *(Hyssopus officinalis)*
    Lavender *(Lavandula angustifolia)*
    Lemon Balm *(Melissa officinalis)*
    Mint *(Mentha* spp.)
    Rosemary *(Rosmarinus officinalis)*
    Thyme *(Thymus* spp.)
    Wintergreen *(Gaultheria procumbens)*

Echinacea root

The medicinal part of Echinacea is the root, but the beautiful flower is medicine for the soul.

The Flowering Herb Garden

Throughout history practicality was the first priority of the herb garden, with attractiveness usually stumbling along far behind. Gardens were always well tended, which in itself adds beauty, but no amount of primping can make some herbs easy on the eye.

The flowering herb garden is a more modern invention that blends practicality with floral beauty. It consists of plants that bear very attractive flowers — some, such as lavender and Apothecary's rose, with enchanting scents as well. In addition to the flowers, each of the plants is also useful for teas, home remedies, lotions, potpourris, or cooking. The herbs flower at different times from spring to late summer, and many attract honeybees, butterflies, hummingbirds, and beneficial insects.

Flowering herbs can be arranged into their own garden or scattered among existing plantings. The tall, stately flowers of echinacea and yarrow are at home in the perennial border as well as the herb garden. Thyme is lovely as an accent to a rock garden or creeping along crevices and between stepping-stones. Some species, such as sweet violet, can even be grown in the natural lawn. Sweet woodruff can be used as a ground cover beneath trees where it brightens shady places with constellations of star-shaped, vanilla-scented flowers. Others, such as scented geraniums and passionflowers, make good container plants and can be set just about anywhere, from the deck to the garden.

When designed into a single garden, flowering herbs create a special environment of color and fragrance that is a dynamic addition to the yard. Even a small planting where bee balm, lavender, pineapple sage, and scented geranium mingle is an unforgettable aromatic and visual treat. Herbs that also grace the garden with beautiful flowers are a bonus that should not be overlooked when planning the season's plantings.

♦ **Plants for the Flowering Herb Garden**

Anise hyssop (*Agastache foeniculum*)
Apothecary's Rose (*Rosa gallica 'Officinalis'*)
Bee balm (*Monarda didyma*)
Calendula (*Calendula officinalis*)
Echinacea (*Echinacea* spp.)
Hyssop (*Hyssopus officinalis*)
Lavender (*Lavandula angustifolia*)
Lavender cotton
    (*Santolina chamaecyporissus*)
Nasturtium (*Tropaeolum majus*)
Passionflower (*Passiflora incarnata*)
Pineapple sage (*Salvia elegans*)
Roman chamomile (*Chamaemelum nobile*)
Scented geranium (*Pelargonium* spp.)
Sweet goldenrod (*Solidago odora*)
Sweet violet (*Viola odorata*)
Sweet woodruff (*Galium odoratum*)
Thyme (*Thymus* spp.)
Yarrow (*Achillea millefolium*)

Bee balm

The Scented Herb Garden

The scented garden has been around in one form or another for hundreds of years. In times past, groups of aromatic plants were gathered into formal arrangements to decorate the gardens of the well-to-do. Such gardens gradually lost favor but have reemerged in the last few decades. In their new incarnation teachers and other caregivers use them to reach out to troubled youth, the blind, shut-ins, or those confined to nursing homes. The results can be astounding. When people are surrounded by aromatic plants, their sense of smell comes alive. This in turn seems to revitalize the other senses, especially the sense of touch. Folks interact with the plants, caressing them to release the fragrances.

Although usually small, scented gardens are wonderfully rich in aromas and make lovely retreats that can enrich everyone's life. One can occupy a small section of your backyard, deck, or patio, or even be brought indoors during the long winter months, where selected pots can occupy a sunny windowsill.

Scented gardens are commonly constructed on a terrace or other platform that is waist high and about three feet wide. This puts all the plants within easy reach — which is essential for their complete enjoyment. Many times the herbs are grown in containers and arranged on appropriate surfaces. Rearranging them periodically allows you a different, though equally rewarding, experience. If planted outdoors, ground-cover herbs, such as thyme and chamomile, can be sited in walkways, so that you release their fragrance as you enjoy your other plants.

♦ **Plants for a Scented Herb Garden**
(Numbers in parentheses refer to number of plants required for plan shown below.)

1. Costmary (1)
2. Wormwood (1)
3. var. Pineapple mint (1)
4. Catnip (1)
5. Anise hyssop (1)
6. Pineapple sage (1)
7. Lemon thyme (2)
8. Pennsylvania-Dutch tea thyme (2)
9. Golden lemon thyme (2)
10. Caraway thyme (1)
11. Oregano thyme (1)
12. Corsican mint (1)
13. Lavender (2)
14. Rock rose (2)
15. Lemon verbena (1)
16. Scented geranium (2)
17. Tangerine southernwood (1)
18. Peppermint (1)

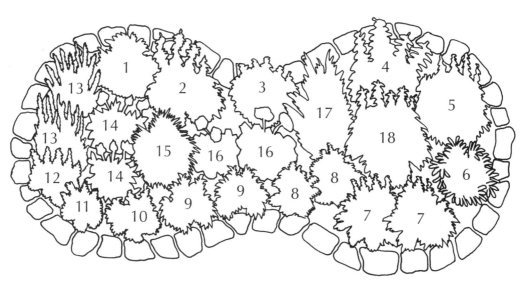

Plan for a Scented Herb Garden

The Kitchen Herb Garden

The kitchen garden is the epitome of the practical planting, for all the plants must earn their keep. Nothing is there just for show. Historically, cooks planted the kitchen garden just outside the kitchen door, where its herbs could be both gathered quickly and taken care of without leaving the proximity of the house. It was usually divided into small plots separated from each other by access paths. Today the plantings often take the form of raised beds, which give the garden a formal, decorative character while preserving its practical nature. As in the scented garden, the beds of the kitchen garden are kept narrow enough that none of the plants are beyond reach from the path.

The traditional kitchen garden wasn't limited to culinary herbs, for the kitchen was much more than just the site of food preparation: It also served as the place where first aid was administered, soap and candles made, and cloth dyed. Accordingly, the kitchen garden was home to the soft, wonderfully fuzzy leaves of lamb's-ears *(Stachys byzantina)*, which were used as colonial Band-Aids, and the St.-John's-wort *(Hypericum perforatum)*, which dyed cloth in shades of metallic yellow. Soapwort *(Saponaria officinalis)* was grown to aid in the making of soaps, with lavender *(Lavandula angustifolia)* there to scent soaps and candles.

Modern kitchen gardens maintain this tradition of individuality and self-reliance. To plan yours, simply observe what herbs you use the most in your kitchen. Then separate out the ones that are easy to grow in your area and use that list as a template for your garden.

Two Plans for a Kitchen Herb Garden

Back: sage, peppermint, marjoram, dill

Middle: oregano, thyme, tarragon, parsley, rosemary

Front: chives, thyme, basil, thyme, chives

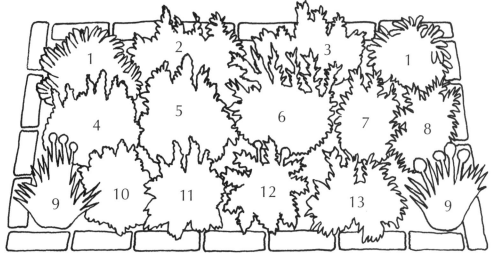

1. Sage (2)
2. Peppermint (1)
3. Spearmint (1)
4. Oregano (1)
5. Marjoram (1)
6. Tarragon (1)
7. Lemon balm (1)
8. Rosemary (1)
9. Chives (2)
10. Dot Wells upright thyme (1)
11. Lemon thyme (1)
12. Burnet (1)
13. French thyme (1)
(Numbers in parentheses refer to number of plants required.)

The Container Herb Garden

A great many herbs seem to enjoy growing in containers. This makes having a great herb garden even easier, because containers have advantages of their own. They come in many different materials, styles, and colors, and, because they are portable, the garden can be rearranged whenever the urge strikes or even brought indoors for the winter. In addition, soil mixes can be tailored to each plant, for instance, so that bee balm can grow in rich, fertile soil that stays evenly moist, and catnip can sink its roots into sandy, well-drained soil. Shade-loving plants can grow beneath trees without competing with them, and herbs that love the sun can be moved throughout the season to the brightest spots.

Even the containers themselves can accentuate herb growing: Plants that prefer well-drained soils that dry quickly can be grown in clay pots; those that like moister conditions in plastic. Containers also make gardens possible in more urban environments, bringing flowers and greenery to rooftops, balconies, and porches.

The choice of containers is determined by the priorities of the grower. If you need portability but cannot lift heavy clay pots, then plastic is the obvious choice for you. If you grow your plants in small pots on the windowsill and want the healthiest herbs all winter long, then clay is best. In general, clay pots grow better, healthier plants and are more decorative; plastic pots are less expensive and weigh less. There are now plastic pots that look like they are made of clay, however, which are thus just as decorative as terra-cotta. These pots are not as expensive as clay containers, but are more expensive than traditional plastic pots.

Still, certain plants do grow better in certain containers. Here is a brief list to help you choose.

- ◆ **Herbs That Grow Best in Clay Pots**
  Anise hyssop (*Agastache foeniculum*)
  Calendula (*Calendula officinalis*)
  Catnip (*Nepeta cataria*)
  Dill (*Anethum graveolens*)
  Fennel (*Foeniculum vulgare*)
  Garden sage (*Salvia officinalis*)
  Hyssop (*Hyssopus officinalis*)
  Lavender (*Lavandula angustifolia*)
  Lavender cotton
     (*Santolina chamaecyparissus*)
  Marjoram (*Origanum majorana*)
  Rosemary (*Rosmarinus officinalis*)
  Scented geranium (*Pelargonium* spp.)
  Sweet bay (*Laurus nobilis*)
  Thyme (*Thymus* spp.)
  Winter savory (*Satureja montana*)

- ◆ **Herbs That Grow Best in Plastic Pots**
  Bee balm (*Monarda didyma*)
  Lemon balm (*Melissa officinalis*)
  Roman chamomile (*Chamaemelum nobile*)
  Sweet violet (*Viola odorata*)
  Wintergreen (*Gaultheria procumbens*)

- ◆ **Herbs That Grow Well in Clay or Plastic**
  Borage (*Borago officinalis*)
  Cayenne pepper (*Capsicum
     annum* var. *annuum*)
  Chives (*Allium schoenoprasum*)
  Lemongrass (*Cymbopogon citratus*)
  Mint (*Mentha* spp.)
  Nasturtium (*Tropaeolum majus*)
  Parsley (*Petroselinum crispum*)
  Passionflower (*Passiflora incarnata*)
  Sweet basil (*Ocimum basilicum*)

COMPANIONS IN CONTAINERS

Many herbs are valued as companion plants. Traditionally, companion plants have been thought of as those that grow in the ground next to other plants. However, the portability of container-grown plants widens this traditional definition. Like the honeybee hives that are brought to orchards in the spring, certain container-grown herbs can be set where needed. Plants that attract honeybees and other pollinators can be placed in the vegetable garden or berry patch to ensure good fruit set. Herbs with daisylike flowers or flat, umbel-shaped blossoms can be placed to attract hoverflies and parasitic wasps, which help control pests.

A Gallery of Herbs

Anise Hyssop
Agastache foeniculum

SOIL: Fertile, well drained, pH 6.0–7.0
LIGHT: Full sun to light shade
HEIGHT: Three feet
PLANT TYPE & HARDINESS: Perennial, Zones 6–9

A relative of mint, anise hyssop is native to the prairies and open spaces of the Great Plains, where Native Americans used the leaves in teas to treat coughs. The plants are stiffly erect, with dusky green leaves and clusters of small, bluish-purple, tubular flowers from July through September. The strongly aromatic leaves blend anise and peppermint scents. The blossoms attract bees, butterflies, and hummingbirds. Honey made from the flowers has a golden color with soft undertones of licorice.

How to Grow: Sow seeds either indoors in spring or on site after danger of frost has past. Transplant or thin plants to 12 inches apart. Water during periods of hot, dry weather. Lower leaves can drop in late summer or during droughts. Propagate from seeds or by division in spring. Anise hyssop can be overwintered in colder areas of Zone 4 and some sections of Zone 3 by covering with a layer of mulch after the ground has lightly frozen.

Harvest and Use: The dried or fresh leaves and flowers make an anise-flavored, slightly sweet tea that is said to help purify the body by inducing perspiration, and is also useful in relieving congestion. Tender leaves gathered from growing tips are used in salads, while dried leaves make fine additions to sauces and potpourris. For the strongest flavor grow plants in full sun, in soil rich in organic matter, and harvest the leaves after flower buds appear but before they open. For subtler flavors, grow in partial shade or harvest during bloom.

Sweet Basil
Ocimum basilicum

SOIL: Fertile, evenly moist, pH 5.5–7.5
LIGHT: Full sun
HEIGHT: 1–2 feet
PLANT TYPE & HARDINESS: Annual

Basil species range from camphor basil, which is used as an insect repellent, to sacred basil, a plant grown in India for its protective influence. The most popular, however, is sweet basil, the leaves of which contain a variety of strongly aromatic oils in combinations that give the many different cultivars their distinctive scents: cinnamon basil (*O. basilicum* 'Cinnamon'), with spicy cinnamon-scented leaves; licorice basil (*O. basilicum* 'Anise'), with an earthy, anise aroma; and lemon basil (*O. basilicum* var. *citriodorum),* whose leaves bear rich scents of citrus. These and many others have become essential ingredients in the cuisine of countless cultures around the world.

How to Grow: Sow seeds indoors in early spring or on site after night temperatures remain above 50°F. Once the plants are a few inches tall, thin them to 6 inches apart and cover the soil around them with a light layer of screened mulch to retain moisture. Pinch out growing tips to induce branching. Other good cultivars include 'Dark Opal', 'Purple Ruffles', and 'Genovese'.

Harvest and Use: The entire plant is used, with the seeds, leaves, and flowers employed most often. The fresh or dried leaves are essential ingredients in tomato-based sauces and as a seasoning for vegetables, meats, and stuffings. A tea made from the leaves produces a warm, restorative feeling; itchy insect bites can be soothed by rubbing fresh leaves over the skin. Basil is said to aid digestion, relax cramps and muscle aches, and reduce fevers. In companion plantings it helps repel aphids. Gather individual leaves anytime. Whole plants should be harvested as flowers begin to open.

Bay, Sweet
Laurus nobilis

SOIL: Fertile, well drained, pH 6.0–7.0
LIGHT: Full sun to partial shade
HEIGHT: 10–50 feet
PLANT TYPE & HARDINESS: Evergreen shrub, Zones 8–10

Sweet bay is a woody shrub native to southern Europe, the Azores, and the Canary Islands. Under optimum conditions it grows into a tree up to fifty feet high. The glossy, evergreen leaves are leathery and pleasantly aromatic. In spring inconspicuous yellow flowers blossom in the axils of the leaves, followed later by dark purple berries. Its Latin name translates to "noble praise"; historically garlands of bay were draped over the heads of notable Romans. Sweet bay continues to be used as a symbol of accomplishment.

How to Grow: In warm regions sweet bay is sometimes grown from seeds, though germination can take up to a year. A better method of propagation is either to transplant suckers from mature plants or air-layer the stems. In northern regions sweet bay is commonly grown in pots filled with a fertile growing medium, such as California mix. Transplant to larger pots as the plant grows, and overwinter in a warm, sunny spot away from cold drafts. Varieties include 'Angustifolia,' with willow-shaped leaves, and 'Aurea,' with golden foliage.

Harvest and Use: The large leaves of sweet bay not only flavor soups, stews, and sauces, but also aid in digestion. Fresh leaves may be used in recipes, though dried ones have an even stronger flavor and remain flavorful for about a year. A tonic made from the leaves is used to treat dandruff. Commercially, figs are packed in sweet bay leaves to repel insects.

Bee Balm, Bergamot
Monarda didyma

SOIL: Rich, evenly moist, pH 6.0–6.7
LIGHT: Full sun to light shade
HEIGHT: Three feet
PLANT TYPE & HARDINESS: Perennial, Zones 4–8

Bee balm is as much at home in the perennial border as it is in the herb garden. Native to much of eastern North America, it forms thick colonies in wetlands and along streambanks. Plants have tall, pliant, four-sided stems draped with aromatic, dusky green leaves and crowned with a distinctive cluster of scarlet flowers in summer. Bee balm attracts butterflies and hummingbirds.

How to Grow: Grow from seeds sown indoors or from purchased transplants. Plants spread very quickly once they're established and should be divided every three years. Bee balm is an excellent plant for a wet meadow. Plant in an area with good air circulation to inhibit powdery mildew, which often appears on the leaves in late summer. Many excellent cultivars of bee balm include: The rich red flowers of 'Cambridge Scarlet' have made it a long-time favorite. 'Raspberry Wine' has scarlet flowers with lilac undertones and resists powdery mildew. 'Marshall's Delight' blooms from July into September and was bred for those who can't get enough of bee balm's unique scarlet flowers.

Harvest and Use: Used to flavor Earl Grey tea, the leaves of bee balm have a fruity, spicy taste. Pick them just before the flower buds open, and dry in the refrigerator to preserve flavor. Teas brewed from the fresh or dried leaves are used to calm indigestion. Gather individual flowers and add to salads. Harvest and dry plants in small bunches for use in dried arrangements. Tomatoes and peppers, in particular, seem to grow better when planted near a patch of bee balm.

Borage
Borago officinalis

SOIL: Rich, evenly moist, well drained, pH 6.0–7.0
LIGHT: Full sun to partial shade
HEIGHT: 2–3 feet
PLANT TYPE & HARDINESS: Annual

Native to Europe, borage has been used and cultivated since ancient times. Its name stems from a Latin word that means "hairy garment" — a reference to the plant's coarsely hairy leaves. Borage is reputed to lift the spirits, induce euphoria, and even create a feeling of courage in those who eat them. Recent research has determined that borage does indeed stimulate the production of adrenaline — which just might account for the sense of well-being and courage some people feel after nibbling on the plant.

How to Grow: Sow indoors in early spring or outdoors after danger of frost has past. Borage develops a taproot rather quickly, and transplanting should be done carefully so that the root is not damaged. Support plants that grow to more than over 2 feet in height. Borage often self-seeds; volunteers that appear the following spring should be transplanted before the long taproot develops too much. The variety 'Alba' has snow-white flowers, while 'Variegata' has gray-green leaves laced with white.

Harvest and Use: The tender leaves have a delicate, cucumberlike flavor. Gather anytime and add to salads, lightly steamed like spinach, or sautéed in butter. The beautiful starlike lavender-blue flowers appear from midsummer until frost and are a tasty and colorful addition to salads; they have traditionally been added to wine as well. A tea made from the leaves and flowers is said to relieve coughs and ease the discomfort of colds. Use borage as an accent and in moderation, however, as some authorities suggest that large amounts of it may cause liver damage.

Calendula, Pot Marigold
Calendula officinalis

SOIL: Fertile, well drained, pH 6.0–7.0
LIGHT Full sun to very light shade
HEIGHT: Two feet
PLANT TYPE & HARDINESS: Annual

A stout, rather floppy plant, calendula has lance-shaped medium green leaves and either single or double orange to yellow flowers from summer until frost. Its name comes from a Latin word meaning "first day of the month" and refers to the plant's long bloom time. It is also known as pot marigold, because English cooks used to throw one blossom into a pot to thicken and color stews or soups.

How to Grow: In Zones 8 through 10 sow seeds outdoors in fall; in other zones seeds can be started indoors two months before last frost or outdoors after the danger of frost has past. Set plants 1 to 2 feet apart, depending on the height of the mature plant. Mulch around them to retain soil moisture and keep roots cool. Cut back spent flowers as they appear. Calendulas are sensitive to heat and crowding; they benefit from light afternoon shade in the South as well as sites with good air circulation. In hot regions plants may die in midsummer. Many varieties are available, ranging from compact, dwarf forms to tall types. Calendulas are sometimes bothered by aphids, slugs, leafhoppers, or whiteflies.

Harvest and Use: Calendula has a long history of use as a medicinal herb added to skin creams and shampoos. Pick flowers when they are dry and about three-quarters open. Dry the petals in a cool, shady place, with good air circulation, on absorbent paper. Dried petals and flowers can be stored in jars. The petals are used as a substitute for saffron, imparting a rich, golden yellow color to rice dishes, soups, breads, cheese spreads, and butter.

Caraway
Carum carvi

SOIL:	Well drained, fertile, pH 6.0–7.0
LIGHT:	Full sun
HEIGHT:	2 to 4 feet
PLANT TYPE & HARDINESS:	Biennial, Zones 3–8

Caraway is one of the most ancient of cultivated plants and has been grown for well over 5,000 years. The plants have upright, hollow stems and deeply cut leaves that resemble those of carrots. During the first season the plant produces a rich display of foliage. The following spring a flush of new foliage appears, followed by a 2- to 4-foot stem topped by an umbel of small white or blush-white flowers. A few weeks after the flowers fade the small, tasty seeds ripen and can be collected.

How to Grow: Sow seeds directly in the garden about 2 weeks before the last frost. Gently press the seeds into the soil surface, and cover lightly with vermiculite. Thin seedlings to stand 6 to 12 inches apart. Caraway does not like to be transplanted or disturbed. Fertilize lightly when seedlings are 3 inches tall and again the following season when the flower shoot appears. Once established the plants are drought tolerant and usually do not need much watering.

Harvest and Use: Cut flowerheads as seeds begin to turn from a yellowish color to brown. Hang stems upside down in a paper bag. Place seeds in a sieve and pour boiling water over them. Dry the seeds in a sunny place for a few days and store in a sealed jar. Use the seeds to flavor breads, cheese, meat, and vegetable dishes or cookies. Chewing a few seeds is said to relieve indigestion. The fresh leaves can be gathered anytime. Chopped and sprinkled over salads, they add a distinctive zing.

Carpet Bugle
Ajuga reptans

SOIL:	Well drained, dry, pH 5.5–7.0
LIGHT:	Full sun to shade
HEIGHT:	3 to 6 inches
PLANT TYPE & HARDINESS:	Perennial, Zones 3–10

Carpet bugle is a vigorous groundcover that is as much at home in the perennial border as in the herb garden. It has attractive, spatula-shaped leaves in a range of colors from green to shades of rose to deep burgundy. Some varieties have variegated leaves of green, red, and white. In spring short, upright stems appear decorated with a spike of small blue or white flowers.

How to Grow: Carpet bugle can be grown by direct sowing seeds in the garden in early spring, but is most often grown from purchased transplants. Space plants 12 inches apart. Carpet bugle is very easy to grow and needs little care. It can spread quickly and can be restrained with garden edging. Some of the best varieties include 'Atropurpurea' with deep reddish purple leaves; 'Burgundy Glow' with leaves randomly stained with rose, white, and green; 'Variegata', bearing deep green leaves edged with white; and 'Cristata', with small, deep green, lightly crinkled leaves.

Harvest and Use: In centuries past species of bugle were used for everything from cures for malaria to treatments for boils and hangovers. Today the plant is used to relieve the discomfort of minor scratches and insect bites. Gather the fresh leaves anytime they are needed. They stay green just about year round, even in cold northern areas. Stack the leaves in a little pile and lightly bruise them with a rolling pin. Place the bruised leaves over the scratch or bite. The fresh leaves can also be chopped and added to ointments.

Catnip
Nepeta cataria

SOIL: Sandy, well drained, pH 7.0–8.0
LIGHT: Full sun to partial shade
HEIGHT: To three feet
PLANT TYPE & HARDINESS: Perennial, Zones 4–9

Catnip has been famous since ancient times for its intoxicating effects on cats. A rather rangy herb with an open growth habit, it has semi-erect stems ornamented with rough-textured, pungently aromatic foliage and spikes of small white flowers bedecked with tiny purple spots. Catmint *(Nepeta x faaseenii),* a more ornamental relative of catnip, is attractive enough for the perennial border but lacks catnip's potent medicinal qualities.

How to Grow: Sow seeds indoors in spring and transplant to the garden, or direct-sow after danger of frost has past. Space or thin the plants to 18 inches apart and cover the soil with a light layer of compost or well-rotted manure. Fertilize lightly every few weeks with an organic fertilizer. Catnip is a very vigorous grower and, once established, can become invasive; bury plant guards around plantings to inhibit its spread.

Harvest and Use: Gather the fresh, tender leaves anytime before the plant flowers to add a nip to salads or make a softly flavored, relaxing tea. The leaves can also be finely minced to add an undertone of mint to sauces or hearty stews. In late summer gather the topmost leaves and dry them in a cool, dry place. A tea from the dried leaves is said to relieve the discomforts of indigestion, fevers, colds, and the flu, as well as induce relaxing sleep. 'Citriodora' is a cultivar with aromatic, lemon-scented leaves that makes an even more flavorful tea than the species. And of course cloth pouches liberally filled with catnip are a turn-on to cats.

Cayenne Pepper
Capsicum annuum var. *annuum*

SOIL: Fertile, evenly moist, well drained, pH 6.0–7.0
LIGHT: Full sun
HEIGHT: 2–2½ feet
PLANT TYPE & HARDINESS: Annual

Columbus brought some long, scarlet fruits of cayenne pepper back to Spain from South America in 1493. The fiery spice became especially popular in the late 1800s, when its warming properties were used to relieve sore joints and muscles, calm the chills of colds, and dispel depression. Cayenne pepper is a lanky plant with thin, medium green, lance-shaped leaves and small white flowers from summer until frost. The slender, 4-inch-long, thin-walled fruit grows abundantly from midsummer until frost.

How to Grow: Cayenne peppers grow best in the heat of summer. Sow seeds indoors in early spring and transplant after danger of frost has past. Space plants about 18 inches apart and cover the soil with mulch. Fertilize regularly with an organic fertilizer, such as fish emulsion. Pinch off the first two sets of flowers to increase yields. Keep the soil moist during dry periods. Cayenne peppers can often withstand a few light frosts in fall; protect them with row covers to extend the season for several days.

Harvest and Use: The active ingredient in cayenne stimulates blood circulation and produces a pronounced warming effect when applied externally or ingested. The dried, powdered fruit is added to a variety of recipes, including sauces, stews, and soups. The fruit also contains a potent antioxidant and is used to relieve migraines and sore throats. Harvest the peppers when they're fully colored, leaving about 1 inch of stem. Split the fruit lengthwise, remove all seeds, and dry in a cool, shady place until crumbly.

Chamomile, Roman
Chamaemelum nobile

SOIL: Evenly moist, pH 6.5–7.5
LIGHT: Full sun to light shade
HEIGHT: Six inches
PLANT TYPE & HARDINESS: Perennial, Zones 4–8

A sweetly aromatic herb called ground apple by Greeks and Romans and believed by Saxons and Vikings to be a gift from the gods, Roman chamomile is a weak-stemmed plant with pale green, wonderfully scented, ferny foliage. The blossoms, which appear from midsummer to frost, are small, daisylike flowers with white rays surrounding a prominent yellow central disk.

How to Grow: Sow seeds indoors in spring, keeping soil at room temperature, or direct-sow after the danger of frost has past. Thin or set plants about 6 inches apart. Use in the crevasses between stepping-stones to add a soft accent. The plants are not vigorous, so weed often. Divide in spring, if needed. Handling the leaves causes dermatitis in some people.

Harvest and Use: Teas made from the dried flowers have been used since ancient times to relieve indigestion, colic, and diverticulitis. A warm infusion taken at bedtime is said to relax the muscles, calm the nerves, and dispel anger. Mixing a tablespoon of flowers with hot water and breathing the vapors relieves congestion and hay fever. Creams made with the dried flowers relieve the itch of insect bites and soothe minor scratches. Infusions of Roman chamomile are also sprayed on seedlings to prevent damping off, and on many mature herbs to prevent powdery mildew. Cut flowers last longer when chamomile tea is added to the vase. Harvest the flowers as they appear and dry them on a screen in a cool, shady place. Store in an airtight jar. Stored blossoms generally keep for about a year.

Chives
Allium schoenoprasum

SOIL: Fertile, well drained, pH 6.0–7.0
LIGHT: Full sun to light shade
HEIGHT: 6–12 inches
PLANT TYPE & HARDINESS: Perennial, Zones 3–9

A member of the remarkably versatile onion family, chives are native to Asia Minor. Their thin, gracefully cylindrical, deep green leaves have a mildly pungent, oniony aroma and arise from equally aromatic bulbs. The leaves are topped with lavender or purple ball-shaped clusters of small cloverlike flowers in late spring to early summer.

How to Grow: Sow seeds indoors in spring, covering them lightly with soil; keep at about room temperature. Once seedlings emerge, harden the plants off and transplant them to the garden in clumps of a few plants each. Space clumps about 6 inches apart. As the plants grow larger, top-dress by sprinkling compost lightly over the clumps. Chives are very vigorous growers and should be divided every three years: Lift the entire clump and separate as needed, then amend the soil with compost or well-rotted manure. The variety 'Forescate' is more vigorous than the species, with longer, thicker leaves and larger flowers. Garlic chives (*A. tuberosum*) is a closely related species with white flowers, flat, solid leaves, and a mild garlic flavor.

Harvest and Use: Harvest fresh green leaves continually from early spring to fall. The diced herb brings a mild onion flavor to salads, soft cheeses, eggs, potatoes, and gravies. The fresh or dried leaves can season soups and stews. Separate the petals from fresh flower heads and sprinkle them over salads. Chives are frequently used as companion plants for certain vegetables and fruits, including carrots, grapes, and tomatoes. In the flower garden they enhance the growth of roses.

Cilantro, Coriander
Coriandrum sativum

SOIL: Fertile, well drained, pH 6.0–6.5
LIGHT: Full sun to light shade
HEIGHT: 1–3 feet
PLANT TYPE & HARDINESS: Annual

Cilantro is mentioned in Egyptian papyri dating to three thousand years ago. The Greeks and Romans used it extensively, and it was quickly adopted by the Chinese when travelers brought it to the Far East nearly a millennium ago. The common name, coriander, which most often refers to the seed, comes from the Greek word for an insect that exudes a disagreeable odor very similar to the one emitted from the herb's unripe fruit. Cilantro has deeply lobed, glossy green leaves and small clusters of white flowers in summer. The fruit is tan colored when the seeds are ripe and ready to harvest.

How to Grow: Direct-sow seeds outdoors after the danger of frost has past, and lightly cover with soil. Thin to about 4 to 6 inches apart. Cultivate to reduce competition from weeds. Cilantro is a good companion plant for anise but not for fennel.

Harvest and Use: The flavorful dried seeds taste of citrus and can be chewed to relieve upset stomachs. The ground seeds are used in seasoning bakery products, eggs, soft cheeses, and sauces as well as in pickling recipes and salad dressings. The fresh leaves, which you can harvest anytime, have a strong flavor reminiscent of sage and lemon combined. They are used extensively in the cuisines of the Middle and Far East. Harvest the seeds when the plants have turned brown but before the seeds scatter. Dry the seeds thoroughly before using; the aroma gets stronger and more pleasing as they dry.

Dill
Anethum graveolens

SOIL: Fertile, well drained, pH 5.5–6.5
LIGHT: Full sun
HEIGHT: To 3½ feet
PLANT TYPE & HARDINESS: Annual

Dill's common name comes from a Norse word meaning "to lull" and refers to the fact that the herb was once used to induce sleep. Similar to fennel, with highly dissected, deeply lobed leaves that have a soft, fernlike texture and pleasing aroma, dill has a tall, single, hollow stem crowned with pale yellow flowers borne in flattened umbels in summer, followed by brown, distinctively aromatic seeds.

How to Grow: Dill dislikes transplanting. Direct-sow in shallow trenches after danger of frost has past. When seedlings are a few inches high thin to about 8 inches apart. Keep soil moist until plants are well established. Dill makes an excellent companion to cabbage but should not be planted near carrots or fennel, with which it can hybridize.

Harvest and Use: Once highly regarded as a medicinal herb that was said to cure everything from flatulence to hiccups, dill is still used to calm digestive disorders and relieve cramps. Fresh dill is used to flavor vinegars and pickles and add a unique taste to salads. The fresh or dried leaves and seeds are also used in seafood recipes, salad dressings, sauces, stews, butter and cheese spreads, egg dishes, grilled and steamed vegetables, and as a seasoning for lamb, pork, and poultry. Harvest the leaves as needed; use them fresh or freeze them for later. The seeds become ripe a few weeks after the plants blossom. Cut the stems when the uppermost seeds are tan in color but before the lower seeds ripen. Hang upside down in a cool, dry place with the heads just inside a brown paper bag.

Echinacea
Echinacea spp.

SOIL: Well drained, pH 5.5–7.0
LIGHT: Full sun to partial shade
HEIGHT: To 3½ feet
PLANT TYPE & HARDINESS: Perennial, Zones 3–9

Generations ago the Native Americans of the Great Plains used echinacea more than any other herb. Of the many echinacea species, the most beautiful and widely grown is the purple cone-flower *(E. purpurea)*, with its tall, strong stems topped in summer with large magenta-colored, daisylike flowers. The large, lightly fragrant flowers are especially attractive to butterflies.

How to Grow: Sow seeds indoors about two months before planting out, keeping the soil moist and at about 75°F. Transplant the seedlings to the garden when the soil is cool and night temperatures still fall into the 30s. Mulch around established plants and water as needed. Propagate by division in spring in the North, and in fall south of Zone 7. There are many excellent cultivars available, including 'Magnus', with stems to nearly 4 feet and very large, raspberry-colored flowers; and 'White Swan', which has large, pure white blossoms on strong stems.

Harvest and Use: Though the most beautiful part of the plant is the flower, the most valuable parts are the roots and rhizomes. The dried roots are used in teas to stimulate the immune system and lessen the symptoms of colds, fevers, and the flu. A warm infusion of the dried root is used to stimulate healing of wounds, as well as to ease the symptoms of skin diseases and lung congestion. The tea has an earthy, slightly bitter taste with a pleasing aroma. Lift the roots in fall after a few hard frosts. Remove them and replant the crown of the plant. Carefully wash the roots and dry.

Fennel
Foeniculum vulgare

SOIL: Rich, well drained, pH 6.0–6.5
LIGHT: Full sun
HEIGHT: 4–6 feet
PLANT TYPE & HARDINESS: Perennial, Zones (4) 5–9

Fennel strongly resembles dill, with its tall, fat, hollow stalks. The fernlike leaves have a sweet, anise flavor and are so fine as to appear as insubstantial as mist. The pale yellow flowers grow in shallow umbels high atop the stems in summer.

How to Grow: Fennel transplants poorly. Direct-sow it in shallow holes spaced 6 inches apart in moist soil in spring. Once plants reach about 6 inches tall, let the soil dry out between waterings. The flowers attract beneficial insects, including hoverflies. Do not plant fennel near beans, tomatoes, kohlrabi, or dill. Fennel does not grow well next to cilantro, and artemisia can inhibit flower formation. Florence fennel *(F. vulgare* var. *azoricum)* has the most flavorful stems, while wild fennel *(F. vulgare)* produces the tastiest seeds. Bronze fennel *(F. vulgare* 'Purpureum') is the most ornamental, sporting attractive plumes of bronze-purple foliage.

Harvest and Use: All parts of fennel are edible, and the leaves can be gathered as soon as the plant is established and growing well. The thick stems are eaten as a vegetable; they reach peak flavor after the flower buds have formed but before the blossoms begin to open. Collect the seeds when the seed head begins to turn from greenish-yellow to brown, letting them fall into a paper bag. Close up the top of the bag and store it in a cool, dry place. The seeds will complete their ripening in the bag. Once they are fully ripe, store them in a jar. Fresh leaves are used in salads, and the fresh stalks eaten like celery. Use the seeds to flavor everything from sausages, fish, and desserts to breads and vegetables.

Garlic
Allium sativum

SOIL: Rich, well drained, pH 5.5–7.0
LIGHT: Full sun to light shade
HEIGHT: 1½–2 feet
PLANT TYPE & HARDINESS: Perennial bulb, Zones (4) 5–9

Garlic is the herb of magic, capable of dispelling evil, repelling vampires, and neutralizing the spells of witches. The small compound bulb produces a cluster of long, deep green, flat leaves wrapped in a papery sheath. In summer a round umbel of white to pink flowers appears atop a pliant stem.

How to Grow: Garlic is planted in fall, about the time the first hard frosts occur, for harvest the following summer, or in spring to harvest a fall crop. Separate the cloves from the bulb; plant 2 inches deep and 6 inches apart in well-worked soil. To increase the size of the bulb, remove any flower stalks as they appear. As harvest approaches, the leaves should begin to turn brown. Lift the plants from the ground and dry them on a screen in a cool, shady place with good air circulation. Shake off any soil and twist off the dried leaves. Store in a dark place in an onion bag until needed. (For more information, see the "Garlic" entry in the "Catalog of Warm-Season Vegetables," page 95.)

Harvest and Use: The pungent bulb was believed by the Romans to instill strength and courage by the Egyptians to relieve headaches and by the Chinese to lower blood pressure. Recent research shows that garlic has strong antibacterial, antiviral, and antifungal properties. It is used to treat respiratory problems and various heart ailments. Plus it is an indispensable ingredient in countless recipes, adding a unique zest to just about everything.

Geranium, Scented
Pelargonium spp.

SOIL: Rich, fertile, well drained, pH 6.0–7.0
LIGHT: Full sun to light shade
HEIGHT: 1–3 feet
PLANT TYPE & HARDINESS: Tender perennial, Zone 10

Scented geraniums are herbs with an identity crisis. First of all, they are not true geraniums but simply share a leaf shape similar to that of members of that genus. Second, the many varieties and species smell like everything else in the garden: lemon, peach, rose, cinnamon, apple, nutmeg, peppermint, chocolate mint, lime, coconut, strawberry, ginger, and orange, to name just a few. Also, they do not even look alike — some have broad leaves and large, showy flowers, while others have small, curly leaves and small flowers.

How to Grow: They are best grown as container plants that can be moved outdoors in summer and overwintered inside. The plants need good air circulation and should not be overwatered. Do not get the leaves wet when you're watering, as the plants are susceptible to the foliage diseases that thrive on moistened foliage. Remove the spent flowers as they shatter. Cut back to maintain shape. The pruned stems can be rooted easily to start new plants. Fertilize the plants with fish emulsion in late winter or spring when new growth begins. Repot every three to five years.

Harvest and Use: The dried leaves make great additions to potpourris and sachets. Of all scented geranium fragrances perhaps the most popular is rose; these sweetly scented leaves can be used to flavor jellies, baked goods, and teas. Harvest the leaves anytime and dry using the refrigerator method. Store in an airtight container.

Goldenrod, Sweet
Solidago odora

SOIL: Well drained, pH 5.5–7.0
LIGHT: Full sun to partial shade
HEIGHT: 2–3 feet
PLANT TYPE & HARDINESS: Perennial, Zones 3–9

Goldenrod, like dandelion, is considered a weed, but many of its sixty species have herbal uses. The easiest to identify and use is sweet goldenrod. It has slender, toothless leaves with distinct parallel veins and tiny transparent dots. The leaves are aromatic and freely emit a delightful licorice scent when bruised. In late summer the plant bears a graceful plume of sunlight yellow flowers.

How to Grow: Goldenrod is increasingly available at nurseries, especially those that specialize in native plants. Set the plants in the back of the garden in soil that has *not* been amended with much organic matter: Soil lean in nutrients actually encourages goldenrod to grow strong, self-supporting stems. Goldenrod is a wonderfully self-reliant plant and thrives without fertilizer, extra water, or extra attention. Other goldenrods worthy of the garden include gray goldenrod *(S. nemoralis)* and European goldenrod *(S. virgaurea).*

Harvest and Use: The bright yellow blossoms add much-needed color to the late-summer garden. Gather the tender leaves of sweet goldenrod as an ingredient in a relaxing, anise-flavored tea. The blossoms are used to create a dye that gives fabrics a gorgeous yellow glow. The entire plant can also be gathered and dried for use in year-round floral arrangements.

Hyssop
Hyssopus officinalis

SOIL: Well drained, pH 6.0–7.0
LIGHT: Full sun to partial shade
HEIGHT: 1–2 feet
PLANT TYPE & HARDINESS: Shrubby perennial, Zones 3–9

Hyssop derives from a Hebrew word meaning "holy herb." The strong, shrubby stems bear numerous spikes of small, purple blossoms from early to late summer that attract bees and butterflies from everywhere. It is primarily grown for its strongly aromatic foliage, which emits a bit of mint, a touch of camphor, and a dash of spicy warmth.

How to Grow: Start seeds indoors about two months before planting out, or direct-sow in spring. Cover the seeds lightly. Space or thin plants to about 1 foot apart. Clip the plants often to encourage a bushy habit. Cut the plants to the ground in fall or early spring and fertilize with a dose of fish emulsion. In the North, divide every four years in spring; in the South, divide every three years in fall. The cultivar 'Grandiflorus' has larger flowers than the species. 'Albus' bears abundant spikes of pure white flowers. 'Sissinghurst' is a dwarf, more compact variety.

Harvest and Use: Gather the fresh leaves and flowers and use sparingly to add zip to garden salads. Toss a few fresh or dried leaves into soups, stews, stuffings, or roasted meats for a warm, sage-mint flavor. Tea made from the flowers is used to control coughs and relieve congestion. An infusion of the leaves and flowers is said to calm nervous stomachs and relieve indigestion. Harvest leaves before the flower buds open; pick the flowers individually and dry with the leaves. Store in airtight containers.

Lavender
Lavandula angustifolia

SOIL:	Well drained, pH 6.5–7.0
LIGHT:	Full sun
HEIGHT:	2–3 feet
PLANT TYPE & HARDINESS:	Perennial, Zones 5–7 (8)

About twenty species of lavender grow over warm hills and alpine ridges from the Mediterranean to India. The shrubby, multi-branched plants are covered with a dense canopy of thin, needle-like gray-green foliage. The leaves are highly aromatic and perfume the air around them with a clean, herbal scent. The flowers are arranged in neat spikes of small lavender-blue blossoms from summer to fall.

How to Grow: Set well-rooted plants in the garden in spring, spacing them about 16 inches apart. Cut established plants back in spring, and remove the flower stalks after the blossoms have faded. Lavender often does poorly in hot, humid weather and is sometimes grown as an annual in the South. The plants are favorites for borders and mass plantings; the most popular varieties are the twenty-inch-tall 'Hidcote' and 'Munstead Dwarf', which reaches to twelve inches.

Harvest and Use: Lavender's Latin name means "to wash" — a reference to its being used to scent soaps and bathwater. Added to smelling salts, cordials, and sachets that repel insects or induce a deep sleep, lavender is also used to flavor vinegar, creams, shampoos, and jellies. Lavender-scented incense creates a restful ambience, and the leaves are essential to most potpourri recipes. Tea made from the flowers is said to induce sleep, relax the body, calm depression, settle upset stomachs, and relieve tension headaches. The most fragrant leaves and flowers come from unfertilized plants grown in full sun. Harvest flowers when they are dry and the buds have begun to break. Gather leaves only from well-established plants.

Lavender Cotton
Santolina chamaecyparissus

SOIL:	Well drained, pH 6.5–7.5
LIGHT:	Full sun to partial shade
HEIGHT:	1–2 feet
PLANT TYPE & HARDINESS:	Perennial, Zones 6–8 (9)

Native to the Mediterranean region, this shrubby perennial has pewter gray, lavenderlike leaves that exude a strong, astringent aroma. In summer the neat, compact plant is peppered with dozens of round yellow or white flowers that contrast nicely to the cool foliage.

How to Grow: Seeds gathered from garden plants should be placed in a plastic bag that also contains a moist growing medium. Seal the bag and chill in the refrigerator for one month. Sow chilled or purchased seeds indoors about two months before planting time. Seeds may also be direct-sown in autumn. Thin or transplant, leaving about 18 inches between plants. Lavender cotton grows well without a lot of attention. Deadhead spent flowers to keep the plants looking neat. Propagate by layering in spring. Transplant to containers in fall and overwinter on a sunny windowsill.

Harvest and Use: In ancient times, the herb was used to cleanse the body of illness and as a fumigant in rooms and dwellings. It was not until the plant became popular in northern Europe and England that its present-day use revealed itself: Lavender cotton is very tolerant of shearing and is easily trimmed into low formal hedges or topiary. When knot gardens and other formal plantings became popular, lavender cotton became the herb of choice for lining gardens. It is still used this way in modern herb gardens, its soft gray foliage serving as a subtle frame for other more colorful plants. Gather the top 10 inches of the plant when the flowers are fully open. Collect the stems into bunches and hang them upside down to dry. You can then use the plants in fragrant holiday wreaths or to make distinctive potpourris.

Lemon balm
Melissa officinalis

SOIL: Well drained, pH 6.5–7.5
LIGHT: Full sun to partial shade
HEIGHT: 1–2 feet
PLANT TYPE & HARDINESS: Perennial, Zones (4) 5–9

The scientific name for lemon balm comes from the Greek word for honeybee, because honeybees come from miles around to sip the flower's sweet nectar. The plant has weak, four-sided stems that give it a floppy appearance. The small whitish flowers appear in clusters in the leaf axils in summer. The leaves are coarsely toothed and rough to the touch, with an intoxicatingly rich lemon scent.

How to Grow: Sow seeds indoors about two months before planting time, or direct-sow in fall. Set plants (or thin them) about 2 feet apart to induce good air circulation and inhibit powdery mildew. After a plant has flowered, cut it back to encourage a second crop of leaves. In fall cut the plant back to the ground. The variety 'Aurea' has deep green leaves edged in gold. 'All Gold' has bright gold young leaves that mature to golden green.

Harvest and Use: The fresh, rough leaves can be rubbed on the skin to repel insects or take the itch from insect bites. An infusion from fresh or dried leaves has a cool, citrus taste that induces restful sleep, lowers fevers, relieves headaches, and calms upset stomachs. The herb is also said to have antiviral and antibacterial properties. The lower leaves have a stronger aroma, gather in summer to add to garden and fruit salads or to season fish and poultry dishes. Use fresh leaves: Lemon balm loses much of its flavor when dried.

Lemongrass
Cymbopogon citratus

SOIL: Rich, well drained, pH 6.5–7.0
LIGHT: Full sun to partial shade
HEIGHT: To six feet
PLANT TYPE & HARDINESS: Tender perennial, Zone 10

Lemongrass is an essential ingredient in many commercially prepared herb teas. It grows in clumps with wide, dark green leaf blades that grow to 36 inches long, in a graceful arch.

How to Grow: Purchase transplants and set them out after the danger of frost has past and night temperatures no longer drop below 50°F. Fertilize every few weeks with an organic fertilizer, such as fish emulsion, and mulch to retain soil moisture. Be sure to keep the soil evenly moist, with extra water during hot, dry periods. North of Zone 10, lift the plants in fall and transplant them to containers; use fresh potting soil around the edges of the rootball. Overwinter indoors on a sunny, draft-free windowsill. In Zone 10 remove old, tattered leaves or those beginning to turn brown. Propagate lemongrass by dividing the clump every few years.

Harvest and Use: The leaves of lemongrass are used either fresh or dried to flavor herb teas, especially those infusions that also incorporate some of the more bitter medicinal herbs. Lemongrass is also a favorite ingredient in many Thai recipes. Gather the fresh leaves from the outside of the clump and dry on a screen in a cool, shady place, or by use of the refrigerator method. Crumble the dried leaves, or use scissors to cut them into small pieces. Store in an airtight jar.

Lemon Verbena
Aloysia triphylla

SOIL: Rich, evenly moist, pH 6.0–6.5
LIGHT: Full sun
HEIGHT: To 10 feet
PLANT TYPE & HARDINESS: Shrubby perennial, Zones 9–10

Lemon verbena is a multi-stemmed woody shrub native to warm regions of Chile and Argentina. In the eighteenth century the plant was brought to Europe by the Spanish and Portuguese. In Victorian times lemon verbena's sweet scented oil was used to create popular perfumes and colognes reputed to induce passion in anyone who smelled them. The herb has long, woody stems with highly aromatic, lance-shaped leaves. The flowers consist of small spikes of tiny white blossoms.

How to Grow: Grow lemon verbena in a container so that you can move it outdoors in summer and indoors in winter. It thrives in rich potting soil amended with compost and fertilized regularly. This vigorous plant should be tip-pruned often to keep it compact and encourage branching. Don't overwater, especially in winter. Plants brought indoors for the winter will drop their leaves and rest for about a month before beginning to grow again.

Harvest and Use: In years past, a popular ingredient in soaps and bath products, lemon verbena has a sweet, earthy, long-lasting lemon fragrance. Tea made from the fresh or dried leaves was said to ease stomach pains and reduce fevers. The oil has insecticidal as well as antibacterial properties. Fresh leaves were also added to stuffings or (sparingly) garden salads. Recently it was discovered that lemon verbena can make skin sensitive to sunlight. Consequently, the herb has fallen out of favor and is now generally replaced in recipes and teas by lemongrass.

Marjoram, Sweet
Origanum majorana

SOIL: Well drained, pH 6.5–7.5
LIGHT: Full sun
HEIGHT: 1–2 feet
PLANT TYPE & HARDINESS: Tender perennial, Zones 9–10

Marjoram is known as one of the subtle herbs. A square-stemmed member of the mint family (called by Greeks "the joy of the mountains"), sweet marjoram is not only an aromatic kitchen herb but also an attractive addition to the garden. The plant has compact, multibranched stems densely covered with small, sweetly fragrant green leaves. Clusters of tiny white or pink flowers are held above the stems in late summer.

How to Grow: Sow the tiny seeds indoors in spring and set them in the garden after the danger of frost has past. When flower buds appear, cut the plant back by about one-third, removing all the flower buds. New leaves will form and extend the harvesttime. Lift the plants in fall before the first frost and repot them in containers. Overwinter on a sunny windowsill.

Harvest and Use: The flavor of sweet marjoram resembles oregano blended with mint. Infusions of fresh or dried leaves relieve congestion and headaches, settle upset stomachs, and instill restful sleep. Its soft flavor enhances stuffings, soups, sauces, and stews, as well as meat dishes and flavored vinegars. Harvest the fresh leaves as needed. The leaves are most flavorful just before the plant blooms. Dry them in the refrigerator for the best flavor. Dried leaves have a softer, almost faint aroma when compared to the fresh leaves.

Mint
Mentha spp.

SOIL: Well drained, pH 6.0–7.0
LIGHT: Full sun to partial shade
HEIGHT: 2–3 feet
PLANT TYPE & HARDINESS: Perennial, Zone 5–9

Mint has found a home in virtually every garden. You can choose from peppermint, spearmint, applemint, gingermint, pennyroyal, lemonmint, and gingermint, to name a few. All mints have square stems graced with toothed, highly aromatic leaves. In summer the small flowers appear clustered in the leaf axils or as a spike on top of the stem.

How to Grow: Propagate transplanting the suckers that rise from the roots, spacing plants about 1 foot apart. To prevent this vigorous plant from taking over the garden, surround with a plastic or metal barrier buried about 10 inches into the ground. When stems become woody, cut them back to encourage more succulent growth. Plant mint in full sun in soil that is evenly moist.

Harvest and Use: Infusions of fresh or dried mint leaves are said to relieve indigestion and reduce cramps. A strong tea can be used as a skin wash, and mint is a favorite ingredient in skin creams and shampoos. Use leaves to flavor drinks, jellies, and desserts as well as soups and sauces. It repels many insects and thus is planted with vegetables and flowers. Gather individual leaves as needed or cut the entire stalk just as the flower buds emerge. Dry by hanging bunches upside down in a cool, dry place. Crumble leaves into airtight jars.

Nasturtium
Tropaeolum majus

SOIL: Evenly moist, well drained, pH 6.0–7.5
LIGHT: Full sun to partial shade
HEIGHT: One foot
PLANT TYPE & HARDINESS: Annual

More than eighty species of nasturtium are native to Central and South America. Spanish conquistadors brought the plant from Peru to Spain, where the tasty flowers became the rage of Europe. Over the centuries many hybrids have been created, some with double flowers, many in brilliant, sunny colors. The stalk attaches to a

base at the center of the leaf blade, a form botanists call *peltate*. The attractive, tubular flowers have a sharp, peppery taste and appear from early summer to frost.

How to Grow: Direct-sow in well-worked soil after all danger of frost has past. Thin plants to about 6 to 9 inches apart for small varieties, 12 to 18 inches for intermediate, and up to 24 inches for large cultivars. Nasturtiums are excellent plants for containers in a sunny spot with good air circulation. Plant seeds in well-aerated potting mix. Once seedlings emerge, keep the soil moist provide afternoon shade. 'Empress of India' is an heirloom variety with dark green leaves stained with lavender and rich red flowers. 'Peach Melba' bears cream-colored flowers marked with a pale red center. The 'Whirlybird' hybrids produce semidouble blossoms in a wide range of colors.

Harvest and Use: Gather nasturtium flowers when they are nearly fully open and add them to garden salads. To make a substitute for capers, gather the green seeds just after the flowers fade and cure them in a jar of seasoned vinegar for six weeks. Plants grown in full sun will produce more flowers and fruit than those grown in shade.

Parsley

Petroselinum crispum

SOIL: Rich, evenly moist, well drained, pH 5.5–6.5

LIGHT: Full sun to partial shade

HEIGHT: One foot

PLANT TYPE & HARDINESS: Biennial

Parsley is like the middle child of the herb garden: always there but never fully appreciated. Three types are commonly grown: Curly parsley *(P. crispum)* has dark green, curled leaves; Italian parsley *(P. crispum* var. *neopolitanum)* has dark green, strongly flavored, flat leaves; and turnip-rooted parsley *(P. crispum* var. *tuberosum)* produces a fleshy, edible root.

How to Grow: Sow seeds outdoors in spring when soil temperatures reach about 50°F. Cover with a light layer of soil. Germination is slow — it can be more than a month before seedlings appear. Thin plants to 8 inches apart. Remove flower shoots and yellowing leaves as they appear. Fertilize with an organic fertilizer or mulch lightly with compost or well-rotted manure. For your winter windowsill garden, sow seeds in a 4-inch pot and place on a sunny sill. Do not overwater. One of the most popular varieties is 'Moss Curled', with its tightly rolled, compact leaves and excellent, zesty flavor.

Harvest and Use: Parsley's leaves contain large amounts of chlorophyll, a natural deodorizer. They can be chewed to eliminate bad breath; in ancient times they were sprinkled in rooms to remove offensive odors. In recipes the herb blends the flavors of disparate seasonings and is used when preparing fish, meats, poultry, sauces, soups, and many other dishes. Use root of turnip-rooted parsley like a turnip or parsnip. Parsley is often planted in the vegetable garden to repel insects. Harvest the leaves anytime they are needed. Dry them in the refrigerator and store in airtight containers.

Passionflower

Passiflora incarnata

SOIL: Fertile, well drained, pH 6.0–6.5

LIGHT: Partial shade

HEIGHT: To 30 feet

PLANT TYPE & HARDINESS: Perennial vine, Zones 7–10

A semivigorous climbing vine, passionflower has soft, glossy, deeply lobed leaves and clasping tendrils that hold the plant to its support. In summer the beautiful flowers consist of lavender-colored petals overlain with numerous reddish-purple filaments and crowned with an attractively complex stigma; these yield to a wonderful tasting yellow, oval fruit about 2 inches long.

How to Grow: Grow plants from seeds or cuttings, or purchase two- to three-year-old container-grown plants from nurseries. Grow plants in soil generously amended with organic matter. Mulch with compost in spring and again in fall. Cut back the plants in early spring to encourage new growth. North of Zone 7, passionflower is best grown in containers that can be moved to the shady patio or deck in summer and overwintered indoors in a sunny spot. Fertilize container-grown specimens with fish emulsion once a month during the warmer months. Prune yearly to contain growth, and remove yellowing leaves as they appear. Repot with fresh soil every three to five years.

Harvest and Use: The dried leaves and flowers of passionflower are quite potent. In very small quantities in infusions they relax the body, relieve pain, calm nervous tension, and induce a restful sleep. Many commercial herb teas use passionflower along with chamomile and valerian to relieve insomnia. The aromatic ripe fruit is eaten fresh, used in fruit salads, or processed into jelly.

Rose, Apothecary's
Rosa gallica 'Officinalis'

SOIL:	Fertile, evenly moist, well drained, pH 6.0–7.0
LIGHT:	Full sun or light shade
HEIGHT:	Three feet
PLANT TYPE & HARDINESS:	Shrub, Zones 4–8

The rose was cultivated by nearly all the major ancient civilizations, from Egypt to India to China. The most valued rose for the herb garden is the apothecary's rose, also called the red rose of Lancaster. It is a bushy, somewhat twiggy shrub with abundant medium green, moderately toothed leaves. In June it is decorated with lush semidouble, soft crimson, intensely fragrant blossoms.

How to Grow: The apothecary's rose is vigorous, hardy, and easy to grow. Plant where it gets full sun with some light afternoon shade. Top-dress with compost in spring, and at the same time fertilize with a balanced organic fertilizer. Once the flowers are past, prune the plant to tidy up its appearance. In early spring remove dead or broken branches as well as any remaining fruit. Another rose suitable for the herb garden is sweetbrier (*Rosa eglanteria*), a rangy shrub with 10-foot-long canes and small, fragrant pink flowers in early summer.

Harvest and Use: Add fresh flower petals to garden salads. Fresh or dried, these petals are also used in infusions to relieve diarrhea and congestion and are said to help depression. The dried petals can be added to potpourris and used to make flavored vinegars, cooking oils, skin creams, rose water, soaps, and shampoos. A strong tea brewed from the fresh petals has been used to relieve itchy, irritated skin. Gather the flowers when they are about half open and gently remove the petals. Dry these quickly on a screen in a cool, shady place or by using the refrigerator method. Store in airtight jars.

Rosemary
Rosmarinus officinalis

SOIL:	Well drained, pH 6.0–6.5
LIGHT:	Full sun
HEIGHT:	2–4 feet
PLANT TYPE & HARDINESS:	Tender perennial, Zones (7) 8–10

Rosemary is an erect, evergreen shrub with thin, needle-like, dark green leaves that are strongly aromatic, penetrating, but pleasantly relaxing. The plant flowers from winter through spring, bearing clusters of small white, pink, or lavender blossoms. There are many varieties, with a range of flower and foliage colors.

How to Grow: Propagate by rooting cuttings or by stem layering. Transplant into well-worked soil after the danger of frost has past. Prune plants after the flowers have faded. In spring remove dead or broken stems. Rosemary may not overwinter well when the weather is wet and cold for prolonged periods. In northern areas it is often grown as a container plant; use a fertile, well-drained potting mix. Rosemary is sensitive to both underwatering and overwatering; you should water only after the soil has dried, but before it *completely* dries out. Control powdery mildew by misting the leaves with cool chamomile tea.

Harvest and Use: The fresh or dried leaves season sauces, stews, soups, and meat dishes. Hot infusions are said to relieve migraine headaches and to relax the body. The herb is also used in lotions and ointments to ease muscle aches and joint pain. Collect the leaves and flowers by snipping 4- to 6-inch sprigs from healthy plants. Sprigs can be gathered into bunches and hung upside down in a cool shady place or placed in freezer bags and frozen. The most aromatic leaves are collected from plants just as they come into flower.

Sage, Garden
Salvia officinalis

SOIL: Well drained, pH 6.0–6.5
LIGHT: Full sun to partial shade
HEIGHT: 1–2 feet
PLANT TYPE & HARDINESS: Perennial, Zones (4) 5–8

The ancients believed that those who used sage would acquire wisdom and achieve immortality. Garden sage is native to the Mediterranean and northern Africa, where it grows into a woody, semi-erect, 3-foot-tall shrub. The evergreen leaves exude a pungent, spicy, slightly sweet scent. Other species include pineapple sage *(S. elegans)*, with its bright red, tubular flowers and pineapple-scented leaves, and Spanish sage *(S. lavandulifolia)*, which has narrow, gray-green leaves with the aroma of lavender and spice.

How to Grow: Propagate from cuttings taken in early fall or divide older, established plants. Sage can be grown from seeds, but it takes at least two years to produce a useful specimen. Plant in well-worked soil and mulch with compost or well-rotted manure. Sage does not grow well when winters are wet or springs are moist and cool. In late fall mound dry mulch over the plants to help them overwinter. Some excellent cultivars include 'Kew Gold', with bright yellow leaves; 'Icterina', with green leaves edged in gold; and 'Purpurea', a vigorous plant that bears large, richly aromatic leaves tinged with violet.

Harvest and Use: The freshly gathered leaves of garden sage make a wonderful addition to omelets, breads, vegetables, meats, sauces, stuffings, and soups. They can also be blended with butter or soft cheese to make aromatic spreads. The dried leaves do not smell as sharp and clean as the fresh but are still quite tasty. An infusion of the fresh leaves is used as a gargle for sore throats; the oil is used in soaps, lotions, creams, and shampoos.

Savory, Winter
Satureja montana

SOIL: Well drained, pH 6.5–7.0
LIGHT: Full sun
HEIGHT: 6–12 inches
PLANT TYPE & HARDINESS: Perennial, Zones 6–9

Winter savory is among the most aromatic of all herbs, with a strong spicy flavor reminiscent of pepper. It is native to the Mediterranean region. The Romans, who used it to flavor many dishes, brought it north to England. Winter savory is a shrubby, compact-growing plant with narrow, dark green foliage. The leaves are evergreen in the southern part of its range, semi-evergreen in the northern.

How to Grow: Many people purchase plants from the garden center to get a jump on the season, but winter savory can also be grown from seeds. Sow indoors in early spring in flats, and cover lightly or direct sow in late spring. Space or thin the plants to about 1 foot apart. Summer savory *(S. hortensis)* is an annual with slightly longer leaves than winter savory, but it is grown and used in the same way.

Harvest and Use: Infusions of winter savory were once used to relieve the discomfort of indigestion and as a gargle for sore throats. A strong tea made from the fresh leaves was also used as a skin wash to relieve the itch of insect bites. Today the leaves season prepared meats, such as sausage, vegetable dishes, and stuffings, and they are often blended with butter or soft cheese. Harvest the fresh leaves as needed. Collect leaves for drying just before the flower buds open; dry them on screens in a cool, shady place, or in the refrigerator. Store in airtight containers.

Tarragon
Artemisia dracunculus

SOIL: Well drained, pH 6.0–7.0
LIGHT: Partial to full shade
HEIGHT: 1–2 feet
PLANT TYPE & HARDINESS: Perennial, Zones (4) 5–7

Tarragon is but one of three hundred species of aromatic herbs belonging to the genus Artemisia and collectively called wormwoods (a German word meaning "preserver of the mind"). Tarragon has a somewhat bitter but pleasing taste and an ability to produce a warm sensation in the body. The plant has pliant, sometimes woody stems and thin, green, aromatic leaves.

How to Grow: Plants should be purchased from commercial nurseries or propagated by dividing established plantings. The name tarragon comes from the French word for "little dragon," and refers to the shape of the roots. These roots tend to entangle themselves over the course of a few growing seasons, making division of the plants not simply a method of propagation, but also a necessity for the continued welfare of the plants. Container-grown tarragon is a good choice for the winter windowsill garden. In acid soils, add some wood ashes to help keep the pH in the appropriate range.

Harvest and Use: Tarragon is used to stimulate the appetite and to flavor mustards, soups, poultry, eggs, dressings, and stuffings. In the bath it is added to soaps, shampoos, and lotions and even toothpaste. To harvest, cut the stems from plants in early summer in the cool of the morning; repeat at the end of the season. Dry the leaves in the refrigerator or freeze for later use, and then store them in an airtight container. Leaves prepared by traditional drying methods often lose a good measure of their flavor.

Thyme
Thymus spp.

SOIL: Well drained, pH 5.5–6.5
LIGHT: Full sun to partial shade
HEIGHT: 2–6 inches
PLANT TYPE & HARDINESS: Perennial, Zones 5–9

The most popular thymes have small, mouse-ear leaves that are strongly aromatic. The scent of common thyme is so pungently spicy that it seems to lend acuity to the senses. Other thymes mimic the aromas of lemon, caraway, and nutmeg. Many thymes are low-growing or creeping plants that are at home in the herb garden, in crevices, or cascading over walls and rock gardens.

How to Grow: Sow seeds indoors in flats, keeping the soil just above room temperature; they can also be direct-sown in late spring. Transplant or thin the plants to 1 foot apart. As the plants become established and woody, they will benefit from being divided every three to five years. If leaf production declines, replace plants rather than divide them. Mulch in late fall with leaves, pine needles, or straw.

Harvest and Use: Thyme has been used since ancient times to treat a number of complaints, including anxiety. Today warm infusions are said to relieve congestion, relieve the pain of headaches, and ease stomach complaints. A blend of sage, lavender, and thyme eases coughs. As a culinary herb, it was a strong but pliant taste that both supports and accents the flavor of many dishes. The fresh or dried leaves can be added to sauces, stews, meats, fish, poultry, eggs, dressings, and stuffings. Thyme also mixes well with other seasonings, such as garlic and lemon. Harvest the leaves anytime and then dry them in the refrigerator for best flavor. Plant near eggplant, potatoes, or tomatoes to help repel unwanted insects. The delicate flowers of thyme also attract honeybees.

Violet, Sweet
Viola odorata

SOIL: Rich, evenly moist, well drained, pH 5.5–6.5
LIGHT: Full sun to full shade
HEIGHT: 4–6 inches
PLANT TYPE & HARDINESS: Perennial, Zones 4–9

Although today violets are thought of more as denizens of the perennial border, the Greeks believed the plant grew from the place where Orpheus slept, and after his exile, Napoleon pledged to the population of France that he would return with the violets.

How to Grow: Propagate by dividing established plantings and transplant to 1 foot apart. Violets do best in cool, partly shaded places with no midday sun in summertime. Plant them beneath deciduous trees or in shady, rocky corners. Sweet violets make excellent plants for a woodland garden or meadow; they also serve as a cheerful companion to aromatic herbs. Some of the best cultivars include 'Royal Robe', a 6-inch-tall hybrid with softly scented, rich purple blooms in spring, and sometimes again in fall; and 'White Czar', with its deep green leaves and large, fragrant white flowers in spring. Johnny jump-up *(V. tricolor)* is a close relative with small but perky, pansylike flowers painted with shades of purple, yellow, and cream.

Harvest and Use: Often used as a catalyst for other herbs, violet is blended with such plants as thyme, mint, or chamomile, for a combined effect greater than the sum of the parts. The fresh flowers are also added to garden salads, where their delicate, slightly sweet aroma is wonderful. The fresh or dried blossoms can be added to herb teas, soaps, lotions, and shampoos, or blended into jellies, desserts, and liqueurs. Collect the flowers and dry them in the refrigerator. Store them in an airtight container; they lose flavor quickly if exposed to air.

Wintergreen
Gaultheria procumbens

SOIL: Rich, evenly moist well-drained, pH 4.5-5.5
LIGHT: Full sun to full shade
HEIGHT: Four inches
PLANT TYPE & HARDINESS: Perennial, Zones 3–6 (7)

Wintergreen is one of my favorite herbs, in part because of its cool candy-like flavor and in part because the wild plant often prefers the less visited, more peaceful places in the forest. The soothing aroma of wintergreen is warm yet cool — an herbal paradox. The plant is a low-growing evergreen with glossy, dark green leaves and white, lantern-shaped flowers in spring and summer. The delectable, shiny red berries have snow-white flesh and are one of nature's nicest nibbles.

Harvest and Use: The leaves and fruit of wintergreen contain methyl salicylate, a compound related to aspirin. A warm infusion relieves headaches and eases the pain of sore muscles and joints. Very strong teas (bruise leaves thoroughly) can also be used as a skin wash that cools as well as soothes tired and sore muscles and joints. The dried leaves have no flavor. Wintergreen essential oil is used in lotions, ointments, soaps, shampoos, and bath oils.

How to Grow: Purchase plants from a commercial nursery that grows its own stock. Do not collect plants from the wild. Once a planting is established, propagation can be accomplished by separation of suckers, layering, or division. The plants grow best in moist woodlands beneath trees that acidify the soil, such as hemlock, pine, spruce, and fir. In the backyard plant wintergreen beneath or near rhododendrons, azaleas, or blueberries. Lightly mulch with pine needles in fall and again in spring. Wintergreen does best with afternoon shade, especially in the southern zones. Give plants extra water during hot, dry periods.

Woodruff, Sweet
Galium odoratum

SOIL: Rich, evenly moist, well drained, pH 5.0–6.5
LIGHT: Partial to full shade
HEIGHT: Six inches
PLANT TYPE & HARDINESS: Perennial, Zones 4–8

Sweet woodruff is an inconspicuous herb most of the time, growing in ground cover profusion beneath the trees. Indeed, it traditionally signified humility, because it grew so unassumingly. The ray-shaped leaves are attached to the stem in whorls to form a lovely blanket. The surprise comes in late spring or early summer, when exquisitely small, star-shaped white flowers appear like myriad miniature constellations above the carpet of green. The blossoms exude a fragrance that is as sweet as dessert.

How to Grow: Sweet woodruff is not easy to grow from seeds, as it takes a long time to germinate. It is thus usually purchased from nurseries or obtained by dividing established plantings in spring or fall. The plants do best in shady, woodland areas, where they grow into a thick but softly textured ground cover, excellent for a natural garden. Sweet woodruff also grows well in crevices along walkways or shady rock gardens.

Harvest and Use: Sweet woodruff gets its name from the Greek word for milk, because the herb was once used in the cheesemaking process. The leaves and flowers are dried and made into infusions said to ease stomach discomforts, relax the nerves, and encourage restful sleep. The fresh flowers are added to white wines to impart a vanilla bouquet; after a few days the wine is strained and served. The herb is also used in potpourris and-linen-closet sachets. Gather the foliage throughout the growing season and dry in the refrigerator or in a warm, shady place. Crumble and store in airtight containers.

Yarrow
Achillea millefolium

SOIL: Rich, well drained, pH 5.5–6.5
LIGHT: Full sun to light shade
HEIGHT: 1–2 feet
PLANT TYPE & HARDINESS: Perennial, Zones 3–9

Yarrow has often been regarded as having spiritual qualities, an aid to clear thought and divine inspiration. Its botanic name honors Achilles, who used the herb to treat his wounded soldiers during the battle of Troy. Yarrow produces clumps of strong stems lightly decorated with ferny, pungently aromatic foliage. The tiny flowers appear in attractive, flat-topped clusters in early summer through fall.

How to Grow: Sow seeds indoors two months before planting out. Set the seeds in a moist medium, but do not cover them. Keep them moist until germination occurs. Transplant in spring, spacing the plants about 1 foot apart. Plants grown in full sun will produce more aromatic leaves and have stronger stems. Divide every three years: North of Zone 7, divide established clumps in spring; do so in fall from Zone 7 south. Two excellent varieties are 'Cerise Queen', which sports sprays of pastel pink flowers, and 'Lilac Beauty', with pale pink blossoms flushed with lavender.

Harvest and Use: Poultices made from the bruised, fresh leaves of yarrow help stop bleeding, reduce swelling, and soothe insect bites and stings. Warm infusions of the leaves induce sweating and purify the body. Note that this bitter-tasting herb does not agree with some people and should be used with caution. Harvest the entire stalk, clipping the stem near the ground just as the flowers are opening. Strip the leaves from the stems and dry them in the refrigerator. Hang the stems and flower heads in a cool, shady place until dry. Use the leaves in infusions, the dried flowers in arrangements.

The Bountiful Berry Patch

Fruit from the backyard berry patch marks the passing of the seasons in ways so pleasant they stay in your memory for years: warm spring evenings when dinner is an oversize serving of strawberry shortcake, mornings when toast with freshly made strawberry jam greets you. Endless summer afternoons picking blueberries are followed by evenings eating slice after slice of tart blueberry pie. Sweet raspberries harvested from drooping canes instantly disappear as often as they get dropped in the berry basket. And in summer and fall bunches of grapes slow cook into jelly for savoring throughout the winter. Fruits and berries soothe the palette like flowers soothe the eyes. Yet these delicious additions to the backyard garden are not planted nearly as often as their floral counterparts. Sometimes these tasty treats are left out of the garden because people think they take up too much room. Actually a bountiful berry patch can be quite unobtrusive. Strawberries can nestle among perennials in the border or cascade from a strawberry jar or other container. Blueberries in the rock garden provide flavorful summertime treats as well as a brilliant display of scarlet foliage in autumn. And a grape arbor in the backyard is as much a shady retreat as source of sweet fruit.

If you once grew berries years ago but gave it up for one reason or another, you just might wish to try growing them again. Research stations across the country have created some wonderful new varieties tailored to a variety of different regions and growing conditions making the berry patch even easier and more bountiful than ever.

In addition to all these reasons to put in a berry patch, grapes, strawberries, brambles, and blueberries are usually inexpensive to buy and easy to grow, and they reward you with a range of delicacies that will make you happy you have taste buds. Just about anywhere you live you can plant berries that will make meals a little sweeter and the passage of the seasons a little more special.

Grapes: An Introduction

There are about sixty-five species of grape in the world, the majority native to the temperate regions of North America. Of these many climbing vines, only a few have become important producers of fruit. The American grape *(Vitis labrusca)*, also called the fox grape or skunk grape, is a highly variable species native to temperate eastern North America. It is from this species that the famous 'Concord' grape arose. The muscadine grape *(Vitis rotundifolia)*, also called the Bullace, is native to southern regions of eastern North America and is one of the few species that thrive in climates with hot, humid summers and cool, moist winters. Muscadine grapes have become synonymous with the South, the most famous variety being the 'Scuppernong', which has been cultivated since about 1760.

The dominant species of the cold regions of northern North America is the aptly named frost grape *(Vitis riparia)*, whose abundance along the cold Canadian coast may have inspired Leif Erickson to name the New World Vinland. The frost grape is not itself a very tasty fruit, but when crossed with the American grape yields varieties that allow northern gardeners to finally enjoy flavorful grapes. The European grape *(Vitis vinifera)*, native to the Old World, is the species that gave rise to the massive vineyards and wineries of Europe. The most economically important grape in the world, many of its primary varieties require specific, precise conditions to grow well.

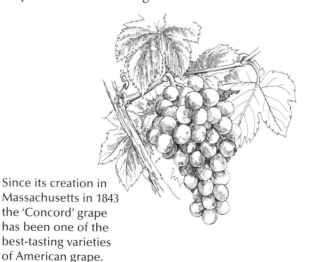

Since its creation in Massachusetts in 1843 the 'Concord' grape has been one of the best-tasting varieties of American grape.

American Grapes (*Vitis labrusca*)

American grapes and their varieties grow best in the temperate regions of North America, including the northeastern states, the Great Lakes region, and sections of many western states. The conditions that determine whether American grapes will thrive in any given location are the climate in general, the microclimate of the vineyard site, and the soil type.

CLIMATE

Varieties of American grapes require cold winters balanced by warm summers to grow well. American cultivars generally need about 160 frost-free days to properly mature; hybrids of American and European grapes need about 10 days longer. Areas where the climate is modified by large bodies of water, such as the coasts and around the Great Lakes, generally provide the conditions American grapes need. In general, though, their range corresponds roughly to Zones 4 through 7. Some cultivars do well even farther south.

MICROCLIMATE

Even a quick glance will tell you that most orchards and vineyards are established on land that slopes. This is, in fact, one of the secrets of growing the best crops. Sloping land does not allow cold air to collect in any one spot but instead channels it downslope, where it pools. Positioning your vineyard on a slope thus reduces the chance of damage from early-spring or fall frosts.

For the slope to best perform its funneling function, it should be as open as possible, with no large obstructions that could hinder air flow. Siting your vineyard on a slope also helps control many of the common diseases to which grapes are susceptible, including black rot, downy mildew, and powdery mildew. The increased air circulation inhibits the growth of these diseases. Many people favor south-facing slopes over others, because southern exposures warm faster in the morning and in early spring and stay warmer later into fall.

SOIL

American grapes grow best in sandy and gravelly soils that have abundant amounts of organic matter. The soil (topsoil and subsoil) should also be deep — at least 4 feet — to ensure the best drainage. Grape varieties grown on sandy loams often ripen faster, have a higher sugar content, and taste better than those grown on other soils. Still, grapes will grow well in many different types of soil, provided they have abundant organic matter and are well drained.

PLANTING THE VINEYARD

Preparation of the soil should ideally begin about a year before the vines are planted. The best results can be expected from sites that have been cultivated regularly and routinely had large amounts of organic matter added over the course of cultivation. The organic matter can come in the form of cover crops turned into the soil, sheet composting of leaves and such, or the addition of compost or manures. Soil pH should be modified to about 6.0.

Purchase one-year-old number-one grade vines and set them into rows in early spring, soon after the soil can be worked. Spacing distance depends on the vigor of the grape variety you choose. The most vigorous cultivars, such as the 'Niagara', 'Fredonia', and 'Concord', should be spaced 10 feet apart for maximum yield. Slower-growing varieties, such as the 'Delaware' and 'Catawba', should be planted 7 feet apart. Most other varieties will grow and produce well when spaced 8 feet apart.

For most home vineyards, the soil 2 to 3 feet in front of and behind the vines should be covered with an organic mulch; use sod to cover the remaining soil between rows. Thoroughly till the soil before planting, and dig a hole twice as large as the rootball of each vine. Trim the roots of bareroot stock to remove any broken or extralong roots. Set the plant in the hole at a depth matching that which it enjoyed at the nursery. Spread the roots evenly in the hole and cover.

SOIL MANAGEMENT

Once your vines are planted, it is essential that you maintain the soil in a fertile state to ensure healthy plants that yield well. The most common way to maintain soil fertility in the vineyard is to regularly add organic matter to the soil. This can be accomplished by raising and tilling under cover crops, or adding a layer of mulch.

Cover crops are most often used in large vineyards. In the Great Lakes region, where their use in vineyards has been honed to an art form, an ingenious and very productive regime employs rotating soybeans and rye grass. Soybeans are planted when the grapes bloom in spring and tilled under in late August when annual rye is sown.

For small vineyards an excellent way to add organic matter to the soil is to add a mulch of well composted, strawy manure around the plants in fall. Good old regular compost is also an excellent mulch for the vineyard, but some people insist — although this is a matter of some debate — that vineyards amended with composted manure produces better-tasting grapes than any other mulch.

THE BEST FERTILIZER FOR GRAPES

If you walk through the fertilizer section of many nurseries and garden centers, the options can overwhelm you. It may comfort you to know, however, that despite all these choices, the best fertilizer for grapes is one that has been around for generations: manure.

Well-rotted manure, or compost made with large amounts of strawy manure, is, quite simply, unbeatable. Apply the compost as a mulch during the growing season. In fall, apply either manure compost or straight, well-rotted manure at the rate of 15 to 20 pounds per 100 square feet. In most cases no other fertilization is required. Vineyards given this treatment consistently yield up to 30 percent more fruit than those fertilized with commercial preparations.

For fairly small plants grapes have a lot of parts, each with its own name. Knowing these names is important so that you don't snip something you shouldn't.

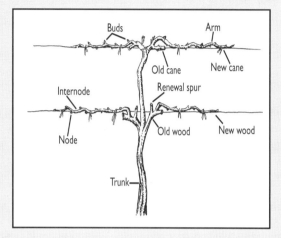

Trunk: the unbranched portion of the grape vine's primary stem

Arm: a branch extending from the trunk

Old wood: the parts of the grape vine older than one year

New wood: the parts of a vine that are younger than one year

Shoot: new growth that bears leaves

Cane: a leafless shoot that has gone dormant

Node: the joint on a shoot or cane where buds develop

Internode: the smooth section of stem between two nodes

Primary bud: the largest bud at the node

Secondary bud: a bud at the node that is smaller than a primary bud

Eye: the collective name for all the buds on any given node

Lateral: a side branch on a shoot or cane

Spur: a cane that has been pruned back to one or two buds

TRAINING THE VINES

There are almost as many ways to train grape vines as there are varieties. So many, in fact, that at first glance it may be difficult to determine just how you should train your vines. In the end, though, selecting a training system is easier than it looks, because each method was invented to maximize the production of specific types of grapes growing under specific conditions. The choices for growing great American grapes in most regions can be whittled down to three: the Four-Arm Kniffen System, the Hudson River Umbrella System, and the Munson System.

The Four-Arm Kniffen System

This is the most popular system for training American grapes, though not always the most productive. It *is* good for those areas that have optimum climates for grape growing.

To build a Four-Arm Kniffen System, start with wooden posts 8 to 10 feet long with a diameter of about 6 inches. Set the end posts into holes spaced 25 to 30 feet apart and deep enough to allow 6 feet of post to remain above ground. Bracing the end posts will inhibit them from sagging toward each other. String two lengths of metal wire (9 to 11 gauge) between the end posts on the upslope side of the post, one length 6 feet above the ground, the other 3 feet. Secure the wire to the end posts with fence staples. Build the trellis before you plant the vines, if possible.

Pruning techniques under the Kniffen System vary, depending on the season. After planting, select the strongest cane and cut it back to two buds. Remove all other canes. Erect a 5- to 6-foot stake near the vine so the new growth can be trained to it throughout the growing season. Some people allow only one shoot to develop; others allow two, in case one shoot should die. Do no other pruning during the first season.

In the second season prune away all side branches from the cane and remove the stake. If the cane reaches above the top wire, cut the vine a few inches above the wire and tie the cane to the wire with twine. If the vine has not reached the upper wire but seems vigorous, remove all side branches from the strongest cane. Cut the cane above the top of the lower wire and secure it with twine. Leave

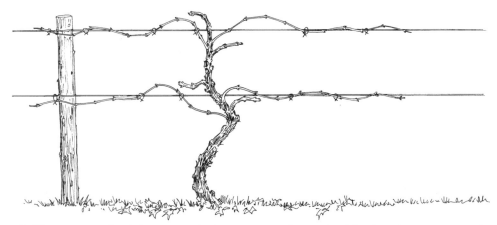

The Four-Arm Kniffen system of training grapes is the most popular method for American grapes such as 'Concord' and 'Niagara'. It provides reliable support for the fruiting vines while maximizing production.

the stake in place to train the stem to the top wire. If the vine has not reached the upper wire and seems weak, remove all but the strongest cane, cutting it back to two buds; begin the process again.

For the third season select the four strongest canes nearest and to either side of the wires. Remove all other growth, leaving a spur just below each of the four selected canes. Cut back the selected canes on the lower wire to six buds, those on the upper wire to four. As the season progresses, tie the canes to the wire with twine.

The Hudson River Umbrella System

Long ago it was noticed that the most fruitful vines of wild American grapes were those that dangled and swung from the treetops. The Hudson River Umbrella System thus begins with the support of the Kniffen method, but adapts it to create

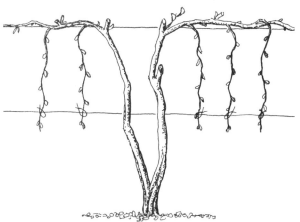

The Hudson River Umbrella system imitates the way wild grapes grow with fruiting vines hanging beneath sturdy, older canes.

an environment similar to that in the treetops. Vines trained to the Hudson River System are easier and faster to prune, and often more productive, than vines trained to other methods. This system is especially recommended for vigorous varieties, such as the 'Concord'.

Pruning differs from the Kniffen System in that two primary canes are used. These canes are allowed to grow to the top wire, where they are attached. Arms are then allowed to grow along the top wire, while shoots hang from the arms and are tied to the lower wire. This method of training provides excellent air circulation as well as maximum infiltration of sunlight. The vines are also easier to prune, because most cuts are made at eye level and fewer are needed.

The Munson System

This method consists of posts mounted with crossbars so that the finished structure resembles a telephone pole. Two to four lengths of wire are strung between the crossbars. The arms of the vines are then trained along the wires, with the fruiting shoots allowed to hang down. This type of support system is popular with many homeowners who grow a variety of grape cultivars because vines with different growing habits can be trained to the same support and do equally well. As an added bonus other garden plants, such as leafy vegetables, can be grown beneath the vines, making this system ideal for folks with small spaces.

PRUNING MATURE VINES

Pruning the vineyard for three or more years while the vines are getting established initiates the gardener into the art of grape pruning. During this time the individuality of each vine becomes evident; some are strong and vigorous, while others only a few feet away may be much weaker. No general rule can tell you how many buds to leave on each vine. Only experience can do that. There *are* some general principles to follow, however, as you learn the intricacies of your beloved vines:

- Each arm of your vines must have a complementary spur near its base, to provide fruiting wood for the next growing season.
- The best time to prune is in late winter or early spring, when the vine lies dormant and the buds have yet to show signs of swelling.
- Remove all unnecessary wood. The number of buds you leave on each cane will vary according to the training system you use and the vigor of the vine. Vigorous vines trained to the Kniffen System can have as many as ten buds per cane, while the same vines trained to an Umbrella System should have five.

Pruning Neglected Vines

Vines just aren't happy standing still. If left to their own devices they would climb to the tops of the highest trees in search of the perfect sunny spot. This viney habit is why grapes must be pruned every year. If they're not, the best fruit will be produced farther and farther from the main stem, and within a few years a once-tidy vine will become a rangy beast. The rejuvenation process is not a quick fix; it takes as long to complete as it does to train new plants.

In spring select the four best-fruiting canes that are close to the main trunk and remove the rest. Trim these four canes to three to five buds each and allow them to grow as usual. The next spring, again select the best canes that are close to the main stem, trim to three to five buds, and grow as usual. After the third or fourth season of this regimen, your vine should once more be manageable.

Even neglected grapevines, with a little help, can be brought back to a productive, healthy state.

WHEN TO PICK

Believe it or not, it isn't always easy to tell when a grape is ripe. Unfortunately, once it is picked, it will neither develop any deeper color nor get any sweeter. So it is very important to know just when to harvest your crop. There are indications to tell you just when your grapes have fully ripened. Many varieties do not ripen uniformly but a little at a time, which means that frequent checking of your vineyard is essential.

Grapes that are to be used fresh for eating should be picked when a few of them begin to loosen and fall from the bunch. Another way to gauge ripeness is to sneak a taste of a berry or two from bunches that you suspect are ripe. I like this method the best.

The harvest time for grapes used for wine or juice is later than for grapes used for fresh eating. Wine and juice grapes can be left on the vine a few days longer than those for fresh eating, which allows a maximum amount of sugars to be deposited in the fruit. Grapes used for jelly should be picked a few days *before* those for fresh eating. These slightly sour grapes produce an attractive, clear jelly with no cloudiness or crystals. This knowledge can come in handy in regions where early frosts often end the growing season before the grapes are fully ripe. These can then be harvested and processed into jars and jars of tasty grape jelly.

Muscadine Grapes (*Vitis rotundifolia*)

Muscadine grapes are one of those plants, like okra and pecans, that are fondly identified with the South. In appearance, muscadine fruits are large compared to other species; the berries of some varieties resemble small plums more than they do grapes. Their flavor is as distinctive as their size, the juicy pulp replete with complex mixtures of sweet and earthy aromas. Some folks love the flavor of muscadines right away, while for others it is an acquired taste. Muscadines produce smaller but more numerous clusters of fruit than other grapes, with yields per vine ranging from around thirty pounds to more than seventy.

The plants are quite vigorous and are hardy in Zones 6 through 9; fruits ripen from mid-September to early October. They grow best along a belt extending from North Carolina southwest to Texas, roughly corresponding to Zone 8. The vines are extremely resistant to disease, and very few insects bother them. Some varieties are self-pollinating, though other, all-female cultivars need to be planted with another pollinating variety.

SOIL AND FERTILITY REQUIREMENTS

Muscadine grapes grow best in a fertile, well-drained sandy loam with a pH of about 6.0, but they will tolerate a wide range of soils, from moist to dry and sandy to clayey. Like other grapes, muscadines do not require extensive applications of fertilizer, but they do need a bit more than their northern cousins. Mulching with rotted manure or rich compost in spring and again in fall is all they require for the first three years. Older vines may need an application of an organic, high-nitrogen fertilizer, such as fish emulsion, just after fruit set. Chlorosis of the leaves is common in alkaline soils and can be remedied by applying chelated iron.

TRAINING AND PRUNING

Whereas American grapes should be planted in early spring, muscadine varieties are best planted in winter, between late December and early February. Select one- to two-year-old plants and set them out in the same way as described for American grapes, but space them 15 feet apart.

Train the vines to a single wire strung between posts spaced 20 feet apart or to an overhead trellis system. This consists of an arbor built of strong vertical posts set at the corners of a 15-foot square. Crossbeams are then attached to the posts 6 or 7 feet above the ground. Ten-gauge wire is strung at 3-foot intervals between the crossbeams. Trail the vines up the posts to the overhead wires.

Prune in the same way as American grapes, with the exception of allowing the spurs on muscadine vines to branch. Prune the spurs to the strongest three or four stems, then prune these to two buds when dormant.

HARVESTING AND STORING MUSCADINES

The yield of muscadines increases with the age of the vineyard, reaching its maximum at about six years. The individual berries in the small clusters ripen at different times, so the vines must be checked almost daily at harvest time. The grapes of most varieties change color as they mature, and the skin of ripe berries yields slightly to the touch of a finger. Store the fruit in a cool place at 55 to 60°F.

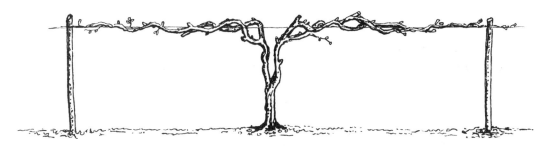

An easy-to-build training system for muscadine grapes consists of a single wire strung between posts set 20 feet apart.

European Grapes
(Vitis vinifera)

European grapes are grown throughout the warmer regions of the world, where their distinctive juices are used to produce myriad flavorful wines. Some of the most famous grape varieties are Europeans, including 'Chardonnay', 'Chenin Blanc', 'Pinot Noir', 'Zinfandel', and the delicious table grape 'Thompson Seedless'.

Despite their fame these grapes have a reputation for being temperamental to grow, with exacting climate requirements and a penchant for diseases and pests. European grapes do best in semi-arid, subtropical or Mediterranean climates where the summers are warm and dry (75-85°F) and the winters cool and wet (35-50°F). Worldwide they grow well in Europe, Africa, the Middle East, North and South America, and Australia. In North America, European varieties do best in California, Arizona, and parts of Texas, though they are planted in many other states as well.

SOIL AND FERTILITY

Like other grapes, European varieties grow best in deep sandy loam soils liberally amended with organic matter. Apply a mulch of rotted manure or compost at the beginning of the growing season. An application of an organic source of nitrogen, such as fish emulsion, is used just after fruit set, and another layer of rotted manure or compost is spread after harvest. Zinc deficiencies have been noticed in grapes grown in some arid soils. Correct by painting pruning cuts with a solution of four ounces of zinc sulfate dissolved in one quart of water.

TRAINING AND PRUNING

Prepare and plant European grapes in the same manner as American varieties. European grapes are often trained to a Kniffen System, but small vineyards frequently use another system called the Vase Support. After planting, the vine is trained to a 6-foot stake. It's pruned to about four canes, each with about ten buds. The spurs are small and located at the base of each cane, though not all varieties have fruitful spurs at the cane base. For the latter varieties — for example, 'Thompson Seedless' and such small-fruited varieties as 'Pinot Noir' and 'Chardonnay' — the vines are pruned using a technique called cane pruning where from twenty-five to thirty buds are left on each vine after cutting. After six to ten years, when the vines have become self-supporting, the stakes are removed.

TOP GRAPE PRODUCING STATES

Grapes are produced all over the United States yet different kinds of grapes are grown in different regions. American grapes, which include such varieties as 'Concord', 'Niagara', 'Delaware', and 'Catawba', are most popular in the Northeast, Great Lakes, and Northwest. The top-producing states are New York, Washington, Michigan, Pennsylvania, Ohio, Iowa, and New Jersey.

European grapes, which favor the warm, dry regions of the country, make up the bulk of grape production, sometimes constituting over 90% of each year's total harvest. The top-producing states of European grapes include California and Arizona with notable yields in Michigan, Arkansas, Ohio, Pennsylvania, Washington, and New York.

Muscadine grapes tolerate the heat and humidity of the Gulf and South Atlantic coasts. The top-producing states of muscadines include North Carolina and South Carolina.

THINNING EUROPEAN GRAPES

The climates that European grapes favor are also subject to years of drought. To guard against this, more buds are left on the vine after pruning than are needed to produce a good crop in years of normal rainfall. If the subsequent season is dry, all the fruit clusters are then left on the vine to ensure as large a crop as possible. If there is adequate rain, however, up to 25 percent of the clusters are removed shortly after fruit set. This increases berry size and thereby improves the overall quality of the fruit produced on the vine.

Gallery of the Best Grapes

AMERICAN GRAPES
(VITIS LABRUSCA)

V. 'Beta'

HARDINESS:	Zones 3-6
FLAVOR:	Tangy, definite wild quality
FRUIT COLOR:	Blue
FRUIT QUALITY:	Good, medium-size berries
RIPENS:	Early to mid-Sept.

The product of a cross between American and frost grapes, 'Beta' is noted for being one of the hardiest of all varieties; it survives -40°F. Vines are vigorous and yield dependable crops year after year, even in the North Country. Crops ripen well even during cool summers. Needs a growing season of just over 100 days. Not a good table grape. This is a good grape to train to an arbor where it is both productive and decorative.

Best Uses: Juice, jelly, wine

V. 'Canadice'

HARDINESS:	Zones 5-7 (8)
FLAVOR:	Sweet, fruity, with a touch of spice
FRUIT COLOR:	Red
FRUIT QUALITY:	Excellent, medium-size seedless berries in large clusters
RIPENS:	Mid-Aug. to late Sept.

Often planted as a replacement for 'Delaware', this variety bears reliably good crops of outstanding quality. Produces large bunches with high-quality flavor similar to 'Delaware', though vines of 'Canadice' are much more vigorous. Fruit ripens over a long period and keeps well on the vine. Introduced in 1977, the vines have some resistance to mildew and black rot.

Best Uses: Eating, juice, jelly, wine

V. 'Catawba'

HARDINESS:	Zones 5-7 (8) (-10°F)
FLAVOR:	Sweet, rich
FRUIT COLOR:	Copper-red
FRUIT QUALITY:	Excellent, large to medium-size berries
RIPENS:	Late Sept. to early Oct.

'Catawba' produces good crops of berries in well-formed clumps. The vines are moderately vigorous though susceptible to powdery mildew in warm, humid summers. These grapes store well.

Best Uses: Eating, wine, jelly, juice

V. 'Concord'

HARDINESS:	Zones (4) 5-8
FLAVOR:	Excellent; sweet and clean grape taste
FRUIT COLOR:	Blue-black
FRUIT QUALITY:	Excellent, medium-size berries
RIPENS:	Late Sept. to early Oct.

Derived from native wild grapes around Concord, Massachusetts, in 1843, 'Concord' has been the most popular North American grape for well over a century. It is vigorous and grows well in many soils.

Best Uses: Eating, wine, jelly, juice

V. 'Concord Seedless'

HARDINESS:	Zones 5-9
FLAVOR:	Excellent; sweet, clean
FRUIT COLOR:	Blue-black
FRUIT QUALITY:	Excellent, medium-size berries
RIPENS:	Mid to late Sept.

This tasty (similar to 'Concord') seedless grape is good for northern and southern growers. The vines are slower to establish than those of the 'Concord', but the berries ripen a bit earlier.

Best Uses: Eating, pies, jelly, juice, wine

V. 'Fredonia'

HARDINESS:	Zones (3) 4-9
FLAVOR:	Excellent; sweet and spicy
FRUIT COLOR:	Blue-black
FRUIT QUALITY:	Excellent, large to medium-size berries
RIPENS:	Early to mid-Sept.

A very hardy hybrid, 'Fredonia' produces heavy crops of sweet berries on strong vines. The entire bunch usually ripens at the same time, before the first hard frosts of northern areas.

Best Uses: Eating, wine, jelly, juice

V. 'Himrod'

HARDINESS:	Zones 5-8
FLAVOR:	Excellent; sweet, clean, and delicate
FRUIT COLOR:	Yellow-green
FRUIT QUALITY:	Excellent, large berries
RIPENS:	Mid-Aug. to early Sept.

Hardy seedless variety bears very heavy crops of sweet fruit in late summer. Stores very well, for as long as three months if harvested when fully ripe.

Best Uses: Eating, juice, excellent raisins

V. 'Niagara'

HARDINESS:	Zones 5-7 (8) (-15°F)
FLAVOR:	Delicately sweet, slightly tart, with a subtle wild flavor
FRUIT COLOR:	Green
FRUIT QUALITY:	Excellent, large berries
RIPENS:	Late Aug. to mid-Sept.

Bears tight clusters of good-size berries a week or two ahead of 'Concord'. A vigorous grower with attractive foliage, its vines are self-fruitful and do not need a pollinating variety. A good variety for a decorative arbor, but slightly less hardy than the 'Concord'.

Best Uses: Eating, wine

V. 'Reliance'

HARDINESS:	Zones 4-8
FLAVOR:	Excellent; very sweet, rich, and fruity
FRUIT COLOR:	Pink
FRUIT QUALITY:	Excellent, medium-size seedless berries in large clusters
RIPENS:	Early to mid-Aug.

Strong vines yield heavy crops of very flavorful, extremely high quality fruit. This variety adapts easily to many conditions and reliably weathers temperatures down to -34°F. This hardiness extends to the fruit as well; the grapes last up to three months in storage. The vines resist mildew and anthracnose, though they are susceptible to black rot. One of the very best seedless varieties. Introduced in 1965.

Best Uses: Eating, jelly, juice

V. 'Swenson Red'

HARDINESS:	Zones (3) 4-7
FLAVOR:	Very sweet
FRUIT COLOR:	Red with blue tinge
FRUIT QUALITY:	Excellent for fresh use
RIPENS:	Late Aug. to early Sept.

'Swenson Red' produces long clusters of medium-size berries that are nicely sweet even before they are fully ripe. Berries are small in newly planted vines but increase in size as plants become established. With winter protection it will grow in Zone 3. Reliably hardy to -30°F, the fruit ripens 3 weeks before 'Concord'. The fruit stores well. 'Swenson Red' was introduced by the University of Minnesota in 1980.

Best Uses: Eating, jelly, juice

MUSCADINE GRAPES
(VITIS ROTUNDIFOLIA)

V. 'Dixie Red'

HARDINESS:	Zones 7-9
FLAVOR:	Well balanced, sweet
FRUIT COLOR:	Pale red
FRUIT QUALITY:	Excellent, large berries in large clusters
RIPENS:	Midseason

Perhaps the best of the muscadines, this self-fertile variety consistently yields heavy crops of very high-quality fruit.

Best Uses: Eating, wine, juice, jelly

V. 'Hunt'

HARDINESS:	Zones 7-9
FLAVOR:	Very sweet
FRUIT COLOR:	Black
FRUIT QUALITY:	Very good, large to medium-size, juicy berries
RIPENS:	Mid-Sept.

The female vines produce excellent yields of very sweet fruit. Grapes can be harvested in bunches instead of picking each berry individually. Stores well. Very versatile fruit can be used for just about everything a grape can be used for. Pollinate with 'Triumph' for best fruit set. Berries ripen uniformly and cling well to the vine.

Best Uses: Eating, wine, juice, jelly

V. 'Scuppernong'

HARDINESS:	Zones 7-9
FLAVOR:	Variable from very sweet to lightly tart
FRUIT COLOR:	Light bronze-red
FRUIT QUALITY:	Very good, large, thick-skinned berries
RIPENS:	Mid-Sept.

Introduced in 1760, this is the oldest muscadine variety but still the most popular. Vigorous, very productive female vines yield good crops of juicy berries with a sweet, slightly wild flavor. It does not fruit well in the Northwest but is excellent in the South. For best fruit set, pollinate with 'Triumph'.

Best Uses: Eating, wine, juice, jelly

V. 'Triumph'

HARDINESS:	Zones 7-9
FLAVOR:	Sweet
FRUIT COLOR:	Bronze-green
FRUIT QUALITY:	Good, medium-size berries
RIPENS:	Mid- to late Sept.

Very vigorous vines grow rapidly and consistently set large quantities of fruit. This is the pollinating variety to plant to ensure best fruit set of all female types.

Best Uses: Eating, wine, juice, jelly

V. 'Welder'

HARDINESS:	Zones 8-9
FLAVOR:	Very sweet
FRUIT COLOR:	Bronze
FRUIT QUALITY:	Excellent, medium-size berries
RIPENS:	Early to mid-season

This is one of the best-quality muscadines, with fruit that is good for fresh eating and excellent for wine making. Vigorous vines grow quickly and consistently set good quantities of fruit. Equally popular with commercial and backyard growers, 'Welder' has the ability to produce sweet, high-quality fruit even when grown in partial shade.

Best Uses: Eating, wine, juice, jelly

EUROPEAN GRAPES
(VITIS VINIFERA)

V. 'Baco Noir'

HARDINESS:	Zones 5-7
FLAVOR:	Fruity, light, high acid
FRUIT COLOR:	Blue-black
FRUIT QUALITY:	Good, small berries in long clusters
RIPENS:	Late Aug. to early Sept.

This French hybrid's vigorous vines produce heavy crops, even in poorly drained soils. The juice ferments quickly into a clear, full-bodied red wine.

Best Uses: Wine

V. 'Chardonelle'

HARDINESS:	Zones 5-8
FLAVOR:	Dry, clean
FRUIT COLOR:	Green
FRUIT QUALITY:	Excellent, small to medium-size berries
RIPENS:	Sept.

This French hybrid produces a clean, white wine with a 'Chardonnay' flavor. Although hardier than the 'Chardonnay', it is susceptible to disease.

Best Uses: Wine

V. 'Foch'

HARDINESS:	Zones 5-9
FLAVOR:	Low acid, clean
FRUIT COLOR:	Blue-black
FRUIT QUALITY:	Good, medium-size berries in long clusters
RIPENS:	Late Aug.

'Foch' is a hardy French wine grape that makes a tasty fresh juice or a full-bodied red Burgundy-type wine. Like 'Baco Noir' and 'Chardonelle', this is a good grape for cooler regions.

Best Uses: Juice, wine

V. 'Thompson Seedless'

HARDINESS:	Zones 7-9
FLAVOR:	Very sweet, clean
FRUIT COLOR:	Green to greenish-yellow
FRUIT QUALITY:	Excellent, medium-size berries in long clusters
RIPENS:	Aug. to Sept.

This very famous variety grows best in warm regions with low humidity and long growing seasons. It is planted most extensively in a belt extending from Southern California to the Pacific Northwest.

Best Uses: Eating, wine, jelly, juice, raisins

COMMON NUTRIENT DEFICIENCIES IN GRAPES

NUTRIENT	DEFICIENCY SYMPTOMS
Boron (more common in parts of the South)	deformed new leaves; very small fruit (shotberry); no fruit set
Iron (more common in high-pH soils)	uniform yellowish color of younger leaves
Magnesium (more common in low-pH soils)	whitish interveinal chlorosis of older leaves
Manganese (more common in high-pH soils)	pale green color between veins of shaded leaves
Nitrogen	uniformly pale green leaves
Potassium	scorch of leaf edges and interveinal chlorosis of leaves at vine's midpoint; black leaves; reduced yield; small berries; late maturity of fruit
Zinc (more common in sandy soils)	small berries and deformed clusters; stunted growth of leaves (little leaf); whitish interveinal chlorosis of foliage, with some leaves having wavy margins

Common Grape Pests and Diseases

Bud Mite

The microscopic bud mite is most common in western states on American and European grapes. Symptoms include flattened and zigzag growth of canes, little or no fruit set, and dead terminal buds.

Control: None

Grape-Berry Moth

Small brown worms appear in grapes of infested plants. Most common on American, European, and muscadine grapes. Infested berries color up prematurely, split open or shrivel up, and drop from vine.

Control: Pheromone-baited trap

Grape Phylloxera

The very small yellow insects inhabit galls on leaves and roots. They appear only on European grapes not grafted onto American rootstock. Galls form on undersides of leaves as well as on root tips; vines appear stunted, and yields are less than normal.

Control: Grow only European grape varieties that are grafted onto American grape rootstock.

Grape Root Worm

These small brown beetles are most common on American and European grapes; adult beetles chew leaves, leaving chainlike damage.

Control: Neem

Grapevine Flea Beetle

The larva of this flea beetle is a small brown worm; the adult is a small blue beetle. Most common on American, European, and muscadine grapes, beetles damage new spring growth; worms feed on upper surface of leaves in summer.

1/16"-1/8"
1.6-3.2mm

Control: Neem

Japanese Beetle

Adults are beetles with shells colored in shades of metallic blue and green. They are common on all grape types and in most areas; adults skeletonize leaves.

1/2"/1.3cm

Control: Handpick from plants

Leafhopper

Adults are small insects with yellow and red markings. Most common on American and European grapes. Leafhoppers transmit Pierce's disease (see page 178). They leave a speckled appearance on upper leaf surfaces and hop when disturbed.

1/4"/6mm

Control: Populations are usually low; use neem for heavy infestations.

Bitter Rot

This fungus, which is most common on muscadine grapes, is sometimes very troublesome in Georgia and adjoining states. Infected fruit has a dry, bitter flavor. Some berries are reduced to shells of dry skin.

Control: Copper-based fungicides

Black Rot

The black rot fungus can be very troublesome on grapes with European parentage, but it also affects American and muscadine grapes. Red spots on leaves turn brown as they enlarge; they have gray centers with tiny black dots. Berries rot, shrivel, and mummify.

Control: This fungus overwinters in diseased plant material. Destroy infected leaves and fruit. Spray with copper-based fungicide one week before bloom, one week after bloom, and again two weeks later. Keep vines well pruned to increase air circulation. Cultivate in early spring to destroy previous season's mummified berries.

Dead-Arm Disease

Most common in the East, the Midwest, and California on American and European grapes, dead-arm disease appears as small dark spots with yellow margins on leaves and canes. The spots enlarge into diamond-shaped cankers on canes, slowly killing the vine or, more typically, one side, or arm, of the vine. Infections are often spread through unsterilized pruning tools.

Control: When removing infected wood, make cuts six inches below each canker. Disinfect your pruning tool after each cut. Spray with a copper-based fungicide.

Downy Mildew

This false mildew most commonly shows up in eastern and midwestern states on American and European grapes. Yellowish areas appear on upper leaf surfaces, white downy patches on undersides.

Control: Plant resistant varieties. Prune out and destroy infected plant parts. Do not plant susceptible varieties near Virginia creeper or Boston ivy. Use copper-based sprays one week before bloom, one week after bloom, and once at midseason.

Pierce's Disease (Southern Grape Decline)

First noticed in California vineyards in 1892, Pierce's disease can devastate entire vineyards and is especially destructive of varieties of European grapes. In spring or summer the leaves appear brown, while their veins remain green. As the disease advances, the tips of the canes die back in late summer or early fall. Fruit shrivels, new growth is dwarfed and stunted, and the root system progressively dies back.

The virus that causes Pierce's disease exists harmlessly in a number of plants, including such herbs as rosemary, such annuals as zinnias, and many commonly grown cover crops, including clover and alfalfa. Leafhoppers feed on the infected plants, especially alfalfa, then transmit the disease to grapes. The disease seems particularly virulent in the Gulf states.

Control: None. Limit infection by not planting host species near vineyards. Obtain plants from disease-free stock that is certified as heat-treated. Rouging of diseased plants does *not* stop the spread of the disease.

Powdery Mildew

Most common in midwestern and eastern states on American and European grapes, powder mildew is also often a major problem in California. Leaves, canes, and young fruit have patches of white, felt-like growths; these typically appear on upper leaf surfaces late in the growing season.

Control: In California, sulfur dust is used. Sprays of one tablespoon baking soda to one gallon water are also effective.

Strawberries

The strawberry's long history extends back to Roman times, when the fruit of the wild plant (*Fragaria vesca*) was gathered throughout Europe. This fruit was tart, of good quality, with a strong strawberry aroma, but small. When Europeans began to colonize North America, they brought their strawberry with them. Once here, however, they discovered a native strawberry growing in open spaces, one quite different from the species they were used to. The Virginia strawberry (*Fragaria virginiana*) — larger, juicier, and sweeter than the wild strawberry — quickly found its way into Colonial gardens. Specimens of this new species were returned to Europe, where they were planted alongside the European strawberry.

In the 1700s the beach strawberry (*Fragaria chiloensis*) was discovered growing along the coasts of California and Chile. It bore poor-quality but very large fruit, and it, too, was brought back to European gardens. There, as honeybees did their thing, new hybrids formed over the years that combined the strawberry aroma and long fruiting time of the wild strawberry, the juicy sweetness of the Virginia strawberry, and the large fruit size of the beach strawberry. In 1838 the first modern variety was developed in Massachusetts and named the 'Hovey' after its creator.

Since that time scores of varieties have been introduced, with great advances made in lengthening the season, increasing yields, and improving fruit quality. Today strawberries are one of the most popular plants grown in the garden, supplying people from Canada to California with these delicious fruits of spring.

The large, sweet strawberry of today's berry patch has a complex ancestry involving the European wild, Virginia, and beach strawberries.

SOIL TYPE AND PREPARATION

Strawberries need a well-drained, fertile soil high in organic matter. The pH should be between 5.5 and 7.5, with 6.0 to 6.5 being optimum. Sandy loams warm faster in spring than most other soil types; they can produce ripe fruit up to one week earlier than clay or silt soils. Planting in raised beds is recommended because it helps control a number of diseases and pests as well as aid in soil drainage.

If possible, avoid previously cultivated soil on which strawberries, potatoes, tomatoes, peppers, beets, peas, corn, or brambles have grown in the last three years. These soils can harbor nasty pests and soilborne diseases that could turn your strawberry patch into an intensive care unit. Soil beneath sod is generally free of problems. In northern regions large plantings should be on land with a gentle slope, to reduce the danger of frost damage.

It is important to amend any soil annually with compost or well-rotted manure. Apply either one as a mulch, or cultivate it into the soil.

BUYING PLANTS

Various nurseries pack and ship their plants in different ways. Some are careful and some aren't. Even if you purchase your new strawberries from the local garden center, chances are good that the center originally purchased them from a main supplier and grew them on site for just a little while.

Healthy bareroot strawberry plants should have firm roots; look for a light yellowish color on the thickest ones. Sometimes the roots of plants grown on muck soils are darker in color, but even these should be firm. Old plants that have gone too long without a home have black roots that are soft and sometimes a little slimy. These often find their way to the discount rack a week or so before they are tossed out with the garbage. Don't buy them. In addition to looking healthy on the outside, plants should be healthy on the inside; make sure of this by buying only the certified kind.

PLANTING STRAWBERRIES

Strawberries have a healthy mat of fibrous roots that begins directly beneath the crown of each plant. In tilled, evenly raked soil dig a hole larger than the root system. Set the plant so that its crown is even with the soil surface. Fluff the roots, spreading them evenly around the hole, and cover with soil. Gently firm the soil around the roots; do not compress it. Water the soil well.

Double Hill System

Many gardeners plant strawberries using the double hill system, a versatile method that is also very effective in raised beds. To plant using the double hill system, begin by removing any runners from the mother plants. Set plants 10 to 12 inches apart in paired, hilled rows that are themselves 10 to 12 inches apart. Space pairs of rows 18 inches apart.

A variation on the hill system requires raised beds, usually of timbers, that are 24 inches wide. Fill the beds with sandy loam amended with compost or rotted manure, and adjust the pH to between 6.0 and 6.5. Set plants in twin rows 6 inches from the edge of the timbers and 12 inches apart. This also leaves 12 inches between the rows.

Snipping off runners as they appear increases the size of the mother plants along with the size of the berries. Strawberries grown using the double hill system frequently produce larger plants than those grown under the matted row system.

Matted Row System

If you want a large bed, the matted row system is an easy way to grow strawberries. Plant rows of strawberry plants 12 inches apart, with 12 inches between rows. Allow the plants to put forth as many runners as they wish to. As the runners form, arrange them in a roughly circular pattern around the mother plant. Once you've achieved strawberry plants every 3 to 4 inches, begin snipping off any additional runners, to make sure the plants don't become overcrowded. Matted row systems produce good crops, but berries are smaller than those grown by the double hill system.

WHEN TO PLANT

Strawberries are planted at different times in different parts of the country. In central California plants can be set out in midsummer, while in southern California and areas of the Southwest they are planted in late summer. In the Northwest set plants out in April through May. In the Deep South, including southern Texas, the Gulf Coast, and Florida, strawberries are often planted in December and grown as annuals; in cooler areas of the South plant about a month or so earlier, in October and November. In the remainder of the country, planting traditionally takes place in spring, though some folks set their strawberries out in late summer and protect them through the first winter with mulch.

  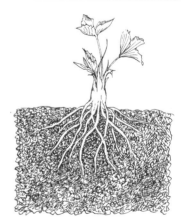

Strawberries must be planted at the correct depth to thrive. The plant at the left is planted too deep, while the one on the far right is set too shallow. Proper planting, shown in the center illustration, has the crown even with the soil surface.

The First Summer

This first year, strawberries need to establish a strong root system. If flowers are allowed to stay on the plants, the maturing fruit will divert energies away from root and leaf growth, resulting in weaker plants and lower yields in subsequent years. You should therefore remove all blossoms.

Plants grown by the hill system will grow larger and produce heavier yields if the runners are removed as they appear — during this first growing season only.

Either use mulches or swing your hoe to keep weeds out of the berry patch. Strawberries need soils high in fertility and do not yield well when they must compete for moisture and nutrients with weeds.

During the first summer of growth any flowers that appear should be removed to encourage vigorous root and leaf growth.

LOTS OF FLOWERS BUT NO FRUIT

Strawberry flowers are *dioecise,* meaning that each blossom contains both male and female parts. In some varieties the male and female organs are functional: The pollen from the male anthers can pollinate the female parts of the same flower, resulting, a few weeks later, in a ripe strawberry. These varieties are called self-pollinating. In other cultivars the male parts of the flower are present but their pollen cannot pollinate the flowers. These cultivars are called self-sterile. When buying strawberries be sure to match self-sterile cultivars with a pollinating variety so that your plants bear as many berries as flowers.

FERTILIZATION

Strawberries are often grown with vegetables as companion plants (see the box on page 184), in part because strawberries nutrient requirements are more like those of vegetables than those of fruits. Beginning in the spring of your plants' first year and continuing into fall, watering every other week with a low-analysis fertilizer, such as fish emulsion, will give great rewards. Normally, in fact, this will supply the plants with all the nutrients they need. In some soils of the South, East, and Midwest, extra phosphorus is needed. In the Northwest applications of trace minerals, such as boron, sulfur, and manganese, are sometimes required. From their second season on, fertilize the plants at the beginning of the growing season and when the blossoms open.

WATERING

Strawberries do not like to dry out. The best strawberries grow in soil that is kept evenly moist and not allowed to dry out for extended periods. Adequate soil moisture can increase yields substantially. Overhead watering can also be used to cool plants in temperatures over 85-90°F, and to protect them from frosts.

While the fruit is ripening, strawberries need about 1 inch of water per week. This will produce large, juicy berries, but don't get greedy: Too much water at this time will yield large fruit that has a watery, diluted flavor. In general, it's best to water in ways that moisten the soil while leaving the leaves dry. This greatly reduces the spread of foliar diseases.

Strawberries need soil that is evenly moist. If you grow them by the hill system, you can water thoroughly between the rows, then mulch with straw to keep the bed moist.

COLD AND FROST PROTECTION

Mulch helps keep moisture in the soil, which protects root systems. It also reduces heaving of soil in late winter and early spring from alternate freezing and thawing. In areas where the temperatures drop to about 0°F without a cover of snow, a thick straw mulch can save your berry patch from severe damage.

Sometimes, however, the best way to fight frost is not to fight it at all. It's true that late-spring frosts can kill early blossoms and devastate a berry crop. To prevent this, large farms use mist nozzles and rows of mulch. A much easier solution, however, is either to plant varieties that blossom after the last frost dates for your area, or to plant everbearing varieties that will reblossom and yield a good crop even if the first flowers get nipped.

HARVESTING

When ripe, some strawberries have firm flesh while others have a much softer feel. All underripe strawberries have firm flesh. So when is it time to pick the berries? As strawberries ripen the fruit changes color, from white to pink to red. This can happen very quickly during warm June days. As the color changes, sugars are deposited in the fruit. Berries

picked before they are fully ready will not have as much sugar as ripe ones. Another harvesting tip is that strawberries don't ripen after they're picked, so if a berry was tart when you picked it, it will be tart when you eat it.

Pick strawberries in the cool of the morning, when the berries are firm. If you must pick them in the heat of the day, place them in the refrigerator for a few hours before washing or slicing them; they will stay firm and juicy without getting mushy. To pick a berry from the plant, don't pull on it or grasp it too firmly. Snip the stem between your fingers so that the cap remains on the berry.

THE CALL OF THE WILD

Even with hundreds of varieties of cultivated strawberries available, there is a priceless pleasure in sitting amid a patch of the wild kind and picking and nibbling on the tart, tasty fruit. Four species of wild strawberry commonly grow in North America; the two most common are the European wild strawberry and the Virginia strawberry.

The European wild strawberry, also called the woodland strawberry (F. vesca), has small white flowers from spring to late summer and small, conical berries usually held above the leaves from late spring to fall. The seeds of the wild strawberry appear on the surface of the fruit. The plant was brought to North America in the 1600s and is now established in fields and open places from eastern Canada through the northeastern states to the southern Mississippi Valley.

The Virginia strawberry, also called the common strawberry or scarlet strawberry (F. virginiana), is a wonderfully variable species that produces white flowers in spring followed by bright red berries in late spring. The round fruit is usually held beneath the leaves and the seeds are recessed in shallow pits. The Virginia strawberry is native to most of North America.

Strawberries (*Fragaria* x *Ananassa*) by Region

THE SOUTH AND GULF COAST

F. 'Chandler'

FRUIT SIZE: Large
FLAVOR QUALITY: Good

Vigorous plants produce many runners and bear large, deep red, firm fruit that is good for freezing and fresh use. This variety is susceptible to red stele, leaf spot, and leaf scorch (see page 187).

F. 'Sunrise'

FRUIT SIZE: Medium to large
FLAVOR QUALITY: Good

A very vigorous, drought-tolerant variety, 'Sunrise' produces many runners and bears firm, very aromatic fruit with a pale red color. It is resistant to red stele, verticillium wilt, leaf scorch, and mildew, but not to leaf spot. The fruit stores very well.

F. 'Tangi'

FRUIT SIZE: Medium to large
FLAVOR QUALITY: Excellent

An old variety from Louisiana famous for its high-quality flavor, 'Tangi' resists most foliar diseases.

F. 'Tioga'

FRUIT SIZE: Medium to large
FLAVOR QUALITY: Very good

Very productive, vigorous plants bear firm, well-shaped fruit that is excellent for fresh use. 'Tioga' resists leaf spot and blight but is not resistant to red stele.

THE MID-ATLANTIC COAST

F. 'Pocahontas'

FRUIT SIZE: Medium to large
FLAVOR QUALITY: Excellent

Very vigorous plants produce bright red fruit with good sweetness and texture throughout the season; the berries are excellent for fresh use, freezing, and jams. This variety resists leaf scorch.

F. 'Raritan'

FRUIT SIZE: Medium to large
FLAVOR QUALITY: Excellent

'Raritan' produces many runners and bears bright red, firm fruit but is susceptible to red stele, verticillium wilt, powdery mildew, leaf spot, and leaf scorch.

F. 'Red Chief'

FRUIT SIZE: Medium to large
FLAVOR QUALITY: Very good

A longtime favorite, producing numerous runners and bearing medium red fruit with a full, rich flavor, 'Red Chief' is good for fresh use and freezing. It resists red stele, leaf scorch, and mildew.

F. 'Surecrop'

FRUIT SIZE: Medium to large
FLAVOR QUALITY: Excellent

A very vigorous variety producing dark red berries, that are colored to their centers, 'Surecrop' is excellent for fresh and frozen use. It produces good crops even on poor, dry soils or during drought and resists red stele, verticillium wilt, leaf spot, and leaf scorch.

THE NORTHEAST

F. 'Darrow'

FRUIT SIZE: Medium to large
FLAVOR QUALITY: Good

Moderately vigorous plants bear few runners but fine crops of deep red berries, which are good for fresh use. This variety is very resistant to red stele but needs a slightly longer growing season.

F. 'Earliglow'

FRUIT SIZE: Medium to large
FLAVOR QUALITY: Excellent

A very vigorous, highly productive variety that sends out many runners, 'Earliglow' bears deep red fruit. Unrivaled flavor makes it good for fresh use, jams, and freezing. It is resistant to botrytis blight, red stele, verticillium wilt, leaf scorch, and leaf blight.

F. 'Red Coat'

FRUIT SIZE: Medium to large
FLAVOR QUALITY: Excellent

This very hardy variety is well suited for the colder regions of the Northeast. Stout, very vigorous plants yield exceptionally sweet, firm berries that are good for fresh use as well as for freezing. 'Red Coat' is resistant to leaf scorch and leaf spot.

F. 'Sparkle'

FRUIT SIZE: Medium to large
FLAVOR QUALITY: Excellent

'Sparkle' does well in clay soils and blooms late enough to almost never be troubled by frost. The berries are dark red and excellent for fresh use, freezing, and jams. 'Sparkle' resists red stele and leaf spot.

THE MIDWEST

F. 'Chief Bemidji'

FRUIT SIZE: Large
FLAVOR QUALITY: Good

Vigorous, very large plants produce ample runners and heavy crops of evenly red, sweet berries. This variety is extremely hardy.

F. 'Guardian'

FRUIT SIZE: Large
FLAVOR QUALITY: Excellent

Moderately vigorous plants produce good crops of light red berries with excellent flavor that are good for fresh use and jams. This variety is resistant to verticillium wilt, red stele, leaf scorch, and mildew.

F. 'Midway'

FRUIT SIZE: Medium to large
FLAVOR QUALITY: Excellent

A vigorous plant producing ample runners, 'Midway' bears good crops of juicy, dark red berries over a long season. The fruit flavor is mild and sweet, making this variety good for fresh use and freezing. Resistant to red stele and verticillium wilt, it grows well on loams and heavier clay soils; however, it does poorly on dry, sandy soils.

F. 'Sparkle'

See preceding column.

THE SOUTHERN PLAINS

F. 'Cardinal'

> FRUIT SIZE: Very large
> FLAVOR QUALITY: Excellent

Vigorous plants produce many runners and bear richly flavored, red fruit that is good for fresh use, freezing, and jams. 'Cardinal' resists leaf spot, leaf scorch, powdery mildew, and anthracnose.

F. 'Trumpeter'

> FRUIT SIZE: Medium to large
> FLAVOR QUALITY: Excellent

The vigorous variety produces many runners and bears very heavy yields of bright red fruit, which is good for fresh use, freezing, and jams.

F. 'Pocahontas'

> FRUIT SIZE: Medium to large
> FLAVOR QUALITY: Excellent

Very vigorous plants produce of bright red fruit with good sweetness and texture throughout the season; the berries are excellent for fresh use, freezing, and jams. This variety resists leaf scorch.

F. 'Tennessee Beauty'

> FRUIT SIZE: Medium to large
> FLAVOR QUALITY: Good

These vigorous plants produce abundant runners and bear heavy crops of bright red, slightly tart berries in all types of soils. The fruit is good for fresh use, freezing, and jams. The variety is resistant to leaf scorch and leaf spot.

THE UPPER PLAINS AND ROCKIES

F. 'Chief Bemidji'

See preceding page.

F. 'Crimson King'

> FRUIT SIZE: Very large
> FLAVOR QUALITY: Good

Very vigorous, hardy plants produce nicely colored fruit, softer than many varieties; good for fresh use and freezing. Resistant to all leaf diseases.

F. 'Cyclone'

> FRUIT SIZE: Large
> FLAVOR QUALITY: Excellent

A very hardy, vigorous, and extremely productive variety, 'Cyclone' bears heavy crops of bright red, richly flavored berries. Resistant to leaf spot, it does well in high-altitude gardens.

F. 'Dunlap'

> FRUIT SIZE: Medium to large
> FLAVOR QUALITY: Excellent

Very vigorous plants produce copious runners and bear good crops of dark red, very sweet, flavorful berries that are good for fresh use. This variety grows well in all soil types, is drought-tolerant, and is resistant to many leaf diseases.

F. 'Sparkle'

See preceding page.

F. 'Trumpeter'

See preceding column.

THE NORTHWEST

F. 'Hood'

> *FRUIT SIZE:* Very large
> *FLAVOR QUALITY:* Excellent

Vigorous plants produce heavy crops of dark red, sweet berries that are excellent for fresh use, freezing, and jams. This variety is resistant to red stele and mildew.

F. 'Shuksan'

> *FRUIT SIZE:* Large
> *FLAVOR QUALITY:* Good

Large, vigorous plants produce good crops of bright red berries, which are good for fresh use and freezing. Tolerant of viral diseases and red stele, 'Shuksan' is also very cold-tolerant. It grows well even on poorly drained soils.

F. 'Totem'

> *FRUIT SIZE:* Medium to large
> *FLAVOR QUALITY:* Excellent

Moderately vigorous plants produce ample runners and bear high yields of bright red, tasty berries.

F. 'Tribute'

> *FRUIT SIZE:* Medium to large
> *FLAVOR QUALITY:* Good, slightly tart

This everbearing, vigorous variety produces large spring crops of firm, bright red fruit. The nicely shaped, conical fruit is equally good for fresh use or jams.

CALIFORNIA AND THE SOUTHWEST

F. 'Chandler'

> *FRUIT SIZE:* Large
> *FLAVOR QUALITY:* Good

Vigorous plants produce many runners and bear large, deep red, firm fruit that is good for freezing and fresh use. This variety is susceptible to red stele, leaf spot, and leaf scorch (see page 187).

F. 'Quinault'

> *FRUIT SIZE:* Enormous
> *FLAVOR QUALITY:* Very good

This variety bears enormous fruit — perhaps the largest of any variety — over a very long season. The plants are vigorous, very productive, and resistant to leaf scorch and leaf spot. The fairly soft berries are good for fresh use and jams.

F. 'Tillikum'

> *FRUIT SIZE:* Small to medium
> *FLAVOR QUALITY:* Excellent

Perhaps the heaviest producer of all, 'Tillikum' bears tart berries from spring to fall, setting fruit even during the hottest months. The fruit is soft but an excellent choice for a small garden patch.

F. 'Tioga'

> *FRUIT SIZE:* Medium to large
> *FLAVOR QUALITY:* Very good

Very productive, vigorous plants bear firm, well-shaped fruit that is excellent for fresh use. 'Tioga' resists leaf spot and blight but is not resistant to red stele.

Strawberry Pests and Diseases

Cyclamen Mites

These pests are nearly invisible. They usually hide and feed in new buds, causing dwarfing and crop loss. Infestations are worst in the north.

Control: Some suppliers treat their strawberries for mites before selling them. Destroy infested plants.

Leaf-Rollers

These small green worms feed on leaves in spring, then roll each leaf into a little hideaway held together with whitish webbing. They continue to feed from inside the leaf.

Control: Hand-pick rolled leaves and destroy.

Root Weevils and Crown Borers

These pests appear as white grubs around the roots and inside hollowed-out sections of the crown. The stem can be girdled and the roots sufficiently damaged to kill the plants.

Control: Destroy infested plants. Move your strawberry bed to a new location.

Strawberry Weevils

Small, dark-colored insects, these weevils lay eggs in the flower buds, which they then girdle. Larvae feed on the buds.

Control: Pull weeds from strawberry beds.

Leaf Scorch

Multiple purplish spots about ¼ inch in diameter appear on the upper surfaces of leaves and then enlarge to cover the entire leaf. Lesions sometimes appear on leaf stalks and can girdle the main stem. The disease is most prevalent in the South and during periods of hot, humid weather.

Control: Spores overwinter on diseased leaves, so collect and destroy all dead leaves at the end of the growing season. Plant resistant varieties.

Leaf Spot (Black-Seed Disease)

Small, purplish spots appear on leaves, turning reddish with pale centers. Black spots occur on unripe fruit. Fruit yields decrease and runners are noticeably less vigorous than normal. Although it occurs everywhere, leaf spot is more severe in the Gulf states.

Control: Plant resistant varieties when possible. Remove and destroy any diseased leaves. Set plants in raised beds in a sandy, well-drained soil. Spray with a copper-based fungicide, if needed.

Red Stele (Brown Core Rot)

First noticed in the Midwest in 1930, red stele is one of the most serious of strawberry diseases. It first destroys the fine root hairs, inhibiting moisture and nutrient uptake. The centers of the roots appear red. Leaves wilt easily, and the largest ones curl and dry up. New growth is often small and blue-green in color. Plants often die quickly during dry spells. Red stele is most severe in California and all northern regions, especially in poorly drained soil and during times of cool, wet weather.

Control: Plant resistant varieties, purchasing only certified plants. Plant in well-drained raised beds.

Strawberry Anthracnose

Light brown, sunken spots appear on the petioles of leaves or on the stems of runners. The disease is most severe in the South, especially along the Gulf Coast during August and September or extended periods of warm, moist weather. Severe infections can girdle and kill runners.

Control: Grow plants in raised beds in well-drained soil. Water the soil, not the leaves. Spray plants with a copper-based fungicide.

The Alpine Strawberry

The alpine strawberry, also called the fraise du bois, is a small, upright-growing plant that bears small, conical fruit from late spring to fall. The ripe berries possess an enchanting, aromatic strawberry flavor. The many cultivars of the alpine strawberry are all grouped as varieties of the European wild strawberry *(F. vesca);* the main difference between the two is that the alpine produces no runners. Varieties of the alpine also differ significantly from almost all other strawberry cultivars in that alpines come true from seed — that is, plants grown from seed are virtually identical to the parent plant.

The alpine strawberry is gaining in popularity as its versatility becomes more widely appreciated. It makes an excellent and unique edging plant and also grows well in patio containers and window boxes, affording tidy beauty as well as tasty nibbles.

Over the years a number of varieties of alpine strawberries have been introduced. Plants labeled fraise du bois can actually be any of a number of varieties that share these characteristics: The plants are runnerless; the berries are small, and conical, with excellent flavor; and the plants come true from seed. Notable Alpines include 'Mignonette', which bears inch-long, very tasty, bright red fruits. 'Pineapple' has inch-long creamy yellow berries with a tropical fruit flavor. 'Alba' is a white-fruited form; the berries are of lower quality than red ones but have the advantage that birds do not eat them.

RAISING ALPINES FROM SEED

Before collecting the seed berries, construct a box from wooden boards that measures about 1 foot on each side. Cover it with a sheet of metal window screen stapled into place. Now you can collect the berries; the best come from flowers produced from late spring to early summer.

Remove any caps from the fruit. Place a sheet of newspaper on a table near a sunny window and put the wooden box atop the paper. Spread the berries over the screen, making sure they do not touch each other. Allow them to dry in the sun, gently rolling them over the screen with your hands every few days. As the fruit dries its seeds loosen, and when it is rolled against the screen the seeds will fall onto the paper for collection.

The process takes about two weeks on average. The seeds can be sown immediately in propagating medium. Those sown in March will produce bearing plants by June.

Brambles

Brambles include raspberries, blackberries, loganberries, boysenberries, and trailing blackberries (dewberries). As a group they have perennial rootstocks but biennial growth and fruiting habits. They produce fruits on long erect or trailing canes.

Brambles are a diverse lot, with many forms and varieties, flavors and colors. A large number of the 250 species are gathered locally, but only a few have produced noteworthy varieties and so moved into extensive cultivation. The fruit is used fresh, frozen for later use, processed into jams and jellies, and made into juice and wine.

Generations ago bramble fruits were extensively cultivated in small plots and sold at roadside stands. Unfortunately, careless propagation techniques introduced viral diseases that reduced the vigor of the plants and significantly lowered the amount of fruit they produced. Today, certified virus-free varieties have brought brambles back to grocery stores and roadside stands in many areas of the country. Although different brambles grow best in different parts of the country, there is such a cornucopia of species and varieties that just about anywhere you live, your backyard can include a little bramble patch that will supply you with tasty fruits for many years to come.

CLIMATE

Raspberries grow best in cool, temperate regions from eastern Canada and New England down the Appalachians to northern Virginia, and west through the Great Lakes states and areas around the Ohio and central and upper Mississippi Valleys. They also grow well in British Columbia, the Pacific Northwest, and parts of California. However, varieties have recently been introduced that grow well in much warmer regions. Blackberries generally prefer a warmer climate than raspberries, doing best in the South, the Southern Plains, and regions of California. Dewberries, or trailing blackberries, prefer a cooler climate and thrive in areas from New England and New York west through the Great Lakes as well as sections of the Pacific Northwest. Loganberries and boysenberries, which are types of trailing blackberries, thrive in the cool climate of the Pacific Northwest.

RASPBERRIES

Most varieties of red raspberries are descended from the European red raspberry *(Rubus idaeus)* and the American red raspberry *(Rubus idaeus* var. *strigosus)*. The European is noted for its large, conical fruits, while the American has more rounded berries. In addition to the red-fruited varieties, there are also yellow- and white-fruited types. Black raspberries *(Rubus occidentalis)* are native to eastern and central North America and bear dark purple-black berries with more seeds and flavor than red raspberries. Purple-fruited raspberries are hybrids between red and black raspberries; they resemble the black kind in growth and fruiting habits. Everbearing raspberry varieties bear a crop of fruit in late spring and again in fall, or a nearly continual crop from late spring to fall.

Certified viral-free plants are more vigorous and produce larger crops than infected plants.

SITE AND SOIL

Like many other berry crops, brambles do best on ground that slopes slightly, allowing cold air to drain away from the berry patch and thereby reducing the chance of damage from late-spring frosts. Gentle slopes also aid in reducing disease problems and winter injury. Northern slopes are preferable, because they stay cooler through the summer months. Windy places and those with southern exposures can precipitate excessive water loss from the plants.

Brambles will grow on a wide range of soils — as long as they are well drained. It should be noted that brambles lose water through their leaves more quickly than most other fruit crops. Soils that are well drained and contain high amounts of organic matter, such as sandy loams, hold moisture well and thus help the plants thrive in during hot, dry periods. In soils less water-retentive, brambles may need regular watering throughout the growing season. Brambles also need a soil with a pH of between 5.5 and 7.5; 6.0 to 6.5 is optimum.

PROPAGATING BRAMBLES

Many bramble diseases are caused when infections are transferred from one plant to the next during propagation or maintenance procedures. To avoid infecting your berry patch, begin with certified stock from reliable nurseries. Politely decline the freebies offered by neighbors. Once disease-free plants are established in your patch, they can be propagated easily.

To propagate red raspberries and blackberries, transplant one-year-old suckers that arise from the roots of the mother plant. For black and purple raspberries and for trailing blackberries in late summer to fall layer canes by inserting each tip about 2 inches deep into the soil so that the upper few inches poke out. The plants will be ready to transplant the following year.

PLANTING BRAMBLES

Brambles are best transplanted on cloudy, moist days with little or no wind. Soak purchased plants in a bucket of warm water as soon as they arrive. If planting cannot be done for a day or so, remove the plants from the water after a few hours and cover the roots with wet burlap. Place the plants in a cool, dry place. If you're planting when the brambles arrive, take the bucket of water and plants with you to your planting site.

Dig a hole in the soil and place a plant in it, spreading the roots evenly. Set plants an inch or two deeper than they grew in the nursery, but do not cover the tips of the emerging buds with soil. Firm the soil gently and water well.

Once the plants begin to grow, cultivate around them lightly and carefully to remove weeds; work by hand with a hoe when possible, scraping only the top inch or so of soil. Be careful not to damage emerging shoots. Many people spread a layer of straw or other organic mulch over the row after planting to hold moisture in the soil, reduce weed growth, and reduce the need for cultivation.

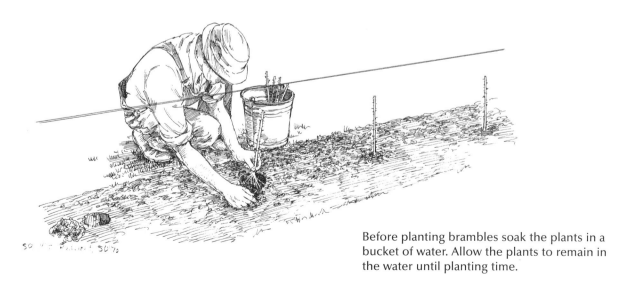

Before planting brambles soak the plants in a bucket of water. Allow the plants to remain in the water until planting time.

Planting Systems

Most commercial berry patches are planted using either a linear or a hedgerow training system; both are very productive, but at the expense of berry size. The hedgerow method consists of a 2-foot-wide planting containing mother plants and suckers. The linear method is similar but has only mother plants.

The most popular system for home growers is the hill method, in which strawberries are planted in a long raised bed about 1 foot tall and 2 to 3 feet wide. Although the yield per plant is not quite as great as with other planting systems, the berries are usually larger and of higher quality.

FERTILIZING

Brambles, like strawberries, benefit enormously from the addition of organic matter to their soil. The added moisture-retention, fertility, and aeration that organic matter provides produce healthier plants, heavier yields, and tastier berries.

Over the years it has been found that the best results are obtained using either well-rotted manure or compost. While brambles do occasionally respond to fertilization, they often do not respond predictably. In general they respond to nitrogen more than other nutrients (though boysenberries do not seem to need as much as other types). In warm, humid climates or in sandy loam soils you may need to apply a complete fertilizer. The trace nutrient boron can pose some interesting considerations. In some areas soils are deficient in boron and the element needs to be added. In other soils boron levels may exceed what brambles require.

PRUNING AND TRAINING

Brambles produce canes that grow vegetatively the first season; the next, they bear fruit and die. The vegetative canes are called primocanes, while the fruiting kind are called florocanes. Prune out old florocanes after they have borne fruit and remove weak or diseased canes.

Topping: When the new canes of black and purple raspberries and upright blackberries have reached about 2 feet, pinch off the top 3 to 5 inches. This encourages new shoots to develop and keeps the plants more stout and manageable. Cut back the resulting laterals the following spring. Do not top red raspberries.

Dormant pruning: Snip the top few inches of red raspberry canes in late winter or early spring while the plants are still dormant. After pruning, the canes should be no taller than 5 feet. These canes will produce many lateral fruiting shoots during the growing season.

Training: Train red raspberries and trailing blackberries (including logan- and boysenberries) to 6-foot posts to which crossbars have been attached; string two strands between the crossbar ends. Train erect blackberries to a two-wire trellis strung between posts 2 and 3 feet above the ground. Tie the fruiting canes to the wire and after a cane blossoms, cut back the laterals to 18 to 30 inches.

HARVESTING AND YIELDS

Brambles last only a few days after they are picked because the fruit bruises easily; gather it very carefully and handle as little as possible. Pick in the cool of the morning, when berries are firm. Ripe raspberries slip from their receptacles cleanly and easily. Blackberries hang on to their receptacles but separate easily from their clusters. They feel firm but not soft and are evenly colored.

Once picked, do not expose blackberries to the sun, as this will produce bitterness. Place all berries in the refrigerator for a few hours before using, to allow them to recover their firmness.

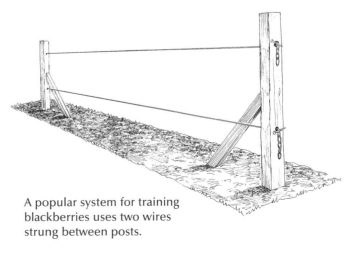

A popular system for training blackberries uses two wires strung between posts.

Rambles through Brambles: A Regional Gallery

RASPBERRIES FOR THE SOUTH

R. 'Bristol'

TYPE:	Black raspberry
FRUIT SIZE:	Large
FRUIT QUALITY	Excellent

This vigorous, very productive variety has a full, nicely sweet flavor. Plants are compact and upright, the canes strong enough to not need support. Fruit is excellent for fresh use as well as jams, canning, and even freezing.

R. 'Cumberland'

TYPE:	Black raspberry
FRUIT SIZE:	Large
FRUIT QUALITY	Excellent

This vigorous plant produces enormous crops of juicy berries. One of the best flavored raspberries, 'Cumberland' is good for fresh use, freezing, and jams and jellies. An excellent variety for Zones 5 through 9, especially in the Upper South.

R. 'Dorman Red'

TYPE:	Red raspberry
FRUIT SIZE:	Large
FRUIT QUALITY:	Very good

Vigorous plants produce very long canes that bear heavy crops of sweet, full-flavored, yet mild fruit, even during hot, dry conditions. One of the best varieties for the Deep South, 'Dorman Red' resists disease.

R. 'Heritage'

TYPE:	Everbearing red raspberry
FRUIT SIZE:	Large
FRUIT QUALITY:	Excellent

Strong, self-supporting canes of this vigorous variety bear heavy crops of sweet, mild-flavored fruit. A small crop in July is followed by a heavier, better-quality crop in fall. Although not as juicy as many other varieties, the berries are good for fresh use, freezing, and jams, and jellies.

R. 'Sodus'

TYPE:	Purple raspberry
FRUIT SIZE:	Large
FRUIT QUALITY:	Very good

Vigorous, nearly thornless, disease-resistant plants bear heavy yields of sweet, burgundy-red berries, which are excellent for freezing. This variety is easy to grow.

R. 'Southland'

TYPE:	Everbearing red raspberry
FRUIT SIZE:	Large
FRUIT QUALITY:	Very good

'Southland' is known for vigorous plants that produce reliably heavy crops of bright red, sweet fruit in late June and again in fall. Very tolerant of hot, dry periods and disease-resistant, the berries are good for fresh use, freezing, and jams and jellies.

R. 'Sunrise'

TYPE:	Red raspberry
FRUIT SIZE:	Large
FRUIT QUALITY:	Excellent

Vigorous plants yield very heavy crops of great-tasting berries. Good for fresh eating and jams.

RASPBERRIES FOR THE NORTHEAST

R. 'Allen'

TYPE: Black raspberry
FRUIT SIZE: Large
FRUIT QUALITY: Excellent

Vigorous, very productive plants bear shiny black, juicy berries. Good for fresh use, jams and jellies, and freezing. Very hardy and disease resistant.

R. 'August Red'

TYPE: Everbearing red raspberry
FRUIT SIZE: Large
FRUIT QUALITY: Excellent

Very hardy and compact, 'August Red' produces 30-inch-tall canes. Crops of juicy, red, very flavorful berries ripen in early summer and again in September. This cultivar is good for fresh use, freezing, and jams and jellies.

R. 'Brandywine'

TYPE: Purple raspberry
FRUIT SIZE: Very large
FRUIT QUALITY: Very good

This very vigorous, thorny variety bears good crops of tart, juicy purple berries that are good for fresh use and excellent for jellies and jams.

R. 'Heritage'

See preceding page.

R. 'Latham'

TYPE: Red raspberry
FRUIT SIZE: Very large
FRUIT QUALITY: Excellent

One of the most popular varieties, 'Latham' offers vigorous growth and heavy yields of high-quality, aromatic red berries that are good for fresh use, freezing, and jams and jellies, and excellent for pies. The plants are disease resistant and the fruit ripens over a month-long period in early summer.

R. 'Meeker'

TYPE: Red raspberry
FRUIT SIZE: Large
FRUIT QUALITY: Excellent

A vigorous, very productive plant, its long, pliant canes bear heavy crops of richly flavored, juicy fruit. The berries are good for fresh use, freezing, and jams and jellies. One of the best.

R. 'Royalty'

TYPE: Purple raspberry
FRUIT SIZE: Very large
FRUIT QUALITY: Excellent

Vigorous plants bear good crops of sweetly aromatic berries that are good for fresh use when picked fully ripe; when picked in their red stage, they are good for freezing and jams and jellies.

◆ **More Excellent Raspberries for the Northeast**
  R. 'Fall Red'
  R. 'Haut'
  R. 'Jewel'
  R. 'Newburgh'
  R. 'Success'

RASPBERRIES FOR THE MID-ATLANTIC

R. 'Fall Gold'

TYPE: Everbearing gold raspberry
FRUIT SIZE: Large
FRUIT QUALITY: Excellent

This vigorous variety produces heavy yields of sweetly flavored, soft fruit in July and again in late August. 'Fall Gold' adapts to a wide range of soils. The berries are good for fresh use and freezing.

R. 'Jewel'

TYPE: Black raspberry
FRUIT SIZE: Very large
FRUIT QUALITY: Excellent

Very vigorous plants produce heavy crops of richly flavored, shiny black berries that are good for fresh use, freezing, and jams and jellies, and excellent for pies. This is one of the most disease resistant of all black raspberries.

R. 'Sentry'

TYPE: Red raspberry
FRUIT SIZE: Medium to large
FRUIT QUALITY: Excellent

Vigorous, nearly thornless plants bear good crops of richly flavored, bright red berries that are good for fresh use, freezing, and jams and jellies.

◆ **More Raspberries for the Mid-Atlantic**
R. 'Brandywine'
R. 'Reveille'
R. 'Scepter'

RASPBERRIES FOR THE MIDWEST

R. 'Black Hawk'

TYPE: Black raspberry
FRUIT SIZE: Very large
FRUIT QUALITY: Excellent

These very vigorous plants bear heavy crops — even during hot, dry conditions — of firm, deep black berries with a sweet, rich flavor. They are good for fresh use, freezing, and jams and jellies.

R. 'Durham'

TYPE: Everbearing red raspberry
FRUIT SIZE: Medium to large
FRUIT QUALITY: Excellent

Vigorous, hardy plants bear good crops of firm, full-flavored red berries in both summer and fall. Use fresh, freeze, or make jams and jellies.

R. 'Jewel'

See preceding column.

R. 'Sodus'

TYPE: Purple raspberry
FRUIT SIZE: Large
FRUIT QUALITY: Very good

Vigorous, nearly thornless, disease-resistant plants bear heavy yields of sweet, burgundy-red berries, which are great for freezing and easy to grow.

◆ **More Raspberries for the Midwest**
R. 'August Red'
R. 'Brandywine'
R. 'Fall Red'

RASPBERRIES FOR
THE SOUTHERN PLAINS

R. 'Indian Summer'

Type: Everbearing red raspberry
Fruit Size: Large
Fruit Quality: Excellent

Strong plants bear wonderfully sweet, bright red berries in early summer and again in fall; the fall crop is especially heavy. The fruit is good for fresh use, freezing, and jams and jellies.

R. 'Jewel'

Type: Black raspberry
Fruit Size: Very Large
Fruit Quality: Excellent

Very vigorous plants produce heavy crops of richly flavored, shiny black berries that are good for fresh use, freezing, and jams and jellies as well as pies. This is one of the most disease resistant of all black raspberries.

R. 'Southland'

Type: Everbearing red raspberry
Fruit Size: Large
Fruit Quality: Very good

'Southland' is known for vigorous plants that produce reliably heavy crops of bright red, sweet fruit in late June and again in fall. Very tolerant of hot, dry periods and disease-resistant, the berries are good for fresh use, freezing, and jams and jellies.

RASPBERRIES FOR THE UPPER PLAINS
AND ROCKIES

R. 'Durham'

See preceding page.

R. 'John Robinson'

Type: Black raspberry
Fruit Size: Large
Fruit Quality: Very good

Very hardy, long-lived plants bear good crops of juicy, flavorful berries. This variety will bear reliable crops well into Canada. The fruit is good for fresh use, freezing, and jams and jellies.

R. 'Latham'

Type: Red raspberry
Fruit Size: Very large
Fruit Quality: Excellent

One of the most popular varieties, 'Latham' offers vigorous growth and heavy yields of high-quality, aromatic red berries that are good for fresh use, freezing, and jams and jellies, and excellent for pies. The plants are disease resistant and the fruit ripens over a month-long period in early summer.

R. 'Nordic'

Type: Red raspberry
Fruit Size: Medium
Fruit Quality: Very good

Extremely hardy plants bear heavy crops of aromatic, slightly tart berries well into Canada. In addition to being good for fresh use and excellent for freezing, the fruit is resistant to many fungal diseases.

RASPBERRIES FOR
THE PACIFIC NORTHWEST

R. 'Chilliwack'

TYPE:	Red raspberry
FRUIT SIZE:	Large
FRUIT QUALITY:	Very good

These strong plants adapt well to wet areas and bear good crops of very sweet, red berries. They are good for fresh use and freezing.

R. 'Munger'

TYPE:	Black raspberry
FRUIT SIZE:	Large
FRUIT QUALITY:	Excellent

Strong canes yield good crops of very sweet, glossy black berries that are good for fresh use, freezing, and jams and jellies. 'Munger' is resistant to some fungal diseases.

R. 'Willamette'

TYPE:	Red raspberry
FRUIT SIZE:	Very large
FRUIT QUALITY:	Excellent

One of the most productive varieties, 'Willamette' bears good crops of full-flavored, slightly tart fruit that is good for fresh use, freezing, and jams and jellies. It grows well into northern California.

BLACKBERRIES FOR THE
MID-ATLANTIC AND SOUTH

R. 'Chester'

TYPE:	Semi-erect blackberry
FRUIT SIZE:	Large
FRUIT QUALITY:	Very good

Long, thornless canes bear heavy crops of glossy black, good-flavored berries. This variety produces good yields from the Midwest to the Deep South. The fruit does not soften even in the middle of summer.

R. 'Comanche'

TYPE:	Erect
FRUIT SIZE:	Large
FRUIT QUALITY:	Very Good

The plants are excellent for backyard growing with somewhat soft, very flavorful berries. Fruit is best for fresh eating but is also good for pies, jams, and freezing. Hardy from the Ohio valley south to the Gulf coast.

R. 'Floragrand'

TYPE:	Trailing
FRUIT SIZE:	Large
FRUIT QUALITY:	Good

The plants bear large yields of flavorful berries even in dry soils and hot climates, but they do well only in Florida and the Deep South.

BLACKBERRIES FOR THE NORTHEAST AND MIDWEST

R. 'Chester'

See preceding page.

R. 'Darrow'

Type: Erect blackberry
Fruit Size: Large
Fruit Quality: Good

Plants bear very heavy crops of rich, slightly sweet fruit with a touch of wild flavor; it is good for fresh use, freezing, jams, and pies. In addition to being very winter-hardy, this variety sometimes bears a second crop in September.

R. 'Illini Hardy'

Type: Erect blackberry
Fruit Size: Medium to Large
Fruit Quality: Good

Plants are very vigorous bearing good crops of attractive, black berries with a distinctive, wild blackberry flavor. Good for fresh eating and makes very good jams. Introduced in 1990 by the University of Illinois.

R. 'Youngberry'

Type: Trailing blackberry
Fruit Size: Large
Fruit Quality: Excellent

Youngberry is a thornless variety that bears sweet, richly flavored berries. Excellent for fresh use, wine, jams and jellies, and freezing. Very disease resistant and hardy.

BLACKBERRIES FOR THE PACIFIC NORTHWEST

R. 'Black Satin'

Type: Semi-erect blackberry
Fruit Size: Large
Fruit Quality: Excellent

Long, thornless canes bear heavy crops of deliciously sweet berries that are good for fresh use, freezing, jams, and pies. Resistant to many diseases. This variety does well in all regions of Zones 6 through 9 except along the coast.

R. 'Dirksen'

Type: Erect blackberry
Fruit Size: Large
Fruit Quality: Excellent

Very vigorous plants produce long canes that bear large clusters of very sweet, tasty berries. They are good for fresh use, freezing, jams, and pies. This variety is resistant to many diseases.

R. 'Marion'

Type: Semi-erect blackberry
Fruit Size: Medium to large
Fruit Quality: Excellent

Strong, vigorous plants that bear high yields of shiny black berries with a pleasant, slightly wild flavor. Produces over longer period than many varieties. Good for fresh use as well as pies and jams. Developed for the climates of western Oregon and Washington.

Common Bramble Pests and Diseases

Raspberry Cane Borers

Small galls appear at the base of a wilted section of cane. Small white grubs are found inside the galls.

Control: Remove and destroy infested canes.

Raspberry Crown Borers

Larvae tunnel into the bases of canes, stunting growth and sometimes killing the canes. These borers are most common in the western states.

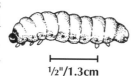

½"/1.3cm

Control: Spray with pyrethrins.

Raspberry Fruit Worms

These small worms feed on the light green receptacle at the berry's center. Infested fruit drops. Infestations are more common on red raspberries.

Control: Spray with pyrethrins.

Raspberry Sawflies

Foliage is eaten by small greenish larvae on the undersides and margins of the leaves. Sawflies are most common in the northern Great Plains and Rocky Mountains.

Control: Spray with neem or pyrethrins.

Spider Mites

These barely visible pests produce thin webs on the undersides of leaves. The foliage appears pale or is speckled with tiny yellow spots. Infestations are worst in hot, dry weather.

less than ¹/₅₀"/ .5mm

Control: Spray with neem and insecticidal soap.

Bramble Anthracnose (Spot Anthracnose)

Although it occurs on all bramble fruits, bramble anthracnose is most common on black raspberries. Sunken purple spots with gray centers appear on new canes. Old canes develop large lesions and can be completely girdled by them. Fruit on these old canes dries up; the leaves yellow and then drop prematurely.

Control: Remove fruiting canes from black raspberries after harvest.

Cane Gall

Cane gall occurs most commonly on blackberries and black and purple raspberries. Small white galls form on fruiting canes in mid to late spring, turning brown several weeks later. The canes often split open and yield small, dry berries.

Control: Cane gall is less of a problem than crown gall but is controlled in similar fashion. Destroy infected plants and do not replant brambles in the same spot for three to five years.

Crown Gall

Crown gall infects many plants, including grapes, roses, fruit trees, euonymus, honeysuckle, turnips, beets, asters, daisies, and chrysanthemums, to name a few. Of the brambles, it appears most often on red raspberries. Small to large rough-surfaced galls or tumors appear on the plant near the soil line, expanding until the plant eventually declines and then dies.

Control: The bacteria that cause crown gall can live in the soil for two to three years without a host plant and thrive best in slightly acid to alkaline soils. Thus you should destroy infected plants and avoid placing susceptible plants in the same location for three to five years. Inspect all nursery stock before buying plants as well, and keep soil at the lower end of the acceptable pH range for your species.

Orange Rust

Orange rust is very destructive to blackberries and dewberries and occasionally to black raspberries. Bright orange dots appear on the undersides of leaves in spring.

Control: The disease appears most often in a belt from the Northeast across the Midwest and on to the Pacific Northwest; it has been known for nearly two hundred years. The only known control is to destroy infected plants.

Spur Blight

Most common on raspberries, spur blight also occurs on black- and dewberries. Dark purple spots turn gray on the canes at the nodes, then enlarge to encompass the buds. Shoots developing from the infected buds are weak and rarely yield fruit. The leaves often become chlorotic. Known in North America for over a century, it most often appears in regional outbreaks.

Control: The spores germinate on moist leaves and canes and penetrate even healthy tissues; thus you should space plants to encourage good air circulation and rapid drying of leaves and canes. Remove and destroy infected and old fruiting canes. For persistent outbreaks spray dormant plants with lime sulfur followed by a Bordeaux mixture; spray when the canes are 6 inches high and again two weeks later.

Verticillium Wilt (Blue Stem)

Most often seen on black raspberries, the disease attacks over three hundred different types of plants. In summer the canes turn bluish and their tips bend downward. Lower leaves wilt and dry up. Plants usually die after leafing out the following spring. This disease can be severe in the Pacific Northwest.

Control: Remove and destroy infected plants.

Viral Diseases

BLACK RASPBERRY NECROSIS, RASPBERRY STREAK, YELLOW MOSAIC, TOMATO RING SPOT (CRUMBLY FRUIT), TOBACCO RING SPOT

Symptoms depend on the particular disease. These diseases are most destructive of purple and black raspberries. On red raspberries, they may be contagious but asymptomatic.

Control: Many viral diseases are spread by insects, such as aphids, or other pests, such as nematodes. There is no cure for any of the viral diseases. Plant new patches at least five hundred feet away from the old. Remove and destroy infected plants. Purchase only certified nursery stock.

Blueberries

Blueberries are one of the few plants whose wild and cultivated crops are both economically important. That rather unique situation stems directly from the blueberry's natural vitality. Long before North America was colonized by Europe, the blueberry was an important ingredient in the diets of Native Americans. They would gather the berries each year, sometimes mixing them with meal and dried meat to form an ancient equivalent of the Cliffbar, a snack bar favored by modern hikers. There are scores of species of blueberry, every one native to America.

When colonists first arrived here, the bright, tasty, blueberries were brand new to them. As they explored the continent they realized that the array of native blueberry species was staggering. There were highbush blueberries, lowbush blueberries, rabbit-eye blueberries, mountain blueberries, dryland blueberries, evergreen blueberries, velvetleaf blueberries, black highbush blueberries, elliot blueberries, low sweet blueberries, southern blueberries. There were so many blueberries that huge supplies could be gathered each summer from wild patches. With all this bounty, the settlers felt little need to create cultivated varieties, as they had for grapes, apples, strawberries, and almost every other of fruit.

It wasn't until 1906 that F. V. Coville, a scientist with the U. S. Department of Agriculture, began a selection program to improve on the wild species with new varieties. This and subsequent programs relied primarily on three species — the highbush, lowbush, and rabbit-eye — to create the plethora of cultivars now available. Yet after nearly a century of such work, bogs, barrens, and mountains still yield amounts of wild blueberries every year that challenge the value of all the cultivated plantations put together. Each year Native Americans still climb the mountains of the Cascades and pick berries from wild patches their families have harvested for centuries. And the fruit for the very best blueberry pie I have ever had was picked not from a plantation, but from a wild patch of lowbush blueberries in the Berkshire Hills of Western Massachusetts on a summer afternoon.

CLIMATE AND SOIL

The best way to get to know cultivated blueberries is to get to know wild ones. The cultivated blueberries that grow in backyard berry patches are for the most part descended from three major species of wild ones: the highbush blueberry (*Vaccinium corymbosum)*, the rabbit-eye blueberry (*Vaccinium ashei)*, and the lowbush blueberry (*Vaccinium angustifolium)*.

THE DIFFERENCE BETWEEN BLUEBERRIES AND HUCKLEBERRIES

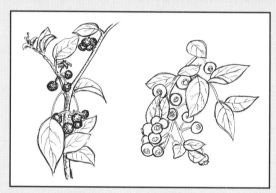

In the mountains of Washington, Oregon, and Idaho the local blueberries are called huckleberries. They're not really huckleberries, though; they're blueberries. The *real* huckleberries grow back East with other real blueberries. Nevertheless, even in the East some people call a blueberry a huckleberry and a huckleberry a blueberry. In an effort to put an end to the confusion, let me give you the way to tell a real blueberry from a real huckleberry.

Blueberries belong to the genus *Vaccinium* and are characterized by fruit that ranges in color from blue to black. Huckleberries belong to the genus *Gaylussacia* and have fruit that is also colored blue to black. However, the bottom part of a blueberry fruit has a starlike pattern on it, formed from a section of the flower called the calyx, while the bottom part of a huckleberry fruit is smooth, with no such pattern. A real blueberry also has many small, soft seeds that are inconspicuous when you open the berry. A real huckleberry has ten good-size, hard, stony seeds that are easy to notice when you open the berry.

Highbush Blueberries

Highbush blueberries are native to the Atlantic coastal plain and neighboring uplands from Maine south to northern Florida,  as well as much of the area surrounding the Great Lakes. The plants are often multistemmed shrubs reaching nearly 15 feet in height in temperate regions and about 6 feet in the northern parts of their range.

Highbush blueberries prefer soils that are rich in organic matter, consistently moist but not wet, and very acid, with a pH of between 4.3 and 4.8. These conditions are not usually found in the typical backyard, so to make cultivars derived from highbush blueberries happy, a little soil amendment must be done. In clayey or sandy soils add organic matter in the form of compost or well-rotted manure to increase fertility and enhance moisture-retention. In wet soils add organic matter and build raised beds to encourage better drainage.

The acidity needed by highbush blueberries is so extreme that few other plants grow well near them. Thus you should separate your berry patch from lawn grass, vegetables, and other higher-pH plants with a 5-foot strip of ground thickly mulched with pine needles or bark. On fertile soils sulfur is often used to lower the pH to the required level, while in sandy soils ammonium sulfate lowers pH as well as supplying nitrogen. Once your soil's pH is at the proper level, it can be maintained by mulching and top dressing the patch with acidic mulch or compost.

Highbush blueberries, like many temperate species, need a cold period in winter to grow well. This chill requirement differs from north to south; some varieties developed for Florida need less winter chill, for instance, while others selected for the North need a bit more. Scientists can tell you all the numbers, but there is a simple and practical way to determine if your climate is suitable for growing highbush blueberries: If you can grow Elberta peaches, then your climate is also right for growing highbush blueberries.

Rabbit-Eye Blueberries

Rabbit-eye blueberries grow wild along streams and at the edges of clearings and fields throughout the Southeast, from North Carolina to Louisiana. They prefer soil that is slightly less acid — about pH 5.0 — than their highbush buddies and are much more tolerant of hot, dry conditions. As with highbush types, amend the  soil with compost or rotted manure, and add an acidic mulch over the soil to retain moisture. Rabbit-eye blueberries are not as hardy as many other species; they grow best in Zones 7 through 9, though some are hardy to Zone 6.

Lowbush Blueberries

Lowbush blueberries grow wild across wide areas of the Northeast and Upper Midwest. They are remarkably adaptable, colonizing vast patches of abandoned pasture, mountaintops, and coastal wetland. They grow from 1 to more than 2 feet tall, with fruit that varies from pale blue to black. Lowbush blueberries spread via underground shoots, so once a colony is established it is very difficult to grow anything but blueberries on it. Indeed, lowbush species do so well at establishing themselves on wasteland that these patches are often called blueberry barrens.

The wild lowbush blueberry has been so productive that until very recently no cultivars were developed. Now, however, it has been used in breeding programs with the highbush type, and the resulting cultivars blend the best qualities of the two species. These hybrids have brought the unmatched wild flavor of the lowbush blueberry from the mountaintop to the backyard. The lowbush hybrids require essentially the same soil conditions as highbush blueberries do, but they are much hardier. Many of the lowbush hybrids thrive in Zone 4; some produce reliable crops in Zone 3.

PRUNING

Once established, blueberries will produce fruit on second-year wood; the more vigorous stems yield better than the thin ones. Do not prune plantings until their third year, when you should thin the base of the bush. In the fourth year remove dead or broken branches as well as four-year-old wood. Make as few cuts as possible, and do not remove more than a third of a plant during any one season. In subsequent years remove only branches that are four or more years old; these tend to be the bushiest.

On some varieties it may be necessary to thin the fruiting stems so that the plants don't overset the fruit. Too much maturing fruit reduces the size of the berries. Prune these varieties in winter, cutting the next season's fruiting stems back to about five buds.

A pruning secret: Heavily pruned bushes produce smaller crops of very large berries that ripen earlier than normally pruned bushes of the same variety. Lightly pruned plants, on the other hand, produce heavy crops of smaller berries that ripen later than normally pruned bushes.

HARVESTING

As blueberries mature they turn from light green to red to either blue or black (at full ripeness). Unripe fruit is sour, but the sugar content of the berries increases rapidly in the last days of ripening. Clusters do not ripen evenly, and ripe berries must be picked individually from the bush. When the fruit is picked an open wound, called a scar, is usually left on the top of each berry. Varieties with large scars, such as 'Herbert', can leak juice from them, which makes their fruit more perishable and prone to spoilage. Small-scar varieties generally keep better than large-scar.

As with all berries, harvest blueberries in the cool of the morning when they are dry. Place them in the refrigerator for a few hours after picking to allow them to firm up and reduce scar leakage. When you're ready to use them, fill the bowl with cold water and remove any unripe berries, which will tend to float to the top. Drain and use.

A Gallery of Cultivated Blueberries

HIGHBUSH BLUEBERRIES (V. CORYMBOSUM)

V. 'Berkeley'

FRUIT SIZE:	Very large
RIPENING TIME:	Midseason
FRUIT FLAVOR:	Good
HARDINESS:	Zones 4-8

This vigorous variety flowers in early spring, making the blossoms susceptible to late frosts. The foliage is dark green on yellow stems. Fruit set can be variable, with berries ripening to a pale powder blue. Some berries drop before fully ripe. Excellent for fresh eating and good for freezing, 'Berkeley' needs good air circulation.

V. 'Blue Chip'

FRUIT SIZE:	Large
RIPENING TIME:	Early
FRUIT FLAVOR:	Good
HARDINESS:	Zones 6-7

This variety was developed at North Carolina State University and grows best along the Southeast coast. The plants are upright, with flowers appearing a week or so later than most varieties. The fruit is pale blue with a very small picking scar. Good for pick-your-own operations and home gardens.

V. 'Bluecrop'

FRUIT SIZE:	Very large
RIPENING TIME:	Early to midseason
FRUIT FLAVOR:	Good
HARDINESS:	Zones 4-8

An excellent all-around blueberry. Plants are vigorous, growing to about 5 feet in height, with medium red stems and excellent red autumn foliage, but they can overset fruit, leading to crops of smaller berries. The fruit ripens to bright blue, with a mild blueberry flavor. Drought resistant.

V. 'Bluejay'

FRUIT SIZE:	Medium to large
RIPENING TIME:	Mid
FRUIT FLAVOR:	Very good
HARDINESS:	Zones 4-7

This very vigorous variety has an upright habit with slender, pliant stems and open clusters of light blue fruit. The berries have a mild flavor that makes them excellent for fresh eating. If mummy berry is a problem in your area this is a good variety to plant. Pollinate with 'Northland'. Good for backyard berry patches and pick-your-own operations as well as commercial plantings.

V. 'Blueray'

FRUIT SIZE:	Very large
RIPENING TIME:	Early to midseason
FRUIT FLAVOR:	Very good
HARDINESS:	Zones 4-8

This vigorous variety grows up to 5 feet tall, with glossy green leaves. Fruit has soft blue skin and a fine, sweet flavor. Good for fresh use, freezing, and pies. Plants withstand hot summers and are a good choice for Zones 7 and 8. An excellent pollinator for 'Bluecrop'.

V. 'Collins'

FRUIT SIZE:	Large
RIPENING TIME:	Early to midseason
FRUIT FLAVOR:	Very good
HARDINESS:	Zones 5-7

Attractive bushes grow up to 5 feet tall with nicely red-colored stems. Yields are not as heavy as 'Blueray' or 'Bluecrop'. The fruit has a good, medium blue color and aromatic, sweet blueberry flavor. Good for fresh use, freezing, and pies. Very resistant to fruit drop.

V. 'Coville'

FRUIT SIZE:	Large
RIPENING TIME:	Late
FRUIT FLAVOR:	Very good
HARDINESS:	Zones 5-8

These very vigorous bushes reach about 5 feet in height and are covered with dark green leaves that turn brilliant red in fall. They yield very flavorful, blue berries, which are good for fresh use and excellent for freezing and jellies. Pick only when the berries are fully ripe. Pollinate with 'Bluecrop'. Susceptible to anthracnose.

V. 'Duke'

FRUIT SIZE:	Medium
RIPENING TIME:	Early
FRUIT FLAVOR:	Very good
HARDINESS:	Zones 5-7

These very vigorous plants form open but upright, 6 foot tall bushes with strong branches. The fruit is pale blue, high quality, firm and produced in large quantities. The mild flavored berries ripen early and are good for fresh eating. 'Duke' grows best in the middle Atlantic and southern midwest regions.

V. 'Earliblue'

FRUIT SIZE:	Large
RIPENING TIME:	Early
FRUIT FLAVOR:	Good
HARDINESS	Zones 5-7

Vigorous, 5-foot-tall bushes produce dark green leaves and bright red stems. Fruit resists cracking and is light blue with a rich, full flavor. Good for fresh use and freezing, yields are consistent but average. It does best in Zones 5 and 6, but avoid growing it on poorly drained soils. Pollinate with 'Bluecrop'. Susceptible to canker.

V. 'Eliot'

FRUIT SIZE: Medium
RIPENING TIME: Late
FRUIT FLAVOR: Very good
HARDINESS: Zones 4-7

Vigorous, upright growers reach 6 feet in height, with attractive red stems. Good crops of mild-flavored, pale blue berries can be very tart if they are picked before fully ripe. 'Eliot' does not do well along the Pacific Coast.

V. 'Herbert'

FRUIT SIZE: Very large
RIPENING TIME: Late
FRUIT FLAVOR: Excellent
HARDINESS: Zones 4-7

Producing some of the largest, most flavorful highbush berries, these vigorous plants grow to about 5 feet in height and have strong stems that hold the entire crop of fruit without drooping. Berries are dark blue and very sweet. Yields can be low but are excellent for fresh use and very good for freezing and baking.

V. 'Jersey'

FRUIT SIZE: Small to medium
RIPENING TIME: Late
FRUIT FLAVOR: Good
HARDINESS: Zones 5-8

This very vigorous variety quickly grows into a 6 foot tall bush with a very open, upright habit of pliant, yellow branches. The light blue, mild flavored fruit is produced in loose clusters. The foliage turns an attractive shade of yellow in the fall. An excellent variety for the backyard berry patch, pick-your-own, and commercial operations.

V. 'Late Blue'

FRUIT SIZE: Large
RIPENING TIME: Very late
FRUIT FLAVOR: Very good
HARDINESS: Zones 4-7

Introduced in 1967, 'Late Blue' is the result of a cross between two outstanding varieties, 'Herbert' and 'Coville'. The bushes are vigorous and large, growing to over 6 feet in height. They provide average yields of full-flavored, nicely sweet berries that ripen very late, usually around mid-August, and are very good for fresh use, freezing, and baking. Long spells of hot weather can ripen the berries prematurely and simultaneously.

V. 'Meader'

FRUIT SIZE: Medium to large
RIPENING TIME: Mid
FRUIT FLAVOR: Very good
HARDINESS: Zones 5-8

This variety was developed by the New Hampshire Experiment Station and has a number of excellent qualities. The vigorous, 6-foot-tall plants consistently produce heavy yields of excellent quality berries. The blue fruit is firm, and mild flavored. Excellent for backyard patches and pick-your-own operations. Very hardy for highbush type.

V. 'Patriot'

FRUIT SIZE: Medium
RIPENING TIME: Mid
FRUIT FLAVOR: Very good
HARDINESS: Zones 3-7

This attractive variety has an upright, slightly open habit with bright red branches. The plants are extremely hardy and tolerate poorly drained soils better than most varieties. The blue, nicely flavored berries are born in clusters. Developed by the University of Maine.

HIGHBUSH AND LOWBUSH HYBRIDS
(V. CORYMBOSUM X ANGUSTIFOLIUM)

V. 'Northblue'

Fruit Size:	Medium
Ripening Time:	Midseason
Fruit Flavor:	Excellent
Hardiness:	Zones 3-7

Developed at the University of Minnesota in 1983, 'Northblue' is a small bush, growing to between 2 and 3 feet in height. Its yields are smaller than many highbush types but the fruit is superior — dark blue berries with a fine wild flavor. They keep well and are very good for fresh use, freezing, jellies, and pies. Yields are best when 'Northblue' is planted with 'Northcountry'. In northern regions buds are often winterkilled if snow cover is absent.

V. 'Northcountry'

Fruit Size:	Medium
Ripening Time:	Midseason (one week before 'Northblue')
Fruit Flavor:	Very good
Hardiness:	Zones 3-7

Developed at the University of Minnesota in 1983, 'Northcountry' is a small bush — it grows to only 2 feet in height, though it has a greater spread. Yields are smaller than highbush types but best in areas with a consistent snow cover in winter. The berries are pale blue and sweet with a hint of wildness; they are very good for fresh use, freezing, jellies, and pies.

V. 'Northland'

Fruit Size:	Small
Ripening Time:	Midseason (one week before 'Northblue')
Fruit Flavor:	Very good
Hardiness:	Zones 3-7

The large, vigorous bushes of this variety grow to 4 feet in height, with pliant branches that resist breaking under heavy snow loads. The variety is very productive, with yields equal to highbush types. The fruit is dark blue and has all the flavor of wild blueberries; it is excellent for fresh use, freezing, jellies, and pies. 'Northland', which needs to be planted with a pollinating variety, was developed at Michigan State University.

V. 'Northsky'

Fruit Size:	Small to medium
Ripening Time:	Midseason
Fruit Flavor:	Very good
Hardiness:	Zones 3-7

These very small plants (they grow to only 12 inches in height, though they spread to 2 feet) have dark green leaves that turn bright red in fall. Despite very low yields, the bright blue fruit have an excellent, rich wild blueberry flavor. A very hardy variety, and an excellent choice for far northern regions, it was developed at the University of Minnesota.

V. 'Ornablue'

Fruit Size:	Small to medium
Ripening Time:	Midseason
Fruit Flavor:	Very good
Hardiness:	Zones 4-7

Plants grow to 3 feet tall with spread of 4 to 5 feet, and pliant branches covered with attractive foliage. Very heavy yields are common. Plants are as decorative as they are productive. Good for natural landscape and rock gardens.

RABBIT-EYE BLUEBERRIES (V. ASHEI)

V. 'Bluebelle'

> FRUIT SIZE: Large
> RIPENING TIME: Early to midsummer
> FRUIT FLAVOR: Excellent
> HARDINESS: Zones 6-10

Upright plants bear very good yields of dark blue, flavorful berries that ripen over a long period — up to one month.

V. 'Brightblue'

> FRUIT SIZE: Medium to large
> RIPENING TIME: Early to midsummer
> FRUIT FLAVOR: Excellent
> HARDINESS: Zones 6-10

Short, vigorous, drought-tolerant bushes bear long clusters of light blue, rich berries. Yields are a bit smaller than highbush types.

V. 'Delite'

> FRUIT SIZE: Medium to large
> RIPENING TIME: Mid to late summer
> FRUIT FLAVOR: Excellent
> HARDINESS: Zones 6-10

Attractive, upright shrubs grow to 8 feet in height and bear good yields when irrigated. The fruit is light blue with reddish undertones; it is richly sweet even when not completely ripe.

V. 'Tifblue'

> FRUIT SIZE: Medium to large
> RIPENING TIME: Midsummer
> FRUIT FLAVOR: Excellent
> HARDINESS: Zones 6-10; best in 7-9

This has long been the best rabbit-eye. Bushes grow to over 12 feet in height, with layers of thick foliage. The pale blue fruit ripens in midsummer and has a full, rich flavor. The hardiest of the rabbit-eyes, plant it with 'Woodward' for best pollination.

V. 'Woodward'

> FRUIT SIZE: Very large
> RIPENING TIME: Early summer
> FRUIT FLAVOR: Excellent
> HARDINESS: Zones 7-9

Medium-size plants bear good crops of pale blue, very flavorful berries that are nicely sweet with a hint of tartness. Yields decline as the plants age. Pollinate with 'Tifblue'. 'Woodward' does not do well in mountainous areas.

MORE NATIVE BLUEBERRIES

- **Evergreen blueberries** (*Vaccinium ovatum*) are native to open woods of the Pacific coastal plain from southern British Columbia to northern California. The shrubs grow 3 to over 10 feet tall, with shiny, dark, evergreen leaves and shiny black berries. The fruit, with a sharp though sweet flavor, is gathered in September and October, most often for baking. The branches, called leatherleaf or huckleberry, are harvested for florists. Evergreen blueberry also makes an attractive ornamental shrub and is hardy in Zones 8-9.

- **Mountain blueberries** (*Vaccinium membranaceum*) grow wild from southern Ontario northwest to Alaska and south through the mountains of British Columbia to northern California. The bushes grow from 3 to 5 feet in height, with attractive exfoliating bark and medium green leaves. The fruit — black and distinctively pear shaped — with a sweet flavor and rich aroma is gathered extensively, an event that many westerners turn into an annual holiday.

- **Dryland blueberries** (*Vaccinium pallidum*) grow throughout the southern Appalachians and in the Ozarks. The bushes are small — from 1 to 3 feet tall — and thrive in the dry, gravelly soils of mountain ridges. They spread via underground stems and form large colonies. The fruit is pale blue and full flavored.

Common Blueberry Pests and Diseases

Birds

While I have difficulty seeing birds as pests, they do sometimes help themselves to more blueberries than is their fair share. Birds have a less defined sense of taste than people do and don't mind stealing berries that are far from ripe. When they are feeling especially greedy a flock of birds can relieve a berry patch of its fruit in a surprisingly short amount of time.

Control: Cover bushes with bird netting before the berries begin to show color.

Black-Vine Weevils

Adult weevils feed on leaves, cutting small, semicircular notches from the leaf margins in early to midsummer. The larvae are whitish grubs that feed on stems and roots near or under the soil line. These grubs can sometimes girdle entire bushes.

Control: Wrap the base of each bush in plastic wrap painted with Tanglefoot or petroleum jelly to trap adults.

Blueberry Maggots

Blueberry maggots are small, whitish worms that hatch from eggs laid by a type of fruit fly. The maggots feed on the berries, turning them soft. Infested fruit drops before it is fully ripe.

Control: Do not pick berries until they are fully ripe. Cover bushes with very fine netting after fruit set to impede flies from laying eggs on the fruit.

Cranberry Fruit Worms

Small, greenish caterpillars appear inside webs that hold fruit clusters together.

Control: Hand-pick and destroy infested fruit. Spray plants with pyrethrins after fruit set.

Anthracnose

Small, light-colored lesions appear on fruit and expand as the berries rot.

Control: Anthracnose thrives in moist conditions, especially when foliage remains wet for long periods of time; thus you should keep leaves dry as much as possible. Set plants on a gentle slope, to both maximize air circulation and provide them with eastern and southern exposures.

Bacterial Blueberry Canker (Stem Canker)

Most severe in the Pacific Northwest, reddish to black cankers appear on second-year wood, sometimes girdling stems. Buds near the cankers die.

Control: Remove diseased stems and disinfect pruning tools. Rake and remove plant debris from beneath bushes. Add mulch around plants in fall. Plant resistant varieties and avoid susceptible ones.

Note: There are at least four other canker diseases that can attack blueberry. All have similar symptoms and controls.

Blueberry Cane Canker (Stem Canker)

Most severe in the Southeast, this disease causes reddish swellings to appear on the branches. The following season these swellings enlarge into black lesions that encircle each branch, killing the portion of the stem above the canker.

Control: Remove diseased stems and disinfect pruning tools. Rake and remove all plant debris from beneath bushes. Add a layer of mulch around plants in fall. Plant resistant varieties.

Blueberry Mildew (Powdery Mildew)

Severe infections are characterized by patches of white, powderlike mildew on upper leaf surfaces; mild infections, by barely noticeable whitish threads on leaf undersurfaces. This mildew appears late in the season, usually after berry harvest.

Control: Sulfur dusts have been used in the past, but spraying with solutions of baking soda has recently gained favor. Plant blueberries away from other host plants, such as lilacs, whenever possible.

Blueberry Necrotic Ring Spot Virus

Bushes appear stunted, with distorted growth.

Control: None. Transmitted by dagger nematodes.

Blueberry Stunt Virus

Bushes appear dwarfed, with smaller leaves than normal. The leaves turn color earlier in fall than those of healthy plants. The fruit is small and of poor quality.

Control: The virus is spread by leafhoppers. Control of these insects can reduce incidence. Wild blueberries are sometimes reservoirs of infection. Destroy infected plants, both wild and cultivated, and control leafhoppers with organic pesticides.

Blueberry Twig Blight

This fungus disease is caused by the same organism that infects cranberries with twig blight. The disease most often appears during the spring while the plants are rapidly growing. The fungus first infects the growing tip of new shoots, causing wilting in young leaves. As the disease spreads down the stem the leaves and stem die back.

Control: Prune out diseased stems as they appear. Cut the infected branch 2 to 3 inches below the diseased area and discard. Disinfect pruning tools after each cut by dipping the blades in a 4:1 solution of water and bleach. The disease is usually not serious.

Double Spot

This viral disease seems to have originated in a population of wild highbush blueberries in North Carolina, where it remains most severe. Small brown circular spots appear on leaves in spring or summer. In late summer a dead area forms along the margin of the original spot, giving a double-spot appearance. Extensive defoliation can result.

Control: None. All varieties of highbush blueberry are susceptible to this disease, with some much more affected than others. Plant resistant varieties such as 'Dixie', 'Cabot', or 'Pioneer'.

Fir-Huckleberry Rust

This fungus invades twigs, mutating buds and causing dense, dwarfed, multibranched growths called witches' brooms. Although symptoms only appear on twigs, the disease is systemic and present throughout the plant.

Control: Destroy infected plants. Fir trees are alternate hosts, so avoid planting blueberries near them. There is evidence that in some sections of the northeast and upper midwest spruce trees can also serve as an alternate host as well as fir trees. Do not site Christmas tree plantations near blueberry operations.

Mummy Berry (Brown Rot)

Most common on the highbush blueberry and its varieties, mummy berry causes flowers and leaves at the tips of twigs to wilt. Infected berries develop normally for a few weeks, then dry up and fall to the ground.

Control: Practice good sanitation in the berry patch. Rake and remove as many fallen leaves and berries as possible. Mulch around plants in fall to cover any infected berries left behind.

Easy and Beautiful Annuals and Biennials

To young children there are few things as magical as the first time they enter a greenhouse full of bedding plants in flower. You can see it in their eyes. The mosaic of color that flows over the benches is spellbinding in a way that is new and wonderful to them. Yellow and orange marigolds, scarlet salvia, pastel impatiens, blue ageratum, and petunias of all the colors in the rainbow cover every inch of growing space, transforming the building into a garden that, for this moment and these eyes, has no equal.

Some of us find the enchantment of annual flowers lasts a lifetime. They are easy to grow, bloom all season long, and can turn a barren patch of yard into a solid mass of flowers in just hours. They have always been popular additions to gardens across the globe, yet over the years the nature of the plants has changed significantly.

Annual flowers have always been a favorite subject for plant breeders. It became commonplace for breeding programs to strive not only to improve the plants, but to change them drastically. There was the much publicized search for the first all-white

marigold, the race to produce a petunia that did not need to be deadheaded, and the ongoing challenge to cross a painted-tongue with a petunia. The result of all this work is a cornucopia of plants for every need and want. If you want an annual groundcover, there is the petunia variety 'Purple Wave'. For pest control, a marigold called 'Nema-gone' repels nematodes. There are yellow nasturtiums, eyed geraniums, pansies with faces and pansies without, red sunflowers and white marigolds. The variety is staggering.

Yet when all is said and done, the most enduring trait of annuals is something that goes beyond their variety or ease of culture. Think about it for a moment. Every spring gardeners haul flats of marigolds and petunias out to the garden and plant them all one more time. They know every plant will be dead by fall, but they do it anyway. Every year. On the surface such behavior may seem contrary to logic. But it isn't really. The desire to fill the world with long-lasting flowers is quite logical. And for many gardeners annuals just do the best job.

Bloom and Bust:
The Uniqueness of Annuals

Annuals don't do anything halfway. All summer long each plant produces abundant bouquets of flowers, and each autumn the first frosts kill them all. Beautiful gardens go from bloom to bust in a matter of hours. This all-or-nothing quality of annuals drives some gardeners crazy. They love the seemingly inexhaustible supply of flowers but hate planting new beds every spring. Unfortunately, you can't have one without the other.

In nature success is often measured by how many offspring are produced, and different plants have developed different strategies to maximize the numbers of their progeny. Some plants, such as perennials, produce small amounts of seed over many years. Others, such as annuals, produce large amounts of seed over a much shorter time. To produce as much seed as possible, annuals direct their energies toward flowers and away from root growth and food storage. Thus, the flowering plants simply use more energy than they make. It would be as if every time you burned ten gallons of gas in your car, you put in only nine. That is how annuals work: They produce lots of flowers and seeds, but pretty soon they just run out of gas. The frosts of autumn only hasten the process.

Categories of Annuals

Annuals are grouped into three categories, based on their ability to withstand frost and cold. A *tender* annual is the most cold sensitive, the plant and seeds often succumbing as soon as the temperature touches 32°F. A *half-hardy* annual is just as sensitive to cold as a tender but produces seed that can tolerate some subfreezing weather. A *hardy* annual can survive light frosts — down to about 29°F — and produces seeds that can often overwinter in the garden.

◆ **Some Tender Perennials Often Grown as Annuals**
   Black-eyed Susan vine *(Thunbergia alata)*
   Flowering tobacco *(Nicotiana alata)*
   Madagascar periwinkle *(Catharthus roseus)*
   Petunia *(Petunia* x *hybrida)*
   Snapdragon *(Antirrhinum majus)*

◆ **Some Tender Annuals**
   Butterfly flower *(Schizanthus pinnatus)*
   Cockscomb *(Celosia argentea)*
   Four o'clock *(Mirabilis jalapa)*
   Garden balsam *(Impatiens balsamina)*
   Morning glory *(Ipomoea purpurea)*
   Nasturium *(Tropaeolum majus)*
   Swan River daisy *(Brachycome iberidifolia)*

◆ **Some Half-Hardy Annuals**
   Cosmos *(Cosmos bipinnatus)*
   Marigold *(Tagetes* spp.)
   Nemesia *(Nemesia strumosa)*
   Painted tongue *(Salpiglossis sinuata)*
   Spider flower *(Cleome hassleriana)*

◆ **Some Hardy Annuals**
   Morocco toadflax *(Linaria maroccana)*
   Pot marigold *(Calendula officinalis)*
   Rose mallow *(Lavatera trimestris)*
   Sweet alyssum *(Lobularia maritima)*
   Sweet pea *(Lathyrus odoratus)*

Gallery of Fifteen Popular Annuals

Ageratum, Floss Flower
Ageratum houstonianum

HARDINESS: Tender annual
HEIGHT: 4-15 inches
LIGHT: Full sun to light shade
SOIL: Moist, well drained (pH 6.0-7.5)
BEST USES: Borders, containers

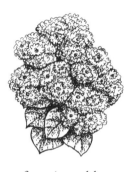

How to Grow: Ageratum prefers cool weather, both for seed germination and growing. Sow seed indoors in February or early March (keep soil near 70°F) and plant outside in May. Warm-weather gardeners can start plants in late summer for winter bloom. Pinch plants to encourage branching and keep soil evenly moist. Aphids and mites are sometimes a problem in warm weather or late in the growing season.

Selected Cultivars: 'Blue Hawaii' produces compact eight-inch-high mounds of light green leaves covered with dense sprays of snowflake-shaped blue flowers. 'Capri' is a heat-tolerant variety with beautiful white flowers edged in blue fringe.

Cockscomb
Celosia argentea

HARDINESS: Tender annual
HEIGHT: 12-36 inches
LIGHT: Full sun
SOIL: Well drained, slightly moist to dry (pH 6.0-7.5)
BEST USES: Borders, dried flowers, cut flowers

How to Grow: Cockscomb plants are light sensitive and should be transplanted to the garden after the last frost but before the plants have set buds. If

transplanted when in flower, the plants quickly set seed and die. Cockscombs love hot weather, are drought tolerant, and do not like to be fertilized, which makes their care, once you get them to the garden, easy indeed.

Selected Cultivars: 'Chief' is excellent for cut flowers, with strong, three-foot stems topped with colorful crested flower heads. *Celosia* Century Series produces large plumes of rose, yellow, or red flowers atop sturdy, 20-inch stems.

Cosmos
Cosmos bipinnatus

HARDINESS: Half-hardy annual
HEIGHT: 24-48 inches
LIGHT: Full sun to light shade
SOIL: Well drained, slightly moist to dry (pH 6.0-7.0)
BEST USES: Borders, cut flowers, butterfly gardens

How to Grow: Cosmos, derived from the Greek word for "beautiful," is one of the easiest annuals to grow. Sow seed directly in the garden after danger of frost has past. Do not fertilize, as the plants are sensitive to excess salts in the soil. Stake when plants reach about twenty-four-inches tall; avoid planting in windy areas.

Selected Cultivars: 'Early Vega' produces abundant bouquets of daisy-shaped flowers in shades of red, pink, or white atop three-foot tall stems. 'Seashells' produces flowers with unique tubular petals in a wide range of colors.

Flowering Tobacco
Nicotiana alata

HARDINESS:	Tender perennial
HEIGHT:	12-24 inches
LIGHT:	Full sun to partial shade
SOIL:	Well drained, moist (pH 6.0-7.0)
BEST USES:	Borders, hummingbird gardens

How to Grow: Flowering tobacco's scientific name, *Nicotiana,* was given to honor Jean Nicot, who introduced tobacco to France in the sixteenth century. Seeds of flowering tobacco are sensitive to light and germinate best under natural light from March to June. Sow seeds indoors in late March and transplant to the  garden after the last frost, or direct-sow after the last frost. Flowering tobacco does well in warm, humid areas and is especially disease-resistant. Because the plants need twelve or more hours of light each day to bloom, they are not a good choice for the warm-weather winter garden.

Selected Cultivars: *Nicotiana* Domino Series produces sturdy, 12-inch stems topped with fragrant flowers in red, pink, white, or purple.

Impatiens
Impatiens wallerana

HARDINESS:	Tender perennial grown as an annual
HEIGHT:	12-16 inches
LIGHT:	Partial shade to deep shade
SOIL:	Moist to wet, well drained (pH 6.0-6.5)
BEST USES:	Borders, containers

How to Grow: Sow seed indoors in February, but be patient, for the seed can take from three to four weeks to germinate. Plant in the garden after dan-

ger of frost has past. Fertilize lightly or not at all. Too much fertilizer produces lush foliage and few flowers. Container-grown plants can be brought indoors before the first frost, where they will flower all winter long. In the Deep South plants often overwinter. The name *Impatiens* comes from a Latin word meaning "to be impatient" and refers to the explosive discharge of the seeds when the ripe fruit capsule is touched.

Selected Cultivars: *Impatiens* Deco Series sports 12-inch-tall mounds of dark green foliage flecked with burgundy and loads of intensely colored flowers. *Impatiens* Pride Series has large, 2-inch-wide flowers in a wide variety of colors.

Lobelia
Lobelia erinus

HARDINESS:	Tender perennial grown as an annual
HEIGHT:	4-8 inches
LIGHT:	Full sun to partial shade
SOIL:	Well drained, moist to wet (pH 6.0-7.5)
BEST USES::	Borders, containers

How to Grow: Lobelia is not a plant that germinates well when direct-sown in the garden. Plant seeds indoors about ten weeks before the last frost and keep seed flats at about 70°F for best germination. The seedlings will appear in about two weeks,  but then they often seem to just sit there and refuse to grow. Be patient, and keep them in a cool (55 to 60°F), bright spot. They do eventually grow, honest. Lobelias can get leggy in hot weather but respond to shearing with new growth and abundant flowers. Container-grown plants can be brought indoors and overwintered; they will continue to flower. Lobelia was named in honor of Mathias de Lobel, who was the personal physician to James I of England.

Selected Cultivars: 'Crystal Palace' has dainty 6-inch-high mounds of green foliage smothered with small flowers of vivid blue. 'Complete Colors' has a trailing habit; the tidy, heat-tolerant plants are decorated with abundant white, lilac, rose, or blue flowers.

Marigold
Tagetes spp.

HARDINESS: Half-hardy annual
HEIGHT: 6-36 inches
LIGHT: Full sun
SOIL: Well drained, moist (pH 6.0-7.5)
BEST USES: Borders, background, cut flowers, containers

How to Grow: Marigolds are some of the easiest annuals to grow. In the South sow seed in late December or early January for flowering plants in late March or April. Seed sown in early February will be ready to plant outside in early May, and those up  North who sow seed in early March will have flowering plants around June 1. Marigolds grow best when the days are warm and the nights are cool. In the heat of summer the plants often stop flowering until cooler weather returns. Midday shade in the South helps bloom last longer.

Selected Cultivars: *T. erecta* Discovery Series (African marigold) produces large flowers on compact, stout stems. *T. patula* 'Gypsy Sunshine' (French marigold) bears abundant flowers atop small mounds of dark green leaves.

Petunia
Petunia x *hybrida*

HARDINESS: Tender perennial grown as an annual
HEIGHT: 6-18 inches
LIGHT: Full sun to light shade
SOIL: Well drained, rich (pH 6.0-7.5)
BEST USES: Beds and borders, containers, ground cover

How to Grow: Expose young plants to ten or fewer hours of light per day for first four to six weeks to promote stout growth and branching. This can be done by starting plants in January and February or by using timed grow-lights. After this, allow plants thirteen or more  hours of light per day to promote bud formation. Branching can also be encouraged by pinching terminal buds. Petunias grow best during warm days and cool nights in soil that is kept on the dry side.

Selected Cultivars: *Petunia* 'Purple Wave' grows about 4 inches tall but spreads up to 4 feet in a season, making it an excellent ground cover. 'Pink Wave' has the same growth characteristics as 'Purple Wave' but with rose pink blossoms. 'Caprice' has stunning rose-pink double blooms that resemble roses more than petunias. 'Chiffon Morn' is a beauty with large, cotton candy pink flowers that hold up well to rain. The plants are vigorous growers reaching 9 to 12 inches tall. *Petunia* Daddy Series produces large, four-inch-wide flowers on strong stems in a range of colors. 'Blue Daddy' is one of the best of this series with large, pale blue flowers with veins etched in navy blue. 'Global Grandiflora' has beautiful single blossoms in almost every color imaginable. 'Summer Sun' grows to 9 inches tall with orange-yellow flowers.

Pot Marigold
Calendula officinalis

HARDINESS: Hardy annual
HEIGHT: 12-24 inches
LIGHT: Full sun to light shade
SOIL: Well drained, moist (pH 6.0-7.5)
BEST USES: Cut flowers, containers, borders; flower petals make a tasty garnish for soups and salads

How to Grow: In warm regions seed can be sown in the garden in late summer for winter blooms. In cool and cold areas sow seed indoors in February for planting in spring. Pot marigolds grow best when the weather is cool and the soil is kept evenly moist. Seeds sown in the garden in warm or hot weather develop weak root systems and stems.

Selected Cultivars: 'Kablouna' is mildew resistant and has yellow or orange blossoms sprinkled over dark green, 18-inch stems. 'Bon Bon' is an early variety that produces bright yellow or orange blossoms even in warm weather.

Scarlet Sage
Salvia splendens

HARDINESS: Tender perennial grown as an annual
HEIGHT: 12-36 inches when grown as an annual
LIGHT: Full sun to partial shade
SOIL: Well drained (pH 6.0-7.5)
BEST USES: Borders, containers, butterfly and hummingbird gardens

How to Grow: Scarlet sage can be grown as a perennial in the Deep South and warm areas of the Southwest, though old plants can look wild and

rangy. In warm areas seed can be sown in the garden in fall or winter. Northern gardeners should start seeds indoors in late winter. Scarlet sage grows best in warm days (70 to 85°F) followed by cool nights (55 to 60°F). The plants are quite sensitive to salts and do poorly in some saline soils of the West or if overfertilized.

Selected Cultivars: *Salvia* Hotline Series gives the gardener a choice of intense colors, from fiery red to cool white, violet, and pink. Flowers adorn stout, 12-inch-tall heat- and drought-tolerant plants accented with dark green leaves. *Salvia* Wine Series produces clusters of wine-red or creamy white flowers on 12-inch-tall spikes.

Snapdragon
Antirrhinum majus

HARDINESS: Tender perennial grown as an annual
HEIGHT: 6-36 inches
LIGHT: Full sun to light shade
SOIL: Well drained (pH 5.5-7.0)
BEST USES: Borders, cut flowers, background

How to Grow: In the Deep South and warm areas of the Southwest, snapdragon seed can be sown in the garden in fall. In northern regions, sow the seed indoors in mid-February, keeping the flats cool (55 to 65°F). Snapdragons grow best in cool weather when nights are below 70°F, and in soil that is kept evenly moist. Softwood cuttings root easily.

Selected Cultivars: 'Liberty' grows to 18 inches tall with abundant, well-formed flower spikes in a variety of colors. 'Tahiti' has flowers in a wide range of colors on stems only 8 inches tall.

Spider Flower
Cleome hassleriana

HARDINESS: Half-hardy annual
HEIGHT: 36-48 inches
LIGHT: Full sun or light shade
SOIL: Well drained, slightly moist to dry (pH 6.0-7.0)
BEST USES: Borders, cut flowers, butterfly and hummingbird gardens

How to Grow: Spider flowers are one of the few annuals that thrive in the heat of summer. They are drought tolerant, and their tall stems are strong enough that staking is not required. In northern areas sow seed indoors in late winter, keeping the soil at about room temperature. In warm regions sow directly in the garden in spring.

Selected Cultivars: *Cleome* Queen Series produces forty-eight-inch-tall plants topped with spidery trusses of violet, red, or pink flowers. 'Helen Campbell' grows to 36 inches in height with clear white blossoms.

Wax Begonia
Begonia x *semperflorens-cultorum*

HARDINESS: Tender perennial grown as an annual
HEIGHT: 6-12 inches
LIGHT: Light to partial shade
SOIL: Well drained, moist, rich (pH 5.5-7.0)
BEST USES: Borders, containers

How to Grow: Wax begonias are also called everflowering begonias, for the seemingly endless supply of blossoms each plant can produce. Sow seed indoors in late December or early January, keeping the soil moist and at about 70°F. The tiny seeds take about a month to germinate. Grow the young plants in a cool place (about

55°F). Plant in the garden after danger of frost has past and fertilize regularly. In areas with hot summers plant bronze-leafed varieties; plant the green-leafed varieties in cool northern regions.

Selected Cultivars: *Begonia* Cocktail Series is a bronze-leafed hybrid that grows about 6 inches tall with sprays of white, red, or rose flowers. 'Stara' is a green-leafed hybrid with 12-inch mounds of emerald foliage covered with rose, white, or pink flowers.

Zinnia
Zinnia elegans

HARDINESS: Tender annual
HEIGHT: 8-36 inches
LIGHT: Full sun
SOIL: Well drained, moist, rich (pH 5.5-7.5)
BEST USES: Borders, cut flowers, containers

How to Grow: Sow seed indoors in early April for planting outside in late May, or direct-sow in the garden when the danger of frost is past. Pinch plants when they are about 4 to 6 inches tall to promote branching. Zinnias like hot, sunny weather, but be sure not to let the soil dry out. In humid regions powdery mildew is sometimes a problem, but it's less so in breezy spots.

Selected Cultivars: 'Blue Point' is a European variety noted for its strong 3-foot stems and striking double flowers, traits that make it an excellent cut flower. 'Dreamland' is an 8-inch-tall dwarf with dark green leaves and large double flowers in a range of colors.

Zonal Geranium
Pelargonium x *hortorum*

HARDINESS: Tender perennial grown as an annual
HEIGHT: 10-15 inches
LIGHT: Full sun to light shade
SOIL: Well drained, moist to slightly dry (pH 6.0-7.5)
BEST USES: Borders, containers, mass plantings

How to Grow: Many people still buy their zonal geraniums in packs from garden centers each spring, but some folks have started to grow these old-time favorites from seed at home. Sow seed indoors about twelve to fourten weeks before the last frost. Germination is often erratic, with seedlings popping up here and there around the flat. Every few days prick out the largest plants and transplant them into containers. Zonal geraniums grown from seed are often more heat tolerant than those produced from cuttings, which means better flowering through the hot summer months. Keep plants well watered and fertilized, then stand back and watch the show.

Selected Cultivars: 'Tetra Scarlet' is a disease-resistant tetraploid (a plant having twice as many chromosomes as normal) with strong, vigorous stems and large flower heads of vivid red. *Pelargonium* Orbit Series grows to 14 inches tall with richly zoned leaves and long-lasting flowers in white, pink, red, or violet.

Secrets of Growing Biennials

Biennials are more patient than annuals. Instead of burning themselves out over just one season, as annuals do, biennials make life last for two growing seasons before collapsing from exhaustion. They spend their first season growing an impressive root system topped by a neat rosette of leaves. The roots and leaves accumulate food, which the plant stores over winter. During the second growing season the neat, leafy rosette bolts into a strong stalk decorated with flowers. At the end of this second season the plant dies.

At least, that's the way things are supposed to work. But if biennials are patient creatures, gardeners sometimes aren't. Over the years people have tinkered with nature, trying this and that technique, until today it is possible to trick most biennials into going from seed to flower in one season.

HOW TO GET BIENNIALS TO FLOWER IN ONE SEASON

Biennials, like many plants, are sensitive to the intensity and duration of light. This quality, called photoperiodic response by scientists, means that these plants can determine how long daylight lasts and whether or not the day length is increasing or decreasing over time. If a plant perceives that the day length is decreasing, it realizes that the colder months are coming and responds by going dormant. Conversely, if the days are lengthening, then the warm months are ahead, and the plant responds by producing flowers and seeds. There are many weeks between late December — when days begin to get longer — and the start of the growing season. It is this window of time that gardeners use to fool biennials.

To encourage a biennial to flower in its first year, sow the seed indoors in January or early February. Keep the seed flats at about 65 to 75°F. When seedlings emerge, transplant and grow them under natural light.

Six Very Popular Biennials

Dame's Rocket
Hesperis matronalis

HARDINESS: Zones 3-9
HEIGHT: 2-3 feet
LIGHT: Full sun to partial shade
SOIL: Well drained, rich, moist (pH 5.0-7.5)
BEST USES: Mass plantings

How to Grow: *Hesperis,* the genus name of dame's rocket, comes from a Greek word meaning "evening," the time when the colorful flowers are most fragrant. Dame's rocket bears beautiful pyramidal clusters of violet, red, or white flowers. Sow the seed indoors in early March. Seedlings will emerge in about three weeks if flats are kept at 70 to 80°F. Transplant to rich garden soil in spring. Dame's rocket freely self-sows and can take over large areas of the garden in just a few seasons. Double-flowered forms do not come true to seed and must be propagated by taking softwood cuttings in late summer.

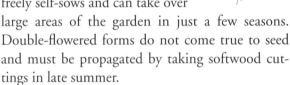

Selected Cultivars: 'Alba' bears clear white blossoms on pliant 2- to 3-foot stems.

Foxglove
Digitalis purpurea

HARDINESS: Zones 4-8
HEIGHT: 2-6 feet
LIGHT: Partial shade to deep shade
SOIL: Moist, well drained (pH 6.0-7.5)
BEST USES: Cut flowers, borders

How to Grow: Foxgloves prefer rich, loamy soil with plenty of compost or leaf mold. Start seed indoors in late winter and transplant to the garden in spring. They will often self-sow, though over repeated seasons the offspring often become less vigorous than their parents were. Foxgloves make excellent cut flowers if collected when the buds are half open.

Selected Cultivars: 'Sutton's Excelsior Hybrids' produce strong four-foot stems graced with numerous slightly drooping tubular flowers in a wide range of colors. 'Giant Shirley' is overpoweringly large, with 4- to 6-foot stems crowded with large, bell-shaped flowers.

Hollyhock
Alcea rosea

HARDINESS: Zones 3-9
HEIGHT: 3-8 feet
LIGHT: Full sun
SOIL: Well drained
BEST USES: Borders

How to Grow: Sow seed indoors in February or March; they will germinate in about two weeks if the flats are kept at about 70°F. Transplant seedlings to the garden in spring. Hollyhocks are very susceptible to rust, which appears as little orange dots on the undersides of the leaves. The disease disfigures the leaves, causing them to curl, turn brown, and die. Control by removing the infected leaves and dusting those that remain with sulfur.

Selected Cultivars: 'Indian Spring' has beautiful semidouble red, pink, yellow, or white blossoms on 4-foot-tall stems. 'Powderpuffs' produces 4-foot-tall stems covered with roselike double blossoms in white, red, yellow, or pink.

Honesty
Lunaria annua

HARDINESS: Zones 6-9
HEIGHT: 2-3 feet
LIGHT: Partial shade
SOIL: Well drained, moist
BEST USES: Dried flowers

How to Grow: Start seeds indoors in early March, keeping the flats at about 70°F. Seedlings will emerge in two to three weeks. Prick out to containers and grow under natural light until ready to transplant to the garden in midspring. Some folks have poor luck trans-planting honesty and prefer to sow seeds directly in the garden in late fall or when the ground can be worked in the spring. The fragrant purple or white flowers grow into fruits by late summer. When the fruits have matured, cut the stems, remove the sheath of the fruit, and hang the stems upside down to dry. Honesty's scientific name, *Lunaria*, derives from the Latin word for "moon" because the plant's round, yellowish seed vessel resembles the full moon.

Selected Cultivars: 'Variegata' bears beautiful flowers of pale violet with medium green leaves edged in creamy white.

Pansy
Viola x *wittrockiana*

HARDINESS: Zones 6-9
HEIGHT: 6-8 inches
LIGHT: Light shade or partial shade
SOIL: Rich, well drained, moist (pH 5.5-7.0)
BEST USES: Borders, mass plantings, containers

How to Grow: Sow seeds indoors in January in flats kept at 60 to 70°F. Seedlings will emerge in two to three weeks. Prick out into containers and harden off as soon as the weather warms. Plant in the garden in spring. Pansies do not like hot weather, but planting them in a shady spot in evenly moist, rich soil will keep them flowering well into summer. Remove old flowers and seed heads to encourage flowering.

Selected Cultivars: 'Chalon' is an heirloom variety cherished for its classic pansy-shaped flowers in gold, violet, or burgundy cheerfully marked with black. 'Maxim Marina' is a heat-tolerant hybrid with abundant sky-blue petals surrounding a central black spot.

Stock
Mathiola incana

HARDINESS: Zones 9-10
HEIGHT: 12-24 inches
LIGHT: Full sun
SOIL: Moist, well drained, fertile (pH 6.5-7.5)
BEST USES: Borders, mass plantings, containers

How to Grow: Sow seeds indoors 6 to 8 weeks before last spring frost in sterile medium such as vermiculite or direct sow in the garden one month before last frost. In zones 9-10 seeds can be direct sown in the garden in fall or early winter. Sow seeds on soil surface as they need light to germinate. Space plants from 8 to 14 inches apart. Close spacing produces earlier flowers. Pinch plants when about 6 inches tall to encourage branching. Water and fertilize regularly. Mulch plants to keep roots cool. Flowering period can be extended by making successive sowings

Selected Cultivars: 'Trisomic Seven Week' produces bushy, 12 inch tall plants bearing large spikes of richly fragrant double flowers in many colors.

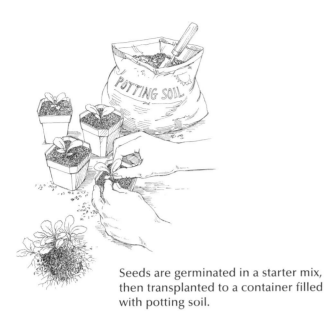

Seeds are germinated in a starter mix, then transplanted to a container filled with potting soil.

Seed-Starting Ingredients and Mixes

Horticultural techniques have been evolving for thousands of years, but over that time surprisingly few materials have been used alone, or in combination, to germinate seeds. They include soil, sand, mosses, and, more recently, vermiculite and perlite. Seed-starting mixes are often made from the same ingredients as growing mixes with two critical differences: seed starting mixes have a finer texture than growing mixes and fewer nutrients. After seeds germinate and produce a set of true leaves, they should be transplanted from a seed-starting mix to a growing mix. The two mixes that have become seed-starting benchmarks are the John Innes Seed Compost Mix and the Cornell Peat-Lite Mix C.

SOIL AND SAND

Soil is a complex blend of inorganic and organic substances mixed with air and water. The properties of a soil depend on how much of each ingredient is present.

The inorganic part of soil consists of weathered particles of rock. The size and relative abundance of these particles determine whether the soil is a sandy loam, a clay loam, or another of the myriad soil types. (For more information on soil types see page 2.)

The organic portion of soil consists of living and dead organisms. Decayed organic matter,

called humus, supplies fertility and aids in retaining water. The liquid portion of soil, called the soil solution, contains dissolved minerals and other nutrients that aid in plant growth. The remainder of the soil is made up of air, which helps supply needed oxygen to plant roots.

Taken together, soil is what nature intended plants to grow in, but its lack of uniformity can pose problems for the gardener by making seed germination unpredictable.

Horticultural-grade sand consists of rock grains (primarily quartz) 0.05 to 0.5 millimeters in diameter. It contains almost no nutrients and typically weighs up to 100 pounds per cubic foot. Sand is sometimes used alone but more commonly is mixed with other materials. Many seeds germinate well in sand, but young seedlings left a bit too long in a flat of sand quickly turn pale and feeble.

MOSSES

Commercial peat moss is the remains of bog vegetation commonly cut from bogs in northern Canada. Peat moss contains many types of moss, all of which have an amazing ability to hold water: one pound of peat moss can hold five gallons of water. It is very acid as well, with a typical pH of 3.8 to 4.5, little nitrogen, and almost no phosphorous or potassium. The acidity and poor nutrient value of peat moss make it a poor germination medium by itself; still, its ability to retain water makes it an excellent addition to composite mixes.

Pure sphagnum moss can retain more water than even standard peat moss, one pound absorbing up to ten gallons of water. It is usually a bit more acidic than peat moss, with a pH value of 3.5 to 3.8. Milled sphagnum moss is frequently used in seed mixes because it contains fungistatic and antibiotic substances that inhibit damping-off disease in seedlings. However, some people are allergic to sphagnum moss and develop an itchy rash after touching it.

VERMICULITE AND PERLITE

Vermiculite is made from mica rock that is ground up and heated in an oven. At about 2,000°F the rock's hundreds of layers expand, producing tiny pellet-shaped nuggets that look like little accordions. Vermiculite is very light and water-absorbent; a cubic foot weighs about 8 pounds and is able to hold nearly 4 gallons of water. It is a good source of magnesium and potassium, and is disease-free. Grade 4 vermiculite consists of particles about 1 millimeter in diameter and is the best grade for germinating seeds.

Perlite is made from volcanic rock that is crushed and screened before being run through a 1,500°F oven. The heated grains then pop like popcorn into small kernels of lightweight perlite. Perlite weighs about the same as vermiculite and holds about the same amount of water. Perlite does not have any inherent nutrient value, however. Its pH is about 7.0, and it is often added to mixes containing peat moss to provide aeration.

MAKING AN OLD-FASHIONED SEED MIX

Horticulture is close to a religion in England, where the John Innes Horticultural Institution is located. Many years ago this facility developed a series of soil-based mixes for use in seed starting and container growing. The folks at the Innes Institution were not in a hurry for their seed mix — it typically took six months to a year to make one batch and age it properly. But then good soil, like good wine and cheese, shouldn't be rushed.

The John Innes Seed Compost Mix

20.25   cubic feet loam soil
6.75   cubic feet strawy manure
1   pound ground dolomitic limestone
14   cubic feet sphagnum peat moss
13   cubic feet washed sand

The best place to make an Innes mix is in a cement-block compost bin, but it can be produced just about anywhere you have the room. An Innes mix starts with well-drained loam soil that has a pH of about 6.0. Mark out an area 3 feet by 3 feet, and cover it with a 9-inch-deep layer of soil. Cover the soil with 3 inches of strawy manure and dust with ground dolomitic limestone. Water until moist, then add another 9-inch layer of soil to the pile, followed by another 3-inch layer of manure and a dusting of limestone. Water well and add one more layer of soil, manure, and lime. Water well, cover with 8-mil clear plastic, and wait.

Make your Innes pile in spring. In the South, Northwest, and Southwest your Innes pile will be ready in fall. In northern regions it will be ready the following spring.

When the pile has properly aged, turn it well and screen through ⅜-inch hardware cloth. Add 12 cubic feet of sphagnum peat moss and 12 cubic feet of washed sand to the soil. Mix well and screen again. Store in clean garbage cans or other large containers. The recipe makes about 2 yards of mix.

You can replace the sand with grade 4 vermiculite to reduce the weight, if you wish. The recipe can also be cut to make smaller batches, as long as the ratios of ingredients are maintained. Be sure to pasteurize the mix before sowing seed.

MAKING A MODERN SEED-STARTER MIX

If you would like to plant seeds the same year you make your seed-starter mix, then the Cornell Peat-Lite Mix C is just what you want. Easy to make and store, this mix, developed at Cornell University in New York, has been the most popular seed-starting medium for decades.

Cornell Peat-Lite Mix C

  8   gallons shredded sphagnum moss
  8   gallons grade 4 vermiculite
  4   level teaspoons ammonium nitrate
  2   level teaspoons superphosphate
10   level teaspoons dolomitic limestone

Because of the dust inherent in vermiculite and peat moss, it is best to make this mix outside wearing a dust mask and plastic gloves. Lay a clean 6- or 8-mil sheet of plastic on a level spot. Using a clean plastic gallon milk container with the bottom neatly cut out, scoop the 8 gallons of shredded sphagnum peat moss onto the center of the plastic. Water the peat moss until it is uniformly moist. Add the eight gallons of grade 4 vermiculite. Sprinkle on the ammonium nitrate, superphosphate, and dolomitic limestone. Mix thoroughly until the medium is uniform. Store in any clean container. Cornell Peat-Lite Mix C is sterile and does not need to be pasteurized before use.

PASTEURIZATION

Pasteurization differs from sterilization in that it kills most organisms, good and bad, in the soil, while sterilization kills *all* the organisms, good and bad, in the soil. At first glance it may seem that sterilization is better, but often it isn't. Because pasteurization leaves a small but (usually) balanced population of beneficial and harmful organisms, their populations compete, neither one dominating the other. A soil that has been sterilized, on the other hand, has no organisms, and, hence, no balance. Whatever organism happens to establish itself first in sterilized soil often undergoes an unchecked population explosion, and if that organism is one harmful to plants, a great deal of trouble can ensue.

Pasteurization consists of heating moist soil to 180°F for thirty minutes. For years gardeners thought the only way to pasteurize soil at home was to use the kitchen oven. I wouldn't wish that on anyone. No matter how carefully you do it, you just can't avoid making the whole kitchen smell like a superheated muddy sauna. There is a better way: the boiling water method.

BOILING WATER METHOD OF SOIL PASTEURIZATION

1. Fill a large, small-screen sieve three-fourths full of soil mix.

2. Pour boiling water over the soil until it is thoroughly saturated.

3. Drape with plastic wrap and wait 15 minutes.

4. Remove the plastic and repeat step 2.

5. Cover with plastic again and wait until the soil is cool. You're done.

STERILIZING CONTAINERS AND TOOLS

Whether you use seed flats, plastic multiflats, or pots, your containers should be sterilized before each use. The easiest way to accomplish this is to wash them in a solution of water and chlorine bleach in a ratio of 9:1 and rinse. Tools, such as dibble sticks, should be washed in a 4:1 solution and rinsed.

Seed Sowing

A long, hot day hoeing thousands of weed seedlings from the garden is enough to convince you that seeds need no help from people to germinate. Yet an entire summer's armada of sprouting weeds represents only a fraction of the seeds that actually occupy the soil in your garden. Disease and environmental factors manage to thin the weedy horde substantially. Seeds *do* need our help to maximize their germination rate, and a little knowledge can allow you to consistently produce bumper crops.

USING SEED-STARTING CONTAINERS

These directions apply to starting annuals, biennials, perennials, vegetables, and so on.

1. Fill each container completely with starter mix and level with a straight board.
2. Gently tamp with the board until the mix is recessed ½ inch beneath the container rim.
3. Water gently until the mix is evenly moist.

Blend small seeds (petunia, begonia) with grade 4 vermiculite and sprinkle this mixture evenly over the soil surface. Water evenly and place the container in a plastic bag with a few pinholes poked in it. Put in a warm spot.

For medium seeds (pansy) use the tip of a dibble stick or pencil to make small trenches down the length of the container. Be sure each trench is about twice as deep as the diameter of the seeds. Drop seeds into the trench at regular intervals and cover.

For large seeds (marigold) use a dibble stick to poke evenly spaced holes in rows along the length of the container. Plant individual seeds into holes that are one and a half to two times their diameter and cover.

For light-sensitive seeds, place the seeds on the surface of the mix, gently pressing them. Cover with a fine dusting of vermiculite. Water evenly and place the container in a plastic bag with a few pinholes poked in it. Put in a warm spot.

HOW SEEDS GERMINATE

The seeds you purchase for your garden are made up of three parts: a quiescent plant embryo, a food supply, and a protective seed coat. When the seed is planted, a three-stage germination process begins.

During the first stage the embryo becomes active. Water is absorbed, which swells the seed and awakens the embryo. The plant's metabolic rate increases and its cells begin to manufacture the substances that the plant will need to begin its growth process.

The second stage of germination involves the breakdown of fats and carbohydrates into simpler substances, and the movement of those substances from food-storage tissues to the plant's growing points.

In the final stage of germination the plant begins to actively grow, and the root and stem emerge from the protective seed coat.

When your seedlings begin to emerge from the soil, untie the plastic bag to allow a degree of air circulation. When most seed leaves, or cotyledons, have opened, remove the flat from the bag and place it under grow-lights or on a windowsill.

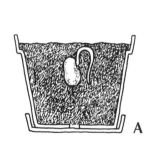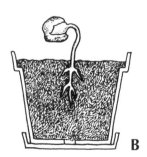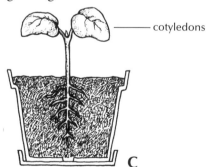

cotyledons

When a seed is planted in moist soil it swells with absorbed moisture and becomes metabolically active. The first active growth sees the root emerge from the seed (A). While the root provides anchorage the stem pushes through the soil (B). When the seedcoat is shed the seed leaves, called cotyledons, begin photosynthesis (C).

Growing and Transplanting Indoors

Once the seeds have germinated and the first true leaves have appeared, it's time to move the seedlings from the seed flat to a growing container. This process is called *pricking out* and is one of the more delicate tasks a gardener performs. We'll discuss it later (see page 225). First, though, you have two decisions to make: what type of growing mix to use, and what type of container to select.

GROWING MIXES

Growing mixes differ from seed-starting mixes in that growing mediums have a coarser texture, a wider range of organic additives, and a higher concentration of nutrients. Some are formulated for specific crops, such as rhododendrons, for when the plants are grown in containers for prolonged periods. Other mixes suit a wide range of seedlings until they are ready to be transplanted to the garden. The latter is what the following mixes are designed to do.

California Growing Mix

Some years ago the University of California designed several growing mixes based on easily obtained, uniform ingredients. These recipes allow gardeners to create uniform mixes at home over and over again. Of all the U.C. formulations, the best for growing plants that eventually will be transplanted into the garden is this:

8	gallons shredded sphagnum peat moss
24	gallons fine sand
4	tablespoons plus 1 teaspoon potassium nitrate
4	tablespoons plus 1 teaspoon potassium sulfate
7	ounces single superphosphate
28	ounces ground limestone

Because of the dust inherent in peat moss, it is best to make this mix outside wearing a dust mask and plastic gloves. Lay a clean 6- or 8-mil sheet of plastic on a level spot. Using a clean plastic gallon milk container with the bottom neatly cut out, scoop the shredded sphagnum peat moss onto the center of the plastic. Water the peat moss until it is uniformly moist. Add the fine sand. Sprinkle on the potassium nitrate, potassium sulfate, single superphosphate, and ground limestone. Mix thoroughly until the medium is uniform. Store in any clean container. California Mix is sterile and should not be pasteurized before use.

Modified Cornell Peat-Lite Growing Mix

Some people love the California Growing Mix or any of a number of similar ones. My favorite, however, is a modified Cornell Peat-Lite Growing Mix. I was introduced to it many years ago and have yet to find anything better:

9	gallons shredded sphagnum peat moss
5	gallons grade 2 vermiculite
4	gallons horticultural-grade perlite
½	pound dolomitic limestone
2	tablespoons superphosphate
1	pound 5-10-5 granular fertilizer

As with the California Growing Mix, it is best to make this mix outside wearing a dust mask and plastic gloves. Lay a clean 6- or 8-mil sheet of plastic on a level spot. Use a clean plastic gallon milk container with the bottom neatly cut out to scoop the shredded sphagnum peat moss into a pile on the center of the plastic. Water the peat moss until it is uniformly moist. If the moss is very dry it can become almost water repellant. To moisten dry sphagnum moss add a tablespoon of Murphy's Oil Soap to 2 or 3 gallons of water and moisten the moss with the solution of soap and water. (The soap reduces the surface tension of the water making it more readily absorbed by the moss). Add the vermiculite and horticultural-grade perlite on top of the moss. Sprinkle on the dolomitic limestone, superphosphate, and 5-10-5 granular fertilizer. This mix contains enough fertilizer to supply growing plants for four to five weeks. Organic growers can skip the fertilizer but should begin a regime of organic fertilizing as soon as the plants are potted up. Mix thoroughly until the medium is uniform. Store in any clean container.

CONTAINERS TO GROW IN

A growing container is where a plant lives when it isn't in the garden. Containers come in a vast array of sizes and materials, all designed to hold enough soil to keep a plant's roots healthy. Some do this better than others; clay pots, followed closely by heavy-gauge plastic pots, are best.

Clay Pots

Clay pots have been used to grow plants for thousands of years, by many diverse cultures. They are perhaps the oldest reusable growing containers in the world. Today they are available in myriad sizes, ranging from tiny things about one inch across to giant containers suitable for interior landscaping. The most popular are round in shape with 3-, 4-, 5-, 6-, and 8-inch rim diameters.

Benefits

- Allow both moisture and air to pass through the pot walls, resulting in better root growth
- Can be sterilized with very hot water (200°F for three minutes)
- Reusable and made from natural materials

Drawbacks

- Heavier than most other containers
- Easily broken or cracked
- Toxic levels of salts forming on pot walls as moisture wicks through; must be periodically removed by soaking in hot water

Used clay pots should be sterilized in a bath of very hot water before being filled with growing mix.

Plastic Pots

Plastic pots are the most popular type of growing container now in use. They are inexpensive and come in an assortment of sizes and shapes. Unlike clay pots, however, plastic pots cannot be sterilized with very hot water without damaging them. Soaking in 160°F water for three minutes kills most harmful pathogens without, however, harming the pot.

Benefits

- Lightweight and easy to store
- Reusable and recyclable
- Come in different shapes and colors

Drawbacks

- Nonporous, which inhibits air and moisture exchanges and sometimes allows salts to develop on the soil surface or inside the rim of the pot
- Inhibited root growth in some white pots that allow light to transfuse through pot walls
- Overheat soil when some dark-colored pots left in direct sunlight
- Cannot be sterilized with very hot water

Fiber Pots

Fiber pots are made of a combination of peat and wood fiber molded into the shape of a container. They are biodegradable, inexpensive, and easy to store. The most common sizes are three- and four-inch rounds.

Benefits

- Negligible damage to roots when transplanting, since pots are set in the soil
- Biodegradable and inexpensive

Drawbacks

- If pots kept too wet, pots fall apart before plants large enough to transplant
- If pots kept too dry, plant roots unable to penetrate the sides, resulting in weak, deformed root growth

Drinking Cups

Drinking cups of either Styrofoam or waxed paper make very inexpensive growing containers. All they lack are some drainage holes, which can be punched into the bottom of each with a nail.

Benefit

- Very inexpensive

Drawbacks

- Styrofoam: not environment-friendly and cracks easily
- Waxed paper: can fall apart before plants are ready to transplant

Plastic Multipacks or Divided Flats

Plastic multipacks have become the container of choice for commercial nurseries growing bedding plants and vegetables in the spring. They are inexpensive, readily available, and easy to use; they maximize growing space as well.

Benefits

- Inexpensive
- Maximize growing space

Drawbacks

- Cannot be sterilized
- Usually cannot be reused
- Easily broken during use

HOW TO PRICK OUT SEEDLINGS

Of the many tools that can be used for pricking out seedlings, the pointed end of a plastic garden label has served me best over the years. Hold the label at about a forty-five-degree angle, with the tip resting on the soil about half an inch from the seedling's stem. Insert the label into the soil and loosen the rootball while gently holding one of the plant's seed leaves, or cotyledons. When the plant is free of the flat, move it immediately to a growing container prefurnished with a hole in its soil slightly larger than the size of the rootball. Place the seedling in the hole. Firm the soil gently and water lightly.

GROWING PLANTS USING NATURAL LIGHT

In the Northern Hemisphere plants grow best in late spring and early summer when natural sunlight lasts for more than twelve hours each day and is near its seasonal peak of intensity. Conversely, the intensity of natural light is lowest in winter, when many people try to start their spring plants. Thus even under the best of conditions, using only natural light in winter produces weaker plants than a well-managed regimen of artificial light.

To put it bluntly, growing strong, healthy plants on a windowsill in late winter is like trying to get a suntan in a cave. With a little modification, however, even a windowsill can produce good-looking plants.

1. Use a window with a southern exposure that gets unobstructed sunlight.
2. Place an incandescent light about 12 inches above and directly behind the plants. Leave the light on about twelve hours a day. This setup strengthens the intensity of the light the plants receive and enhances the red wavelengths that promote sturdy growth.
3. Turn the growing containers 180 degrees each day.

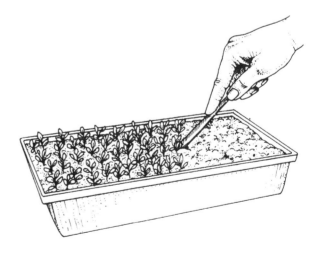

Pricking out is the term that describes the technique of transplanting seedlings from the germination area to the growing area.

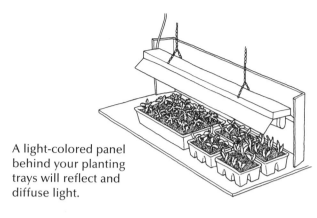

A light-colored panel behind your planting trays will reflect and diffuse light.

GROWING PLANTS UNDER ARTIFICIAL LIGHT

Since the discovery of fire people have tried to duplicate natural light. We haven't done it yet, but we're getting closer all the time. Today it's relatively simple to make a bank of artificial lights that will grow plants almost as well as the best natural light.

1. Most artificial light units consist of two forty-watt incandescent bulbs alongside four fluorescent tubes. The incandescent bulbs provide light with abundant red and orange wavelengths, while the fluorescent tubes yield violet and blue light. In combination they almost duplicate natural light. Grow-lights are single-bulb units that supply all the wavelengths present in natural light; thus they are often more convenient to use than fluorescent/incandescent light banks.

2. Set the lights about 6 inches above the tops of the plants and leave them on for a minimum of twelve hours a day — preferably fourteen to sixteen hours. Timers can be added to the light units to make turning them on and off easy.

TRANSPLANTING FROM CONTAINER TO GARDEN

I once had a professor who taught that transplanting was as traumatic to a plant as surgery was to people. As true as this may be, proper transplanting techniques can reduce that trauma and ease a plant's transition to its new home.

The act of transplanting most often damages the roots of a plant. If they are injured, their resulting inability to provide the rest of the plant with water can lead to wilting or death. Because plants lose water most quickly on hot, sunny days, these are the worst times to transplant. The best time is on a cool and drizzly day, for water loss is then at a minimum.

Prepare the garden by watering the soil the previous night. Just before transplanting, water the plants and loosen the soil of the garden with a rake. Remove each plant from its growing container. With a trowel, dig a hole slightly bigger than the rootball of the transplant, pulling the displaced soil toward you into a low mound. Set the plant in the hole and push the soil around the rootball. Firm the soil gently around the plant and water.

HOW ELECTROMAGNETIC RADIATION LIGHTS UP YOUR LIFE

The sunlight that warms us each day is a small part of a grand thing called electromagnetic radiation. There are many types of this radiation, including cosmic waves, radio waves, and microwaves, but of the many forms this energy takes the one that most influences life on earth is visible light.

Visible light occupies a small section of the electromagnetic spectrum and is itself divided into the six regions that we know as the colors of the rainbow: violet, blue, green, yellow, orange, and red. When most forms of electromagnetic radiation strike a plant, the majority is reflected back into space. When visible light contacts a plant, however, chlorophyll inside the plant absorbs the violet, blue, yellow, orange, and red wavelengths and uses that electromagnetic energy to drive the process of photosynthesis. The unused green light is reflected back from the plants, which is why they appear green to us.

In addition to fueling photosynthesis each wavelength of visible light helps the plant grow in a certain way. Violets and blues stimulate tall, thin, unbranched stems with large, thin leaves. Reds and oranges produce stout, well-branched stems with small, thick leaves. Too much or too little of any one color, or of all colors, results in abnormal plant growth.

Pinching is the removal of the growing tip of a plant. The growing tip is called the apical meristem, and when it is removed the buds along the stem break and grow into new branches. This happens because as the meristem grows, it produces hormones that travel to nearby buds, telling them to just sit tight and do nothing. By removing the meristem, you remove these inhibiting hormones, and the buds are free to grow.

Meristems of different plants produce different quantities of inhibiting hormones. Usually plants that naturally grow straight and tall with little side-branch development have large amounts of inhibiting hormones, while plants that naturally branch freely have low levels. Consequently, the only plants that need encouragement to branch are the tall, straight types that would not do so naturally. Examples of plants commonly pinched back include snapdragon, lisanthus, and dahlia.

Starting Seed Outdoors: Direct Seeding

As we have seen, tender plants, or plants that need a longer growing period to flower, are started indoors in late winter. Plants that need shorter growing seasons to bloom, or that are more cold-tolerant, are often sown directly in the garden.

PREPARING THE SOIL

If you have average garden soil, water it well the night before and let it dry until afternoon. Rototill the soil to a depth of 6 to 12 inches until it looks uniform. Rake the area smooth and plant the seeds.

Arid garden soil is common in the West, where low rainfall, frequent irrigation, and high water tables encourage the deposition of toxic salts in the upper layers of the soil. Water the garden well the night before. Rototill to a depth of 6 to 10 inches until uniform. Rake the soil into a gently sloping mound and again water it well. Let the seed bed dry overnight. The next day, lightly rake it to break up the soil. Plant seeds along the slope of the seed bed but not at its crest. Over the course of the growing season, salts are more likely to accumulate at the crest of the slope than along its sides.

If you have clay garden soil, cultivate the seed bed to a depth of 8 to 12 inches when the soil is dry. Rake the soil smooth and water for four to eight hours (about 1 inch of water). Allow the soil to dry until it seems evenly moist, and then rototill again, this time to a depth of 4 to 6 inches. Rake the soil smooth and plant the seeds.

PLANTING SEEDS

To plant small seeds (petunia, begonia), blend them with grade 4 vermiculite, sprinkle the mixture evenly over the soil surface, and water evenly.

For medium seeds (pansy), use the tip of a dibble stick or pencil to make small trenches down the length of the seed bed. Be sure the trench is about twice as deep as the diameter of the seeds. Drop seeds into the trench at regular intervals and cover.

For large seeds (marigold), use a dibble stick to poke evenly spaced holes in rows along the length of the seed bed or scrape a shallow trench. Plant individual seeds into holes or space them in the trench and cover.

For light-sensitive seeds, place the seeds on the surface of the soil, gently pressing them in. Cover with a fine dusting of vermiculite and water evenly.

Large seeds can be planted in a trench dug along the seedbed. Proper spacing at sowing eliminates the need to thin plants later on.

Growing On

Once your plants are happily growing in the garden, you can usually spend less time tending to them and more time enjoying their beauty. Of the things that still require your attention, watering and fertilizing are two of the most important.

Gardens in general need about one inch of water per week to meet their needs, though during hot spells that amount can easily double or triple. The best time to water the garden is in the early morning when it is cooler and the strengthening sun can dry any wet foliage before diseases can take advantage. If you must water at other times be sure not to wet the foliage. Don't water during the hot portion of the day.

Plants grown for their flowers need higher levels of phosphorus and lesser amounts of potassium and nitrogen than plants grown just for their leaves. Once the plants are established, two applications four weeks apart of half-strength 20-20-20 liquid fertilizer helps them get off to a good start. After that, a sidedressing of granular 5-10-5 will see them through the flowering season.

Some annuals grow better without added fertilizer. These include nasturtium, spider flower, portulaca, cosmos, gazania, and salpiglosis. Simply amend the soil with a little compost or rotted manure before planting and water as needed.

HOW TO MEASURE HOW MUCH WATER YOUR GARDEN RECEIVES

If the garden requires about an inch of water each week, just how are you supposed to know how much water equals an inch? Here's the answer. Use a permanent marker to mark the inside of a clean, empty coffee can in one-inch gradations. Place the can halfway between the sprinkler and the farthest point the spray of water from the sprinkler reaches. By timing how long it takes to fill the can to the first mark, you can gauge how long the sprinkler needs to be on each week if it doesn't rain.

Controlling Common Pests and Diseases

It's common belief that there are more plant pests than there are plants in the world. At least some days it seems that way. It's foolish to think we can control creatures as versatile and diverse as bugs and slugs. We should be content if we just slow them down a bit. Here are a few very safe concoctions that the bugs haven't caught up with yet.

SAFE INSECT CONTROL

Soap sprays are a very safe method of controlling many types of insects and mites. Be sure to use soft water (rainwater is great) when making a soap spray, as hard water inactivates the soap. When using these sprays, cover all plant surfaces thoroughly with the solution. The following recipes can provide good control of spider mites, whiteflies, caterpillars, aphids, and other insects. In cool weather spray plants every ten days. In warm or hot weather spray plants every four to six days.

Ivory Soap Spray

    3   tablespoons Ivory Soap powder
    1   gallon warm soft water

Mix the soap with the water until soap dissolves. Pour the solution into a hand sprayer and apply to plants.

Murphy's Oil Soap Spray

    2   fluid ounces Murphy's Oil Soap
    1   gallon warm soft water

Pour the soap into the water and stir gently. Pour the solution into a hand sprayer and apply to plants.

Neem is an organic pesticide derived from the seeds of the neem plant (*Azadirachta indica*), a tree native to India. Neem is effective against at least 150 different insect pests, as well as black spot on roses, and perhaps even powdery mildew. It also has low toxicity to beneficial insects, animals, and people. Neem sprays are available in oil-based and oil-free formulations and have been registered for use on ornamentals as well as edible crops. Some of the neem sprays presently available include Bioneem, Azatin, Turplex, and Margosan-O.

SAFE SLUG AND SNAIL CONTROL

Methods of controlling slugs and snails are famous for being unorthodox. They range from placing saucers of beer in the garden to liberal applications of diatomaceous earth around plantings. Recent studies have shown that both of these techniques, along with mulching with wood chips, are only slightly more effective than doing nothing at all. Saucers of sugar water (water with 5 percent table sugar added) perform better than beer; saucers of water containing dissolved Nutrasweet, however, catch only a few flies. As discouraging as this sounds, there are some safe techniques that work.

If you have any copper piping — the type used for household water pipes — you have more than pipes, you have a great slug controller. Place the pipes in the garden about one foot from the plants. Make sure they contact the ground. Most slugs won't cross the pipes — except perhaps the King Kong-size ones along the Pacific Coast.

Another option is a garlic spray. Some folks believe that if you spray at night, especially during a waning moon, you can achieve even better control.

Garlic Spray

    5   cloves garlic
    1   quart hot water
    1   tablespoon Murphy's Oil Soap

Mash the garlic cloves with mortar and pestle and place them in a clear one-quart bottle. Pour in the Murphy's Oil Soap, followed by the hot water. Stir gently and cap loosely. Allow to sit for twenty-four to forty-eight hours. Strain and pour into a hand sprayer. Spray the leaves of your plants thoroughly, as well as any slugs you may see.

SAFE POWDERY MILDEW CONTROL

For years disease control has been left largely to the chemical companies. That's a pity, for there are ingenious ways to control many common problems. Annuals, such as zinnias, routinely suffer from powdery mildew. Many people just let this disease take its course, but they don't have to. Almost everyone is familiar with chamomile (*Chamaemelum nobile*). It makes a flavorful tea and smells delightful. In addition, chamomile is an excellent control for powdery mildew.

Chamomile Spray

    3-4   tea bags of pure chamomile
      1   pint hot water

Heat the water to boiling. Place the tea bags in the water and allow to brew until the solution is cool. Pour the solution into a hand sprayer and spray infected plants completely, covering all sides of the leaves. Repeat every day for advanced infections, and once every four to six days for preventative control. Do not spray plants in full sun.

Collecting and Storing Seed

No matter how many times you grow a garden of annuals, you never quite get comfortable with its transience. Its beauty ends with the autumn frosts. One way to soften the loss is to collect seeds from your favorite plants, store them, and plant them in spring. Seed collection is an enjoyable pastime and links your years of gardening into a beautiful genealogy of flowers. Here are five favorites to try:

Ageratum
(*Ageratum houstonianum*)

Collect the abundant amounts of tiny ageratum seeds when seed heads turn brown. Screen to separate the seeds from the chaff. Dry the seeds on paper towels for about a week, and then store them in labeled and sealed paper envelopes. Place the envelopes in a jar and keep in the refrigerator.

Cosmos
(*Cosmos bipinnatus*)

Collect the seed heads when ripe and dry them indoors on a screen or paper towels for a week to ten days. Then separate the seeds from the seed heads and dry for another three to four days. Store in labeled and sealed paper envelopes. Place the envelopes in a jar and keep in the refrigerator.

Marigold
(*Tagetes* spp.)

Many of the most popular marigold varieties are hybrids that produce largely infertile seed. Still, there are many others that can produce abundant amounts of fertile seed. Collect the dried seed heads and dry them indoors for about a week. The seeds themselves are large and easily pulled from the heads. Dry the seeds for another four days, then store in a labeled, sealed envelope. Place the envelopes in a jar and keep in the refrigerator.

Nasturtium
(Tropaeolum majus)

Collect the 3-sided seed pod of the nasturtium when dry and separate the individual cells. Do not try to separate the seed from the individual cell. Allow the seeds to dry for about a week, then store in labeled, sealed envelopes. Place the envelopes in a jar and keep in the refrigerator.

Pansy
(Viola x wittrockiana)

Many pansies are hybrids that produce what many gardening experts call inferior forms. Inferior or not, I like them. The flowers of these seeds are not the giant happy faces of the hybrids, but they are pretty just the same. The seeds are found in small, dry capsules. Collect the capsules before they shatter, and dry them for about a week. Then separate the seeds and store them in labeled, sealed envelopes. Place the envelopes in a jar and keep in the refrigerator.

SPECIAL PROJECT: MAKING A CHILDREN'S GARDEN OF ANNUALS

Adults take for granted what children do not — that the world is new and mysterious and waiting to share its secrets. Some of those secrets are found in every garden, but a garden designed just for children holds enchanting treasures that their innocent curiosity readily embraces. This is a garden where kids can play and learn, and even grown-ups, if given enough time, can rediscover a bit of magic. Here are some basic rules to keep in mind when creating a garden for children:

Keep flower beds narrow, so that little arms can reach across; any furnishings, such as tables or pergolas, should be small as well. Tools should be kid-size and sturdy, with items such as watering cans small enough for kids to carry even when full.

Add a few items that seem out of scale. If you have a garden path in the children's garden, pave it with small stepping-stones surrounding large ones. Or leave areas of the path without stones, so kids can jump across. One or two climbing-size boulders are fun to have as well.

Plants with interesting textures can keep a child's attention for hours. The best of these is fuzzy lamb's ears (*Stachys byzantina*), which is a perennial and not an annual but too nice to leave out.

Children like to see things happen, and watching grass grow is slow and boring. Choose

plants for the garden that grow quickly: petunias, marigolds, nasturtiums, hollyhocks, zinnias.

Plants that smell good are always a hit with kids. Flowers with rich fragrances include blue petunias, sweet alyssum, snapdragons, four o'clocks, stocks, and spider flowers. Some plants, such as fragrant geraniums and many herbs, also have fragrant leaves.

With a little string and some wooden poles it's easy to make a tepee-shaped trellis, perfect for a hideaway. Plant scarlet runner beans at the base of the strings and watch the fast-growing vines transform the trellis into a leafy fort.

10

Versatile Perennials

When I was growing up, annuals were much more popular garden plants than perennials. Each spring the garden centers would overflow with flats of colorful marigolds and petunias. These were bought by the carload and methodically planted about every yard in the neighborhood. French marigolds were used as edging along walkways. Petunias cascaded from windowboxes and hanging baskets. And impatiens brightened the shady places beneath the trees.

Our yard was no different, except for a small side garden my mother cared for at the edge of the woods. In spring there were clumps of tall bearded iris in shades of lilac, yellow, and violet. In summer daylily blossoms swarmed like clouds of orange butterflies. But to my very young eyes the most stunning sight was when the cardinal flower came into bloom. Its flowers were of a shade of scarlet so bright it seemed they could set the world on fire.

In a way I suppose they have, for perennials have become the backbone of the garden. Peonies, irises, daylilies, and phlox share space with delphiniums, cone flowers, daisies, and scores of others. Where they once occupied a page or two in the seed catalogs or a small space in the garden center, perennials now dominate. This change does not imply that perennials are better than annuals. Both should have space in the garden. But annuals, no matter how beautiful, are visitors to the garden. Perennials live there.

In early summer some years ago I found myself walking through the remains of a walled garden that lay behind an abandoned New England estate. At its heyday in the early 1920s, the place had been a beautiful formal garden with manicured flower beds and carefully pruned apple trees. As the years of neglect melted into decades, the flower beds slowly disappeared beneath a mantle of weeds. The apple trees were splintered by winter storms and the stone walls were enveloped in a blanket of bittersweet vine. I was just about convinced that all of this garden's splendor had vanished many seasons ago when I noticed a bright spot of color poking above the weeds. Upon investigation, I discovered a patch of lemon daylilies in full bloom.

It is inspirational to find something with the ability to survive and even prosper under difficult conditions. As the loyal dog returns unerringly to its master despite obstacles, so perennials return each spring to the garden, even when there is no apparent garden to return to. If you have a need for tough, low-maintenance plants, these are the best.

Some Very Reliable Perennials

ACHILLEA

Achillea is the scientific name for a group that includes the yarrows and sneezeworts. Drought- and heat-tolerant, they thrive in full sun in poor, dry soils with a pH of 5.5–7.0. They do not do well in poorly drained places. Three of the eighty-five species are very reliable:

Fernleaf yarrow *(Achillea filipendulina)*
Fernleaf yarrow is known for deeply cut, fernlike leaves that are richly aromatic. Strong 2- to 3-foot stems hold large flat-topped flower clusters in bright shades of yellow. In cooler areas, propagate by dividing plants after they flower. In the South, divide plants in fall. Sow seeds indoors in late winter or outdoors in fall. Do not cover, as they need light to germinate. Fernleaf yarrows make excellent cut or dried flowers. Hardy in Zones 3 through 8.

Sneezewort *(Achillea ptarmica)*
Sneezewort is one of those plants that is so successful it can cause problems. A small planting can, in just a few seasons, overtake large areas. Control by dividing the clumps after they flower and moving the extra plants to spots needing a touch of white in summer. Hardy in Zones 3 through 8.

Common yarrow *(Achillea millefolium)*
Common yarrow's lacy, aromatic leaves line 2-foot, pliant stems topped with flat clusters of white, pink, or red flowers. Clumps spread quickly, so divide every two to four years after the flowers fade in late summer. In the South, divide plants in the fall. Sow seeds indoors in late winter or outdoors in fall. Do not cover, as they need light to germinate. Common yarrows make excellent cut or dried flowers. Hardy in Zones 3 through 9.

♦ **The Best of the Achilleas**
> *Achillea filipendulina* 'Coronation Gold'
> *A. millefolium* 'Cerise Queen'
> *A. ptarmica* 'The Pearl'

ANEMONE

Anemones, sometimes called windflowers, belong to the buttercup family and are native to the North Temperate zones across the world. They prefer to grow in rich, woodland soils (pH 6.0-7.0) in full sun or partial shade, conditions that allow the vigorous plants to quickly spread into enchanting mass plantings.

Snowdrop anemone *(Anemone sylvestris)*
Snowdrop anemones have medium-green, deeply lobed leaves and pliant, 18-inch stems that bear enchantingly simple, pure white, fragrant flowers in spring. The plants naturalize easily, quickly forming mats of rich foliage. Hardy in Zones 4 through 8.

Japanese anemone *(Anemone x hybrida)*
Japanese anemone is a hybrid producing two-foot mounds of deep green foliage with pink or white flowers held high above the leaves in late summer. It prefers rich, well-drained woodland soils (pH 6.0-7.5) with morning sun. Once established, Japanese anemone reliably produces abundant flowers every year. Hardy in Zones 5 through 9.

Grape-leafed anemone *(Anemone tomentosa)*
Native to Tibet, grape-leafed anemone is perhaps the most vigorous of the anemones, producing abundant numbers of bright pink flowers held above the large, deeply toothed leaves in late summer. The plants prefer open woods or shady gardens and rich soils (pH 6.0-7.0). They do especially well in the eastern United States. The species is hardy in Zones 4 through 9, while most of the varieties are hardy in Zones 5 through 9.

♦ **The Best of the Anemones**
> *Anemone sylvestris* 'Flore Pleno'
> *A. tomentosa* 'Superba'
> *A. x hybrida* 'September Charm'

BOLTONIA

Boltonia asteroides is native to the tall-grass prairies of the American Midwest, where the strong, 3- to 4-foot-tall plants are covered with white or pink asterlike flowers in late summer and early fall. The plants naturalize easily, thriving in full sun and average soil (pH 5.5-7.0).

◆ **The Best Boltonias**
  Boltonia asteroides 'Pink Beauty'
  B. a. 'Snowbank'

ECHINACEA PURPUREA

Purple coneflower is native to eastern meadows and grasslands. The plant has large, lance-shaped leaves on 3- to 4-foot stems topped with large, daisylike flowers in pink or purple in summer to early fall. Coneflowers tolerate poor, dry soil but prefer average, well-drained soil (pH 5.5-7.0). Propagate by dividing in spring in the North, fall in the South.

◆ **The Best Purple Coneflowers**
  Echinacea purpurea Bressingham Hybrids
  E. p. 'Magnus'
  E. p. 'White Star'

HEMEROCALLIS

Hemerocallis is the scientific name for the daylily, one of the most beloved of all garden plants. Daylilies adapt to a wide range of conditions: soils from dry to wet, temperatures from hot to cold. The plants produce strap-shaped leaves and abundant, trumpet-shaped flowers from early summer to fall. Today's hybrids offer flowers in every color of the rainbow except blue.

Tawny daylily *(Hemerocallis fulva)*
The tawny daylily originated in the Orient and came to Europe via the trade routes in 1567. From there it hitched a boat ride to America, where it quickly jumped the garden gate and became naturalized throughout vast areas of the country. Tawny daylilies are triploids — they have thirty-three chromosomes instead of the normal twenty-two — and do not produce seed. They spread by sending out abundant underground shoots, or rhizomes, and can create an extensive ground cover in only a few seasons. The plants will grow in shade or sun and in a wide variety of soil types. Hardy in Zones 3 through 9.

Purple mountain daylily *(Hemerocallis altissima)*
The giant of daylilies, purple mountain has flower stalks reaching from five to seven feet high. The flowers open during the day and close at night; they are a delicate yellow color with a pleasing fragrance. Purple mountain daylilies are famous for being able to look fresh and perky even on hot summer days in full sun. Hardy in Zones 4 through 9.

Lemon daylily *(Hemerocallis lilioasphodelus)*
Lemon daylily is a dainty plant with thin, grasslike leaves and small, clear yellow blossoms that perfume the air in early summer. Native to Asia, the lemon daylily came to America with the first European settlers and has been a part of the landscape ever since. The plants like sunny places in the North, partial shade in the South, but seem to grow well wherever they are planted. Hardy in Zones 3 through 9.

◆ **The Best of the Daylilies**
  Hemerocallis altissima 'Autumn Minaret'
  H. fulva 'Europa'
  H. fulva 'Kwanso'
  H. lilioasphodelus

Great Perennials People Don't Use Enough

Every once in a while a plant becomes so popular that you see it just about everywhere. It seems that every year every mother gets zonal geraniums on Mother's Day, and every shady patch of every garden is planted with some kind of hosta. The trouble with popularity is that it works against imagination, and imagination is what makes any beautiful garden beautifully unique. To help make your perennial border just a little different, add these interesting, underused plants.

Beach Wormwood
(Artemisia stellerana)

If you've ever walked the beaches of the Atlantic Coast, you've probably seen beach wormwood. It clings to the sandy hills and dunes above the high-tide mark, poking its deeply lobed silver-gray leaves into the sea breeze. On the beach the plant grows to about 18 inches tall and is hardy to Zone 4. Recently the British Columbia Botanic Garden introduced a dwarf variety, *A. s.* 'Silver Brocade', with a finely cut, chrome gray leaf. Plant 'Silver Brocade' in well-drained, sandy loam in full sun. It is excellent for summer moon gardens or as an edging accent along garden paths.

Bloody Cranesbill
(Geranium sanguineum)

Native to Europe and Asia, bloody cranesbill produces 10- to 15-inch mounds of deeply lobed leaves richly decorated with brilliant magenta-purple flowers in spring and summer. *G. s.* var. *striatum* has blush pink blossoms accented with veins of deep rose. Bloody cranesbill prefers moist, rich soils in full sun or partial shade. Cut back after flowering in spring to encourage plants to spread. A planting of bloody cranesbill interspersed with beach wormwood is stunning. Plants are hardy in Zones 5 through 7.

Fragrant Solomon's-Seal
(Polygonatum odoratum)

This lovely plant produces long, nodding stems lined with lily-of-the-valley-shaped leaves and rows of creamy white, fragrant, bell-like flowers in spring. Solomon's-seal does best in rich, woodland soil in bright shade and is a natural companion to ferns and wildflowers. *P. o.* 'Variegatum' has shiny green leaves marked with white margins. Plants are hardy in Zones 3 through 9.

Kamchatka Bugbane
(Cimicifuga simplex)

This stately plant is native to the subalpine meadows of the Kamchatka peninsula on the Pacific coast of Russia. It produces large green leaves stained with bronze and strong 3- to 5-foot-tall flower stalks adorned with creamy white bottlebrushlike flowers in late summer through fall. Plant Kamchatka bugbane in moist, rich soil in partial shade. Hardy to Zone 3. Some of the better varieties are *C. s.* 'White Pearl', *C. s.* 'Brunette', and *C. s.* 'Atropurpurea'.

Yellow Corydalis
(Corydalis lutea)

The fernlike foliage of yellow corydalis resembles bleeding heart. Yellow corydalis grows to about 10 inches tall and produces small, thinly tubular yellow flowers from late spring to fall. It prefers shady locations in moist woodland soils but will tolerate dry, sun-baked spots as well. Yellow corydalis is hardy to Zone 5; excellent with Solomon's-seal.

Glorious Goldenrods

An old maxim states that abundance breeds contempt. There is no better illustration of this statement's truth than goldenrod. There are between 60 and 130 species of goldenrod (*Solidago* spp.) in the world, most found in North America. The individual species range from alpine forms only a few inches tall to giants reaching nearly 8 feet. They can live almost anywhere, from the ruined soils of urban lots to boggy wetlands and windswept mountaintops. They are adaptable and rugged and sport beautiful plumes of golden blossoms each summer and fall. They also can be used to produce a reliable, bright dye for yarn, cloth, or basketry (see page 236). All this and most Americans call them weeds. Sometimes we just don't appreciate the beauty before us. If you would like to experiment with goldenrod in the garden, here are a few of the best species to try.

Canadian Goldenrod
(Solidago canadensis)

This is a stately plant with strong 4- to 6-foot stems, plentiful medium green toothed leaves, and large plumes of bright yellow flowers in late summer through early fall. Canadian goldenrod is the species most frequently cultivated in the garden. It grows well in almost any soil, isn't demanding about fertilizer or water, and adds a striking accent to the back of a border. Hardy in Zones 3 through 9.

Cutler Goldenrod
(Solidago cutleri)

This is the goldenrod for the rock garden, though it's sometimes difficult to find in the trade. Native to the alpine mountaintops of New York State, this charming plant grows only 4 to 6 inches tall. It has rich green leaves topped with diminutive plumes of golden yellow flowers. Hardy in Zones 4 through 7.

Seaside Goldenrod
(Solidago sempervirens)

Seaside goldenrod is native to the meadows and salt marshes of the Atlantic Coast, where it is routinely pounded by salt spray and whipped by storms. Consequently, this plant is as tough as nails. Seaside goldenrod has exceptionally sturdy 4- to 7-foot stems with smooth, lance-shaped leaves and a one-sided flower cluster of golden blossoms that persists from late summer into late fall. Hardy in Zones 4 through 9.

Sweet Goldenrod
(Solidago odora)

Sweet goldenrod deserves a place in both the perennial border and the herb garden. It grows from 2 to 4 feet tall, with distinctive lance-shaped, untoothed leaves that yield a delightful anise scent when crushed. The flowers appear in one-sided clusters and bloom in late summer and early fall. Hardy in Zones 3 through 8.

◆ **Additional Goldenrod Cultivars**

In addition to these versatile species there are also some excellent cultivars that will add a sunny dimension to any garden. Here are some of the best:

Solidago 'Baby Gold'
S. 'Golden Baby'
S. 'Golden Fleece'
S. 'Golden Lace'
S. 'Goldenmosa'

GOLDENROD DOESN'T MAKE YOU SNEEZE

For generations people have confused ragweed and goldenrod. Ragweed makes you sniffle and sneeze because its pollen is light and dry and the slightest breeze blows it all over the place. Goldenrod pollen is sticky, so that it can adhere to the legs of the bees that pollinate it. It doesn't blow around, so it doesn't make you sneeze.

There are many ways to transform the transient beauty of a flower into a long-lasting treasure. Some folks dry blossoms or add flowers to jams. And others save summer in the clothes they wear.

Dyeing cloth with goldenrod blossoms isn't all that difficult to do and adds a wonderful activity to autumn afternoons. You will need two large, nonreactive pots and a plastic bucket of equal size; a colander and a wooden stirring stick; alum, which you can purchase at most grocery stores and drugstores; a length of clean, white cloth; and lots of goldenrod flowers.

Fill the pot three-quarters full of water. Add an ounce of alum for every gallon of water. Stir until dissolved. Weigh the fabric on a scale, then add it to the pot and bring the liquid to a low boil. Reduce heat and simmer for one hour. Remove from heat and let the liquid cool to room temperature. While it cools, gather goldenrod flowers equal to three times the dry weight of the cloth. Try to collect only flowers, as leaves and stems will impart a greenish hue to the final cloth.

Put the goldenrod flowers in the second pot. Gently mash them until all are bruised. Cover the flowers with water and simmer for about two hours. As they simmer, continue to add enough water to keep the blossoms covered. Strain the yellow dye through the colander into the plastic bucket. Remove the cloth from the alum solution and gently squeeze out the excess liquid. Put the cloth in the dye bucket and stir gently. Let it stay in the dye until the dye solution is cool.

Remove the cloth and rinse with clear water. Hang in the shade until dry. Whatever you choose to make from the cloth, it will always hold the brilliance of that autumn day, and that is very special.

Pruning Perennials

If you asked people to define the word *pruning*, you would probably get many different answers. To many, the word conjures up visions of cutting branches from trees with loppers and sharp-toothed saws — though I had one whimsical student who insisted that pruning was the process of collecting dried plums. In a practical sense, though, pruning is the removal of part of a plant. Whether you cut off a branch or snip off a dead flower, you are pruning.

The types of pruning required for the above-ground portions of herbaceous perennials usually fall into these categories: deadheading, pinching, disbudding, and cutting back.

DEADHEADING
Deadheading is the removal of flowers after they have opened. In most circumstances an open flower is removed from a plant when it is spent or dead. Removal of flowers from a plant encourages the formation of additional flower buds by inhibiting seed production, thus prolonging the plant's bloom-

ing season. Old flowers are also excellent places for such diseases as gray mold to find a home, so regular deadheading keeps your plants healthier as well as better looking.

To deadhead, use a pair of scissors or small pruning shears. For such plants as daylilies, with many buds clustered at the end of a stalk, carefully nip out individual flowers as they go by. For such plants as phlox, whose flower heads consist of many smaller flowers, or peonies with solitary large blossoms, wait for most of the flowers in the flower head, or most of the petals in the large flowers, to go by, then snip the flower stalk back to the first leaf.

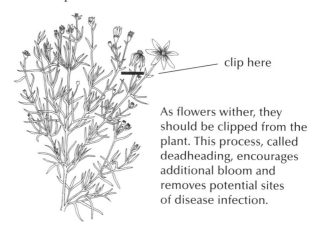

— clip here

As flowers wither, they should be clipped from the plant. This process, called deadheading, encourages additional bloom and removes potential sites of disease infection.

PINCHING

Pinching is the removal of the growing tip of a plant. The growing tip is called the meristem, and when it is removed the buds along the stem break and grow into new branches. This happens because as the meristem grows, it produces hormones that travel to nearby buds and tell them to just sit tight and do nothing. When the meristem is removed, so are these inhibiting hormones, and the buds become free to grow. Pinching in perennials is usually done in spring, when the plants first begin to grow actively. To pinch, simply remove the section of plant above the topmost set of leaves.

Not all perennials should be pinched, but those that need a bit of encouragement to form rounded, bushy plants are prime candidates. These include aster, boltonia, and chrysanthemum.

DISBUDDING

Disbudding is the removal of a flower bud. Some perennials, such as peonies, produce a large terminal flower bud with two axillary buds on either side. In many plants the terminal bud is female and the axillary buds are male. As it happens, the terminal female flowers are often larger and much showier than the axillary male flowers. However, if the male flowers are disbudded, the terminal female bud often responds by producing an even bigger and more beautiful flower than it normally would have.

CUTTING BACK

Cutting back is the horticultural equivalent of a haircut. It's the uniform cutting of a plant to reduce its height. Cutting back improves the appearance of straggly plants and, in some plants, encourages flowering. Examples of plants that are frequently cut back include lavender, yarrow, and geranium.

Perennial Profiles

Perennials are an incredibly large and diverse group of plants. There are, however, some perennials that form the backbone of the group as well as the garden, plants that always seem to pop up in discussions of landscape design, sunny gardens, shady gardens, or just plain gardening. They are replete with diversity, versatility, and beauty, traits they then transpose to any garden they grace.

Astilbe
Astilbe spp.

An astilbe in full bloom looks as inviting as a clump of cotton candy and feels as soft as a clump of goose down. The free-flowing flower spikes are held on upright, sometimes gently nodding stems. This combination of stem and flower creates a beautiful effect in the garden, a mass of blooming astilbe being compared to a colorful earthbound cloud. There are only about fourteen species of astilbe in the world, most native to eastern Asia, yet these species and their hybrids have proven indispensable in the garden. The various types range in height from a few inches to over 4 feet, can grow in full sun or shade, come in a wide range of colors, are easy to grow, and are virtually pest-free. They make wonderful companions to daylilies, ferns, hosta or lilies.

The Best Astilbes: The following listing is organized by species or hybrid groups:

Astilbe x *arendsii*

This is the name given to a group of hybrids created in Germany in the first half of the twentieth century. They prefer a rich, evenly moist but well-drained soil with good amounts of peat or other organic matter. The plants can grow in full sun in cool regions as long as the soil is rich in organic matter and remains evenly moist. In general, however, astilbe prefers fertile, evenly moist soil and partial to full, light shade. The plants are vigorous and look stunning when planted in groups of three or more. *A.* x *arendsii* 'Avalanche' has deep green leaves and large snow-white sprays of flowers on 30-inch stems in summer. The flower spikes all lean slightly in one direction, giving the effect of a steady, soft breeze moving over the flowers. *A.* x *arendsii* 'Bridal Veil' has large lacy white flowers held high above a sea of deep green foliage in summer. This variety is similar to 'Avalanche' in size and color but has slightly fuller flower spikes. *A.* x *arendsii* 'Rheinland' produces pink clusters of flowers on 2- to 3-foot stems in summer. *A.* x *arendsii* 'Fanal' bears deep red blossoms on 30-inch stems in summer. *A.* x *arendsii* 'Feur' (also called 'Fire') produces stems from 24 to 30 inches tall topped with tufts of bright coral flowers above dense, dark green foliage. Hardy in Zones 4 through 8.

A. chinensis

Native to China and Japan, this group naturally likes the moist, cool conditions found in shady wetlands but also adapts to gravelly soils. The plants bloom in late summer and are the last of the astilbes to flower. Once established the plants can become moderately drought tolerant. *A. chinensis* 'Pumila' is a dwarf with light pink, late-summer flowers atop neat, foot-tall stems. *A. chinensis* 'Finale' bears light pink blossoms on stems that grow from 12 to 18 inches tall. *A. chinensis*. var. *taquetii* 'Superba' grows to nearly 4 feet tall and bears upright, pale pink flower clusters in late summer. Hardy in Zones 4 through 8.

A. japonica

Japanese astilbe is an early blooming species flowering in early to mid-summer. The plants have deep green, glossy leaves, often touched with a blush of red or pink, and pyramidal spikes of flowers. *A. japonica* 'Deutschland' has stems reaching just 20 to 24 inches tall with creamy white flowers in early summer. *A. japonica* 'Europa' is a tidy, low growing variety with stems just 18 to 20 inches tall and clear pink, puffy flower spikes in summer. *A. japonica* 'Koblenz' produces 20- to 24-inch stems decorated with bright red flower spikes.

A. japonica 'Red Sentinel' is similar to 'Koblenz' in form with flowers of deep red. *A.* x *japonica* 'Cologne' has rich green, sharply toothed leaves beneath upright stalks of pastel red flowers. Hardy in zones 4-8.

A. x rosea

This hybrid features deeply cut, fernlike foliage and pink flowers on 2-foot stems in summer. *A.* x *rosea* 'Peach Blossom' has large flowers that open a light pink and gently fade to antique white in summer. Hardy in Zones 4 through 8.

A. simplicifolia

This interesting species has simple leaves and a very open flower cluster. It prefers moist, shady places and rich soils. *A. simplicifolia* 'Sprite' was introduced in 1978 and has become one of the most popular cultivars of astilbe. The plant produces 12-inch-tall mounds of rich green foliage decorated in summer with gently arching plumes of pink flowers. In northern regions, plant 'Sprite' in full sun in rich, well-drained, evenly moist soil. In the South, plant in the shade, and water during hot, dry spells. *A. simplicifolia* 'Aphrodite' has deep green leaves with a hint of bronze beneath 24- to 30-inch stems and reddish pink blossoms. *A. simplicifolia* 'Bronze Elegans' has strong 2-foot-tall stems topped with medium red flowers and green foliage marked with a bronze cast. Hardy in Zones 3 through 8.

Astilbe x hybrida

These plants, which number nearly two dozen cultivars, have been created by crossing a variety of species and hybrids. They all thrive in evenly moist, fertile soil rich in organic matter. Most varieties are tall, reaching between 30 and 36 inches high. *Astilbe* x *hybrida* 'Bressingham Beauty' bears plumes of light pink blossoms in summer on strong, 3-foot-tall stems. *Astilbe* x *hybrida* 'Snowdrift' has stems reaching 30 inches tall and linen white flowers in summer. *Astilbe* x *hybrida* 'Betsy Cuperus' is one of the largest astibles with deep green leaves and gently arching stems reaching 36 to 40 inches tall topped with plumes of light pink blossoms in summer. Hardy in zones 4-8.

Daylilies
Hemerocallis spp.

Daylilies have been planted in gardens for as long as there have been gardens to plant. They have bloomed along with our civilizations and become as diverse as our cultures. Earlier in the chapter we explored some of the fifteen species of *Hemerocallis*. Now we will examine some of the thirty-two thousand daylily cultivars.

The scientific name for the daylily *(Hemerocallis)* is a combination of the Greek words for "day" and "beauty," and reflects the fact that each flower lasts for about one day before fading. The flowers are all lily shaped but come in a wide range of forms, including flaring, with the ends of petals appearing flat; recurved, with the tips of the petals slightly reflexed; circular, with very wide petals that give the flower a rounded appearance; star, with narrow petals and pinched tips; and spider, with long, very narrow petals. Flower color is also diverse; varieties come in every shade of the rainbow except blue. There are varieties with flowers of a single color, a blend of similar colors, and two contrasting colors; some have eyed flowers with a dark-colored ring in the center of the blossom. There are so many different types that if you get bored growing daylilies, you just aren't trying.

Hardiness is another area where daylilies show diversity. The hardiest varieties are called dormants, because the foliage dies back to the ground in winter. Dormants do well in most areas of country, the exceptions being the Deep South and the warmest regions of the Southwest. Evergreen daylilies stay green all winter in the South but brown significantly in the North. Some evergreens can grow well in northern gardens if they are well mulched and protected from extreme temperatures. Many evergreens have more colorful flowers than the dormant varieties. Between dormants and evergreens are the semi-evergreen types, which have largely resulted from crosses between dormants and evergreens. The hardiness of semi-evergreen forms can really be a mystery. As a general guideline, plant dormant forms in areas where the ground freezes hard each winter, and evergreens where it does not. Gardeners who live where winters are short can plant many evergreens if they mulch the plants well and provide cover, such as a blanket of pine boughs, to protect them during winter and early spring.

How to Grow: Daylilies are perhaps the easiest of all perennials to grow. They need very little help from us to provide years of pleasure. Plant daylilies in fertile, well-drained soil with a pH of from 5.5 to 7.0 that has been cultivated to make it loose and friable. Water after planting. Supplemental watering while the plant is in bloom encourages larger flowers. Plant in full sun or light shade and divide in fall every four years.

How to Divide: Daylilies are just about as easy to divide as they are to grow. People have their preferred times to divide daylilies; mine is fall, about a month or so before the ground begins to freeze.

1. With a garden fork or shovel, lift the daylily clump from the soil and gently shake off any loose soil.
2. With a sharp shovel, split the clump into three or four pieces.
3. With your hands, gently pull groups of fans from the clump.
4. Cut the leaves about 6 inches above the crown and plant.

Daylilies are as easy to divide as they are to grow. The plants are simple to lift, separate, and replant. Once divided, daylilies often are noticeably more vigorous.

Levering clumps apart with a pair of garden forks does less damage to the plants than cutting them.

The Best Daylily Cultivars: It is perhaps arrogant of anyone to think he could whittle a list of thirty-two thousand varieties of daylilies down to the ten best. So instead I offer nine very good cultivars, and one that I will defend as being the very best:

Hemerocallis 'Candy Apple'

Flowers are a rich shade of melon-pink accented with a central heart of orange. 'Candy Apple' begins to bloom in midsummer and continues for many weeks.

H. 'Catherine Woodbury'

This cultivar produces large, light orchid flowers touched with fragrance on strong 30-inch stems. Plants blossom from mid to late summer.

H. 'Happy Returns'

The progeny of a cross between beautiful 'Suzie Wong' and the charming 'Stella de Oro', 'Happy Returns' is an exceptional variety growing to about 20 inches. Its pale yellow blossoms cover it from midsummer to fall.

H. 'Haunting Melody'

This cultivar has a wonderfully unique color reminiscent of crushed strawberries. The plant flowers in midsummer on 30- to 36-inch stems.

H. 'Hyperion'

Introduced in 1925, this daylily is still one of the best ever created, with large, clear yellow flowers that freely share their enchanting fragrance. The plant blooms in midsummer on strong, 36 to 40-inch stems. In addition to bearing some of the most beautiful blossoms of all daylilies, 'Hyperion' is also one of the tastiest. They are excellent additions to any summer salad. To use in a salad pick the blossom when fully open and the petals are firm and crisp. Snip the petals from the base of the flower and toss on top of salad. The petals have a light, floral flavor and the texture of fresh lettuce. They are great plain and even better when sprinkled with a light flavored vinaigrette

H. 'Ice Carnival'

Creamy white flowers with ruffled petals form on 28-inch scapes in midsummer. This variety holds up very well even in very hot summers.

H. 'Mary Todd'

A semi-evergreen tetraploid, 'Mary Todd' has stout 26-inch stems topped by thick, ruffled petals in early summer.

H. 'Red Reward'

Flowers are an incredibly rich crimson, touched with soft yellow-green at their centers. This variety stands the heat well, though it holds its best color in light shade.

H. 'Stella de Oro'

This variety showers the garden with a nearly continuous display of small, golden yellow flowers from early summer to fall. It is, without a doubt, one of the very best daylilies.

H. 'Black-Eyed Stella'

The best of the best. Bearing beautiful flowers for more than 250 days a year in some regions, this is the closest thing yet to an ever-blooming perennial. Hardy in Zones 5 through 9. Enjoy.

Delphiniums
Delphinium spp.

When you see delphiniums in the garden you will have no doubt that they herald from royalty. They blend dignity and grace into a flawless presence that dominates the late spring garden. But as beautiful as these plants are, many people have never even tried to grow them. It seems that, over the generations, delphiniums have acquired the reputation of being hard to grow, and that scares a lot of folks off. Do not despair; here is the recipe for growing great delphiniums.

How to Grow: Delphiniums know what they want, and if you give them what they want, they like you. Northern gardeners should prepare and plant in spring, southern gardeners in fall. The first thing the plants want is soil that is rich in organic matter, well drained, fertile, loose and friable, and evenly moist. Spread about 4 inches of well-rotted manure or compost onto the area where you wish to plant your delphiniums (make sure this area gets full sun). Rototill the manure or compost into the soil to a depth of 8 to 10 inches and water well. Let the soil dry for about a day, rototill again, and rake smooth. In wet areas, plant delphiniums in raised beds to aid drainage.

Delphiniums need staking and some folks do this before they plant so the roots of maturing plants are not damaged. Set 6-foot stakes into the ground so that about 4 to 5 feet of stake remains aboveground. Set the plants a few inches away from the stakes. Allow them to grow for about four weeks, then side-dress with half the recommended strength of 10-10-10 granular fertilizer, or fish emulsion at full strength. Repeat in four weeks. As the plants grow taller, tie them loosely to the stakes.

Once the plants have flowered, cut the flower heads back to the first leaves. When the leaves begin to yellow, cut the flower stalk back to the ground. At this time you should notice new shoots sprouting from the crown of the plant. These second shoots will be shorter and somewhat weaker than those of spring; they will flower in late summer. Cut back the plants after the ground begins to freeze, and cover the planting with a layer of straw mulch.

The Best Delphiniums: For tall, strong plants with beautifully dense spikes of flowers, it is hard to beat the Round Table Series of the Pacific Coast Strain of delphinium. The varieties of the Round Table Series were named for the characters of Camelot, so your garden can be graced with the likes of *Delphinium* 'King Arthur', which has flowers of deep royal blue with a tuft of white petals in the center, called a bee; *D.* 'Guinevere', with petals in shades of lavender and blue, accented with a white bee; and *D.* 'Galahad', with flowers of pure white. Other excellent delphiniums worth trying include the Blackmore and Langdon Strain from England; the Magic Fountain group, which are dwarf forms of the Pacific Coast Series; and the Connecticut Yankee Series. Most delphiniums are hardy in Zones 4 through 7.

Delphiniums are not the easiest perennials to grow, but they are among the most beautiful. One of the secrets to growing great delphiniums is to support the stems throughout the growing season by loosely tying them to sturdy stakes. Begin tying stems when they are about 12 inches tall. Fix more ties at 12-inch intervals as the plant grows. Add an extra tie along the flower spike to help prevent breakage in rain or wind.

Iris
Iris spp.

In Greek mythology Iris was the goddess of the rainbow, and the petals of her namesake often seem to hold all the attendant colors. That alone makes this group of plants special, but there is more. There are about eleven different divisions of iris, from the noble bearded iris to Siberian iris and water iris. The plants of each division  bear blossoms that are slightly different from those of any other. The exacting standard of loveliness remains constant, but each flower manages to convey that beauty in a unique way. Having irises in the garden is like having both the rainbow and the pot of gold in the same place.

Iris blossoms consist of uniquely shaped petals. The three outer petals, called falls, seem to cascade from the center of the flower much the way a waterfall flows over a cliff. The three inner petals are called standards and often stand upright, sometimes sweeping back on themselves to form a floral cage.

Irises are either rhizomatous or bulbous. Rhizomatous types grow from large, sausage-shaped underground stems called rhizomes, while bulbous forms grow from rounded onion-shaped stems called bulbs.

Bearded Iris

Bearded irises are so called for a fuzzy pattern of hairs in the center of each fall. Several species have contributed to this group, most notably the German iris *(Iris germanica)*. Today bearded irises consist almost entirely of hybrids in a vast array of colors, heights, and flower forms, making them almost a mandatory part of any perennial garden. Bearded irises are hardy in Zones 3 through 7.

How to Grow: Bearded irises prefer fertile soil with plenty of compost, peat moss, or other organic matter. The soil should be well drained and evenly moist. The plants tolerate hot, dry conditions, though they may go dormant during these times. Soil that is overly wet weakens them and can cause the rhizomes to rot. Bearded irises prefer full sun with some light shade.

How to Propagate: Bearded irises should be divided and planted in the fall. Lift the clump from the soil and gently separate the rhizomes. Healthy rhizomes are firm, thick, and usually light colored. Discard any that appear soft or rotted.

Replant divisions by first digging a hole that is larger than the spread of the rhizome and about 6 inches deep. Refill the hole with a mound of loose soil. Place the rhizome on the soil, pressing it gently into the earth about an inch before filling the hole.

When you are done, part of the top portion of the rhizome should be visible above the soil. Water in but do not mulch.

Some Excellent Bearded Irises: The following varieties offer all you could want from the bearded iris:

Iris **'Blue Staccato'**
Clear white petals are edged with lacy tracings of violet-blue. The flowers are held high over the garden on strong, 40-inch stems in early summer.

Iris **'Edith Wolford'**
A stunning bicolor with lemon chiffon standards perched on falls of rich violet, the plant grows to about 40 inches and flowers in early summer.

Iris **'Skating Party'**
Three-foot stems are topped with icy white flowers in early summer.

Iris **'Vanity'**
This variety has a right to be vain. The fragrant flowers are a wonderful shade of clear pink with undertones of linen white on 3-foot stems.

DIVIDING AND REPLANTING IRIS

1. Carefully lift the clump from the earth by first loosening the soil, then levering the plants free. Iris rhizomes are large and brittle and easily damaged so take care.

2. To replant divisions, dig a hole about 6 inches deep and refill it with a mound of loose soil. Set the plant atop the mound, pressing it into the soil about an inch.

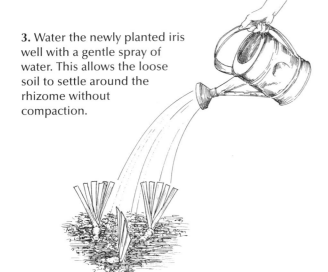

3. Water the newly planted iris well with a gentle spray of water. This allows the loose soil to settle around the rhizome without compaction.

Iris 'Black Dragon'

Introduced in 1982, this variety has strong, three-foot-tall stems with both standards and falls colored a rich blue-black with a velvet-like texture.

Iris 'Blue Luster'

This midseason variety grows from 34 to 38 inches high with both standards and falls a solid cobalt blue. Stunning color and excellent form.

Iris 'Cloud Adrift'

A midseason iris with lovely snow-white blossoms atop 3-foot-tall stems.

Iris 'Chief Hematite'

Large, lightly ruffled flowers with copper-red falls and slightly paler standards. The blossoms appear in midseason on strong 36-inch stems.

Iris 'Extravagant'

The flowers of this iris are a delicate, lavender-satin with all the ruffles and elegance of Scarlett O'Hara's most beautiful gown. Introduced in 1983, this flower naturally exhibits perfect form with straight, strong 3-foot stems and mid- to (fashionably) late-season bloom.

Iris 'Hilltop View'

This is a plant that offers excellent form combined with striking color. The tall 38-inch, well-branched stems are topped with lightly ruffled, azure-blue flowers.

Iris 'Lace Jabot'

A variety that lives up to its name, this iris is the definition of lacy, with wide falls and standards crimped and ruffled to the maximum. Introduced in 1990, this variety has falls that are pale, creamy lilac, while the standards are a deeper but soft shade of lavender.

Iris 'Tangerine Dream'

This iris sounds more like a dessert than a flower, and it truly does look good enough to eat. The flowers are a solid, light orange-yellow with broad, lightly ruffled falls and standards. Blooms early to midseason.

Beardless Iris

Instead of a beard, most beardless types of iris have a bright streak of color called a signal on the topmost portion of the fall. Of the many species and hybrids that make up this group the most popular are the Siberian irises *(Iris sibirica)* and the Japanese irises *(I. ensata).*

Siberian irises have long slender leaves and strong pliant stems that bear flowers rich in blues, purples, and whites in late spring and early summer. They prefer wet, boggy spots but also do quite well in drier soils. The plants are vigorous and form dense clumps that need to be divided every three to five years. Siberians like full sun or partial shade. Divide the same way as bearded iris, but plant about two inches deeper. Hardy in Zones 3 through 8.

Japanese irises have large flowers with wide petals and orchidlike markings on the falls. The leaves are long and thin, nearly grasslike, and the pliant stems commonly reach 40 inches. Japanese irises flower later than Siberians or bearded irises, sometimes waiting until midsummer. They prefer full sun and fertile, moist to wet soil. Divide the same as Siberians. Hardy in Zones 4 through 9.

Some Excellent Siberians: The colors offered by these irises range from yellow and white to blue and violet.

I. s. 'Butter and Sugar'

An eye-catching bicolor, 'Butter and Sugar' has creamy yellow falls and pure white standards on sturdy 2-foot stems.

I. s. 'Orville Fay'

Although it resembles the species in color, with violet-blue petals marked with a bright central signal, 'Orville Fay' bears much larger blossoms, some reaching 4 to 5 inches across. The stout, very strong stems grow to an impressive 36 inches.

I. s. 'Super Ego'

This variety has broad falls of pale blue etched with violet beneath spreading translucent baby-blue standards. The plants grow to a height of 30 inches.

Some Excellent Japanese Irises: Of the Japanese irises, these can't be surpassed.

Iris ensata 'Ise'

Large 6-inch-wide blossoms of pale pastel blue top 3- to 4-foot stems in early summer.

I. e. 'Nara'

This variety produces huge 8-inch-wide blossoms on 40-inch stems in midsummer.

I. e. 'Queen of the Blues'

This iris should really be "queen of the lavenders," for it bears large lavender flowers touched with tracings of white.

Water Irises

The water irises, as their name implies, like to grow in wet, boggy places. They are excellent choices for water gardens, wet meadows, and plantings along streams and ponds. Plant in full sun and very moist to wet soil. Set rhizomes about 2 inches deep in fall. Hardiness in this group varies widely, with some being excellent for the Deep South and others suitable for northern gardens. When purchasing plants, note that those labeled Louisiana hybrids or Louisiana group are good choices for southern gardens, while those called Pacific Coast irises are good for California and northwestern gardens.

◆ **Water Irises to Consider:**
Abbeville Red *(Iris x nelsonii)*
Blue Flag *(I. versicolor)*
Copper Iris *(I. fulva)*
Giant Blue Flag *(I. giganticaerulea)*
Lance Iris *(I. brevicaulis)*
Prairie Blue Flag *(I. hexagona)*
Yellow Flag *(I. pseudacorus)*

Peonies
Paeonia lactiflora

There are about thirty species of peonies native to various areas of the Northern Hemisphere. Of that number, three have had a profound influence in the garden. One, the tree peony *(Paeonia suffruticosa),* is actually a shrub.

The common peony *(P. officinalis)* is native to Europe, where it has been grown since ancient times. When Europeans began migrating to America in the early seventeenth century, the common peony came with them. Each spring, for generations, this peony blossomed in cottage gardens across colonial America. It was a pretty plant with deeply divided leaves and a large single red flower accented with a tuft of bright yellow stamens in its center. Today it is a rare thing to see a common peony in someone's garden, for centuries ago an even more beautiful peony found its way to Europe and then America.

The garden peony *(Paeonia lactiflora)* is native to China, where the plants were grown in the imperial gardens of the emperors. The flowers were so esteemed that people would hold umbrellas over the blossoms during rainstorms so they would not get wet. From China the garden peony came to Europe and America in the late 1700s, reaching its peak of popularity in the early years of the twentieth century. Today there are thousands of cultivars in an amazing array of colors and flower forms. Though no longer regarded as highly as it once was, the garden peony is still one of the most popular perennials in the world. Hardy in Zones 4 through 8.

How to Grow Garden Peonies: Peonies like full sun in the North, light shade in the South. Plant in rich, well-drained soil that has been thoroughly cultivated to a depth of about 12 inches. Peonies are often purchased as roots, which look like big brown hot dogs with eyes, or as crowns with a few roots radiating from a central stem dotted with large pink buds.

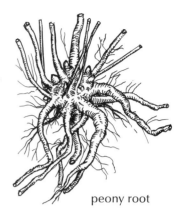

peony root

Plant roots about 2 inches below the soil surface, crowns just deep enough so the pink buds poke out of the soil. Firm gently and water well. In spring the plants will sport lovely-dark-green leaves topped with a large round flower bud. Ants find these buds much to their liking and crawl over them in a seemingly endless parade. They do no harm, however, so you can just let them be. Stake the stem when the flower bud appears.

Many people say that peonies do not like to be transplanted and, once established, should be left alone. If you want to move peonies, just follow the directions for planting and you should do fine. The transplants will hold a grudge the first year by producing lots of leaves and few flowers, but after that they should bloom even better than before.

Some of the Best Garden Peonies:

P. 'Bowl of Beauty'
This variety's truly huge single blossoms, some up to 12 inches across, feature rose-pink petals surrounding creamy yellow stamens. An excellent choice for the South.

P. 'Festiva Maxima'
One of the oldest heirloom peonies still in cultivation, this variety was introduced in 1851. It is noted for producing in midspring large numbers of fragrant antique-white double flowers stained in the center with flecks of crimson.

P. 'Sarah Bernhardt'
Introduced during the height of the garden peony's popularity in 1906, this remains one of the most beautiful varieties. The plants produce a large mound of deep-green foliage decorated with very large, fully double, fragrant, pastel pink blossoms in late spring.

Phlox
Phlox spp.

There are over sixty species of phlox in the world, but of these only five make excellent garden plants. All phlox have dainty, five-petaled flowers in a variety of colors; types range from creeping ground covers to 3-foot-tall beauties. Whatever garden you have, you may rest assured that there is a phlox that will feel perfectly at home in it.

Thick-Leaf Phlox

The thick-leaf phlox *(Phlox carolina)* that gardeners love is not the wildflower native throughout the Midwest and southeastern United States, but a hybrid. *P.* 'Miss Lingard' is one of the finest phlox ever created, sporting rich green leaves and large, open clusters of beautiful white flowers in early summer. It is hardy in Zones 4 through 8 and is an excellent choice for southern gardens, where other phlox are prone to powdery mildew. Plant care is the same for garden phlox, but you rarely need to divide 'Miss Lingard', which gives you more time to relax and smell the flowers.

Wild Sweet William

Wild sweet William *(Phlox maculata)* is native to the woodlands and meadows of the eastern United States, where its red or purple flowers blossom in midsummer. The plant prefers full sun or light shade and fertile, well-drained soil. Over the years a number of cultivars have been introduced; the best is perhaps *P.* 'Rosalinde', a variety with 3-foot stems loaded with conical clusters of deep-lilac flowers. Hardy in Zones 4 through 8.

Woodland Phlox

Woodland phlox *(Phlox divaricata* var. *laphamii)* is another American native that brightens the eastern woodlands each spring from Canada to the southern Appalachians. Unlike other phlox, it loves shady places and is virtually carefree. A vigorous grower, it produces plentiful 12-inch-tall stems topped with pastel lilac flowers in late spring.

Garden Phlox

Garden phlox *(Phlox paniculata)* is a wonderfully fragrant plant native to eastern North America. It was introduced to Europe in 1730; since then hybrids have been developed on both sides of the Atlantic. Garden phlox needs full sun, though the sharpest pinks do best in very light shade. It is hardy in Zones 4 through 9. Plant in fertile, well-drained soil well amended with organic matter. Clumps of phlox should be divided every other year in spring or fall. Separate large clumps into small clusters of five to eight stems and replant.

Great Garden Phlox Varieties:

Phlox 'Bright Eyes'
Strong three-foot stems feature lovely clusters of pale blush-colored flowers dotted with a central drop of deep pink. Flowers bloom in mid- to late-summer.

P. 'David'
Very long-blooming, this mildew-resistant variety displays large clusters of linen white flowers from midsummer to early fall.

P. 'Orange Perfection'
A vigorous grower, this variety reaches three feet in height with bright orange-pink flowers in late summer.

P. 'Starfire'
Radiant fire-engine-red flowers appear on three-foot stems in late summer.

P. 'Franz Schubert'
As beautiful to the eyes as a Schubert symphony is to the ears, this variety has round clusters of soft pink flowers lightly accented with a rose-colored eye. The strong stems reach 36 inches tall, and the medium-green foliage fends off mildew better than most.

It is natural to enjoy beautiful gardens and vases of cut flowers in the warm months of spring, summer, and fall. And it is just as natural to think of winter as a time devoid of both. The easiest way to make the flowers of summer last through winter is by drying them. The process of old-fashioned air drying naturally steals a little color from the flower. To compensate for this, dry only the brightest-colored flowers of any genus or species.

- Astilbe *(Astilbe* spp.) is a very diverse genus with many different flower forms and colors. The feathery flowers lend a unique texture to dried arrangements. Astilbes lose more color than some other flowers, so dry only the most vivid reds.

  The best reds include *A.* x *arendsii* 'Fanal', *A.* x *a.* 'Granat', and *A.* x *a.* 'Spartan'.

- Delphinium *(Delphinium* spp.) is available in shades of lilac, blue, violet, and white; the whites, blues, and violets are the best for drying.

  The best blues include *D. grandiflorum* 'Blue Mirror', *D. g.* 'Blue Butterfly', *D.* x *belladonna* 'Wendy', *D.* x *belladonna* 'Bellamosum', and *D.* 'Blue Bird'.

  The best violets include *D.* 'Black Knight' and *D.* 'King Arthur'.

  The best whites include *D.* x *belladonna* 'Casa Blanca' and *D.* 'Galahad'.

- **English lavender** *(Lavandula angustifolia)* comes in a wide array of colors, from pale pink to deep violet. While sachets can be made from any color lavender, the best types for drying are the deeply colored violet varieties, including *L.* 'Hidcote' and *L.* 'Atropurpurea'.

- **Gayfeather** *(Liatris* spp.) produces large spikes of hundreds of tiny flowers covered with threadlike petals. They come in a wide

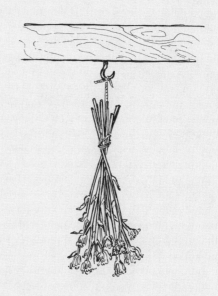

range of colors, with the purple and reddish violet varieties being the best for drying.

The best reddish purples include *L. ligulistylis.*

The best purples include *L. pycnostachya* and *L. spicata* 'Kobold'.

- **Yarrow** *(Achillea* spp.) has fernlike, richly aromatic foliage, strong stems, and large flat clusters of flowers. The best varieties for drying are the golden yellows.

  The best yellows include *A. filipendulina* 'Coronation Gold', *A. f.* 'Parker's Gold', and *A. taygetea* 'Moonshine'.

- **Other Perennials Suitable for Drying**

  Baby's breath *(Gypsophila paniculata)*

  Chinese lanterns *(Physalis francheti)*

  Garden peony *(Paeonia lactiflora)*

  Purple coneflower *(Echinacea purpurea)*

Drying Perennials for Winter Arrangements

PRESERVING PERENNIALS

Preserving perennials by drying is easy as well as enjoyable. And the end result, a vase of beautiful dried summer blossoms, can warm even the coldest, dreariest winter day.

The secret to gathering flowers for drying is to pick them before they have been pollinated and before they have completely opened. Both pollination and age change the chemistry of the flower, making the blossom more prone to shattering and fading. Many flowers are not receptive to pollination before they have fully opened. Collect flowers when they are about three-fourths open. Flowers that come in spikes or clusters, such as delphiniums and yarrows, should be gathered when the bottom flowers (in spikes) or the outermost flowers (in clusters) are fully open.

Remember to gather flowers when they are absolutely dry. This is best done in the afternoon of a sunny, cool day after the dew has evaporated from even the inner recesses of the bloom.

Tie the flowers by type (astilbes with astilbes and yarrows with yarrows) in bunches of five to ten. Secure the stems with a rubber band and hang upside down from the ceiling or rafters in a completely dark room. If you are drying many bunches, be sure to leave a foot or two of space between each hanging clump. The best drying rooms are large enough to encourage good air circulation as well as warm and dry enough to speed drying and discourage the growth of molds. Attics are perfect, but basements will do if they are not overly humid. A small fan placed in the room greatly aids the air circulation.

The room must be dark so the flowers retain as much of their original color as possible; even indirect light can cause them to fade. Dry the flowers from two to three weeks, depending on conditions. Once they are dry you can trim the stems to the length you desire and arrange the flowers in a vase for months of enjoyment. To keep the dried flowers looking as fresh as possible, be sure to keep them away from direct sunlight.

Special Project: Making a Moon Garden

When people design their gardens, they select colors and textures with an eye toward how they will appear in sunshine or shade, not how they will look at night. A moon garden is different: It is designed to be enjoyed during both night and day. Plants must be selected and situated to best use and reflect the subtle light of the stars and moon as well as bright sunshine. The result is a magical place where colors fade into shades of silver, and refuge and mystery exist side by side.

Moon gardens first achieved popularity in New England during the nineteenth century, when people like Emerson and Thoreau were beginning to view nature as something to learn from, not just control; a place of adventure and insight, not just of danger and death. The moon garden offered a place where the mysteries of the night could be explored without leaving the safety of the garden path.

A SENSIBLE DESIGN

When designing a moon garden the primary consideration is light. Or, more correctly, the lack of light. Many of us have become overly dependent on sight to explore the world around us. But if we reduce our ability to see, we then increase our ability to perceive the world through our other senses — hearing, touching, smelling, tasting. Sounds and textures become more distinct, fragrances and tastes more intense. Here is how each of the senses can aid in designing your moon garden:

Taste: Edible Flowers

Taste is an optional addition to a moon garden, for while the other four senses seem to seek us out, the sense of taste asks us to find it. It would be a pity, however, to enjoy a feast of the senses and leave one uninvited. My favorite moon garden nibble is daylily blossoms; the pale yellow varieties touched with a hint of fragrance, such as 'Hyperion' or 'Ice Carnival', taste the best.

Sight: White on Black

The best time to begin planning a moon garden is the middle of winter when snow is on the ground, the sky is clear, and the moon is full. The visual beauty of the moon garden relies in large part on the contrast of white and black. Snow reflects moonlight in much the same way that white flowers will in summertime. As you observe moonlight on snow, try to picture where a patch of pure-white flowers would look best in summer. Notice how the shadows cast by trees, structures, or rocks fall over the garden.

- In winter the moon is high in the sky, while the sun is low in the south. In summer the reverse is true: The sun is high, the moon low in the south. Plan your moon garden so that there are few obstructions to the southeast, south, and southwest; that way, summer moonlight will illuminate the garden.
- Use a series of string trellises covered with quick-growing annual vines, such as morning glory, for background to white flowers.
- Put a bench at the north end of the garden so that you can see the moon and the flowers while enjoying a peaceful evening moment.
- Because the flowers in the garden will all be various shades of white, use height instead of color to add a sense of depth. Place tall plants to the rear of the bed and in front of large, dark elements. Place low-growing plants so that they accent the front of the flower bed and outline the paths and walkways with shades of white and silver.
- Plan your moon garden to be at peak bloom in midspring and late summer, when the moon is higher (the moon is lowest and gives the poorest light in June).
- Garden sites that get full sun during the day, with no part truly shady, generally get more moonlight at night.

Fragrance

Fragrance in a moon garden should be as prominent as moonlight. Select at least some plants for their ability to perfume the air of warm summer evenings.

Texture

While texture certainly relates to how leaves and flowers appear, texture in the moon garden refers to a direct sense of touch. You should feel a moon garden as you walk through it, and one of the best ways to do this is by way of a garden path. The subdued light of the moon asks people to walk more cautiously, and this slowed pace allows garden visitors to feel the earth underfoot more exactly than they would otherwise.

Hearing: Listening for Visitors

The night garden may be dark, but it isn't quiet. In the evening the moon garden attracts insects that chirp and sing and some that fly from flower to flower, including beautiful night-flying moths. The sounds are often musical and as subtle as the moonlight.

Use tall evergreens or dark fencing as background for the northeast, north, and northwest portions of the garden. These dark areas balance the light of the moon as well as provide contrast to the bright white flowers planted around them.

Plant	Height	Bloom Time	Frag-rance	Flower Color	Hardiness Zones	Best Cultivar	Comments
SHRUBS							
Catawba Rhododendron (*Rhododendron catawbiense*)	10 ft.	mid- to late spring	no	red, pink, yellow, white	4-8	'Cunningham's White'	
Exbury Azalea (*Rhododendron* Exbury Hybrids)	8 ft.	spring	intense, unique	red, pink, yellow, white	5-7	'White Swan'	attracts butterflies
Korean Spice Viburnum (*Viburnum carlesii*)	5 ft.	early to mid-spring	very intense	pure white	5-7	'Compactum'	burgundy leaves in fall
Yaku Shima Rhododendron (*Rhododendron yakusimanum*)	3 ft.	spring	no	light pink to white	4-7	'Yaku Princess'	
PERENNIALS							
Astilbe (*Astilbe* x *arendsii*)	3 ft.	summer	none	white, pink, red	4-8	'Bridal Veil'	great for borders
Beach Wormwood (*Artemisia stellerana*)	1 ft.	none	none	none	3-7	'Silver Brocade'	heat- and drought-tolerant; silver foliage complements just about anything
Daylily (*Hemerocallis* spp.)	3 ft.	early to late summer	subtle	various	3-9	'Hyperion'	a vigorous grower; divide every few years for new plants
Delphinium (*Delphinium* x *belladonna*)	4 ft.	late spring to early summer	none	various	4-7	'Casa Blanca'	cultivar snow-white; needs staking
Foxglove (*Digitalis purpurea*)	3 ft.	late spring to early summer	no	various	4-8	'Alba'	excellent border plant; self-sows freely
Garden Peony (*Paeonia lactiflora*)	2 ft.	late spring	good	various	3-9	'Festiva 'Maxima'	large, white flowers on cultivar; divide every 4 to 5 years
Garden Phlox (*Phlox paniculata*)	3 ft.	summer to fall	good	various	4-8	'David'	white flowers on cultivar; divide every few years
Hakonechloa Grass (*Hakonechola macra*)	1 ft.	none	none	none	5-8	'Aureola'	a beautiful ornamental grass with white leaves
Lily (*Lilium* spp.)	2-4 ft.	summer	good	various	4-8	'Casa Blanca'	white, very fragrant flowers on cultivar
Loosestrife (*Lysimachia clethroides*)	3 ft.	summer to fall	none	white	3-8	species	very vigorous; unique, wavelike curve to flowers, easy to naturalize and divide
Peachleaf Bellflower (*Campanula persicifolia*)	2 ft.	late spring to early summer	none	purple, white	5-7	'Grandiflora Alba'	naturalizes quickly; easy to divide and transplant
Purple Coneflower (*Echinacea purpurea*)	2-3 ft.	all summer	none	purple, white	3-9	'White ' Swan	very long bloom time, attracts butterflies; seed heads attractive in winter
Shasta Daisy (*Chrysanthemum* x *superbum*)	2 ft.	early summer to early fall	light	white with yellow center	5-9	'Snow Lady'	good for borders; long bloom time; very easy to divide; vigorous
Siberian Iris (*Iris sibirica*)	2 ft.	late spring to early summer	light	various	4-9	'Butter and Sugar'	pale yellow and white flowers on cultivar; divide every few years

11

Easy-Care Roses for Every Garden

When Howard Carter first entered the tomb of the Pharaoh Tutankhamen in 1928, he found himself surrounded by the treasures of ancient Egypt. These were gold, precious gems, lavishly decorated furniture, and a small bundle of roses.

We have cultivated roses for as long as we have cultivated civilization. Over the course of thousands of years the flower has come to mean many different things to many different cultures. The Greeks revered the rose as the queen of all flowers. The Romans saw the blossom as a synonym for a woman's beauty. Muslims regarded the white rose as a symbol of Muhummad, and Christians made strings of prayer beads, later called rosaries, from dried rose petals.

Even though the rose was regarded as the flower most close to perfection for centuries, people tried to improve it. In the nineteenth century breeders crossed Tea Roses, China Roses, and Hybrid Perpetuals to create what many believed was the perfect rose, the Hybrid Tea.

Hybrid Tea Roses had long stems, elegant flower buds, and very long bloom times, traits that made them immensely popular. This popularity also attracted scores of reckless breeders who selected plants just for flower appearance. As a result, they introduced a number of cultivars that were more susceptible to insects and diseases, were less vigorous and less hardy — but boy, did they have nice-looking flower buds!

Unfortunately for the home gardener, the varieties of roses that deserved their attention became lost amid the flood of inferior ones that did not. These temperamental plants were increasingly seen as not worth growing.

As some people were losing faith in roses, however, others were rediscovering them. In the last half of the twentieth century a new generation of plant breeders revitalized the queen of flowers, deftly crossing the best of the antique, species, and modern roses. The resulting creations range from disease-resistant plants that can survive temperatures of -40°F to exquisite varieties that blend the best qualities of antique and modern roses. In addition to these new roses, many gardeners are finding pleasure planting antique and species roses, turning the garden into a refuge from centuries past.

Today there are so many excellent, low-maintenance roses for every area of the country that the question gardeners should ask is not whether they should grow roses, but which roses should they grow.

251

Species Roses

Species roses are the wild forms from which all cultivated types descend. As a group they are hardy, disease- and pest-resistant, tough plants. But in addition to being survivors, many of them also have a softer side, producing beautiful, often fragrant, single flowers in late spring and early summer and abundant, brightly colored fruits in fall.

Species roses naturalize easily and are often used as informal hedges, in wildflower meadows, and in shrub borders, where their flowers attract butterflies in summer and their fruit brings songbirds in fall and winter. The wild rose is a wonderful example of simple beauty and self-reliance.

♦ **The Best Species Roses for the South and Southwest (Zones 7-9)**

    Cherokee Rose *(Rosa laevigata)*

    Himalayan Musk Rose *(R. brunonii)*

    Musk Rose *(R. moschata)*

    White Lady Bank's Rose *(R. banksiae 'Alba Plena')*

    Yellow Lady Bank's Rose *(R. banksiae 'Lutea')*

♦ **The Best Species Roses for the North (Zones 5-6)**

    Father Hugo Rose *(Rosa hugonis)*

    Redleaved Rose *(R. rubrifolia)*

    Scotch Brier *(R. spinosissima)*

    Sweetbrier *(R. eglanteria)*

    Virginia Rose *(R. virginiana)*

♦ **The Best Species Roses for the Far North (Zones 3-4)**

    Austrian Brier *(Rosa foetida)*

    Meadow Rose *(R. blanda)*

    New England Shining Rose *(R. nitida)*

    Redleaved Rose *(R. rubrifolia)*

    Virginia Rose *(R. virginiana)*

SOIL AND SOIL PREPARATION

Species roses as a group prefer a well-drained soil with good organic content, though many adapt to a wide range of conditions. The type and condition of the soil often directly affect the number and severity of disease and pest problems you will see later on. When those species roses that are susceptible to black spot and powdery mildew are planted in soil that is poorly drained, overly dry, or low in organic matter, they will develop more severe cases of these diseases, and earlier in the year. Poorly drained soil has reduced oxygen content, overly dry soil has too little water and low nutrient accessibility, and soils low in organic matter are less fertile and often low in soil water and/or oxygen. In essence, poor soil conditions rob the plant of one or more of the essential components needed for healthy growth. Without the essentials, the plant can easily slip into a stress condition that allows diseases to enter and establish themselves in plant tissues more readily.

♦ **Species Roses That Need Well-Drained, Very Fertile Soil**

    Moyes Rose *(Rosa moyesii)*

    Redleaved Rose *(R. rubrifolia)*

Plants in this group need liberal amounts of peat moss or compost added to the soil before planting and additional compost added as a topdressing each year.

Species roses are the cornerstone of many modern rose-breeding programs. Yet these tough but elegant plants do not need to be improved to hold an esteemed place in the garden.

◆ **Species Roses That Prefer Well-Drained Soil with Average Fertility**

  Cherokee Rose *(Rosa laevigata)*

  Chestnut Rose *(R. roxburghii)*

  Helen Rose *(R. helenae)*

  Himalayan Musk Rose *(R. brunonii)*

  Meadow Rose *(R. blanda)*

  Musk Rose *(R. moschata)*

  Prairie Rose *(R. setigera)*

  Sweetbrier *(R. eglanteria)*

  Virginia Rose *(R. virginiana)*

  White Lady Bank's Rose *(R. banksiae 'Alba Plena')*

  Yellow Lady Bank's Rose *(R. banksiae 'Lutea')*

Plants in this group can benefit from the addition of some peat moss or compost to the soil at planting time, but they do not need additional topdressing.

◆ **Species Roses that Prefer Well-Drained, Dry Soil with Low Fertility**

  Austrian Brier *(Rosa foetida)*

  Father Hugo Rose *(R. hugonis)*

  Scotch Brier *(R. spinosissima)*

Plants in this group have adapted to poor soils and do best in conditions of low fertility. If planted in rich soils, they may respond with more vigorous growth but will also become more susceptible to attack and infection from pests and diseases.

◆ **Species Roses that Prefer Wet or Boggy Soil**

  Memorial Rose *(Rosa wichuraiana)*

  New England Shining Rose *(R. nitida)*

  Swamp Rose *(R. palustris)*

Plants in this group can grow in other conditions but thrive in the wet, heavy soils of meadows, marshes, and shorelines.

PLANTING INSTRUCTIONS

For bare-root plants dig each hole 4 inches wider than the spread of the roots and about 18 inches deep. Mix ½ gallon of peat moss or compost with the soil from the hole. Refill the hole partway with a pyramid-shaped mound of soil. Position the plant on the mound of soil so that the crown of the plant is even with the soil line, and spread the roots evenly around the mound. Finish filling the hole with soil and firm gently. Prune any canes back to about 4 to 6 inches, and water well.

For container roses dig a hole 4 inches wider than the container and 4 inches deeper. Add about ½ gallon of peat moss or compost to the soil. Add a 2-inch layer of soil to the bottom of the hole. Remove the plant from its container and place in the hole. Add soil around the edges of the plant until the hole is filled. Water well.

Container-grown roses suffer less damage during transplanting than bare-root plants and establish vigorous root systems more quickly.

PRUNING

The self-reliant nature of species roses also extends to pruning — as a group they need very little. Pruning of species roses can be divided into four categories: removal of deadwood; removal of old, large canes; light pruning of all canes to maintain plant shapes; and heavy pruning to rejuvenate old plants. There are only two absolutes when pruning species roses:

1. All species should have deadwood removed each spring.
2. All species used as hedges or as specimen plants should be lightly pruned to keep in bounds or retain desired shape.

Plan to prune in very late winter or early spring when removing deadwood or large-caliber nonproductive canes, or to rejuvenate. Plants that need pruning to be shaped or kept in bounds should be trimmed right after they have completed flowering.

Removing Deadwood

Thin-caliber deadwood can be removed with hand pruners, while larger canes can be removed with long-handled loppers or a pruning saw. Dead canes are tan or brown, or green but shriveled. From the dead section, move down the cane to a live bud and cut about one-quarter inch above the bud.

Pruning to Shape

Keeping a plant well shaped or in bounds requires the removal of only those canes or sections of canes that need it. Many species roses have long canes that gracefully arch out from the plant's center. If these are trimmed back too severely, the remaining section of cane will appear stubby, compromising the gracefulness of the plant.

◆ **Species Roses That Need**
  to Be Pruned to Shape
  Cherokee Rose (*Rosa laevigata*)
  Meadow Rose (*R. blanda*)
  Memorial Rose (*R. wichuraiana*)
  Musk Rose (*R. moschata*)
  Sweetbrier (*R. eglanteria*)

Thick, old canes can rob a rose of its vitality. Remove canes larger than 1 or 2 inches in diameter in spring.

Removing Large Old Canes

In some species roses old canes (those greater than 1 or 2 inches in diameter) become less vigorous, and their thick girth is noticeably less graceful. Remove thick, older canes in the spring with long-handled loppers or a pruning saw. Remove the largest canes first, but do not remove more than a quarter of the canes at any one time.

◆ **Species Roses That Benefit**
  from Removal of Older Canes
  Chestnut Rose (*Rosa roxburghii*)
  Father Hugo Rose (*R. hugonis*)
  Memorial Rose (*R. wichuraiana*)
  Moyes Rose (*R. moyesii*)
  New England Shining Rose (*R. nitida*)
  Prairie Rose (*R. setigera*)
  Redleaved Rose (*R. rubrifolia*)
  Scotch Brier (*R. spinosissima*)
  Swamp Rose (*R. palustris*)
  Sweetbrier (*R. eglanteria*)
  Virginia Rose (*R. virginiana*)

Rejuvenation

As roses grow older, the canes can become so thick that they crowd out younger ones. In addition, older canes are often less vigorous and have fewer new shoots than their younger counterparts. Some species roses benefit from rejuvenation pruning, a simple technique that entails cutting back the entire plant. With a pruning saw, cut every cane to within 2 inches of the ground in spring. Then stand back and watch as the plant reforms itself, often within the first season.

◆ Species Roses That Respond to Rejuvenation Pruning

Meadow Rose *(Rosa blanda)*
New England Shining Rose *(R. nitida)*
Swamp Rose *(R. palustris)*
Virginia Rose *(R. virginiana)*

WATER AND FERTILIZER REQUIREMENTS

As a rule of thumb, species roses grow best and retain their vitality when they receive about an inch of water per week during the growing season. This is especially true during the few weeks they are in bloom. The additional moisture also promotes larger fruit in the fall.

One of the benefits of growing most species roses is that they do not require much attention in return for looking beautiful year after year. Fertilize all types with a well-balanced organic fertilizer, such as fish emulsion, once at the very beginning of the spring growing season and once when flower buds first appear. Only a few types need or will benefit from any more attention.

In addition to fertilizing at the beginning of spring and when flowerbuds appear, some species will benefit from another application in midsummer.

◆ Species Roses That Benefit from Extra Fertilization

Moyes Rose *(Rosa moyesii)*
Redleaved Rose *(R. rubrifolia)*

SPECIES ROSES FOR PARTIAL SHADE

- Redleaved Rose *(Rosa rubrifolia)* needs afternoon shade.
- Scotch Brier *(R. spinosissima)* can adapt to partial shade.
- Virginia Rose *(R. virginiana)* will take light shade.

PROPAGATION

Species roses can be propagated from seed and, in some cases, from suckers.

Propagating from Seeds

Propagating species roses from seed is an economical as well as enjoyable pastime. To gather the seed, wait until the fruits, or hips, on the rosebush have turned from green to their ripened color. This can be orange, red, or even black, depending on the species. Collect the hips when they have completely changed color but before they begin to soften.

With a sharp knife, carefully open each hip and expose its pale-colored seeds. Remove the seeds from the hip, being careful to remove any bits of fruit pulp from the seeds. Fill a plastic bag (one bag for each species rose you are propagating) half full of moist, sterile seed-starting mix. Label the bag, add the seeds, and seal securely with a twist tie.

For the Dog Rose *(Rosa canina)*, store the seeds at room temperature for eight weeks, then in the refrigerator for eight more. For most other species roses, including the Father Hugo Rose *(R. hugonis)*, store the seeds in the refrigerator for two to four months. For the Meadow Rose *(Rosa blanda)*, store in the refrigerator for eight to ten months.

After the chilling period is complete, separate the seeds and sow them in flats filled with moist seed-starter mix. Cover lightly with vermiculite. When the seedlings have their first set of true leaves, transplant them into individual containers.

Propagating from Suckers

Some species roses, such as Swamp Rose *(Rosa palustris)* freely produce suckers from roots near the crown of the plant. These suckers are excellent sources of new plants that cost nothing.

The secret to removing suckers from species roses with a minimum amount of damage to the mother or daughter plants is an old pruning saw. Hold the blade at a slight angle and about 4 to 6 inches from the base of the sucker. Insert the blade into the soil and saw a circle around the sucker. When you have finished, the cone-shaped section of soil containing the sucker and its roots can be lifted from the ground and replanted wherever you want it to go.

Easy-Care Antique Roses

The antique rose group encompasses all the rose cultivars developed before the introduction of the Hybrid Teas around 1867. It's a very large group, containing both hardy and tender, resistant and susceptible varieties, resulting in a confusing maze of plants.

◆ **Antique Roses for the North**

    Rosa 'Celsiana'
    R. 'Charles de Mills'
    R. 'Empress Josephine'
    R. 'Louise Odier'
    R. alba 'Jeanne d'Arc'

◆ **Antique Roses for Small Northern Gardens**

    Rosa 'Gloire de France'
    R. 'Salet'
    R. 'Superb Tuscan'
    R. 'White Bath'

◆ **Antique Roses for the South and Southwest**

    Rosa 'Alister Stella Gray'
    R. 'Blush Noisette'
    R. 'Maman Cochet'
    R. 'Mary Washington'

◆ **Antique Roses for Small Gardens in the South and Southwest**

    Rosa 'Archduke Charles'
    R. 'Bon Silene'
    R. 'Hermosa'
    R. 'Jacques Cartier'
    R. 'Perle des Jardins'
    R. 'Rose du Roi'

GROWING ANTIQUE ROSES

Antique roses prefer to grow in a sunny spot in well-drained, fertile soil amended with good amounts of peat moss or compost. Fertilize with a well-balanced, organic fertilizer in spring, once the plants have completely leafed out, and again in midsummer. Add a topdressing of compost in spring. Water antique roses often during dry periods and at least once a week (if it doesn't rain) while the plants are blooming. Prune after the plants have finished blooming, cutting back the canes by one-quarter to one-third of their lengths. Remove deadwood and old, unproductive canes as needed when the plants are dormant.

Basic planting instructions for antique roses are identical to those for species roses; see page 253. The same pruning techniques are also used; see pages 254–255.

◆ **Companion Plants for Herb Garden Roses**

    Beach Wormwood (*Artemisia stellerana* 'Silver Brocade')
    English Lavender (*Lavandula angustifolia* 'Hidcote')
    Lavandula x *intermedia* 'Grosso'
    Lavandula x *intermedia* 'Provence'
    Artemisia ludoviciana 'Silver-King'
    Artemisia ludoviciana 'Silver-Queen'

SOME ROSES FOR THE HERB GARDEN

Roses have been part of the herb garden for thousands of years. The petals of the flowers are used to make rose water, potpourri, teas, and sometimes in cooking. The following varieties produce high-quality petals that have been used in herbal preparations for generations:

- *Rosa gallica* var. *officinalis* ('Apothecary's Rose') is a 3-foot-tall shrub with crimson-pink, semidouble, very fragrant flowers in late spring to early summer. It is disease-resistant. Dried petals even more fragrant than fresh. (Zones 3 through 8)

- *R. gallica* var. *versicolor* ('Rosa Mundi') grows to about 3 feet tall, with large, semidouble, very fragrant white flowers striped with crimson in early to midsummer. It is very vigorous. Suckers are easily transplanted. Very susceptible to powdery mildew in late summer. Cut back plants to about 1 foot after flowering. (Zones 3 through 8)

- *R.* 'Superb Tuscan' produces richly double, very fragrant, velvety red flowers in late spring to early summer. The dried petals are very fragrant. (Zones 4 through 8)

Easy-Care Rugosa Roses

The Rugosa rose *(Rosa rugosa)* is a species rose native to Siberia, northern China, and Japan. First introduced to Europe in the late 1700s, the Rugosa rose soon found its way to America, where it jumped the garden gate. Today it can be found not only in gardens all over the country, but also naturalized in great colonies on sandy dunes and beaches all along the Atlantic Coast.

The Rugosa rose has a unique, textured leaf with recessed veins and stems covered with spiny thorns. The plant forms a dense, 4-foot-tall, mound-shaped shrub decorated with fragrant, pale pink, single blossoms in late spring and early summer. In autumn its leaves turn antique gold, while the large hips ripen to brilliant red.

Rugosa roses are hardy in Zones 2 through 8 (some cultivars are hardy in Zones 3-8) and can tolerate the hot summers of the South as well as winter temperatures down to -50°F. They thrive in the sea spray along ocean beaches, can tolerate the road salt and compacted soils near sidewalks and streets, and can endure the pollution of urban areas. One of the toughest, most adaptable roses in the world, the Rugosa has given rise to a host of equally tough and adaptable cultivars. They require so little care in exchange for beautiful flowers and tasty fruit that gardeners used to nursing temperamental Hybrid Teas can feel positively guilty.

The Rugosa rose has beautiful, crepe paper-like flowers in summer, brilliant red-orange hips in fall, and a constitution that is as tough as nails.

GROWING RUGOSA ROSES

Rugosa roses as a group prefer a well-drained soil with good organic content. Still, Rugosa are famous for thriving in soil conditions that would kill other, wimpier roses. They will grow well in everything from pure beach sand to gravelly hillsides. Plants growing in a well-drained soil with good organic content, however, are often more vigorous and flower more abundantly than their counterparts at the beach. Fruit set is also higher, an important point if rose hip preserves or tea is on your gardening agenda.

Planting instructions for Rugosas are the same as for species and antique roses; see pages 252–256. Just be sure both bare-root plants and container plants will receive bright sunshine.

PRUNING RUGOSA ROSES

Rugosa roses are so tough and durable that they don't need much attention. Prune all Rugosa roses in late winter while the plants are still dormant by removing deadwood; removing old, unproductive canes; and reducing the overall height of vigorous canes.

Remove deadwood. Thin-caliber deadwood can be removed with hand pruners, while larger canes can be removed with long-handled loppers or a pruning saw. Dead canes are tan or brown, or green but shriveled. From the dead section, move down the cane to a live bud and cut about one-quarter inch above the bud.

Remove large old canes. In Rugosa roses, old canes are less vigorous as well as less productive. Remove older canes in spring with long-handled loppers or a pruning saw. Remove the largest canes first, but do not remove more than a quarter of the canes at any one time.

Prune to reduce overall height. After the older canes are removed, use pruning shears or long-handled loppers to cut back the remaining canes by one-third. This keeps the plant shaped to a neat mound and encourages new growth.

WATER AND FERTILIZER REQUIREMENTS

As a rule of thumb, Rugosa roses grow best and retain their vitality when they receive about an inch of water per week during the growing season, especially when they are in bloom. The additional moisture also promotes larger fruit in the fall. Remember, however, that these plants thrive in the dry sands of the seashore and are quite forgiving if watering chores don't make it to the top of your priority list every week.

In fact, one of the benefits of growing most Rugosa roses is that they do not require much attention in return for looking beautiful year after year. Fertilize all types with a well-balanced organic fertilizer, such as fish emulsion, once at the very beginning of the spring growing season and once when flower buds first appear. Fertilizing more than this can produce more succulent growth that is more easily damaged by Japanese beetles.

TIPS FOR BETTER HIPS

Many roses produce delicious fruits, called hips, in fall, but those from Rugosa roses are definitely among the best. Here are some secrets for growing large, tasty fruit:

- Plant more than one bush. Rugosa roses produce the most abundant crops of fruit when at least two Rugosa bushes are planted near each other.

- The largest fruits are borne on types that bear single flowers.

- Make sure the plants receive about 1 inch of water per week from the time the flowers open to a few weeks before harvest in the fall.

Easy-Care Modern Roses

A few years ago the phrases *easy care* and *modern roses* were a contradiction. There was nothing very easy about caring for modern roses, especially if you gardened north of Zone 6 or in areas where summers were hot and humid.

A modern rose is any cultivar introduced since the advent of the Hybrid Tea in 1867. Modern roses are divided into dozens of more specific categories that, when totaled up, contain literally thousands of cultivars. Nevertheless, relatively few of these cultivars have combined hardy habits, disease- and pest-resistance, beauty, and low maintenance all in one package. Some that have come closest to this goal are the English Roses, Canadian Explorer Hybrids, Morden Hybrids and Buck Hybrids.

English Roses. English Roses are the creations of the English plant breeder David Austin, whose many introductions in the 1980s helped to revitalize modern roses. His breeding program has produced modern roses that preserve the form and fragrance of the best antique varieties. English Roses, which are generally hardy in Zones 5 through 8, are famous for the pastel colors of their flowers, their bewitching fragrances, and their habit of repeat blooming in the fall. As enchanting as these roses are, not all of them exhibit the exceptional disease resistance needed to call them beautiful, fragrant, *and* low maintenance. Of those that do, these are some of the best: 'Abraham Darby' has fragrant pale apricot blossoms on 5 foot plants. 'Constance Spry' is the original English Rose with soft pink, very fragrant flowers. 'Graham Thomas' grows to 5 feet tall with intensely yellow, very fragrant blossoms.

Canadian Explorer hybrids. The Explorer Hybrid roses were created and released under the auspices of the Canadian Department of Agriculture. Over the years these excellent varieties have proven to be very hardy, low-maintenance plants ideal for northern gardens. Without a doubt this group contains some of the best roses for northern areas ever produced. Here are some of the best: 'John Cabot' grows to 6 to 8 feet tall with fragrant, double, deep rose-colored flowers in late spring with rebloom in late summer. 'William Baffin' is a fast-growing climber reaching 10 feet tall with large clusters of pink, double flowers. 'Champlain' has double, deep red, lightly fragrant blossoms on compact 3-foot-tall plants. 'John Davis' grows to 6 feet tall with everblooming, double, fragrant, rose-pink flowers in large clusters.

Buck Hybrids. Griffith Buck was a professor at the University of Iowa who liked to fiddle with roses. The goal of his breeding program mirrored that of the Canadians, and his creations are just as wonderful. 'Prairie Princess' bears soft pink, double, lightly fragrant flowers with good repeat bloom. 'Country Dancer' is an everbearer with rose-pink, fragrant flowers on 3-foot-tall plants. 'Hawkeye Belle' has fragrant, double-blush white flowers.

Morden Hybrids. The Morden Hybrids are the result of the excellent breeding program at the Morden Research Station in Manitoba, Canada. These plants are all everblooming, very hardy, and easy to care for. 'Morden Centennial' bears double, lightly scented rose-pink blossoms. 'Morden Blush' has small, light pink double flowers that fade to ivory. 'Morden Fireglow' has clusters of ember red flowers on small, 24-inch plants. 'Morden Cardinette' bears bright scarlet flowers on compact 24-inch plants.

GROWING MODERN ROSES

English Roses, Explorer Hybrids, Morden Hybrids and Buck Hybrids like a sunny location in soil that is well drained and liberally amended with peat moss or compost. Fertilize with a well-balanced, organic fertilizer in spring once the plants have completely leafed out, again when the flower buds have begun to swell, and one last time in mid-summer. Add a top dressing of compost in spring. Water Buck Hybrids often during dry periods, and at least once a week (if it doesn't rain) while the plants are blooming.

Planting instructions for modern roses are identical to those for species roses; see page 253.

Prune English Roses in late winter while still dormant. Cut back the canes to 1 to 2 feet tall and remove any weak canes or shoots from the area around the crown. In fall lightly cover the crown of the plant with mulch in Zones 5 and 6.

Explorer, Morden, and Buck Hybrids need little or no pruning. If needed remove thin-caliber deadwood with hand pruners and larger canes with long-handled loppers or a pruning saw. Remove less vigorous, less productive older canes, those larger than about 2 inches in diameter, in spring.

Some modern roses, such as those from the Morden Research Station in Canada, are beautiful, hardy *and* highly pest and disease resistant.

EASY-CARE ROSES FOR EVERY GARDEN

259

Pests and Diseases of Easy-Care Roses

Roses have a reputation for attracting and being devoured by just about every pest known to science. In turn, the pest and disease sections of rose books seem as long as a Tolstoy novel.

The easy-care, low-maintenance plants discussed here, however, are simply not troubled by the same legions of pests and diseases as their weaker kin. For example, of the many insects that have developed a taste for roses, only a few bother easy-care roses. (Of these, Japanese beetles, aphids, and cynipid wasps are the most troublesome.) So instead of spending your leisure time trying to control bugs and epidemics, you may actually find yourself with enough time to stop and smell the roses.

Black Spot

Black spot *(Diplocarpon rosae)*, a fungal disease, is the most widely distributed rose sickness. There are several strains of the fungus present in various regions of the world, which explains why a cultivar that is resistant to black spot in New England may become infected if grown somewhere else, such as Texas. As a general rule, yellow varieties are more susceptible to the disease than are other varieties.

Infection occurs when the fungus grows through the protective cuticle of the leaf and enters the leaf cells. The surface of the leaf must remain wet for at least six hours for infection to occur. Once a black spot shows on the leaf, new spores can be produced in as little as ten days. Rain or overhead watering can then spread the disease to other leaves. Severe infections can defoliate the plant — but the disease will remain alive in the fallen leaves and on the canes. In spring new spores are released to infect the lowest leaves as they emerge. Some experts have recommended that overhead irrigation, run for periods of at least five hours at a time, washes spores from the leaves. Unfortunately, spores invade the leaves from all leaf surfaces, so this method, instead of controlling the disease, only serves to spread it. If possible, overhead irrigation of roses should be kept to a minimum.

Controls

Sanitation is one of the cardinal rules of the garden, but its ability to control disease can go only so far. In fall, after the leaves have fallen, rake up as many as possible and discard. Remove all trimmings after any pruning is done, and discard any infected leaves picked off during the growing season. All of this will help, but some fungal spores will undoubtedly remain. After removing all dead plant material in the fall, spread a layer of mulch around the plants just before the ground freezes. This will provide a barrier the spores can't cross in the spring.

Baking soda can also help. Not only does it brighten your teeth and make the kitty-litter box smell fresh, but it can also control black spot on roses. To 1 gallon of warm water add 1 ounce of baking soda and 4 ounces of Murphy's Oil Soap. Stir and pour into a hand sprayer. Cover all leaf surfaces, spraying in the early morning if possible. Repeat every seven to ten days, or as needed. As with any spray, test on a small section of leaves before spraying a large area.

A 1 percent solution of neem oil has recently been shown to slow down black spot infections significantly as well as to control powdery mildew. (Do not confuse neem oil with neem seed extract, the active ingredient in Bioneem and Margosan-O. Neem oil also kills the eggs of spider mites.)

A rose leaf affected with black spot.

Powdery Mildew

There are many different types of powdery mildew, including one that especially likes to infect roses (*Sphaerotheca pannosa* var. *rosae*). This same fungus readily infects apricots and it is best not to plant these plants close together. Powdery mildew is usually found growing over the top surfaces of leaves, but in severe cases it can cover buds and canes with a feltlike mass of white. Cool, moist climates, like that of the Pacific Coast, and semi-arid regions, such as the Southwest, often have extensive mildew problems. Mildew in the eastern states generally makes its appearance in late summer, when the nights begin to get cool. Often red-flowered varieties, particularly ramblers, and hybrid teas are more susceptible than others.

Powdery mildew infection often begins with a slight curling of the leaves. Mildew growing on leaves looks like a light coating of chalk. As the infection worsens the leaves may turn reddish, then black before falling from the canes. Mildew that infects the flower buds can produce bud drop or distorted blossoms. When the fungus grows on the canes it can become quite thick and fuzzy. Fertilizing with high nitrogen fertilizers can make the problem much worse.

Controls

Same as for black spot; see page 264.

Japanese Beetles

Japanese beetles are ½-inch-long, metallic green insects that devour flowers and skeletonize leaves of roses and other plants in summer. Beetle grubs survive the winter underground and move close to the soil surface in early spring to feed on the roots. After a hearty meal they enter a quiescent stage and pupate. In summer the adults emerge from the soil, feed on roses and other plants, then lay eggs in the soil amid the roots of grasses. In a few days the eggs hatch into grubs, which feed on the grass roots until fall, when they burrow deeper into the soil to wait out the winter.

½"/1.3cm

Controls

The best place to begin to control Japanese beetles is lawns, their prime habitat. There are at least two options in habitat control: removal of the habitat (reduce the square footage of lawn) and manipulation of the habitat. If you choose the latter, you may wish to create a natural lawn of native ground covers or a wildlife garden to attract the birds that feed on Japanese beetles.

There are also some other safe, effective controls:

- Hand-pick beetles in the cool of the evening or early morning, when they are especially slow. Drop them into a strong solution of Murphy's Oil Soap.
- Milky spore disease is a bacterium that is deadly to beetle grubs but safe for people and other creatures. Apply milky spore to lawns in late summer.
- Spray with neem oil and neem seed extract (derived from the neem tree, a native of India); the oil acts as a repellent while the extract acts as an insecticide. Both are very safe, effective controls.

Aphids

Aphids are small, soft-bodied, sap-sucking insects also called plant lice. Their life cycle is a fascinating tribute to the adaptability of nature. In fall male aphids mate with females, which then lay eggs. The eggs over-winter and in the spring hatch into a horde of females. These females,

wingless adult
⊢⊣
⅛"/3.2mm

called stem mothers, then clone themselves, giving birth to hundreds more females through parthenogenesis. Please note that males are not needed here. All the aphids you see in summer sucking from your roses are females, exact copies of the original stem mother. A stem mother gives birth to from four to six live young a day, and over one hundred in her short lifetime. When aphid populations become so large that their food supply begins to decline, the females switch from making regular aphids and produce a winged model. These then fly to neighboring plants to begin new colonies. In fall a few token males arise so that the females can lay fertilized eggs, and the cycle starts all over again.

Aphids damage plants by seeking out the most succulent growth, usually near buds and growing points, and inserting their pointy little snouts into single plant cells. The insects then dine on the cell's fluid. Because the injured cells are young ones that have not matured, aphid damage becomes more noticeable as the plant grows, even though that damage may have been done days before.

Controls

Encouraging the natural ecology by introducing predatory insects to feed on prey insects is an excellent, though sometimes expensive, way to control a number of garden pests. Ladybugs, or lady beetles, love to munch on aphids — though they alone cannot control aphid populations. Studies have recently shown that after the beetles are released in a target area, they hang around for a while, then disperse, flying off to other areas where there aren't quite as many other ladybugs to compete with.

Green lacewings also like to eat aphids; they are usually purchased in the form of eggs mixed with rice hulls. Small amounts of this egg/rice mixture are sprinkled

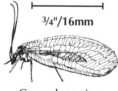

3/4"/16mm

Green lacewing

onto infested plants to distribute the eggs where they are most needed. After the eggs have been applied, do not water for a few days; you want the eggs to hatch without being washed off.

Insecticidal soap is a very safe as well as an easy control. Aphid populations survive as well as they do, not because the insects are tough to kill (they are actually one of the easiest to kill) but because they reproduce so quickly. Their reproduction rate is tied to such conditions as temperature and humidity: The warmer it is, the less time it takes for aphids to reproduce. During warm times in the summer, aphids can mature every five to seven days. In cooler weather it may take two weeks or longer. For soap sprays to work, then, they need to be applied at least once a week in warm weather and every ten to fourteen days during cooler times. Add 4 ounces of Murphy's Oil Soap and 1 ounce of

baking soda to 1 gallon of warm water. Spray all leaf surfaces until the solution drips off.

Gall Wasps

Gall wasps are small cynipid wasps that lay eggs on wild roses throughout much of the northern United States and southern Canada. Galls containing the immature wasps form on a rose stem or on roots that are close to the soil surface in late summer and fall. The wasps develop inside the gall and emerge in spring.

Gall wasps don't fly very well and tend to attack other roses close by.

Controls

The best control is to remove any galls from the roses with pruning shears as they appear in late summer and throughout the fall.

NAME	HARDINESS ZONES	FRAGRANCE	FLOWER	HEIGHT	FORM	BEST USES	PESTS & DISEASES	COMMENTS
Rugosa Rose (*Rosa rugosa*)	2–8	good	single, pale pink	4–6 ft.	dense shrub	hedges, windbreaks, tall ground cover, naturalizing	none	
R. rugosa 'Agnes'	3–8	excellent	double, chiffon yellow	4–5 ft.	dense shrub	hedges, windbreaks, naturalizing, specimen	Japanese beetles	one of the best yellow Rugosas
R. r. 'Blanc Double De Coubert'	3–8	good	double, white in late spring, reblooms in fall	4–5 ft.	dense shrub	hedges, windbreaks, herb gardens, specimen	Japanese beetles	dried petals retain fragrance
R. r. 'David Thompson'	4–8	excellent	double, deep pink	4 ft.	dense shrub	hedges, naturalizing, specimen	none	
R. r. 'Frau Dagmar Hartopp'	3–8	good	single, satin pink from late spring to fall	3–4 ft.	dense shrub	hedges, windbreaks, specimen	Japanese beetles	produces large red hips for jam or tea in autumn
R. r. 'Hansa'	3–8	excellent	semidouble, magenta-purple	6 ft	dense shrub	hedges, windbreaks, naturalizing, specimen, herb gardens	Japanese beetles	dried petals very fragrant; large orange hips ripe in fall
R. r. 'Jens Munk'	3–8	good	semidouble, rose pink from summer to fall	5 ft.	dense shrub	hedges, windbreaks, naturalizing, specimen	Japanese beetles, rose stem girdler	important to prune out canes infected with rose stem girdler each season
R. r. 'Martin Frobisher'	4–7	excellent	double, pale icy pink in early summer to fall	4–6 ft.	dense shrub	hedges, windbreaks, naturalizing, specimen	Japanese beetles	very fragrant blossoms
R. r. 'Schneezwerg'	3–8	good	semidouble, blush white from spring to fall	4 ft.	dense shrub	hedges, windbreaks, naturalizing, specimen	Japanese beetles	hips good for jam or tea
R. r. 'Thérèse Bugnet'	2–8	excellent	double, pink in late spring, repeats in fall	4–6 ft.	dense shrub	hedges, windbreaks, tall ground cover, naturalizing	Japanese beetles	red-colored canes for winter color
R. r. var. *alba*	2–8	good	single, linen white from early spring to fall	4–5 ft.	dense shrub	hedges, windbreaks, naturalizing, specimen	Japanese beetles	large orange hips in fall

SPECIES ROSES

Name	Hardiness Zones	Fragrance	Flower	Height	Form	Best Uses	Pests & Diseases	Comments
Austrian Brier (R. foetida)	3-8	good	single, yellow	5-8 ft.	shrub	informal specimens, naturalizing	black spot	var. *bicolor* with orange-red flowers
Cherokee (R. laevigata)	7-9	good	single, white	5-7 ft.	very loose shrub	naturalizing, informal hedges	none	long bloom time
Chestnut (R. roxburghii)	6-9	none	double, deep pink	4-6 ft.	shrub	informal hedges	none	has a light repeat bloom
Father Hugo (R. hugonis)	4-8	none	single, yellow	5 ft.	shrub	specimens, informal hedges	none	short bloom time
Helen (R. helenae)	5-8	good	single, white	15 ft.	climber	ground cover, trellises	none	bears orange fruit in fall
Himalayan Musk (R. brunonii)	6-8	good	single, white	over 20 feet	spreading shrub	climbers, ground cover	none	very vigorous grower
Meadow (R. blanda)	2-7	good	single, pink	5 ft.	shrub	naturalizing, hedges, specimens	black spot	bright red fruit from fall into winter
Memorial (R. wichuraiana)	5-9	good	single, white	1-2 feet	prostrate	ground cover	none	easy to propagate by tip layering
Moyes (R. moyesii)	5-8	none	single, crimson	6-8 ft.	open shrub	naturalizing	mildew in Southeast	attractive fruit through fall and winter
Musk (R. moschata)	6-9	good	single, white	6 ft.	spreading shrub, loose climber	climbers, informal hedges, naturalizing	black spot	flowers in late summer

SPECIES ROSES (CONT'D)

NAME	HARDINESS ZONES	FRAGRANCE	FLOWER	HEIGHT	FORM	BEST USES	PESTS & DISEASES	COMMENTS
New England Shining (*R. nitida*)	3-7	light	single, pink	3 ft.	shrub	naturalizing	none	can adapt to wet and sea side gardens
Prairie (*R. setigera*)	4-9	none	single, pink	5 ft.	shrub	naturalizing, informal hedges	none	vigorous grower
Redleaved (*R. rubrifolia*)	2-8	light	single, white center, red petals	6 ft.	loose shrub	informal specimens, borders, meadows	none	leaves colored dark purple-red
Scotch Brier (*R. spinosissima*)	4-8	good	single, white or pink	4 ft.	shrub	shrubs, naturalizing	none	abundant flowers in late spring, followed by black fruit
Swamp (*R. palustris*)	3-7	light	single, pink	4-6 ft.	shrub	naturalizing	none	thrives in wet soils
Sweetbrier or Eglantine (*R. eglanteria*)	4-8	good	single, deep pink	3-6 ft.	spreading shrub	naturalizing, hedges	none	leaves smell like apples; birds attracted to red fruit in fall
Virginia (*R. virginiana*)	3-7	none	single, pink	4 ft.	shrub	specimens, naturalizing, herb gardens	none	nice tea from dried fruit
White Lady Bank's (*R. banksiae* 'Alba Plena'	8-9	good	double, white	20 ft.	climber	naturalizing, trellises	none	none
Yellow Lady Bank's (*R. banksiae*)	8-9	good	double, yellow	20 ft.	climber	naturalizing, trellises	none	none

Selected Antique Roses

Cultivar	Type	Hardiness Zones	Fragrance	Flower	Height	Form	Best Uses	Pests & Diseases	Comments
Rosa 'Alba Semi-plena'	Alba	3-7	excellent	semidouble, white	5 ft.	upright shrub	informal hedges, specimens	none	blooms in late spring with no repeat; bears red hips in fall
R. 'Apothecary's Rose'	Gallica	3-8	excellent	semidouble, crimson-pink	3 ft.	shrub	herb gardens, specimens, informal hedges	mildew in fall	blooms in late spring to early summer with no repeat
R. 'Celestial'	Alba	3-8	good	double, white	5 ft.	shrub	informal hedges, mass plantings	none	prefers full sun but can adapt to partial shade
R. 'Celsiana'	Damask	3-8	excellent	double, blush white	4 ft.	shrub	herb gardens, specimens	none	excellent
R. 'Félicité Parmentier'	Alba	3-8	excellent	double, pale pink	4 ft.	shrub	specimens, mass plantings	mildew possible problem in humid summers	easy to grow; blooms in late spring with no repeat
R. 'Harison's Yellow'	Foetida	3-8	light	double, clean yellow	5 ft.	shrub	specimens	none	called the yellow rose of Texas; abundant blooms in midspring
R. 'Henri Martin'	Moss	4-8	excellent	double, red	5 ft.	shrub	specimens, herb gardens	none	blooms in late spring with no repeat
R. 'Ispahan'	Damask	3-8	excellent	semidouble, lilac-pink	5 ft.	shrub	specimens	black spot	intense fragrance

CULTIVAR	TYPE	HARDINESS ZONES	FRAGRANCE	FLOWER	HEIGHT	FORM	BEST USES	PESTS & DISEASES	COMMENTS
R. 'Jacques Cartier'	Portland	4-9	good	double, pale pink	3 ft.	compact shrub	specimen	some black spot	vigorous; blooms in late spring, repeats in fall
R. 'Leda'	Damask	3-8	excellent	double, white splashed with red	3 ft.	rambling shrub	mass plantings	none	blooms in late spring
R. 'Maiden's Blush'	Alba	3-8	excellent	double, pale pink	4 ft.	shrub	informal hedges, mass plantings	none	can grow in light shade
R. 'Queen of Denmark'	Alba	3-8	good	double, pale pink	4 ft.	upright shrub	informal hedges, mass plantings	none	can adapt to light shade; blooms in mid-summer with no repeat
R. 'Reine des Violettes'	Hybrid Perpetual	5-9	light	double, violet-red	5 ft.	shrub	specimen	resistant, but can get black spot	nearly thornless; repeats bloom in the North
R. 'Rosa Mundi'	Gallica	3-8	excellent	semidouble, pink to crimson with white stripes	3 ft.	shrub	herb gardens, informal hedges, specimens	mildew in late summer and fall	blooms in late spring to early summer with no repeat
R. 'Rose de Rescht'	Portland	4-8	excellent	double, red	3 ft.	shrub	mass plantings	none	blooms in late spring, repeats in fall
R. 'Superb Tuscan'	Gallica	4-8	excellent	double, velvet red	3 ft.	shrub	specimens	none	blooms in late spring to early summer with no repeat

MODERN ROSES

Name	Type	Hardiness Zones	Fragrance	Flower	Height	Form	Best Uses	Pests & Diseases	Comments
Rosa 'Bonica'	Shrub	4-8	light	double, pink	4 ft.	shrub	specimen, mass plantings	resistant to black spot and mildew	vigorous growth; repeats bloom in fall
R. 'Carefree Beauty'	Shrub	4-8	light	double, pink	5 ft.	upright shrub	informal hedges, mass plantings, specimen	disease resistant but can get black spot or mildew some years	bears abundant orange hips in fall; repeats bloom in fall
R. 'Carefree Wonder'	Shrub	4-8	light	double, pink	2-3 ft.	low shrub	informal hedges, mass plantings	resistant to black spot and mildew	produces few hips; repeats bloom in fall
R. 'Country Dancer'	Buck Hybrid	4-8	light	double, pink	4 ft.	shrub	informal hedges, specimen	resistant	repeats bloom in fall
R. 'Fair Bianca'	English Rose	5-8	good	very double, snow white	3 ft.	compact shrub	specimen, small gardens, herb gardens	black spot, Japanese beetles	repeat bloom in fall
R. 'Graham Thomas'	English Rose	5-9	excellent	very double, clear yellow	4-5 ft.	loose shrub	informal hedges	black spot, Japanese beetles	prune back the long canes hard each year; short bloom time
R. 'Heritage'	English Rose	5-8	excellent	double, antique white around pale pink center	4 ft.	shrub	specimen	black spot, Japanese beetles	unique scent to the blossoms
R. 'John Cabot'	Canadian Explorer Hybrid	3-9	good	double, magenta	6 ft.	shrub	specimen	none	repeats bloom in fall; one of the best roses, period
R. 'Mary Rose'	English Rose	5-9	good	double, soft pink	4 ft.	shrub	specimen, informal hedges	black spot, Japanese beetles	repeats bloom in fall
R. 'Morden Blush'	Morden Hybrid	4-9	light	double, pale blush	2-3 ft.	compact shrub	specimen, informal hedges	black spot some years	blooms from spring to fall
R. 'Morden Cardinette'	Morden Hybrid	4-9	light	double, red	2-3 ft.	compact shrub	specimen, low informal hedges	black spot in some years	bears flowers from spring to fall
R. 'Morden Centennial'	Morden Hybrid	3-9	light	double, pink from spring to	3 ft.	compact shrub	mass plantings, informal hedges	black spot in some years	bears plentiful, bright red hips in fall
R. 'Sea Foam'	Shrub	5-9	light	double, white	3 ft.	shrub	mass plantings, ground cover	none	blooms from spring to fall

12

Growing the Best Shrubs and Trees

Woody ornamentals — trees, shrubs, and vines — provide the background and backbone of many gardens. Their flowers, foliage, stems, bark, and fruit, can enliven the landscape throughout the year. In addition, many are long-lived plants, providing years of enjoyment. That's the good news. The bad news is that the same longevity that makes them so useful can also lead to problems. Unlike herbaceous plants, which gardeners routinely move or replace, woody ornamentals are considered by many to be permanent parts of the landscape, even if they obviously don't belong where they are. So the red oak on the lawn that was so small twenty years ago is now growing into the electric wires, and the sugar maple near the driveway buckles more of the pavement every year. Whatever type of garden or property you have, though, there are easy-care, beautiful, low-maintenance woody ornamentals that deserve to be thought of as a permanent part of your landscape.

Easy-Care Trees

An easy-care tree is one that is largely pest- and disease free, does not produce a lot of messy fruits or pods to litter the ground, is adaptable to a range of climatic conditions, and does not need much pruning, special fertilizing, or extra watering. All this, and it should be gorgeous and stately, too! Still, there is a surprisingly large number of trees that meet these strict criteria, providing a wide selection to fit your needs no matter where you live. The chart on the following page lists some of the best.

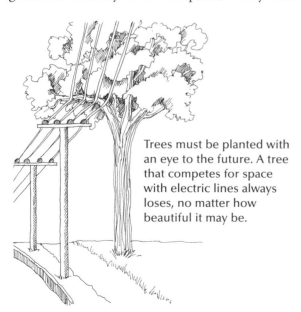

Trees must be planted with an eye to the future. A tree that competes for space with electric lines always loses, no matter how beautiful it may be.

269

TREE	HARDINESS ZONES	HEIGHT	LIGHT	PESTS & DISEASES	LANDSCAPE USES	BEST CULTIVARS	COMMENTS
American Yellowwood (Cladrastis lutea)	4-8	40 ft.	full sun or partial shade	none	shade tree for smaller properties	'Rosea': pink flowers	bears fragrant white flowers in June; likes high-pH soils
Carolina Silver-Bell (Halesia carolina)	4-8	35 ft.	full sun or partial shade	none	small shade tree	'Meehanii': a dwarf form about 10 feet tall	an excellent companion plant for rhododendron; bears white flowers in spring
European Beech (Fagus sylvatica)	4-7	50 ft.	full sun or partial shade	none serious	large shade tree	'Riversii': dark purple leaves; 'Purpurea Pendula': an antique weeping form that only grows to about 10 feet high and has purple leaves	one of the most beautiful shade trees; do not plant near pavement
Ginkgo (Ginkgo biloba)	3-9	60 ft.	full sun or partial shade	none	large shade tree	'Princeton Sentry': male variety with excellent form; leaves yellow in fall	grows slowly but has beautiful fall color; to avoid messy fruit, plant only male trees
Golden Larch (Pseudolarix kaempferi)	4-7	40 ft.	full sun	none serious	specimen tree for large areas	'Annesleyana': a dwarf form	needlelike leaves that turn brilliant golden yellow in fall
Golden Rain Tree (Koelreuteria paniculata)	4-9	30 ft.	full sun	none serious	small specimen tree	'September': hardy in Zones 6 through 9; flowers in late August and early September	bears beautiful chains of yellow flowers in June and July; adaptable to many different soils
Japanese Zelkova (Zelkova serrata)	5-8	65 ft.	full sun or partial shade	none serious	large shade tree	'Green Vase'	closely resembles the American elm but not susceptible to Dutch elm disease; fast growing
Sourwood (Oxydendrum arboreum)	4-9	25 ft.	full sun	none serious	small specimen tree	species	a beautiful tree with fragrant flowers in late June and deep red fall color
Sugar Maple (Acer saccharum)	4-8	60 ft.	full sun or partial shade	leaf scorch during droughts	large shade tree	'Green Mountain': more drought tolerant than the species	a beautiful tree with excellent fall color; do not plant near pavement
White Fir (Abies concolor)	3-7	40 ft.	full sun or light shade	none serious	screens, specimen plant	'Violacea': gray-blue needles similar to the Colorado blue spruce	likes rich, well-drained soil; tolerates drought.

UNUSUAL EASY-CARE TREES

Great gardens are unique places that often convey their beauty and originality through the use of unusual plants. A common misconception about unusual plants in the garden is that *unusual* means difficult to grow. The truth is that many uniquely beautiful trees demand almost nothing for years of splendor.

Dawn Redwood
Metasequoia glyptostroboides

HARDINESS:	Zones 4-8
HEIGHT:	70 feet
LIGHT:	Full sun
PESTS AND DISEASES:	None serious
LANDSCAPE USES:	Large specimen tree

The dawn redwood was first discovered through fossils and thought to be long extinct, but it was later found growing in the wilds of China. The tree has small, deciduous green needles and in overall appearance resembles a bald cypress. It grows very fast, with some trees reaching 20 feet in ten years.

Best Cultivar: Species.

Franklin Tree
Franklinia alatamaha

HARDINESS:	Zones 5-9
HEIGHT:	5 feet
LIGHT:	Full sun or light shade
PESTS AND DISEASES:	None once established
LANDSCAPE USES:	Small specimen tree

The Franklin tree was discovered by John Bartram in 1770 growing along the banks of the Alatamaha River in northern Georgia. Only a few plants were ever found. Within a few years of its discovery the Franklin tree was extinct in the wild, but it has been cultivated in gardens ever since. The tree bears fragrant white flowers in late summer and the leaves turn reddish orange in fall. It grows best in Zones 5 through 7.

Best Cultivar: Species.

Katsura Tree
Cercidiphyllum japonicum

HARDINESS:	Zones - 4-9
HEIGHT:	50 feet
LIGHT:	Full sun
PESTS AND DISEASES:	None serious
LANDSCAPE USES:	Excellent shade tree

Katsura tree is one of the very best shade trees anyone could want. The leaves have a purple cast when young, mature to a soft green in summer, and turn yellowish red in fall, when they have a spicy odor. The tree can adapt to both country and city settings and is at home in any well-drained, evenly moist soil. It must be seen to be appreciated.

Best Cultivar: 'Pendula' has weeping branches covered with blue-green leaves.

Japanese Cedar
Cryptomeria japonica

HARDINESS:	Zones 5-9
HEIGHT:	50 feet
LIGHT:	Full sun
PESTS AND DISEASES:	Some branch dieback in warmer areas
LANDSCAPE USES:	A medium-size, very graceful specimen tree

Japanese cedar is a graceful tree with plumes of evergreen foliage. Like that of the umbrella pine, the foliage takes on a bronze cast in winter. It's one of the best conifers for the South, though it doesn't like windy locations.

Best Cultivar: 'Yoshino' is fast growing with deep green foliage.

Paperbark Maple
Acer griseum

HARDINESS: Zones 4-8
HEIGHT: 20 feet
LIGHT: Full sun or partial shade
PESTS AND DISEASES: None serious
LANDSCAPE USES: Small specimen tree

Paperbark maple is a lovely small tree with cherry-like exfoliating bark and green leaves that turn bronze-red in fall. It grows slowly and prefers soils that are evenly moist but not wet.

Best Cultivar: Species.

Table Top Pine
Pinus densiflora

HARDINESS: Zones 3-7
HEIGHT: 40-60 ft.
LIGHT: Full sun
PESTS AND DISEASES: None serious
LANDSCAPE USES: Specimen tree

A distinguished, slow-growing tree with an attractive form that accentuates any landscape. Grows best in acid, well-drained soils.

Best Cultivar: 'Soft Green', 'Umbraculifera'

Umbrella Pine
Sciadopitys verticillata

HARDINESS: Zones 4-8
HEIGHT: 30 ft.
LIGHT: Full sun or partial shade
PESTS AND DISEASES: None
LANDSCAPE USES: Specimen tree

A handsome conical tree with clusters of soft, broad, needle-shaped leaves arranged like spokes on a wheel. It is slow growing. In cold climates the leaves turn a bronze-green color.

Best Cultivar: Species.

LANDSCAPING AND COCKROACHES

If you live in the South, cockroaches are one of those nasty things that try daily to steal your dignity. It is maddening to spend hours cleaning the kitchen, making sure every crumb has been tossed out and every shiny surface glitters, only to flick on the light at night and watch a herd of little critters scurry for the corners. In addition to making your kitchen a subdivision of roach motels, you can help control roaches by assessing and changing the landscaping that abuts your house.

Growing cockroaches requires many of the same conditions needed to grow good plants, especially even moisture and even, warm temperatures. The more moisture levels and temperatures vary, the less cockroaches like it. Ground cover, such as turf grasses, and mulches, including pine straw and stones, actually create environments that are beneficial to cockroaches. In fact, anything that covers the soil, including trees and shrubs, helps cockroaches survive. A recent study in Alabama concluded that the best surface to have directly adjacent to your house is bare soil or hardscape such as stone.

Attractive hardscapes that abut houses, such as stone patios, can reduce cockroach infestations inside the home.

EASY-CARE WEEPING TREES

Of all the different types of specialty trees, from dwarfs to prostrate groundcovers, perhaps none accents the garden and yard better than weepers. These beautiful trees, also called pendulous varieties, represent scores of species but have one thing in common; they all weep. Weeping trees have long, pendulous limbs that flow down from the upright trunk toward the ground in a sinuous cascade of branches and leaves.

Weeping Katsura Tree
Cercidiphylum japonicum 'Pendula'

HARDINESS:	Zones 4-9
HEIGHT:	15 to 25 feet
LIGHT:	Full sun
PESTS AND DISEASES:	None serious
LANDSCAPE USES:	Specimen tree

This beautiful variety of Katsura tree deserves a place in just about any garden. The branches are pliant but strong and gracefully cascade from the main trunk. The spreading habit accents the small, blue-green foliage giving the plant a stunning, fountain-like appearance. As a bonus it is just as tough as the species making this tree a great value.

Other Weeping Cultivars: *Cercidiphylum magnificum* 'Pendula' is a weeping form of a closely related species. The leaves of this variety are slightly larger than those of weeping katsura tree with stiffer branches and a more upright habit.

Weeping Higan Cherry
Prunus subhirtella var. 'Pendula'

HARDINESS:	Zones 4-8
HEIGHT:	20 to 40 feet
LIGHT:	Full sun
PESTS AND DISEASES:	None serious
LANDSCAPE USES:	Specimen tree

This tree is one of the most beautiful flowering weeping trees you can imagine. They are quite vigorous and are among the longest lived of all the flowering cherries. The slender branches hang like a curtain from the trunk and in early to mid spring are covered with a sea of single pink blossoms. The leaves emerge as the flowers are fading. In late summer small shiny black fruit appear.

Other Weeping Cultivars: *Prunus subhirtella* var. 'Pendula Rubra' has deep pink flowers. *Prunus subhirtella* var. 'Pendula Plena Rosea' grows to about 30 feet high with a spread of 20 feet. Bears double pink fragrant flowers in spring and shiny black fruit in late summer. *Prunus* x 'Snow Fountains' grows to only 10 feet high with abundant single white flowers in spring. Heat and drought tolerant as well as disease resistant.

Weeping White Pine
Pinus strobus 'Pendula'

HARDINESS:	Zones 3-8
HEIGHT:	20 feet
LIGHT:	Full sun
PESTS AND DISEASES:	None serious
LANDSCAPE USES:	Specimen tree

This truly beautiful tree has the same, soft needles as the species, but on a framework of pendulous branches that is as graceful as a veridian waterfall. With time the long branches grow right to the ground. Excellent as a centerpiece in the rock garden or back of the border as well as a specimen tree.

Other Weeping Cultivars: *Pinus flexis* 'Pendula' is a weeping form of Limber pine with a vigorous, spreading habit *Pinus flexis* 'Glauca Pendula' is a low-growing spreading plant with blue-green needles. The plant scrampers along the ground more than weeps. Good in rock gardens. *Pinus banksiana* 'Uncle Fogy' is a variety of Jack pine that forms a weeping tree when grafted to a standard or a wide spreading groundcover if left on its own.

EASY-CARE TREES FOR SMALL SPACES AND NATURAL PLACES

Gardeners who have small properties or seek a beautiful tree that will accent the garden rather than overpower it have some truly magnificent choices. Each one of the following trees bears beautiful flowers in spring or early summer, requires no pruning or special care once established, and is not seriously troubled by pests or diseases.

Downy Serviceberry
Amelanchier arborea

The downy serviceberry likes meadows and fields as well as the backyard. Nurseries almost always label this plant *Amelanchier canadensis* (Shadblow serviceberry), which has similar leaves and bark but is actually a multistemmed shrub that is hardy in Zones 3-7. The true downy serviceberry is a tree that grows to about twenty feet tall and is hardy in Zones 4 through 9. It has a rounded canopy of small, simple leaves, plus abundant small white flowers in midspring. The fruits are small and purplish black, ripening in June; they are used to make serviceberry pies, which some folks claim taste better than blueberry pies. (In most years this debate remains unresolved, because birds eat all the fruit before people can pick any.) In fall the leaves turn bright orange-scarlet.

How to Grow: Plant downy serviceberry in well-drained soil generously amended with organic matter with a pH of 5.0 to 6.0. The plant naturally develops a tidy form and rarely needs pruning. Downy serviceberry is not tolerant of urban conditions. It is an excellent plant for the moist soils along the shores of ponds or streams, but readily adapts to much drier conditions once established. There are many excellent cultivars.

Flowering Dogwood
Cornus florida

Flowering dogwood grows as an understory tree in forests from southern Canada and New England south to Texas and northern Florida. Northern-grown trees are hardy to Zone 5, sometimes Zone 4, but those grown in the South should not be planted north of Zone 6 to avoid winterkill of flower buds. Flowering dogwood is one of the classic trees of the garden. Growing to 15 feet in the North, more than 30 feet in the South, it bears cream white bracts in spring. In fall the leaves turn maroon-red and clumps of crimson berries decorate the tips of the branches.

How to Grow: Plant flowering dogwood in evenly moist, well-drained soil amended with organic matter with a pH of 5.0 to 7.5. It does best in partial shade or full sun with light afternoon shade. Flowering dogwood has a reputation for being susceptible to borer and a leaf disease, anthracnose; outbreaks do seem to occur during droughts or hot, wet summers. 'Cherokee Sunset' has red flowers and excellent vigor; it is resistant to anthracnose.

Kousa Dogwood
Cornus kousa

A stately, well-branched tree, this dogwood grows to 20 feet and is hardy in Zones 4 through 8. Its strong, horizontal branches bear medium green leaves and antique white flowers (formed from large bracts rather than petals) in June or July. The leaves turn scarlet in autumn and persist for many weeks before falling. The pinkish red, round fruits hang like ornaments from the gray branches from late summer until midfall.

How to Grow: Plant Kousa dogwood in a sunny place in sandy loam soil with a pH of 5.5 to 6.5, well amended with organic matter. The tree is quite drought tolerant once established and more cold hardy than flowering dogwood. Many excellent cultivars are available.

Japanese Stewartia
Stewartia pseudocamellia

A particularly beautiful tree, the Japanese stewartia reaches 20 feet in height and hardy in Zones 4 through 7. It has dark green leaves that turn reddish purple in fall, along with white 2- to 3-inch-wide flowers in June or July. Its attractive, exfoliating bark is red-brown, with a transluscence reminiscent of cherry.

How to Grow: Plant in a sunny spot, preferably with early-afternoon shade, in well-drained, evenly moist soil with a pH of between 5.0 and 6.5 and abundant organic matter. Mulch to keep the roots cool.

Lily Magnolia
Magnolia liliiflora

A small tree from central China, this magnolia is hardy in Zones 5 through 8 and rarely reaches more than ten feet in height. It is beautiful in oriental and rock gardens as well as a backyard border. In spring the tree bears large, lily-shaped purple flowers that have a spicy fragrance.

How to Grow: Plant lily magnolia in well-drained soil with a pH of between 5.5 and 7.0. The cultivars of the Little Girl Series arose from crossing *Magnolia liliflora* 'Nigra' with *Magnolia stellata* 'Rosea'. The resulting varieties are truly exceptional plants; perhaps the best is *Magnolia liliflora* x 'Betty', an upright, 10-foot-tall tree with clove-scented red-purple upright flowers that bloom about two weeks later than many magnolias.

White Fringe Tree
Chionanthus virginicus

The white fringe tree is equally at home in a garden and a wildflower meadow. Hardy in Zones 3 through 9, each tree is shaped a little differently from any other. It is native to the mountain valleys and coastal plain of the southeastern United States, where it can be either a shrub or small tree. Commercially grown trees are often much more uniform, reaching 20 feet in height with straight, strong trunks and spreading canopies. White fringe tree is one of the last trees to leaf out, sometimes waiting until late May or early June. The delicate clusters of white flowers appear at about the same time and are lightly fragrant. In fall the leaves turn yellow.

How to Grow: Plant white fringe tree in full sun in spring; soil should be well drained and amended with organic matter, with a pH of between 5.0 and 6.0. This is an excellent tree for the shores of ponds or streams.

TREES AND SHRUBS THAT WON'T MAKE YOU SNEEZE

Flowering plants have been growing on the earth for at least the last 120 million years. If you are one of the millions of people with even a hint of hay fever, you can appreciate the magnitude of that statement: For 120 million years, pollen has been floating through the air. Modern humans showed up about 40,000 years ago, discovered agriculture, and have been sneezing and wiping their watery eyes ever since.

For some of us, life in the garden is a sort of love/hate relationship: We love the beautiful flowers and hate what they do to us. What many of us don't realize, however, is that not all pollen is created equal. Some of it makes us miserable, and some of it leaves us alone. Here are some trees and shrubs (and even a few flowers), that the American Lung Association says are not likely to cause respiratory allergies: firs (*Abies* spp.), redbuds (*Cercis* spp.), dogwoods (*Cornus* spp.), ginkgo (*Ginkgo biloba*), magnolias (*Magnolia* spp.), pines (*Pinus* spp.), pears (*Pyrus* spp.), fire thorns (*Pyracantha* spp.), rhododendrons and azaleas (*Rhododendron* spp.), viburnums (*Viburnum* spp.), yuccas (*Yucca* spp.), begonias (*Begonia* spp.), daffodils (*Narcissus* spp.), poppies (*Papaver* spp.), and tulips (*Tulipa* spp.).

Easy-Care Shrubs

Qualifying as an easy-care, low-maintenance shrub involves more than just the ability to survive cold winters. These plants must also be disease and pest resistant, require little or no attention once established, and provide multiseason interest. That's a tall order, but the following plants do all of that, and sometimes more. The first two are dwarf varieties especially suited for small spaces.

Dwarf Japanese Barberry
Berberis thunbergii var. *atropurpurea* 'Crimson Pygmy'

A beautiful, multibranched little shrub, this barberry grows about 2 feet tall with abundant, small, reddish purple leaves from spring to fall. The brown stems are covered with slender thorns and decorated with small crimson-colored berries from fall through winter.

How to Grow: Plant Japanese barberry in full sun for best leaf color, though it also grows well in partial shade. It can adapt to almost any soil except one that is boggy or wet. Barberry can get a number of diseases but almost never does so under normal conditions. It is hardy in Zones 4 through 8.

Dwarf Koreanspice Viburnum
Viburnum carlesii 'Compactum'

One of the best shrubs available, dwarf Koreanspice viburnum grows to about 2½ feet tall with dark green leaves and clusters of white, intensely fragrant flowers in spring.

How to Grow: Plant in a well-drained soil with a pH of between 5.5 and 6.5, in full sun or light shade. It is hardy in zones 4 through 8.

Japanese Clethra
Clethra barbinervis

Depending on where it grows, Japanese clethra can be a small tree or a large shrub reaching about 10 feet in height, though in southern areas it can reach twice that. The leaves are dark green, turning a collage of red, orange, and pink in fall. In summer long panicles of small, fragrant white flowers emerge that mature into drooping capsules that linger throughout the winter. Japanese clethra is renowned for its beautiful cinnamon-colored, exfoliating bark, which makes the plant especially pretty in winter.

How to Grow: Plant Japanese clethra in well-drained, evenly moist soil with a pH of between 5.0 and 6.0 in full sun or partial shade. It is hardy in Zones 5 through 8 and virtually pest and disease free.

Linden Viburnum
Viburnum dilatatum

For a stunning display from spring through winter, there may be no better pair of plants than two cultivars of the linden viburnum. 'Erie' is a large shrub reaching up to 6 feet in height and nearly 8 feet in width, with dark green leaves that turn reddish bronze in fall. Clusters of white flowers bloom in late spring; in fall the bush is covered with red fruits that last until the birds pick the branches clean. 'Iroquois' is similar to 'Erie' but has leaves of darker green that turn orange-red in fall; it is also a bit taller. The bush is covered with white flowers in late spring and weighted down with red fruit from fall into winter.

How to Grow: Plant both in well-drained soil with a pH of between 5.5 and 6.5 in sun or light shade. They are hardy in Zones 5 through 7.

Mohawk Viburnum
Viburnum x *burkwoodii*

Introduced in 1953 by the National Arboretum, this striking plant is a hybrid between *Viburnum burkwoodii* (Burkwood viburnum) and *Viburnum carlesii* (Koreanspice viburnum). The Mohawk viburum is an upright, many-branched, mounding shrub reaching 7 feet in height and 8 feet in width. The leaves are dark green, turning orange-red in fall; they are disease resistant. In spring the plant bears bright red flower buds that open into clusters of white, clove-scented flowers. The fragrance is so rich it could be dessert.

How to Grow: Plant Mohawk viburnum in well-drained soil with a pH of between 5.5 and 6.5 in sun or light shade. The shrub is hardy in Zones 4 through 8 and tolerates northern cold and southern heat equally well. Excellent for urban as well as country gardens.

Winged Euonymous
Euonymous alata

This is one of the most common plants seen in garden centers and gardens today, precisely because it is extremely versatile and easy to mass-produce. A large, vase-shaped shrub, it grows to 15 feet in height and 10 feet in width, though some cultivars are smaller. The stems are lined with corky extensions called wings that give the plant an interesting winter appearance. The leaves are small and light green in summer, turning bright red in fall — this is the source of the plant's other common name, burning bush. In winter the branches are decorated with small red berries that linger through most of the season.

How to Grow: Winged euonymus does well in almost any type of soil and is equally at home on dry hillsides and the edges of ponds. Plant in full sun for best autumn color, but it will also grow well in shade. It is hardy in Zones 4 through 9.

Growing and Caring For Woody Ornamentals

A gardening corollary to Murphy's Law states that the experts only introduce a new way of doing something immediately after you have mastered the old way. So if you think you can breeze right through this discussion on how to plant ornamental shrubs and trees because you've read the stuff a million times in every other garden book in the world, you're in for a shock. The experts have changed their minds on the proper way to plant shrubs and trees.

For what seems like the past few billion years trees and shrubs have been planted the same way. Here, for the sake of nostalgic review, are the old directions. Dig a hole that is wider and deeper than the size of the tree's rootball. Add a little organic matter to the soil, and fill the hole with a few inches of loose soil. Place the tree in the hole, making sure it is straight, and finish filling in around its rootball. Tamp the soil firmly to remove air pockets, and build a soil berm around the planting area to hold water. Water well.

It seems that recently, however, the American Forestry Association, along with the National Urban Forest Council, took a long and careful look at this age-old technique. They found some serious flaws. Digging a hole in the soil is like creating a large pot for the tree to grow in. The roots grow only to the edge of the original hole; then the compacted soil stops their growth. Instead of penetrating the soil, the roots circle the hole, much the way the roots of a potbound plant circle the sides of the pot. In a few years the tree begins to decline in health until it dies during a summer drought or a winter cold spell, or it succumbs to some disease. The planting recommendations on page 278 are a result of these organizations' efforts to address these problems.

PROPER PLANTING

Instead of a planting hole, the new technique calls for creating a growing area for the tree that is large enough to accommodate root growth for many years. Plant bare-root plants in spring, wrapped plants in spring or fall, and container-grown plants anytime from spring to early fall. Here are the planting guidelines:

1. After you have selected a site, mark out a circle four to five times the width of the rootball. Remove any turf and set aside.

2. Loosen the soil within the circle with a tiller or garden fork to a depth of about twelve inches. Turn some organic matter into the soil.

3. Dig a hole in the center of the circle that is slightly wider than the rootball but exactly the same depth.

4. Place the tree in the hole, making sure it is straight, and remove any wrapping from the rootball. Backfill the hole in stages and *water* the soil, instead of tamping it, to remove excess air.

5. The use of soil berms to create water reservoirs has been eliminated because they worked too well. They held water that moistened the area directly beneath them but left other areas just beyond them too dry. The moist soil promoted root growth but the dry soil inhibited it. The end result was a root system that often did not grow as quickly as the canopy, making the tree top-heavy and prone to windfall. So instead of a soil berm, cover the area with a few inches of mulch.

6. If you're planting on a slope, cover the soil with mulch and make a series of low soil berms in the shape of smiles that extend downslope.

USING TREES AND SHRUBS TO SAVE MONEY

Wherever you live — North, South, East, or West — the proper use of trees and shrubs around your house can save in heating and cooling costs every year. Woody ornamentals reduce temperatures in and near homes, and thereby lower cooling costs, by:

- Shading buildings as well as the areas around them
- Increasing the amount of evapotranspiration in an area
- Altering airflow patterns

Woody ornamentals can also increase the ability of buildings to retain heat in winter by blocking winds. Recent studies have concluded that homes landscaped with an eye to energy conservation can save about 10 percent per year on heating costs and about 25 percent per year on cooling costs.

When transplanting trees use a layer of absorbent mulch over the planting area instead of the traditional soil berm. The water that is applied to the mulch will moisten the soil around the root area of the tree more efficiently than that collected in a berm.

Landscaping Hints for Cold Climates

Use thickly branched, heavily needled evergreens as foundation plantings (under four feet tall) especially around the east, north, and west sides of the house. Good plants include globe arborvitae *(Thuja occidentalis),* 'Aurea' and 'Hetz Midget'; false cypress (*Chamaecyparis* spp.), *obtusa* 'Nana Gracilis', *pisifera* 'Aurea Nana', and *pisifera* 'Mops'; and juniper (*Juniperus* spp.), *chinensis* 'Sea Green' and *horizontalis* 'Bar Harbor'.

Use tall, densely needled evergreens as windscreens, especially to the north, northeast, and northwest. Good plants include spruce (*Picea* spp.), pine (*Pinus* spp.), arborvitae (*Thuja* spp.), and hemlock (*Tsuga* spp.).

Plant deciduous shade trees to the east and west and near paved surfaces to shade buildings and grounds in summer. A favorite here is katsura tree *(Cercidiphyllum japonicum).*

Landscaping Hints for Warm Climates

Plant evergreen shrubs as foundation plantings, and small trees to buffer and shade the east and west sides of the house. Good plants include California incense cedar *(Calocedrus decurrens),* Leyland cypress (x *Cupressocyparis leylandii),* Japanese cedar *(Cryptomeria japonica),* boxwood *(Buxus sempervirens),* and holly (*Ilex* spp.).

Use deciduous shade trees on the south side of the building to shade it in the summer and help warm it in winter: they also help near paved surfaces. Good choices include ginkgo *(Ginkgo biloba)* and katsura tree *(Cercidiphyllum japonicum).*

◆ **Easy-Care Trees for the Southwest and Deep South**

California incense cedar *(Calocedrus decurrens)*

Leyland cypress (x *Cupressocyparis leylandii)*

Live oak *(Quercus virginiana)*

Loquat *(Eriobotrya japonica)*

Mesquite *(Prosopis glandulosa)*

Narrow-leaved black peppermint *(Eucalyptus nicholii)*

Silk tree *(Albizia julibrissin)*

Southern magnolia *(Magnolia grandiflora)*

Deciduous trees planted on the south side of a house will keep the home cooler in summer when the leaves shade the building, and warmer in winter when the sun can pour through the bare branches.

GETTING FORSYTHIAS TO BLOOM UP NORTH

Forsythia (*Forsythia* spp.) is a common garden shrub that has a very flowing, loose habit and bright yellow flowers in early spring. Or at least it's supposed to have bright yellow flowers in early spring. Many years northern gardeners get no flowers at all. Forsythia is hardy to Zone 4, but the flower buds are only reliably hardy to Zone 6.

In the last few years plant breeders have released a host of new cultivars they claim are flower-bud-hardy to Zone 4. The University of Minnesota Landscape Arboretum has evaluated some of them. These proved hardiest of the cultivars tested: 'Meadowlark', 'New Hampshire Gold', 'Northern Gold', and 'Northern Sun'. Thus the way to get forsythias to bloom up North is to plant the toughest cultivars.

CARING FOR WOODY ORNAMENTALS AFTER PLANTING

Large plants, such as trees and woody shrubs, often require from one to as many as four years to become fully established after planting. During this time they need a bit of special care to help ensure that they remain as vigorous and healthy as possible.

- **Staking or bracing** is *not* required or recommended for any woody ornamental properly planted — with the exceptions of trees planted in exposed, windy sites, trees planted in gravelly or heavy clay soils, and those adjacent to sidewalks and other areas where people are likely to physically disturb them (see accompanying box).

- **Wrapping the stem** of newly transplanted trees is also discouraged, for it provides a nice home to a number of insects as well as slowing the natural thickening of the bark. A winter wrap, however, applied after the ground has frozen in fall and removed as soon as the ground thaws in spring, does provide the tree some protection; it helps guard against mice and other animals that can gnaw the bark in winter, as well as against sunscald, a condition in which late-winter sun heats the south side of a trunk during the day, causing the bark to split when the temperature drops quickly after sundown.

- **Watering** of newly planted trees and shrubs is necessary during the period that they are establishing themselves in their new location. The frequency of watering depends on the type of soil,  local rainfall, the altitude of the garden, and the size and type of plant. A good rule of thumb is to apply enough water so that the soil remains evenly moist without ever becoming waterlogged. Be sure to apply water not only around the base of the plant, but also to the soil just beyond the rootball to encourage root growth into the surrounding soil. Signs that a plant is not yet fully established include smaller-than-normal leaves, slower-than-normal growth, smaller or fewer flowers, and early coloration and dropping of leaves in fall.

TO STAKE OR NOT TO STAKE

For many years it has been common practice to stake newly planted trees, decorating them with guy wires and small sections of old garden hose. In theory, the wires and stakes kept the trees from blowing over in the wind, and the sections of hose kept the wires from killing the trees. Many horticulturists stopped staking newly planted trees years ago, however; they felt that staking trees was like spoiling a child. Here's why.

When a breeze moves the stem of a plant, chemicals called cytokinins cause the cells in the stem to thicken and enlarge, strengthening the tissues. If the tree is staked, the stem doesn't move and the cytokinins never do their stuff. Over time the artificial support that the stakes provide actu-

ally encourages weak, thin-caliber stems and top-heavy canopies. When the stakes are removed the tree is more subject to splitting and windfall than it would be if left alone. Plant a tree correctly to begin with, and you will rarely have any need to stake it.

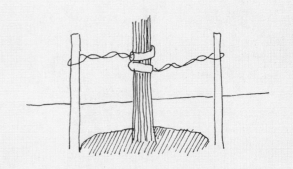

- **Mulching** is advantageous for newly planted as well as most established plantings of woody ornamentals. Applying organic mulches (such as shredded bark, wood chips, or pine needles) keeps the soil cool, modifies soil-temperature fluctuations, reduces water evaporation, reduces the need to weed, and increases the fertility and organic matter content of the soil.

◆ **Trees That Are Easy to Transplant**

Amur cork tree (*Phellodendron amurense*)

Ash (*Fraxinus* spp.)

Elm (*Ulmus*)

Ginkgo (*Ginkgo biloba*)

Linden (*Tilia* spp.)

Maple (*Acer* spp.)

Pin oak (*Quercus palustris*)

Pine (*Pinus spp.*)

FERTILIZING WOODY ORNAMENTALS

The wild relatives of our ornamental trees and shrubs do not require fertilizer. The fallen leaves and other organic matter that pile up on the forest floor conserve the minerals necessary for proper growth, recycling them naturally. Homeowners who annually add compost to the soil around their woody ornamentals and mulch with organic mulches are merely doing what nature does every day. Plantings maintained in such a way rarely need any additional fertilizer. But tidy homeowners — those who collect and toss away leaves and grass

Annual additions of compost around shrubs and trees makes nutrients available to their roots in the same way nature recycles nutrients to shrubs and trees in the forest.

Nutrient Recycling

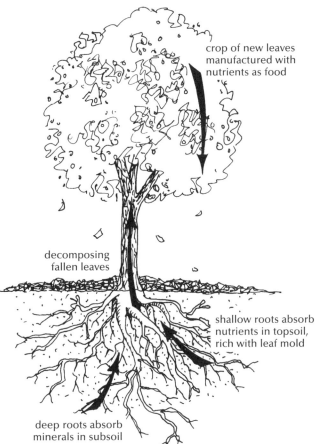

crop of new leaves manufactured with nutrients as food

decomposing fallen leaves

shallow roots absorb nutrients in topsoil, rich with leaf mold

deep roots absorb minerals in subsoil

clippings — often have to amend the soil with additional nutrients to keep all their plants healthy. Both organic and inorganic fertilizers are capable of returning missing nutrients to the soil, and which to use is a matter of personal preference.

Natural fertilizers include fish emulsion; processed municipal sewage; cottonseed, linseed, and soybean meals; and dehydrated animal manure. These fertilizers have relatively low concentrations of nitrogen, phosphorous, and potassium, the three primary plant nutrients, as well as trace minerals. They release their nutrients over a long period of time and cannot damage plant roots.

Inorganic fertilizers have much higher nutrient concentrations, and those nutrients are more quickly available to plants than those in organic fertilizers. If used incorrectly, however, inorganic fertilizers can produce areas of concentrated salts in the soil, which can damage plant roots.

Fertilizing Deciduous Shrubs

Plantings that have layers of organic mulch added yearly rarely need additional fertilizer. Still, flowering and fruit-producing shrubs can benefit from an application of fish emulsion or a similar natural fertilizer in spring as growth begins and again after the shrub has finished blooming. If inorganic fertilizer is used, hand-broadcast a balanced commercial fertilizer, such as a 10-10-10, on the soil surface beneath the branches of the plant at the rate of about 2 pounds per 100 square feet in spring. Water thoroughly.

Fertilizing Deciduous Trees

For young trees, follow the fertilizing guidelines for deciduous shrubs. Fertilize older, well-established trees surrounded by turf in late spring using the *punchbar method:* Use a crowbar to open holes about 1 foot deep and about 2 feet apart in the shape of a circle. Make the first circle about 3 feet from the trunk of the tree and the last about 3 feet beyond the drip line of its canopy. Fill each hole with a solution of fish emulsion, then water the area with a sprinkler for about an hour. After the soil has dried, fill the holes with compost to within 2 inches of the surface and top off with soil.

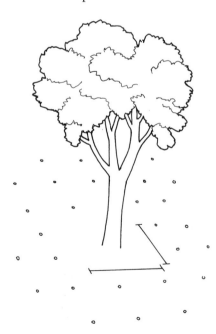

The punchbar method of fertilizer application uses a crowbar to make evenly spaced holes in the soil beneath the canopy of the tree. This method introduces nutrients evenly over the entire root area.

Fertilizing Narrow-Leafed Evergreen Shrubs and Trees

Narrow-leafed conifers include such plants as arborvitae (*Thuja* spp.), hemlock (*Tsuga* spp.), pine (*Pinus* spp.), spruce (*Picea* spp.), juniper (*Juniperus* spp.) and yew (*Taxus* spp.). For the best growth, plants in this group require a well-drained soil containing abundant organic matter. Inorganic fertilizers can cause root damage to narrow-leafed evergreens, especially newly planted shrubs and trees, and their use is not recommended. Instead, apply an organic fertilizer, such as cottonseed meal, at the rate of 5 pounds per 100 square feet in spring. One feeding is usually enough for the year. Many narrow-leafed evergreens, such as pine and spruce, have naturally fast annual growth rates that become exaggerated when too much fertilizer is applied; the result is plants that look stretched and open. Tall evergreen trees with few branches near the ground often have turf growing beneath them. These trees should be fertilized following the directions for deciduous trees.

Fertilizing Broad-Leafed Evergreens

Broad-leaved evergreens include rhododendron (*Rhododendron* spp.), mountain laurel (*Kalmia latifolia*), pieris (*Pieris* spp.) evergreen azalea (*Rhododendron* spp.) leucothoe (*Leucothoe* spp.) and holly (*Ilex* spp.). These plants need an even more acid soil than most narrow-leafed plants to grow well. Add 2 to 3 inches of an acid, organic mulch, such as oak leaf mold, pine needles, or peat moss, annually. In spring add cottonseed meal at the rate of 5 pounds per 100 square feet to the soil around each plant. Do not apply lime or wood ashes to the soil around evergreens, as these raise the pH of the soil and block the availability of iron and other nutrients to the plants. Broad-leafed and narrow-leafed evergreens should not be planted near foundations made of cement as the cement raises the pH of the nearby soil. However, if evergreens are planted near cement foundations and they can't be moved, apply chelated fertilizers and mulch with an acid mulch such as pine needles. Chelated nutrients are available even in high pH environments, and acid mulches help buffer the effect of the cement on the soil.

WHEN TO PRUNE TREES AND SHRUBS

Dead branches can be pruned anytime, but removing live branches should be timed to preserve flower buds and fruit. Do it at a time of year that poses the least risk to the plant's health.

◆ Bleeders

The following plants have a strong sap flow that can begin many weeks before growth in the spring; prune in December or January on a cold, cloudy day:

Birch (*Betula* spp.)
Dogwood (*Cornus* spp.)
Elm (*Ulmus* spp.)
Maple (*Acer* spp.)
Walnut (*Juglans* spp.)
Yellowwood (*Cladrastis lutea*)

◆ Summer Bloomers

The following plants bloom on new growth, also called first-year growth, and develop flower buds after they begin to grow in the spring; prune in winter when they are dormant:

Beautyberry (*Callicarpa americana*)
Bluebeard (*Caryopteris* spp.)
Butterfly bush (*Buddleia* spp.)
Chaste tree (*Vitex agnus-castus*)
Cinquefoil (*Potentilla fruiticosa*)
Coralberry (*Symphoricarpos* x *chenaultii*)
Crape myrtle (*Lagerstroemia indica*)
Five-leaf aralia (*Acanthopanax sieboldianus*)
Glossy abelia (*Abelia* x *grandiflora*)
Hydrangea (*Hydrangea* spp.)
Japanese spirea (*Spiraea japonica*)
Rose mallow (*Hibiscus* spp.)
Rose-of-sharon (*Hibiscus syriacus*)
St.-John's-wort (*Hypericum* spp.)
Summer-sweet (*Clethra* spp.)

◆ Spring Bloomers

The following plants bloom on second-year wood, also called old growth. Their flower buds develop in summer and overwinter. Prune immediately after they bloom:

Azalea (*Rhododendron* spp.)
Beautybush (*Kolkwitzia amabilis*)
Bigleaf hydrangea (*Hydrangea macrophylla*)
Broom (*Cytisus* spp.)
Cotoneaster (*Cotoneaster* spp.)
Deutzia (*Deutzia* spp.)
Flowering quince (*Chaenomeles* spp.)
Forsythia (*Forsythia* spp.)
Fothergilla (*Fothergilla* spp.)
Holly (*Ilex* spp.)
Honeysuckle (*Lonicera* spp.)
Jasmine (*Jasminum* spp.)
Lilac (*Syringa* spp.)
Magnolia (*Magnolia* spp.)
Mock orange (*Philadelphus* spp.)
Mountain laurel (*Kalmia latifolia*)
Ninebark (*Physocarpus* spp.)
Pieris (*Pieris* spp.)
Rhododendron (*Rhododendron* spp.)
Smoke tree (*Cotinus* spp.)
Sweet shrub (*Calycanthus* spp.)
Viburnum (*Viburnum* spp.)
White fringe tree (*Chionanthus virginicus*)
Wisteria (*Wisteria* spp.)

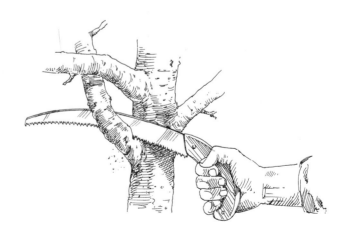

Prune shrubs and trees at the time of year that poses the least risk of injury.

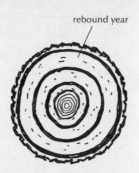

rebound year

Annual rings

Rebound is the term foresters use to describe how trees respond to a specific change in their environment. If trees grow close to one another, they compete for light and nutrients. This competition slows each tree's growth rate, resulting in thin annual rings and small but near-equal amounts of spring and summer wood. If the competing trees are removed, the one that remains suddenly enjoys an abundance of light and nutrients, which spurs increased growth. Its annual rings become much thicker, with as much as four times as much spring wood being produced per year. This growth spurt is the rebound. But rebound is more than an increased growth rate: it is also a different type of growth. A tree experiencing rebound is more apt to produce weak branch crotches and a top-heavy canopy, conditions that can result in damage during stormy weather.

Rebound may be a forestry term, but it is not limited to forests. Many of the landscape-size trees produced in nurseries are grown close together over many seasons. When they come to your yard they are suddenly given lots of room and abundant sunshine, and they grow like crazy. After a few years of rebound growth many of these trees begin to lose branches to storms.

To gauge whether a tree is rebounding, compare the appearance of its lower branches to that of its newer, upper branches. Rebound trees often have weak branch crotches and a top-heavy appearance. By selectively pruning out some of these weak branches you can increase the overall strength of the tree and substantially decrease the chance of its suffering storm damage.

Stormy Weather

As every schoolchild knows, trees have annual rings. The lighter-colored rings are made of spring wood and are formed during spring and early summer, when a tree is growing most rapidly. The dark rings are made of summer wood and are formed during summer as the tree's growth slows before it again enters dormancy. In a nutshell, summer wood is stronger than spring wood.

TREES AND LIGHTNING

There is a certain magic to watching a summer thunderstorm. Because lightning and thunder travel through the air at different speeds, by counting the number of seconds between a lightning flash and the subsequent rumble of thunder, we can determine about how far away the lightning flash was. Every five seconds is equal to just over a mile. It's a fun game to play — until the time when the lightning and thunder arrive at the same moment.

Where lightning strikes seems to be a matter of chance, but some places and things do attract it more than others. As a general rule, the taller something is in relation to its surroundings, the more prone it is to being struck by lightning. In many cases the tallest things in the garden or the backyard are trees, and some trees are more attractive to lightning than others.

Trees with wood that contains high amounts of resin are good conductors of electricity and more likely to attract lightning than trees of low-resin content. High-resin trees include many of the evergreens, such as pine, spruce, fir, and hemlock. Another group of good conductors are those whose wood has a high starch content, including oak, maple, poplar, ash, and tulip trees.

The trees least likely to attract lightning are those whose wood has a high oil content, for these are poor conductors of electricity. Trees in this group include beech and birch. In an unscientific test of this information I poked around until I found seven trees in the nearby hills that had been struck by lightning. Of that number two were ash, one was a poplar, and four were pine or hemlock. If your backyard is subject to frequent lightning strikes, planting beech and birch trees may not be a bad idea.

WINTER INJURY

Many areas of the country are subject to periodic blizzards and ice storms that wreak havoc on shrubs and trees. Heavy, wet snow can weigh down branches until they snap, collapse entire trees, and squash many shrubs. Ice storms can rip branches or snap tops from trees and break unprotected shrubs. Storms of wet snow and ice are most common along a belt extending from the southern Rockies east through the Great Plains and the Mississippi Valley, then across a wide area of the East from the Great Lakes to New England and south to the southern Appalachians. Areas of the Pacific Northwest are also susceptible. But there are ways to minimize damage to plantings before the next storm hits.

Ice and Snow

Upright, multiple-stemmed shrubs, such as Hick's yew, Irish and Swedish juniper, and pyramidal arborvitae, are susceptible to damage when the weight of snow or ice opens up the plant, breaking branches and splitting the main trunk. In fall tie the upright branches together in their natural position using heavy twine. If more protection is required, loosely wrap the shrub with a spiral winding of twine. Remove all twine before growth begins in spring.

Foundation plantings are often damaged when snow and ice slide from roofs, collapsing the plants. For years some homeowners have built plywood roof shields above the shrubs to deflect this assault. It is the best way to protect established, large shrubs, but, frankly, it is a lot of work. An alternative to protecting foundation shrubs is to replace those near the eaves of buildings with perennial gardens. That way the ice and snow fall harmlessly to the ground and the front of your house still looks great in summer.

The damage from the weight of snow or ice on large trees can range from broken limbs to the splitting of the trunk and even the ruin of the entire tree. One way to lessen injury, especially to younger trees, is to restrict each tree to one central leader. If two parallel leaders are allowed to grow, they often form a V crotch, a weak, narrow-angled branch union. Heavy snow loads can easily split this weak union.

Damaged trees and shrubs should be repaired as soon as weather permits. Make flush cuts back to the next larger branch or trunk.

◆ Trees Resistant to Snow and Ice Damage
American hop hornbeam *(Ostrya virginiana)*
American hornbeam *(Carpinus carolianina)*
Bald cypress *(Taxodium distichum)*
Canadian hemlock *(Tsuga canadensis)*
Ginkgo *(Ginkgo biloba)*
White oak *(Quercus alba)*

◆ Trees Susceptible to Snow and Ice Damage
Box elder *(Acer negundo)*
Chinese elm *(Ulmus parvifolia)*
Hackberry *(Celtis* spp.)
Poplar *(Populus* spp.)
Red maple *(Acer rubrum)*
Siberian elm *(Ulmus pumila)*
Silver maple *(Acer saccharinum)*
Willow *(Salix spp.)*

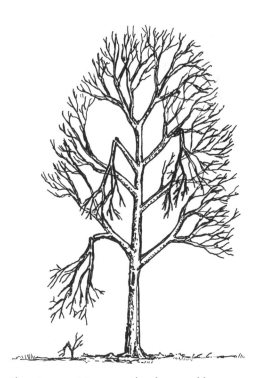

Even the strongest trees can be damaged by severe snow or ice storms. Prompt repair of injured trees improves the chances that the plant will make a good recovery.

Wind and Sun

Broad-leafed evergreens, such as rhododendron and holly, should not be planted where they will be exposed to winter winds and sun. Many of these plants have shallow root systems, and as the ground freezes in winter, the frost line can penetrate deeper than the plant's roots. This in itself causes no damage, but it does stop the roots from absorbing moisture. Then in late winter, when the ground is most deeply frozen, sunlight becomes strong. This can heat the leaves of the plants to a temperature that is warm enough for their pores, or stomates, to open and transpire moisture. The frozen roots cannot replace the lost water, and the leaves scorch. Broad-leafed evergreens should thus be planted in sheltered locations in partial shade on the west, east, or north sides of buildings or other structures that serve as windbreaks and sunscreens.

◆ Plants Susceptible to Winter Leaf Scorch

American yew *(Taxus canadensis)*
Evergreen azalea *(Rhododendron spp.)*
Leatherleaf viburnum *(Viburnum rhytidophyllum)*
Leucothoe *(Leucothoe fontanesiana)*
Mountain laurel *(Kalmia latifolia)*
Pieris *(Pieris* spp.)
Rhododendron *(Rhododendron spp.)*

Frost Cracking

Sometimes thin-barked trees whose trunks are exposed to late-winter sun can develop *frost cracks,* a condition in which a long, slender vertical split appears in the bark, most often on the south side of the tree. Frost cracks form when the sun heats up one side of the tree enough to stimulate sap flow. When the sun goes down, the winter air cools off very quickly, and under certain conditions the trapped moisture beneath the bark freezes, expands, and splits the bark. It helps to wrap trees, especially those newly planted or in a site with an unbroken southern exposure, with white nursery tape during winter months.

◆ Trees Susceptible to Frost Cracking

Apple *(Malus* spp.)
Horse chestnut *(Aescuulus hippocastanum)*
Norway maple *(Acer platanoides)*
Sycamore *(Platanus occidentalis)*

Repairing Winter Damage

At winter's end remove only those branches that are obviously dead. If in doubt, gingerly scrape away a bit of bark to see if the branch shows green underneath. After new growth starts in spring, prune all dead branches and twigs to within one-quarter inch of a live bud or flush with the nearest live branch. If evergreens have turned light brown, they may still regain their green color over the growing season, or new growth may sprout along the stem. Broad-leafed evergreens showing signs of leaf scorch will usually produce a new crop; the older, damaged leaves will eventually drop on their own or can be removed. If any plants have heaved, wait until the soil thaws enough to work. At that time carefully lift each one from the soil and replant.

A screen of burlap placed around broad-leaf evergreens protects the plants from both winter winds and late winter sun.

HIGH AND DRY

In areas such as southern California, where the weather can be hot and dry for months at a time, the trees and shrubs surrounding a home can either increase or decrease the risk of damage from brush fires. Certain plants — those with high resin or low moisture content, for example — provide a fire with fuel that can burn very hot and produce abundant airborne sparks. To reduce fire hazard near your home and outbuildings, *do not* use the listed plants in the landscape.

◆ **Fire-Risk Trees**

Acacia (*Acacia* spp.)
Arborvitae (*Thuja* spp.)
California bay (*Umbellularia californica*)
Cedar (*Cedrus* spp.)
Cypress (*Cupressus* spp.)
Douglas fir (*Pseudotsuga menziesii*)
Eucalyptus (*Eucalyptus* spp.)
Juniper (*Juniperus* spp.)
Pine (*Pinus* spp.)
Spruce (*Picea* spp.)
Yew (*Taxus* spp.)

The types of plants around your home can either slow the progress of a brush fire or enhance it. A broad lawn ofgreen, drought-resistant turf can slow a fire while resin-rich evergreens near a home can accelerate it.

♦ **Fire-Risk Shrubs**

California sagebrush *(Artemisia californica)*
Laurel sumac *(Rhus laurina)*
Manzanita *(Arctostaphylos* spp.)
Rosemary *(Rosmarinus* spp.)
Scotch broom *(Cytisus scorparius)*
Scrub oak *(Quercus ilicifolia)*
Spanish broom *(Genista hispanical)*

A stretch of green lawn around the perimeter of the property is regarded by some experts as one of the best firebreaks. Keeping a lawn green in arid areas is a challenge, though. Try the following turf grass cultivars which stay green using the least amount of water: Kentucky bluegrass *(Poa pratensis),* 'Bristol', 'Challenger', 'Wabash'; Fescue *(Festuca* spp.), 'Aurora' and 'Shademaster'.

Lastly, a word of warning. Some folks try to deal with trees that buckle pavement by pruning the offending roots. In the long run this can prove dangerous, for root pruning many shallow-rooted trees makes the plants unstable and prone to windfall. The larger the tree gets, the greater the chance it will get blown down, and in the crowded spaces surrounding paved places, the sudden windfall of thousands of pounds of tree can be deadly.

THE PRICE PLANTS MUST PAY FOR A ROCKY MOUNTAIN HIGH

If your garden is more than 2,000 feet above sea level, the plants you grow need more water than you might think. Studies in Montana have determined that for every 1,000 feet in elevation gain above about 2,000 feet, plants lose about 5 percent more water through their leaves than they would if grown at lower altitudes. To maintain normal growth the lost water must be replaced — which means that these plants need 5 percent more water over the length of the growing season. Move the garden to about 5,000 feet, and suddenly plants need 20 percent more water; at 10,000 feet, they need nearly 50 percent more water to grow normally. Here is a formula to estimate just how much more water high-altitude gardening requires:

Most garden and landscape plants grow well with about 1 inch of water per week during the growing season; this should suffice for gardens up to about 3,000 feet. At 3,000-4,000 feet, apply 1 inch of water each week and 1½ inches every fourth week. At 4,000-6,000 feet, water the garden with 1 inch of water one week, then 1½ inches the next. For areas over 6,000 feet, give plants 1½ inches of water per week.

ROOTS AND PAVEMENT

Roots are innocent plant parts that anchor trees and shrubs to the ground — at least that's what the plant lobby wants you to think. And there are some roots that perform the mundane jobs of supplying their plants with water, nutrients, and support. But then there are the other roots, those trained by clandestine agencies to worm their way through the ground and heave sidewalks and driveways. It took a long time to discover just which trees those roots belonged to, but now we know. We have names. The following trees all have shallow roots with a proven reputation for heaving the pavement of driveways, parking areas, and sidewalks:

Silver maple *(Acer saccharinum)*
Red maple *(Acer rubrum)*
Sugar maple *(Acer saccharum)*
Norway maple *(Acer platanoides)*
Willows *(Salix* spp.)
Black locust *(Robinia pseudoacadia)*
American elm *(Ulmus americana)*
Catalpa *(Catalpa* spp.)
American beech *(Fagus grandifolia)*
European beech *(Fagus sylvatica)*
Sweet gum *(Liquidambar* spp.)
Ash *(Fraxinum* spp.)
Poplar *(Populus* spp.)
Siberian elm *(Ulmus pumila)*

13

Gardens for Butterflies and Hummingbirds

When people design gardens they tend to design them for other people. The shrub borders are constructed with benches for sitting and a combination of evergreens and deciduous plants that form alcoves for quiet thought. Flower beds have collections of plants savored for blossoms that bring the shades of the rainbow into every sunny nook and cranny. In short, people have for years created gardens as places of refuge for themselves and other people. There is nothing wrong with this. But sometimes there is something missing.

One very cool day last June I found myself wandering about an especially attractive garden. I had no agenda to keep, so my feet just led me along the garden paths with no particular destination in mind. As I strolled by the beautiful borders, however, I couldn't help feeling that this lovely place seemed empty somehow. I passed clumps of white and lavender peachleaf bellflower, the blossoms hanging from the stems like rows of silent chimes. There were penstemons and obedience mingled with the last of the peonies and the first astilbes, roses, and daylilies. A little farther on were masses of Siberian iris with clusters of white, blue, and violet falls that seemed like a cloud of butterflies ready to fly. At that moment I realized what was missing. There were no bees, no butterflies, no hummingbirds, and without them there was no movement and no sound. In their absence the garden just lay upon the landscape like a still-life painting.

A garden is much more than the sum of the plants within it and is attractive to many more creatures than just the people who enjoy it. The next day, when the weather warmed and the sun released the sweet fragrances from the flowers, the garden was awash with life. Honeybees and bumblebees droned above the flowertops, hummingbirds zipped through the air like jeweled streaks, and butterflies gently floated from blossom to blossom on weightless, gossamer wings.

The following pages hold the secrets to creating very beautiful, very special gardens designed to attract butterflies and hummingbirds and the people who love to watch them. I thank Wendy Potter-Springer, who wrote the butterfly garden, and Dale Evva Gelfand, author of the hummingbird garden, for so freely sharing their secrets.

Grow a Butterfly Garden*

Few sights are more delightful than that of a butterfly dancing on the breeze. But sadly enough, butterflies have become all too rare in our rapidly expanding world. The sheer beauty of butterflies has, in the past, prompted the collection and sale of these insects. Twenty years ago this could have been blamed for their disappearance, but it is unusual in this day and age for a collector to capture and kill a butterfly. Most modern day collectors capture their beautiful specimens on film. So where have the butterflies gone?

The disappearance of butterflies must largely be blamed on ourselves. Condominiums and shopping malls have taken over the fields and grassy meadows that served as the breeding grounds for many of our butterflies, and the misuse of backyard pesticides has left them with no alternative environment in which to live and multiply.

By growing a few chosen plants in your yard, you will be making a major contribution toward the preservation of these fragile insects, supplying them with a haven in which to live and breed.

You don't need a large area to have a successful butterfly garden teeming with winged color. A butterfly garden can be grown in a window box, from hanging pots on a terrace or balcony, or from a patch of yard. All it takes is a little planning.

You will, however, need to plant your butterfly garden in a sunny spot, as butterflies are notorious sun-worshippers. But most butterfly flowers are easy to grow and require little care, which affords you plenty of time to sit back and enjoy the view of color, not just on the ground, but in the air as well.

HOW A BUTTERFLY GARDEN WORKS

There are two kinds of butterfly flowers: food plants for caterpillars, and nectar plants for adults. Although butterflies need a shady spot to find respite from the sun during those days we consider scorchers, for the most part they spend their time in the sunshine. This is due to a butterfly's need to raise its body temperature in order to fly. Butterflies perch on flowers and shrubs to bask in the sun and absorb the solar benefits until their bodies reach a temperature of 86 to 104°F.

So it should come as no surprise that most butterfly flowers are those of the sun-loving variety. Many of the plants listed in this chapter are sun lovers, providing butterflies with just the right spot to get going each day.

Colors also play a major role in attracting butterflies. Scientists now know that they have the ability to identify colors. Purple, pink, yellow, and white are the colors most often preferred by butterflies, so when planning your garden you'll want to keep these colors in mind.

ATTRACTING SPECIFIC BUTTERFLIES

You may have noticed the absence of specific butterflies that were once common in your neighborhood. This could very well be due to the use of pesticides. Pesticides have no place in your butterfly garden. Their sole purpose is to destroy insects, and while many who use them are not thinking about killing off their butterflies, this is the inevitable outcome. You can also work to minimize the use of aerial pesticides (used for "mosquito control") and herbicides (used for "roadside weed control") by your local government agencies.

If you would like to help reestablish a rare or endangered species that was once common to your neighborhood, you'll need to do some research. Check in with your local natural history, conservation, or ecological associations for more information about butterfly species native to your area and their population status. You may even be able to assist in programs led by local experts attempting to reintroduce lost species of butterflies to your area.

Another way to help native butterfly species maintain or boost their population is to grow the known food or host plant of those species. If you grow host plants, be sure to leave them intact when the growing season is over. Do not use them for cut flowers or cut them back in the fall — you may destroy hibernating adult butterflies, their pupae, or their eggs.

On the following pages, you will find a list of some known host plants. For more information, consult with your local chapter of The National Audubon Society.

*Adapted from *Grow a Butterfly Garden* by Wendy Potter-Springer (Storey Publishing, 1990)

LIST OF HOST PLANTS FOR CATERPILLARS

The plants on which a butterfly will lay eggs are called host plants. When the eggs hatch caterpillars, the host plant provides the food and shelter that the caterpillars need to survive. Some caterpillars will feed on only one specific plant species, while others can feed on many different plants within the same family. For example, the caterpillars of Black Swallowtail butterflies are found on many different members of the Carrot (Umbelliferae) family, such as carrot, dill, fennel, and Queen Anne's lace. It's important to check with local resources, such as the National Audubon Society, a natural history museum, or any local nature, conservation, or ecological association, for information about caterpillar plant preferences in your area. You can also identify butterflies already present in your garden and consult a butterfly reference book to see what its caterpillars will eat.

Although butterflies may lay hundreds of eggs, very few caterpillars survive — most fall prey to predators and parasites. This is the natural way of balancing the environment. On average, only two to three of every hundred caterpillars live long enough to go through metamorphosis and emerge as butterflies.

On the following pages are some common butterfly species and the plants that are most attractive to them as host plants for their caterpillars. Several of these plants are considered wildflowers and may already be growing in your yard or neighborhood. The butterflies are listed first by their common name, then by their genus. Again, before planting a host plant to attract a specific butterfly, be sure to check with local experts or a butterfly reference guide to make sure that butterfly is common to your area.

SWALLOWTAILS

Giant Swallowtail
(Papilio cresphontes)

Preferred host plants are prickly ash (*Zanthoxylum* spp.), hop tree (*Ptelea trifoliata*), rue (*Ruta graveolens*), and varieties of citrus trees.

Pipevine Swallowtail
(Battus philenor)

Preferred host plants are varieties of birthwort, also known as Dutchman's Pipe (*Aristolochia* spp.).

Black Swallowtail
(Papilio polyxenes)

Preferred host plants belong to the Carrot (Umbelliferae) family, including dill, parsley, fennel, and Queen Anne's lace (*Daucus carota*).

Zebra Swallowtail
(Eurytides marcellus)

Preferred host plant is pawpaw (*Asimina triloba*).

Eastern Tiger Swallowtail
(Papilio glaucus)

Preferred host plants are black cherry (*Prunus serotina*), tulip tree (*Liriodendron tulipifera*), sweet bay (*Magnolia virginiana*), aspen (*Populus tremuloides*), and cottonwood (*Populus deltoides*).

Western Tiger Swallowtail
(Papilio rutulus)

Preferred host plants are aspen (*Populus tremuloides*), willow (*Salix* spp.), alder (*Alnus* spp.), ash (*Fraxinus* spp.), and lilac (*Syringa* spp.).

SULPHURS

Cloudless Sulphur
(Phoebis sennae)

Preferred host plants are varieties of senna (*Cassia* spp.).

Orange Sulphur
(Colias eurytheme)

Preferred host plants are species of the Pea (Leguminosae) family, including alfalfa *(Medicago sativa)*, vetch *(Vicia* spp.), and sweet white clover *(Melilotus alba)*.

Clouded Sulphur
(Colias philodice)

Preferred host plants are clover *(Trifolium* spp.), alfalfa *(Medicago sativa)*, sweet white clover *(Melilotus alba)*, trefoil *(Lotus corniculatus)*, and vetch *(Vicia* spp.).

BLUES

Spring Azure
(Celastrina ladon)

Preferred host plants are shrubs with clusters of flowers, including dogwood *(Cornus* spp.), ceanothus *(Ceanothus* spp., especially New Jersey tea, *Ceanothus americanus)*, blueberry and cranberry *(Vaccinium* spp.), and viburnum *(Viburnum* spp.).

The monarch butterfly's preferred food is milkweed, but you will find they visit other garden flowers such as these asters.

Ceraunus Blue
(Hemiargus ceraunus)

Preferred host plants belong to the Pea (Leguminosae) family, including alfalfa *(Medicago sativa)*, vetch *(Vicia* spp.), and sweet white clover *(Melilotus alba)*.

Eastern Tailed Blue
(Everes comyntas)

Preferred host plants are vetch *(Vicia* spp.), clover *(Trifolium* spp.), alfalfa *(Medicago sativa)*, and other members of the Pea (Leguminosae) family.

HAIRSTREAKS

Mallow Scrub Hairstreak
(Strymon columella)

Preferred host plants are members of the Mallow (Malvaceae) family, including mallow *(Malva* spp.) and hibiscus *(Hibiscus* spp.).

Gray Hairstreak
(Strymon melinus)

Preferred host plants are many, but especially clover *(Trifolium* spp.), vetch *(Vicia* spp.), tick-trefoil *(Desmodium* spp.), mallow *(Malva* spp.), hollyhocks *(Alcea* spp.), and hibiscus *(Hibiscus* spp.).

MILKWEED BUTTERFLIES

Monarch
(Danaus plexippus)

Preferred host plants are varieties of milkweed, also known as butterfly flower *(Asclepias* spp.).

Queen
(Danaus gilippus)

Preferred host plants are varieties of milkweed, also known as butterfly flower *(Asclepias* spp.).

BRUSHFOOT BUTTERFLIES

Hackberry
(Asterocampa celtis)

Preferred host plants are varieties of hackberry (*Celtis* spp.)

Question Mark
(Polygonia interrogationis)

Preferred host plants are elms (*Ulmus* spp.), hackberry (*Celtis* spp.), hops (*Humulus* spp.), nettle (*Urtica* spp.), and false nettle (*Boehmeria cylindrica*).

Milbert's Tortoiseshell
(Nymphalis milberti)

Preferred host plants are varieties of nettle (*Urtica* spp.).

Comma
(Polygonia comma)

Preferred host plants are varieties of nettle (*Urtica* spp.), false nettle (*Boehmeria cylindrica*), hops (*Humulus* spp.), hackberry (*Celtis* spp.), and elm (*Ulmus* spp.).

Mourning Cloak
(Nymphalis antiopa)

Preferred host plants are willow (*Salix* spp.), hackberry (*Celtis* spp.), cottonwood (*Populus deltoides*), birch (*Betula* spp.), elm (*Ulmus* spp.), and quaking aspen (*Populus tremuloides*).

Red Admiral
(Vanessa atalanta)

Preferred host plants are nettle (*Urtica* spp.), false nettle (*Boehmeria cylindrica*), wood nettles (*Laportea canadensis*), and hops (*Humulus* spp.)

American Painted Lady
(Vanessa virginiensis)

Preferred host plants are pearly everlasting (*Anaphalis margaritacea*), hollyhocks (*Alcea* spp.), and everlastings (*Gnaphalium* spp.).

Buckeye
(Junonia coenia)

Preferred host plants are plantain (*Plantago* spp.), snapdragon (*Antirrhinum* spp.), false foxglove (*Aurelaria* spp.), monkey flower (*Mimulus* spp.), and figwort (*Scrophylaria* spp.).

Gulf Fritillary
(Agraulis vanillae)

Preferred host plants are varieties of passion flower (*Passiflora* spp.).

Bordered Patch
(Chlosyne lacinia)

Preferred host plants are members of the Composite (*Compositae*) family, especially sunflowers (*Helianthus* spp.).

Pearl Crescent
(Phyciodes tharos)

Preferred host plants are smooth-leaved asters (*Aster* spp.)

Great Spangled Fritillary
(Speyeria cybele)

Preferred host plants are violets (*Viola* spp.).

Meadow Fritillary
(Boloria bellona)

Preferred host plants are violets (*Viola* spp.).

Regal Fritillary
(*Speyeria idalia*)

Preferred host plants are violets (*Viola* spp.).

White Admiral
(*Limenitis arthemis*)

Preferred host plants are birch (*Betula* spp.) and aspen (*Populus tremuloides*).

Viceroy
(*Limenitis archippus*)

Preferred host plants are willow (*Salix* spp.), aspen (*Populus tremuloides*), cottonwood (*Populus deltoides*), and apple, plum, and cherry trees.

Lorquin's Admiral
(*Limenitis lorquini*)

Preferred host plants are willow (*Salix* spp.), aspen (*Populus tremuloides*), cottonwood (*Populus deltoides*), and chokecherry (*Aronia* spp.).

California Sister
(*Adelpha brewdowii*)

Preferred host plants are varieties of oak tree (*Quercus* spp.).

SKIPPERS

Silver-spotted Skipper
(*Epargyreus clarus*)

Preferred host plants are black locust (*Robinia pseudoacacia*), indigo bush (*Amorpha fruticosa*), and wisteria (*Wisteria* spp.).

Wild Indigo Duskywing
(*Erynnis baptisiae*). ((check Latin))

Preferred host plants are wild indigo (*Baptisia tinctoria*) and false indigo (*Baptisia australis*).

Fiery Skipper
(*Hylephila phyleus*)

Preferred host plants are weedy grasses, including crabgrass (*Digitaria ischaemum*), bermuda grass (*Cynodon dactylon*), bentgrass (*Agrostis tenuis*), and sugar cane (*Saccharum officinarum*).

Long-Tailed Skipper
(*Urbanus proteus*)

Preferred host plants are beans (*Phaseolus* spp.) and other climbing legumes.

MONITORING BUTTERFLY EGGS

After you have identified the host or food plant of a particular butterfly, you may want to witness the various stages of a butterfly first hand. Once you have discovered the eggs, this is a fairly easy thing to do.

When you have found your butterfly eggs, take the whole leaf and a few extra, and place them in a plastic bag until you get them safely home.

To protect your eggs from being devoured by predators and to keep your food plant alive, you can construct a coffee-can home for them. First, remove both the top and bottom of the can. Cover the bottom of the can with a piece of cardboard into which you've made pin holes large enough for the stem of the food plant to fit through. Cut the cardboard wide enough to extend beyond the coffee can and to completely cover a small dish. Place the can over a dish of water so that the cardboard rests on top of the dish. The stems of the leaves should reach the water. This keeps the food plant alive longer and should keep your eggs dry. Cover the can with screening secured with a rubber band. Keep this container in a cool spot but one that receives some sun; not direct sun or the container will become too hot.

Once your caterpillars emerge, you may want to move them to a larger container. An old aquarium or glass cookie jar is fine, just make sure that air can circulate. Caterpillars require very little air, but you don't want to encourage mold.

Supply your caterpillars with plenty of leaves from their food plant and lots of dry twigs or branches on which to climb and pupate (the stage between larvae and adult butterfly). Remove any caterpillar droppings from the container daily.

Remove the top of your container as soon as your butterflies emerge. They will need some time to dry their wings and raise their body temperatures, but soon they will be airborne.

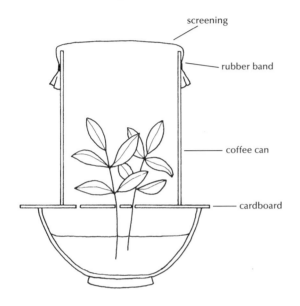

To protect butterfly eggs before caterpillars emerge, place them in a coffee can over a dish of water.

CHOOSING BUTTERFLY FLOWERS FOR YOUR GARDEN

Some of the plant descriptions have been excerpted in part from *From Seed to Bloom*, by Eileen Powell (Storey Publishing, 1995).

An excellent way to gather ideas for laying out a butterfly garden is to first visit local botanical gardens, nature centers, or garden nurseries. Watch carefully to see which plants are attracting the most butterflies, and ask the gardeners at these places which plants they would suggest, based on their experience and expertise, for a butterfly garden.

Butterflies usually prefer plants in full sun. Because color plays such a vital role in attracting butterflies, it is to your advantage to plant groups or masses of a plant in one particular color, rather than single plants of different colors. A group of purple coneflower and a mass of white phlox will have a better chance of attracting butterflies than single flowers in each color. This will also give your garden a more uniform and attractive look to your human visitors. If you want your garden to be populated by butterflies throughout the summer, it is also important to plan your garden so that it has plants that are flowering throughout the growing season — chart the blooming seasons of the plants you decide to include in your butterfly garden and make sure that you'll have at least two or three plants flowering at any given time. Mix together host plants and nectar flowers to increase the number of butterflies visiting your garden.

This list includes good nectar plants — the plants that adult butterflies feed upon. Both perennials and annuals are listed. Whether you choose one or the other, or a mixture of both, is a matter of personal preference. Some perennials will not survive the winter in colder climates, and gardeners in those areas will need to grow them as annuals. For more comprehensive information on any of the plants referenced here, consult a gardening manual.

Herbs are also excellent nectar plants. Grow all your favorite herbs in your butterfly garden, allowing them to flower to attract the butterflies, and trim them in rotation so that there is always at least one herb in flower. Plant extra dill, parsley, and fennel to encourage the Black Swallowtail butterfly to lay eggs on their leaves and take nectar at their flowers.

Aster
(*Aster* spp.)

Zones: 2–9, varying by species
Height: 6"–6'
Blooming season: Spring through late autumn

There are hundreds of varieties of asters. They produce daisylike blooms, most commonly in shades of lavender and purple, but also in white, deep blue, pink, red, and rose. Encourage larger blooms by pruning young shoots in the spring, leaving 6 to 8 shoots per plant to develop. Taller species may need to be staked. Plant in full sun in average soil.

Baja Fairy Duster
(Calliandra californica)

ZONE: 10
HEIGHT: To 4 feet
BLOOMING SEASON: Midsummer

Native to southern California, this tender perennial is most often grown as an annual in the greater United States. It is a showy, spreading shrub with purple blossoms. Plant in rich, moist, but well-draining soil.

Bee Balm
(Monarda spp.)

ZONES: 4–9
HEIGHT: 2–4'
BLOOMING SEASON: Summer

Hummingbirds, bees, and butterflies alike love the shaggy blossoms of bee balm. Most often seen in red, bee balm also blooms in purple, pink, and even white. Deadhead the spent blossoms regularly to keep these easy growers blooming. Plant in moist soil in full sun, and mulch well.

Black-Eyed Susan
(Rudbeckia hirta)

ZONES: 3–9
HEIGHT: 2'–3'
BLOOMING SEASON: Summer

These North American natives will tolerate almost any soil that is well-drained. They have abundant yellow or orange daisylike flowers with prominent brown eyes, and are inclined to become invasive, so pick off the flower-heads after blooming to prevent self-seeding. Plant in full sun, or in partial shade where summers are very hot.

Coneflower
(Echinacea spp.)

ZONES: 3–9
HEIGHT: 2'–4'
BLOOMING SEASON: Early summer to autumn

These easy-to-grow perennials bear white, red, pink, or light purple, daisylike flowers with large pincushion eyes. Although they prefer average, well-drained soil, they will tolerate poor, dry soil. Plant in full sun or light shade.

Cosmos
(Cosmos bipinnatus)

ZONES: 7–10
HEIGHT: 1'–4'
BLOOMING SEASON: Late spring through early autumn

Cosmos will flower more abundantly in poor soil than rich. Their stems and flower foliage are topped with daisylike blooms in pink, red, orange, yellow, and white. Plant in full sun.

Dogbane
(Apocynum androsaemifolium)

ZONES: 3–9
HEIGHT: 1'–4'
BLOOMING SEASON: Midsummer

Dogbane is an herbaceous perennial native to most of the eastern United States. Its pink or white blooms will appear for only a short period in midsummer. Plant in full sun.

Eupatorium
(*Eupatorium* spp.)

ZONES: 3–8
HEIGHT: 2'–10'
BLOOMING SEASON: Midsummer to early autumn

Eupatoriums, native to North America, are all very popular with butterflies. They include white-flowered boneset (*Eupatorium perfoliatum*), pink- and purple-flowered Joe-pye weed (*Eupatorium purpureum*), and lavender-colored mistflower (*Eupatorium coelestinum*). Joe-pye weed may be cut back to encourage branching and more compact plants. Plant in full sun; preferred soil conditions differ between varieties.

Fleabane
(*Erigeron* spp.)

ZONES: 2–9, depending on species
HEIGHT: 4"–36"
BLOOMING SEASON: Summer to early autumn, depending on species

These easy-to-grow annuals and perennials resemble the aster in appearance, with neat foliage and fine-petalled, daisylike flowers of pink, purple, white, yellow, or orange with yellow eyes. Plant in full sun or light shade in average, well-drained soil.

French Marigold
(*Tagetes patula*)

ZONES: Can be grown in any zone as an annual
HEIGHT: 6"–18"
BLOOMING SEASON: Summer through frost

Marigolds prefer moist, well-drained soil enriched with organic matter, but will withstand quite dry soil. Plant in full sun, with afternoon shade where summers are very hot. Deadhead to prolong the blooming season. Single-flowered varieties tend to be the best nectar plants.

Gayfeather
(*Liatris* spp.)

ZONES: 3–10
HEIGHT: 2'–6'
BLOOMING SEASON: Summer to early autumn

Also known as blazing star, these rocket-shaped, pink-purple beauties will perk up any garden. Although preferring a sandy, rich soil, Liatris will tolerate even poor, dry soil, as long as their planting medium is well-drained. Plant in full sun to light shade.

Globe Thistle, Small
(*Echinops ritro*)

ZONES: 3–9
HEIGHT: 1'–3'
BLOOMING SEASON: Summer to autumn

The small globe thistle is an unusual perennial with globelike blue flowers borne atop fleshy white wands. Will tolerate almost any soil that is well-drained, but species grown in very rich soil will require staking. Plant in full sun. Russian globe thistle (*Echinops exaltatus*), which can grow to 5 feet in height, is another good choice for a butterfly garden.

Goldenrod
(*Solidago* spp.)

ZONES: 3–9
HEIGHT: 6"–8'
BLOOMING SEASON: Summer to early autumn

Most goldenrods range in height from 2 to 4 feet, with spikes of tiny yellow flowers. They are inclined to spread rapidly — deadhead after flowering to prevent unwanted self-seeding and cut back completely in autumn. Plant in full sun or partial shade in moist, well-drained soil. Very rich soil will produce lush foliage but few flowers.

Heliotrope
(Heliotropium arborescens)

ZONES: 9–10
HEIGHT: 1'–4'
BLOOMING SEASON: Early spring through early autumn

These violet to deep purple blooms have a sweet vanilla scent. Deadhead regularly to prolong blooming. Plant in full sun in rich, well-drained soil.

Honesty
(Lunaria annua)

ZONES: 6–9
HEIGHT: 1'–3'
BLOOMING SEASON: Summer

Also known as moonwort and moneyplant, honesty is an upright, bushy plant with purple or white blossoms followed by showy, silvery papery seed pods that are popular in dried flower arrangements. Honesty will grow in nearly any soil, and is happiest in partial shade.

Impatiens
(Impatiens spp.)

ZONES: Can be grown in any zone as an annual
HEIGHT: 12"–24"
BLOOMING SEASON: Late spring through first frost

Impatiens are grown as annuals in most of the United States since they are unable to survive frost. With their vibrantly colored, long-lasting flowers, they are ideal for both butterfly and hummingbird gardens. Plant in rich, moist soil. Most species prefer shade, but all will tolerate more sun where summers are cool.

Mexican Sunflower
(Tithonia rotundifolia)

ZONES: Can be grown as an annual in any zone
HEIGHT: 2'–6'
BLOOMING SEASON: Midsummer to frost

The brilliant orange flowers of this annual beauty are eye-catching, and butterflies love them. Deadhead to promote longevity of blooming period. Plant in full sun in average or sandy soil. Is quite tolerant of drought — water only during prolonged dry spells.

This butterfly garden includes butterfly weed (1), tickseed (2), coneflower (3), lupine (4), poppy (5), and butterfly bush (6) to encourage visits from a wide variety of butterfly species.

Milkweed
(*Asclepias* spp.)

ZONES: 3–10
HEIGHT: 1'–6'
BLOOMING SEASON: Summer

North America hosts many different species of milkweeds, which serve as host plants for monarch butterflies and nectar plants for a variety of other butterfly species. These sturdy plants prefer average, sandy soil; most species will tolerate dry soil but not heavy clay or chalky conditions. Plant in full sun to light shade. Bright orange butterfly weed (*Asclepias tuberosa*) is one of the best butterfly nectar plants.

Mountain Mints
(*Pycnanthemum* spp.)

ZONES: 4–8
HEIGHT: To 3'
BLOOMING SEASON: Summer to frost

These members of the mint family have small, pink-flecked white flowers that attract many different species of butterflies. They are long-flowering, and the leaves smell wonderful. They are native to this country but are not easily available from nurseries. Pycnanthemum will tolerate almost any soil. Plant in full sun.

Pentas
(*Pentas lanceolata*)

ZONES: Can be grown as an annual in any zone
HEIGHT: To 4'
BLOOMING SEASON: Early spring to frost

These tropical blooms, one of the best butterfly-attracting plants, are grown as annuals in most of the United States. Also known as starflower, this flower has striking blooms of pink, red, lilac, or white. Plant in full sun to partial shade. Water frequently.

Phlox
(*Phlox* spp.)

ZONES: 3–9, depending on species; some species are annual
HEIGHT: 5"–4'
BLOOMING SEASON: Spring to early autumn, depending on variety

Phlox are well known for their show-stopping floral display with blooms of red, pink, purple, white, or blue. Plant in full sun or partial shade in rich, moist, well-drained soil. Deadhead frequently to extend the blooming period.

Pincushion Flower
(*Scabiosa* spp.)

ZONES: 3–9
HEIGHT: 6"–24"
BLOOMING SEASON: Summer to early autumn

These beauties feature delicate, flowers of purple, pink, light blue, or white borne singly on long stems. Plant in full sun in humus-rich, well-drained soil, and deadhead regularly.

Rabbitbrush
(*Chrysothamnus nauseosus*)

ZONES: 8–10
HEIGHT: 2'–4'
BLOOMING SEASON: Late summer through autumn

This shrubby perennial is native to the western United States. Prune well for better flower production, and water sparingly. Plant in full sun in almost any well-drained soil.

Red Bird of Paradise
(Caesalpinia pulcherrima)

ZONES: 10–11
HEIGHT: To 10'
BLOOMING SEASON: Summer

This tropical woody shrub can spread to a width of up to 10 feet. Its feathery foliage is accompanied by red, orange, and sometimes yellow blooms. Plant in rich, sandy soil.

Red Valerian
(Centranthus ruber)

ZONES: 4–9
HEIGHT: To 3'
BLOOMING SEASON: Spring to midsummer

This hardy perennial has tiny but fragrant deep red blooms. Prefers full sun and well-drained soil. Water plants sparingly. Cut back after flowering to encourage a second bloom.

Scarlet Sage
(Salvia coccinea)

ZONES: 8–10
HEIGHT: 2'–3'
BLOOMING SEASON: Summer to autumn

A tender perennial, often grown as an annual, scarlet sage has profuse bright red (or sometimes white) spikes of tubular flowers which attract hummingbirds. Plant in full sun in well-drained soil.

Sunflower
(Helianthus spp.)

ZONES: 3–10
HEIGHT: 3'–10'
BLOOMING SEASON: Midsummer to mid-autumn

This large genus includes the familiar annual sunflower, as well as a wide variety of perennial sunflowers. They have large, showy, daisylike flowers of yellow, orange, and cream with very large, very flat eyes. Tolerant of both wet and dry soils, but stronger plants will be produced in deep, rich, well-drained soil. Taller species may need to be staked.

Sweet William
(Dianthus barbatus)

ZONES: Can be grown in any zone as an annual, or sometimes a biennial
HEIGHT: 6"–24"
BLOOMING SEASON: Late spring to summer

Choose the crimson variety of this plant with its cushiony, tightly packed blooms. Sweet William self-sows readily and prefers rich, well-drained slightly alkaline soil in the sunny or lightly shaded part of your garden. The taller varieties are wonderfully fragrant and much loved by butteflies.

Tickseed
(Coreopsis spp.)

ZONES: 3–10
HEIGHT: 8"–30"
BLOOMING SEASON: Summer through early autumn

These versatile plants are grown for the reliable abundance of yellow or orange daisylike blooms they produce. Deadhead regularly to prolong the blooming season. Coreopsis prefer a rich, well-drained soil but will tolerate almost any soil condition. Plant in full sun.

Verbena
(*Verbena* spp.)

ZONES: 3–10
HEIGHT: 4"–24"
BLOOMING SEASON: Late spring to frost

These showy plants with tightly packed flower heads are rather short-lived and are best grown as annuals. Choose from pink, white, purple, or red blossoms. Plant in full sun in well-drained soil.

Zinnia
(*Zinnia* spp.)

ZONES: Can be grown in any zone as an annual
HEIGHT: 8"–36"
BLOOMING SEASON: Summer to frost

Zinnias have intensely colored, extravagant double blooms held singly on tall stems. Colors range from light pinks and whites to deep reds and oranges. Plant in full sun in well-drained soil enriched with manure.

GETTING STARTED
If you are going to plant butterfly flowers in an existing garden, you'll simply be adding to the flowers you already have. But if you are planning a brand new garden, you'll need to choose a spot that gets sun for much of the day. A butterfly garden that receives full sun for 5 to 6 hours a day should do well.

The size of your butterfly garden is really a matter of how much time you want to put into it. Although many butterfly flowers require little care, they still need some attention from time to time, so remember, a garden that is 10 feet square is going to require more work than one that is 4 feet square.

If you are unsure of the type of soil you have in your yard, you may want to have it tested. A soil that is deficient in nitrogen, phosphorus, or potassium will need to be adjusted. Testing the soil will also tell you the lead content in your soil, another important factor in a successful butterfly garden, as many gardeners of the past used insecticides containing lead.

Your county agricultural service can give you the address of a lab in your area that will supply you with a soil-test kit.

WINDOW BOX GARDENING
If you are planning a window box butterfly garden you will want to plant annuals. Annuals do beautifully in window boxes, whereas perennials that are left in containers will die over the winter when their root balls freeze.

Butterflies flock to a window box full of morning glories.

There are many excellent bagged commercial soils on the market today and your garden center will be happy to direct you to the soil that is best for your needs.

If you are buying a new window box, or building your own from scratch, be sure to stay away from dark colors. Dark-colored containers absorb the heat of the sun more quickly than light-colored ones, and the roots of your plants may suffer heat damage.

SEEDS

Plan out your garden on paper and know what varieties of plants you want. That way when the seed catalogs start arriving in early winter, you'll be able to order your seeds right away to ensure getting the varieties you want. Seed prices vary, but often there is no difference in the quality of the seed, so you may want to go with the less expensive brand.

Seeds for your butterfly garden may be planted directly in the ground or started indoors. Always keep your seeds stored in a cool, dry place until you are ready to plant them.

For direct planting, the ground must be fairly warm and safe from frost. Tall annuals do best when seeds are sown directly into the garden, although in the North weather doesn't always permit this and starting plants indoors from seed is the only alternative.

Starting seeds indoors is not a difficult process and often results in healthy, sturdy plants with a strong root system for your butterfly garden.

You will want to choose a cool room for your seedlings, such as a basement, as warm temperatures will cause plants to grow long and leggy, and the transition from house to garden will be difficult for them. Temperatures of 50 to 60°F are ideal.

A good seed-starting mixture is important to the proper growth of your plants, as garden soil harbors too many diseases to allow seedlings to flourish indoors. Purchase a soil that has a high vermiculite and sphagnum peat moss content. This mixture will lessen the chance of disease.

Do not use a plant food or fertilizer until the seedlings have been transplanted to the garden.

Plant your seeds in 4- to 6-inch peat wafers or pots, or shallow plastic pots. All are acceptable; the only difference being that with the peat pots you can avoid transplanting. Peat pots are planted directly into the ground.

Fill each pot with the seed-starting mixture and place in a large shallow container of water until the soil has absorbed enough moisture through the drainage holes to make it moist. This is a good way to water your seedlings even after they have sprouted, to avoid damaging them. When using this method, however, be sure to remove excess water so that your seedlings are not sitting in a puddle. The biggest mistake most people make when growing plants from seed is overwatering. Over-watering causes damping-off disease in seedlings.

A good way to tell if your seedlings need water is to pick up the pot and feel if it is heavy or light. If your pot feels light, it probably needs watering; if it feels heavy, leave it alone. Simply feeling the surface soil is not a good indicator.

Place seeds in pots and cover lightly with seed-starting mixture.

Lighting for your seeds should be a good fluorescent light suspended about 2 inches from the seeded pots. Rotate your pots occasionally, as the pots on the end do not receive light as strong as the pots in the center.

Once your seeds have sprouted, raise the lighting to a height of 6 inches above the pots.

HARDENING OFF SEEDLINGS

Hardening off is the term used for acclimating your seedlings to the realities of weather such as strong sunlight, chilly winds, and rain. Seedlings grown indoors are vulnerable, with soft, thin cell walls, and must be watched carefully in the early stages of hardening off.

About a week or so before you may safely transplant your seedlings to your butterfly garden, take them outside and place them on a deck or patio where they will be exposed to sunlight and temperature changes but protected from harsh winds. Unless it is unusually mild, you will need to bring them back inside at night.

After three or four days set them in a spot where they are fully exposed to the weather, but continue to check the night temperatures. Bring them in if temperatures drop considerably.

A way to avoid all this fuss is to use a cold frame for hardening off.

A cold frame is usually a wooden structure covered with a sheet of glass, plastic, or clear fiberglass. It is designed to protect seedlings from the wind and rain yet allow sunlight to pass through. Cold frames have a lid that may be propped open slightly, half open, or fully, depending on how much of the environment you want your seedlings exposed to.

If you will be moving your seedlings to a cold frame, wait for an overcast day and keep the lid down all that first day. This will allow your seedlings to adjust more gradually.

On warm, sunny days open your cold frame to allow your plants the benefit of the sun; but be sure to close the lid early enough in the day so that you are trapping some heat inside for night protection.

After five or six days you will be able to plant your seedlings in your butterfly garden.

Dig a hole for each seedling and, if your seedlings are in plastic pots, carefully lift them out and place into the hole. If you planted your seeds in peat pots, you can simply place the whole pot in. Water thoroughly.

KEEPING A WEATHER DIARY

If this is your first garden, you might want to keep a diary of the weather to assist you in planting next season.

On a calendar or a piece of paper, jot down the temperature highs and lows for the day, the rainfall, winds, frosts, if any. The following season you will be able to refer to this diary when deciding on planting times.

KEEPING A PHOTO RECORD

Once your butterfly garden is in full bloom, take lots of pictures of the butterflies that visit there. The best results can be achieved with a 35mm single lens reflex camera and a slow speed, fine-grade film.

BUTTERFLY TREES AND SHRUBS

There are many trees and shrubs that attract butterflies. Whether you plant a whole hedge or a single shrub, consider the size at maturity. You wouldn't want to plant a small bush in front of a window only to have it soon grow to block the view. In addition, consider the shape, which can be globular, columnar, or horizontal, and plant it in a spot that can accomodate its size at maturity.

When planting a butterfly shrub, use loose, fertile soil that provides adequate drainage and aeration. You may wish to have the soil tested before planting to ensure that the shrub you have invested in will grow well.

Bushes may be purchased in three ways: bare root, the type most often sold by mail; balled in burlap, dug with a ball of soil around the roots and wrapped in burlap; and grown in a container.

Bare-rooted shrubs should be planted in early spring before growth begins, or in late fall after the growing season. These shrubs should be planted immediately after purchase. If this is not possible, keep the roots of the shrub cool and damp by wrapping them in moist newspaper or peat moss.

Dig a hole large enough so that the roots won't be crowded or jammed. Mold a cone shape of soil in the bottom of the hole and set the shrub on top of it. Spread out the roots. Fill the hole about two-thirds of the way full then gently tamp down the soil and fill with water. When all the water has seeped in, fill the hole with soil.

Although balled-in-burlap and container shrubs cost more than bare root, they adjust more quickly to new surroundings because they've already started growing in their root balls.

Water these shrubs well until planting. Dig the hole larger that the root ball and place the shrub in the hole at the same growing level as it was in while in burlap or in the container. If wrapped in plastic, remove covering before planting. Fill the hole in the same manner as the bare root shrub.

After planting your butterfly shrub, prune it back a bit to compensate for any root damage that may have occurred while moving. Start by trimming back young or broken branches.

Newly planted shrubs must be watered well. Mulching will also help conserve moisture.

The following is a list of bushes that butterflies and people find particularly desirable.

Abelia
(*Abelia* spp.)

ZONES: 5–9
BLOOMING SEASON: Late summer through frost

This late-flowering shrub produces small, hanging, bell-shaped flowers in pink and white. Will tolerate almost all soil conditions, but growth may be inhibited by dry soil. Early in the spring, prune some of the older shoots to encourage new flowers. Plant in full sun.

Azalea
(*Rhododendron* spp.)

ZONES: 4–6, with many exceptions
BLOOMING SEASON: Spring to late summer

Azaleas are a group of flowering shrubs within the genus Rhododendron that are particularly favored by butterflies. Blooms come in a variety of colors, including white, pink, apricot, red, yellow, and purple. Plant in full sun to light shade in well-drained soil.

Butterfly Bush
(*Buddleia davidii*)

ZONES: 5–9
BLOOMING SEASON: Midsummer to frost

Also known as summer lilac, butterfly bush is probably the most renowned butterfly-attracting plant. There are many different cultivars available with white, pink, lavender, magenta, purple or yellow blossoms. Deadhead as needed to ensure profuse blooming. Heights of the shrubs vary — some will grow to nine feet — but remember to cut them back hard in the spring. Plant in well-drained soil in full sun.

Buttonbush
(*Cephalanthus occidentalis*)

ZONES: 5–10
BLOOMING SEASON: Summer to early autumn

The creamy white flowers of buttonbush are abundant and extremely fragrant. Prefers moist, sandy soil, but will tolerate most soil conditions if given adequate water. Prune vigorously every two to three years to encourage profuse blooming.

Honeysuckle
(*Lonicera* spp.)

ZONES: Vary by species
BLOOMING SEASON: Varies by species

Lonicera includes a wide range of species whose tubular, fragrant flowers reflect the full spectrum of color. Plant in full sun or light shade.

Lantana
(*Lantana camara*)

ZONES: 8–10
BLOOMING SEASON: Year-round in warm areas; spring to frost in colder areas

This shrub produces compact clusters of orange-yellow, orange, red, or red-and-white flowers. Grow in any well-drained soil in full sun. Water deeply during the summer. Can be invasive in warmer climates.

Lantana, Trailing
(*Lantana montevidensis*)

ZONES: 8–10
BLOOMING SEASON: Mid-summer to frost

This woody shrub is often used as a groundcover. It has long, trailing branches that can extend as much as three to six feet and clusters of small, pink-purple flowers. Plant in full sun. Prefers infrequent, deep waterings.

Lilac
(Syringa vulgaris)

Zones: 3–7
Blooming season: Early spring

This early bloomer, seen in purple, white, pink, and lavender, serves as a nectar source in the spring when little else is available. Deadhead as necessary. Plant in full sun in well-drained soil.

Spicebush
(Lindera benzoin)

Zones: 4–9
Blooming season: Early spring

Also known as wild allspice, snapweed, and fever-bush. Has vibrant yellow flowers that appear stunning against its nearly black bark. Plant in full sun in moist, well-drained soil.

Sweet Pepperbush
(Clethra alnifolia)

Zones: 3–9
Blooming season: Mid- to late summer

This easy-to-grow, late-flowering shrub bears delightfully fragrant white blooms that are favorites among bees and butterflies. Plant in full sun in moist, acidic soil that has been supplemented with organic matter. Prune in the spring.

Viburnum
(Viburnums spp.)

Zones: Vary by species
Blooming season: Varies by species

Beautiful viburnums, with clusters of pink or white flowers, are available in many different varieties. Many have wonderful berries that are enjoyed by the birds in the fall. Viburnums will tolerate almost any soil condition. Plant in full sun.

GARDEN PESTS

We know that pesticides are forbidden in a butterfly garden, but what can we do when pests invade?

First of all, invasions themselves can often be avoided. Many common garden pests can be stopped if their presence is detected early on. A daily inspection of your butterfly garden is helpful.

Keeping the perimeter of the garden free of weeds is often a good idea, as many pests such as aphids first hide among the weeds. But don't forget that weeds are often the plants that butterflies are most attracted to.

If you do detect the onset of aphids in your butterfly garden, a fine spray of the garden hose should get rid of them. The same goes for many beetles.

Beetles are large enough to be picked off by hand, however; aphids are more difficult to see.

ENJOYING YOUR GARDEN

The satisfaction of watching butterflies flirt about your garden is immeasurable. You will want to share it, but how does one share a butterfly?

By encouraging others to take up a butterfly garden, telling them how important it is.

But no matter how important butterfly gardening is for people like you and me, butterfly gardening is a hobby, and hobbies were meant to be fun. Don't let your garden overwhelm you. Who cares if you have a few weeds now and then? Your flowers will always outshine the weeds, and your butterflies will always outshine the flowers.

And that's the whole point of a butterfly garden.

Butterflies of many different species find butterfly bush simply irresistable.

About Hummingbirds*

If asked to name the most ethereal and captivating creature to be found on our planet, most of us would be hard pressed to top the hummingbird. Their minute size (some species weigh only a fraction of an ounce), their beauty (iridescent plumage courtesy of special structures in their feathers), their incredible aerobatic ability (hummingbirds can fly in any direction, including backward), their extraordinary appetites (hummingbirds eat half of their weight in sugar every day), even their aggression (hummingbirds are fierce protectors of their territory and nests) add up to a singularly fascinating family. A little planning of the design of and the plants in your garden is all it takes to make your yard the kind of environment that will readily attract these flying jewels. A perfect hummingbird habitat is also a relatively simple one: food sources, water for bathing (liquid intake is generally provided by nectar), lookout perches, shade and shelter, and nesting sites and materials.

FOOD

Hummingbirds are extremely active creatures with an astonishing metabolic rate that requires high caloric intake of both nectar and insects — which means hundreds of food forays during their waking hours, primarily to flowers. Obviously those flowers that produce lots of nectar and also attract tiny insects are more beneficial, and therefore more appealing, to hummingbirds.

This attraction forms part of one of Nature's many interdependent relationships: Hummingbirds, while stopping for a meal, act as inadvertent pollinators for the plants they rely upon. Depending on their particular shape, the deep-tubed blossoms that are most suitable to a hummingbird's long tongue deliver pollen from the anthers — part of the male organs — onto hummingbirds' heads or bills or chins, and when the nectar-sipping visitors go on to probe neighboring blossoms of the same variety, that pollen is delivered to the stigmas — part of the female organs — for fertilization. In fact, hummingbirds are some of the most essential bird pollinators for flora in North America.

Equally as important as the nectar that the flowers provide are the tiny insects living within them. Insects are an indispensable source of protein in the hummingbird diet and, like the hummingbirds that prey upon them, insects are attracted to the nectar. When hummingbirds aren't catching them on the wing (or, in the case of small spiders, snaring them in their own webs), they find them inside flowers. Happily for gardeners and other outdoors lovers, these insects include many garden pests such as aphids and gnats.

WATER

Like all birds, hummingbirds need to bathe, and they are resourceful in employing water sources that match their tiny size — such as beads of water left on leaves after a rain or the fine spray from a waterfall. Hummingbirds prefer moving water, and are fond of flying through the spray of lawn sprinklers. If you want to set up a sprinkler for a hummingbird bath, use a nozzle that gives off a continuous fine spray. In a pinch, hummingbirds will also use birdbaths, provided they're shallow enough for hummingbirds to stand in. Adding various-size rocks to a birdbath creates different depths for different-size bird species. Hummingbirds prefer not to come to ground for their water, so if you can help them avoid this, they may well use your accommodations.

PERCHES

Having a place from where they can survey their territory is essential to hummingbirds. (For creatures so tiny to be so protective of their domain may seem peculiar, but considering how important ample food sources are to hummingbirds' survival, the ability to oversee their territory and quickly defend it from intruders is crucial.) Hummingbirds prefer a perch that directly overlooks the flowers on which they feed. The male partner of one ruby-throated hummingbird couple that takes up residence in my garden every summer prefers the slender bottom branch of an enormous hemlock tree that anchors the shady end of my garden. From there it's but a short flight to all of the flowers and

---

*Adapted from *Grow a Hummingbird Garden* by Dale Evva Gelfand (Storey Publishing, 1997)

to the nearer of the two hummingbird feeders, as well. It's likely that his mate also perches on the hemlock, but I haven't seen her there, as females generally prefer to remain sheltered within the interior of a tree, shrub, or vine.

SHADE AND SHELTER

Although we think of hummingbirds as being constantly on the wing, in fact they spend about equal amounts of time locating food and resting between meals. Males will rest anywhere from exposed branches to clotheslines to TV antennae, but females and immature birds seek the shade and protection of foliage. Dense foliage for shelter from the elements — evergreens are excellent windbreaks — and for roosting at night is also important to these tiny birds. The ideal balance for a hummingbird habitat is about one-half full sun and one-quarter each shade and partial shade.

NESTING SITES

It's doubtful that you'll ever see a hummingbird nest — or if you do see one, you may not realize what it is. These tiny, usually lichen-covered structures are only 1 to 1½ inches (2½–4cm) in diameter, and are so effectively camouflaged that you would assume they're but a knot on a branch. Hummingbirds nest in both deciduous and evergreen trees, anywhere from 4 to 50 feet (1.2–15m) up but most frequently in the 10- to 20-foot-high (3–6m) range, often bordering or over a stream. Although there are no guarantees in tempting a hummingbird pair to set up housekeeping in your yard, by planting both food sources and those trees and shrubs that provide nesting materials, you'll make it more appealing for them to do so. Primary among the latter is downy plant material, which makes up the bulk of hummingbird nests. An excellent — and favored — source of downy fibers are the filaments of willow seeds; additionally, willow flowers provide both nectar and the insects attracted to it. Consider planting shrub willow in your garden if your yard has a favorable site for this moisture-loving tree. Other trees that provide nesting material for hummingbirds include cottonwoods, aspens, and sycamores.

A Hummingbird Gallery

Hummingbirds are strictly a New World phenomenon, of Central American origin. North America is home to eight common species of hummingbirds and several more rare species. Hummingbirds follow a migratory pattern and are seen in the United States mainly during the summer months, although several species are known to take up permanent residence in coastal California, coastal Oregon, southern Arizona, and southern Florida. In some areas of the country, the ranges of certain species may overlap, although if you live anywhere east of the Mississippi, identification is usually easy: The ruby-throated hummingbird is the only regular resident of that area.

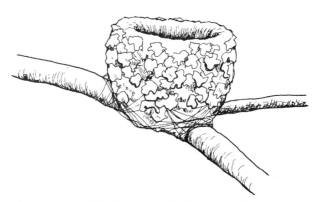

The exterior of the hummingbird's nest is often covered with lichens.

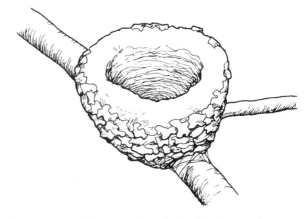

The interior of the nest is packed with downy plant material.

EASTERN AND MIDWESTERN HUMMINGBIRDS

COMMON	UNCOMMON
Ruby-throated	

SOUTHEASTERN AND GULF COAST HUMMINGBIRDS

COMMON	UNCOMMON
Black-chinned	Allen's
Buff-bellied	Anna's
Ruby-throated	Bahama woodstar
	Blue-throated
	Broad-billed
	Broad-tailed
	Calliope
	Magnificent
	Rufous

ROCKY MOUNTAIN REGION HUMMINGBIRDS

COMMON	UNCOMMON
Black-chinned	Magnificent
Broad-tailed	
Calliope	
Rufous	

SOUTHWESTERN HUMMINGBIRDS

COMMON	UNCOMMON
Allen's	Berylline
Anna's	Cinnamon
Black-chinned	Lucifer
Blue-throated	Plain-capped starthroat
Broad-billed	Violet-crowned
Broad-tailed	White-eared
Calliope	
Costa's	
Magnificent	

WEST COAST HUMMINGBIRDS

COMMON	UNCOMMON
Allen's	Ruby-throated
Anna's	
Black-chinned	
Broad-tailed	
Calliope	
Costa's	
Rufous	

IDENTIFYING HUMMINGBIRDS

Listed below are brief descriptions of the hummingbirds that can typically be seen in the United States. For more comprehensive information on common and uncommon hummingbirds — identification, territories, and behavior — consult a hummingbird identification reference book.

Allen's Hummingbird
(Selasphorus sasin)

Allen's hummingbirds are usually about 3¾ inches (9.5cm) in length. An adult male Allen's has rufous (reddish) sides and tail; its gorget (throat) is a deep orange-red bordered below by white. Its green-bronze back distinguishes it from the otherwise similarly colored male rufous hummingbird, which generally has a red back. An adult female Allen's is similarly marked but lacks the gorget — its throat is marked with a small patch of iridescent orange-red feathers and rows of small green dots.

Anna's Hummingbird
(Calypte anna)

Anna's hummingbirds are about 4 inches (10cm) in length. The adult male Anna's has an iridescent rose-colored gorget and crown; its sides are washed with green and its tail is generally dark. The female Anna's has a green-bronze back and a gray-green tail with a dark band; it lacks the gorget but may have instead a patch of iridescent rose-colored feathers in the center of its throat.

Black-Chinned Hummingbird
(Archilochus alexandri)

Black-chinned hummingbirds are typically 3¾ inches (9.5cm) long. The adult male has a black gorget bordered below by an iridescent purple band; it has a dull green crown and a deeply notched black tail. The adult female has an all-white breast and throat and a green back.

Blue-Throated Hummingbird
(Lampornis clemenciae)

Blue-throated hummingbirds are usually about 5 inches (12.5cm) in length. The adult male has a bronze-green crown and back and a white streak that extends back from its eyes, creating a masked look. Its gorget is an iridescent deep blue that is sometimes bordered below by a white stripe. The adult female is similarly marked but lacks the iridescent gorget, having instead a patch of gray on the throat and a white breast. Both males and females have white-tipped tails.

Broad-Billed Hummingbird
(Cynanthus latirostris)

Broad-billed hummingbirds are typically 4 inches (10cm) in length. The vibrantly colored adult male has an iridescent bronze-green back and crown, an iridescent blue throat that melds into green along the breast and belly, and a coral bill tipped with black. The adult female has a bright green crown and back, a subdued gray breast and belly, scattered green spots along the sides, and a black bill with bright orange or pink at its base.

Broad-Tailed Hummingbird
(Selasphorus platycercus)

Broad-tailed hummingbirds are usually about 4 inches (10cm) in length. The adult male has a deep rose–colored gorget, a green crown and back, and a white breast. The adult female lacks the gorget, having instead a small patch of rose-colored feathers in the center of its throat. Both males and females have a long, squared tail.

Buff-Bellied Hummingbird
(Amazilia yucatanensis)

Buff-bellied hummingbirds are typically 4¼ inches (10.8cm) long. The adult male has a bronze-green back, a brighter green throat and breast, and a buff-colored belly. Its bill is coral with a dull-colored tip, and it has a narrow buff-colored band encircling its eyes. Females are similar in appearance, althought not as brightly colored.

Calliope Hummingbird
(Stellula calliope)

Calliope hummingbirds are typically 3¼ inches (8.3cm) long, making them the smallest birds found in the United States or Canada. The adult male Calliope has a vibrant gorget composed of streaks of iridescent rose-purple; the adult female lacks this gorget. Both males and females have iridescent blue-green backs and white breasts.

Costa's Hummingbird
(Calypte costae)

Costa's hummingbirds are typically 3½ inches (8.9cm) in length. The adult male has an iridescent rose-purple gorget and crown, a dark green back, and a white breast. The adult female is similarly marked but lacks the gorget and crown; it may occasionally have a small patch of purple feathers marking its throat.

Magnificent Hummingbird
(Eugenes fulgens)

Magnificent hummingbirds, also known as Rivoli's hummingbirds, are typically 5¼ inches (13.3cm) in length. The adult male has an iridescent blue-violet crown, an iridescent green gorget, and a bronze-green back. Its breast and belly are dark, almost black, but shade to grayish along the edges. The adult female lacks the iridescent crown and gorget and is pale gray along its belly.

Ruby-Throated Hummingbird
(Archilochus colubris)

Ruby-throated hummingbirds are typically 3¾ inches (9.5cm) in length. The adult male has an iridescent ruby gorget, bordered below by a white breast, and an iridescent green crown and back. The adult female is similarly marked but lacks the gorget.

Rufous Hummingbird
(Selasphorus rufus)

Rufous hummingbirds are about 3¾ inches (9.5cm) in length. The adult male has an orange-red gorget bordered below by a white breast and rufous back, sides, and tail. The adult female has green on its back with some rufous on the sides and tail; a small patch of iridescent orange-red feathers marks its throat, accompanied by speckles of dull green dots.

Designing a Hummingbird Garden

Yes, it's true, many hummingbirds have a preference for red flowers, and for a very good reason: They have learned through experience that red flowers frequently have more nectar than others. Ruby-throated hummingbirds in particular have the strongest attraction to red, while this characteristic is less pronounced in many of the western species. However, hummingbirds also feed at pink, orange, purple, yellow, and even white blossoms. In short, there are innumerable tubular-shaped flowers, both cultivated and wild, that can justly be called hummingbird flowers.

With so many flowers to choose from, narrowing down your selection will take some work. Obviously, not all flowers that hummingbirds are attracted to will be hardy to your area, but if you're among those lucky enough to live in a zone suitable to a wide and varied range of plant life, your selections will be limited only by personal preference and space considerations.

CHOOSING PLANTS

When choosing plants for your hummingbird garden, select varieties with overlapping periods of bloom. You can select combinations of annuals, perennials, flowering shrubs and vines, and even some vegetables and herbs. Plant species that are native to your region, especially wildflowers. These will be much better nectar producers than nonnative plants and cultivars.

To ensure an adequate supply of nectar at all times, plant a variety of flower-producing plants in sizable numbers each. Nectar production in some plants can slow or stop altogether when it's too hot, too cold, too wet, or too dry. Having an assortment of plants blooming in your garden at any one time should minimize this problem.

Most gardens have a combination of perennials (herbaceous plants that live at least three years, although most will happily bloom for far longer than that) and annuals (which, as the name implies, bloom for one season only, although many will self-seed for the following year). However, although perennials will reappear year after year, they bloom for only three or four weeks in any one season, whereas many annuals will produce flowers all summer long. Bear in mind, however, that a Zone 8 perennial, such as the zonal geranium, will be available at a Zone 4 garden shop as an annual simply because the plant can't survive that region's cold winters. And some plants, such as begonias, that are designated annuals in colder climes can be dug up in autumn, potted, enjoyed through the winter as houseplants, and then put back in the garden the following spring, after the last frost.

Although not every flower in a hummingbird garden needs to be red, hummingbirds know that red flowers usually offer good nectar. Therefore, to attract hummingbirds to your garden, whether during their summer sojourns or during their long migratory flights, a patch of bright red blossoms will be both highly visible and a good signpost that your garden is an excellent source of food — which is especially important to a tiny bird with limited energy reserves.

Note: The letters "spp." following the Latin name mean that many of the species in that genus attract hummingbirds.

EASTERN WILDFLOWERS

COMMON NAME	LATIN NAME
bee balm	*Monarda* spp.
buttercup	*Ranunculus* spp.
Canada lily	*Lilium canadense*
cardinal flower	*Lobelia cardinalis*
evening primrose	*Oenothera* spp.
fire pink	*Silene virginica*
fireweed	*Epilobium angustifolium*
impatiens	*Impatiens* spp.
Indian-paintbrush	*Castilleja coccinea*
lily	*Lilium* spp.
Maltese-cross	*Lychnis chalcedonica*
phlox	*Phlox* spp.
pink	*Dianthus* spp.
scarlet sage	*Salvia splendens*
smooth phlox	*Phlox glaberrima*
snapdragon	*Antirrhinum* spp.
squill	*Scilla* spp.
Texas plume	*Ipomopsis rubra*
wild columbine	*Aquilegia canadensis*
wood lily	*Lilium philadelphicum*

WESTERN WILDFLOWERS

COMMON NAME	LATIN NAME
bee balm	*Monarda* spp.
buttercup	*Ranunculus* spp.
California fuchsia	*Zauschneria californica*
California Indian pink	*Silene californica*
canon delphinium	*Delphinium nudicaule*
cardinal flower	*Lobelia cardinalis*
coast lily	*Lilium maritimum*
coyote mint	*Monardella villosa*
crimson columbine	*Aquilegia formosa*
evening primrose	*Oenothera* spp.
fireweed	*Epilobium angustifolium*
gentian	*Gentiana asclepiadea*
grand collomia	*Collomia grandiflora*
hummingbird's trumpet	*Epilobium canum*
lily	*Lilium* spp.
longleaf phlox	*Phlox longifolia*
monkey flower	*Mimulus* spp.
paintbrush	*Castilleja* spp.
penstemon	*Penstemon* spp.
phlox	*Phlox* spp.
pink	*Dianthus* spp.
scarlet delphinium	*Delphinium cardinale*
scarlet sage	*Salvia splendens*
skyrocket	*Ipomopsis aggregata*
snapdragon	*Antirrhinum* spp.
squill	*Scilla* spp.
tiny trumpet	*Collomia linearis*
vervain	*Verbena* spp.
Western lily	*Lilium occidentale*
wild columbine	*Aquilegia canadensis*

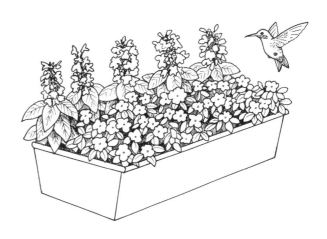

Hanging pots, window boxes, and containers of flowers will lure hummingbirds to your deck, porch, or balcony.

LAYING OUT YOUR GARDEN

Once you have a good idea of the hummingbird-attracting plants that will be appropriate for your region, zone, and soil conditions, you're ready to begin breaking ground for your garden. Remember that hummingbirds prefer areas with trees and/or shrubs that will provide perching locations, sheltering foliage, and protected roosting sites. The ideal hummingbird habitat has about one-half full sun and one-quarter each full shade and partial shade.

Group the plants in your garden so that their blossoms are easily accessible to hummingbirds, with ample room for hovering and flight maneuverability. Flowers are visually more interesting when they're tiered, with the tallest ones in back and the shorter ones in front, and a tiered design will also provide better hummingbird access to all of the blossoms in your garden.

Don't overlook your decks and porches — or even apartment balconies — as potential hummingbird garden sites. Being fearless creatures, hummingbirds will visit container plants and hanging baskets just as often as they do more traditionally embedded flora. In fact, a hanging basket of fuchsia set outside after wintering indoors may well be the only nectar source around during the early warm days of spring, when many hummingbirds return from a winter sojourn in Central America.

Cultivating Wildflowers

It's likely that hummingbird-attracting wildflowers are already established either in or near your yard. Search them out, and if you find any, help them to thrive by eliminating some of their competitors. Thin or prune surrounding trees to let in more light, and provide the wildflowers with water during dry spells. In doing so you'll not only be helping native plants to get a stronger foothold, but you'll also be providing a richer source of nectar for your winged visitors (wildflowers generally produce more nectar than their cultivated cousins), and you'll be saving money to boot.

FLOWERS FOR HUMMINGBIRDS

When planting, consider some of the following flowers for your hummingbird garden, depending on your planting zone and sun and soil conditions. The zone listings specify the zones in which each plant may be grown as a perennial — most plants can be grown as annuals in any zone. The specified heights include flower stalks as well as foliage, which may often be very short by itself. This is followed by the period in which the plant is in flower. For more comprehensive information on any of the plants referenced here, consult a gardening manual.

Beard-Tongue
(Penstemon barbatus)

ZONES: 3–9
HEIGHT: 8"–36"
(20–90cm)
BLOOMING SEASON: Late spring to mid-summer

The individual blossoms of this easy grower are reminiscent of foxglove, although its loose clusters of flower heads are more like annual phlox. Plant in moist, well-drained soil and full sun or light shade.

Bee Balm
(*Monarda* spp.)

ZONES: 4–9
HEIGHT: 2'–4'
(60–120cm)
BLOOMING SEASON: Summer

Hummingbirds, bees, and butterflies alike all love the shaggy blossoms of bee balm. Most often seen in red, bee balm also blooms in purple, pink, and even white. Deadhead the spent blossoms regularly to keep these easy growers blooming, and plant in moist soil in full sun or very light shade.

Begonia
(*Begonia* spp.)

ZONES: 6–10
HEIGHT: 6"–24" (15–60cm)
BLOOMING SEASON: Summer through autumn

Plant begonias in shades of red, pink, or white in your garden or in containers. Give them rich, moist soil in sun where it's cooler and partial shade in hotter climes.

Blazing Star
(*Liatris* spp.)

ZONES: 3–10
HEIGHT: 2'–6' (.6–1.8m)
BLOOMING SEASON: Summer to early autumn

These rocket-shaped, pink-purple beauties (also known as gayfeather and snakeroot) will perk up any garden. Although preferring a sandy, rich soil, Liatris will tolerate even poor, dry soil, as long as their planting medium is very well drained. They prefer full sun to light shade.

Bleeding Heart
(*Dicentra spectabilis*)

ZONES: 3–9
HEIGHT: 2'–3' (60–90cm)
BLOOMING SEASON: Mid- to late spring

This traditionally favorite plant with fernlike foliage and sprays of heart-shaped pink and white blooms at the tips of long, slender stems will impart elegance and charm to your garden. Plant in partial sun or partial shade — more shade is required in hotter areas — in rich, moist, well-drained soil.

Bugleweed
(*Ajuga* spp.)

ZONES: 3–10
HEIGHT: 4"–10" (10–25cm)
BLOOMING SEASON: Mid-spring to midsummer

Carpet bugle (*Ajuga reptans*), a fast-spreading ground cover that's wonderful under trees or other places too shady for grass to grow, sprouts a forest of purple-blue flowers on a carpet of green and bronze-purple leaves. In rock gardens and mixed shade plantings, try Geneva bugleweed (*Ajuga genevensis*) and upright bugleweed (*Ajuga pyramidalis*), which are less invasive. This plant thrives in either sun or shade and just about any soil, even dry, poor soil, provided it drains well (note that in dry soil, bugleweed needs to be shaded).

California Fuchsia
(*Zauschneria californica*)

ZONES: 9–10
HEIGHT: 12"–24"
(30–60
cm)
BLOOMING SEASON: Late
summer to
October

Spikes of vivid red, tubular flowers are a good reason that this plant also goes by the name hummingbird flower. Plant in a warm, sunny spot in light, well-drained soil.

Cardinal Flower
(Lobelia cardinalis)

ZONES: 2–9
HEIGHT: 3' (90cm)
BLOOMING SEASON: Summer

The dazzling red spikes of the cardinal flower are a surefire magnet for hummingbirds. Lobelias do best if given afternoon shade, moist soil (they thrive near running water), and good drainage for regular waterings.

Century Plant
(Agave americana)

ZONES: 6–10
HEIGHT: Varies; can grow as high as 40' (12m)
BLOOMING SEASON: Summer

These bold succulents with fleshy, sword-shaped leaves and giant flower spikes are highly prized desert hummingbird plants. Plant them in well-drained sandy soil in full sun.

Columbine
(Aquilegia spp.)

ZONES: 3–9
HEIGHT: 6"–48" (15–120cm)
BLOOMING SEASON: Mid-spring to early summer

These beautiful spurred flowers are hummingbird favorites. The red-and-yellow-flowered wild columbine native to the East, *Aquilegia canadensis*, will freely reseed itself — be careful it doesn't become a pest. In the West, plant crimson columbine, *Aquilegia formosa*, native to California, Oregon, and Nevada. All columbines like moist soils with light to moderate shade. Columbines do well in rock gardens.

Coralbells
(Heuchera spp.)

ZONES: 3–9
HEIGHT: 12"–36" (30–90cm)
BLOOMING SEASON: Late spring to early autumn

Delicate sprays of small tubular, red, white, or pink flowers rise on tall, wiry stems out of compact clumps of scalloped foliage. Keep this plant neat by removing the flowering stems once they've bloomed. Grow in light, well-drained soil in full sun in northern zones and partial shade in warmer climes.

Creeping Phlox
(Phlox stolonifera)

ZONES: 3–9
HEIGHT: 6"–8" (15–20cm)
BLOOMING SEASON: Early to late spring

These spreading perennials form beautiful beds of star-shaped flowers in varying shades from white to purple to blue, although the bright, hot pink ones will attract hummingbirds most readily. Creeping phlox prefer a rich, well-drained, moist soil and will grow in either full sun or partial shade.

Delphinium
(Delphinium spp.)

ZONES: 3–9
HEIGHT: 18"–84" (.5–2m)
BLOOMING SEASON: Late spring through autumn, depending on species

These statuesque spires of blossoms — some single flowered, some double — are beautiful in any garden. Also known as larkspur, delphiniums bloom in blue, purple, pink, yellow, and white. Plants over 18 inches (46cm) tall will need to be staked to keep them upright. Although short-lived, fading out after only two or three years, delphiniums can be propagated by cuttings from new spring growth. Grow these beauties in rich, moist, well-drained soil.

Fire Pink
(Silene virginica)

ZONES: 4–9
HEIGHT: 10"–24'" (25–60cm)
BLOOMING SEASON: Late spring to early summer

These masses of dark pink and crimson blooms will stay ablaze for quite some time. Plant in well-drained, humus-rich soil in full sun or light shade (more shade in hotter climates).

Four-O'Clock
(Mirabilis jalapa)

ZONES: 8–10
HEIGHT: 24"–48" (60–120cm)
BLOOMING SEASON: Midsummer to late autumn

Coming from the tropics, these lovely blooms, in shades from rosy purple or red to white and yellow, are perennials only in the warmest climates. Elsewhere cultivate as container plants in well-drained soil.

Foxglove
(Digitalis spp.)

ZONES: 3–9
HEIGHT: 24"–60" (60–152cm)
BLOOMING SEASON: Late spring to late summer, depending on species

The tall spires of these plants look majestic in any setting — and depending on the species, if you have a cool, moist climate, they'll grow just about anywhere, from full sun to full shade (the hotter the summer, the more shade necessary). Foxgloves come in creamy yellow, pink, salmon, and orange, with freckled interiors. Give these beauties moist, rich soil, and they'll happily self-seed.

Fuchsia
(Fuchsia spp.)

ZONE: 10
HEIGHT: 1'–6' (30–180cm)
BLOOMING SEASON: Late spring to autumn

With its pendulous blossoms, this plant is much esteemed for hanging baskets and comes in shades of bright red, fiery pink, purple, white, and various combinations of them all. It does best in full or half shade — I hang my fuchsia basket from a sturdy lower pine branch several feet away from a feeder — in a rich, moist soil.

Geranium
(Geranium spp.)

ZONES: 3–10
HEIGHT: 4"–36" (10–90cm)
BLOOMING SEASON: Spring through late summer, depending on species

Geraniums are hardy, carefree plants with lovely lacy leaves and red, pink, or purple blooms, depending on the species and cultivar. They'll grow in average, well-drained soil, but when planted in rich soil, they'll spread rapidly. Plant in full sun in colder climates and in partial shade in warmer southern climates.

Hollyhock
(Alcea spp.)

ZONES: 5–9
HEIGHT: 2'–6' (60–180cm)
BLOOMING SEASON: Summer to early autumn

This wonderful, old-fashioned, upright plant is available in just about every color. Use the older, taller species as back border plantings, along a fence, or against a cottage wall; the newer, shorter species can go anywhere. Although favoring rich, well-drained, moist soil, they'll tolerate dry soil, too — but not excessive heat and humidity.

Impatiens
(*Impatiens* spp.)

ZONES: Can be grown in any zone as
an annual
HEIGHT: 12"–24" (30–60cm)
BLOOMING SEASON: Late spring through first frost

Impatiens are grown as annuals in most of the country since they are unable to survive frost. With their vibrantly colored, long-lasting blossoms, they are ideal hummingbird flowers. Mass them under trees or in containers under your porch overhang, since most species prefer full shade. They also like a rich, moist soil.

Lily
(*Lilium* spp.)

ZONES: 3–9
HEIGHT: 2'–6' (60–180cm)
BLOOMING SEASON: Late spring through autumn,
depending on species

Lilies have large and exquisite, usually multiple, trumpet-shaped flowers on long, strong stems — eye-catching either singly or when massed together in any garden. Lilies require moist, well-drained, usually slightly acidic soil in full sun or light shade.

Lupine
(*Lupinus* spp.)

ZONES: 4–8
HEIGHT: 18"–60" (46–152cm)
BLOOMING SEASON: Spring to midsummer

Lupines give any garden a boost, even when there are only a few. When massed, the effect of the pink, purple, blue, and red flower spikes is spectacular. Many species thrive in areas with relatively cool summers, although others will tolerate hotter climes. Give them a rich and moist but well-drained soil in either full sun or light shade.

Monkey flower
(*Mimulus* spp.)

ZONES: 3–9
HEIGHT: 8"–36" (20–90cm)
BLOOMING SEASON: Spring to autumn, depending
on species

Depending on the species suitable for your location, these trumpet-shaped, lipped flowers come in all sizes and will want either full sun or partial shade. Check a reference guide for more detailed information. Coming in hues of red, orange, pink, and yellow, these plants grow best in moist, rich soil.

Montbretia
(*Crocosmia* spp.)

ZONES: 5–8
HEIGHT: 12"–48"
(30–120cm)
BLOOMING SEASON: Summer

Spectacular branches of funnel-shaped flowers in red, orange, or yellow emerge from fans of stiff, swordlike foliage. Like the iris the foliage resembles, these plants grow from corms and spread to form clumps. Grow in sun to partial shade in average, well-drained soil.

Nasturtium
(Tropaeolum majus)

ZONES: Can be grown in any zone as an annual
HEIGHT: 12"–48" (30–120cm)
BLOOMING SEASON: Summer to late autumn

These annuals have bold and beautiful yellow, orange, and red spurred blossoms that are a wonderful contrast to their rounded green leaves. Nasturtiums prefer summers that are mild and dry with cool nights. They do well even in poor soil so long as it's well drained and slightly acidic. Plant in full sun to partial shade.

Obedient plant
(Physostegia spp.)

ZONES: 2–9
HEIGHT: 12"–48" (30–120cm)
BLOOMING SEASON: Midsummer to autumn

The pink, purple, or white blooms on these vigorous, easy-care plants — also known as false dragonhead — grow in long, regimented rows. Physostegia enjoy any good garden soil in either full sun or partial shade.

Petunia
(Petunia spp.)

ZONES: Can be grown in any zone as an annual
HEIGHT: 12"–18" (30–46cm)
BLOOMING SEASON: Late spring to frost

Petunias are one of the most widely grown garden plants due to their tireless (and seemingly endless) blooming period. The cheery trumpet-shaped flowers are borne on long stems that work well in hanging baskets. To make them bushier, pinch back young plants. When planted in the garden, put them in moist, well-drained soil in full sun or very light shade.

Red-hot-poker
(Kniphofia uvaria)

ZONES: 5–9
HEIGHT: 2'–4' (60–120cm)
BLOOMING SEASON: Midsummer

Also known as torch lily, Kniphofia (knee-FOE-fia) has blossoms of fiery red, yellow, and orange on thickly clustered spikes that are dramatic in any setting. Plant in rich, moist, and well-drained soil. Give full sun in moderate climes, partial shade where summers are very hot.

Scarlet sage
(Salvia splendens)

ZONES: Can be grown in any zone as an annual
HEIGHT: 1'–3' (30–90cm)
BLOOMING SEASON: Summer to autumn, depending on species

Scarlet sage is a tender perennial most often grown as an annual. Its usually bright red spikes are wonderful for creating splashes of color in your garden. Give it well-drained soil and full sun or partial shade.

Spider flower
(Cleome hassleriana)

ZONES: Can be grown in any zone as an annual
HEIGHT: 3'–4' (.9–1.2m)
BLOOMING SEASON: Summer through late autumn

Although annuals, these odd-looking plants will self-seed with wanton regularity, so be careful where you plant them. Give these long bloomers average soil and lots of sun. If your summers are very hot, give them half shade.

Strawberry cactus
(Mammillaria setispina)

ZONES: 9–10
HEIGHT: Various
BLOOMING SEASON: Late spring to summer

This member of the cactus family produces dark red flowers beyond its spines, which makes it a fine place for desert hummingbirds to sup. If you don't live in the Southwest, the mammillaria makes an excellent houseplant that can summer outdoors in half shade. As with most cacti, plant in a light and porous yet stable soil with excellent drainage (a mixture of sandy and clay soils works well).

Sweet William
(Dianthus barbatus)

ZONES: Can be grown in any zone as an annual, or sometimes a biennial
HEIGHT: 6"–24" (15–60cm)
BLOOMING SEASON: Late spring to summer

Choose the crimson variety of this plant with its cushiony, tightly packed blooms. Sweet William self-sows readily and prefers rich, well-drained slightly alkaline soil in the sunny or lightly shaded part of your garden.

Verbena
(Verbena spp.)

ZONES: 3–10
HEIGHT: 4"–24" (10–60cm)
BLOOMING SEASON: Late spring to frost

These showy plants with tightly packed flower heads are rather short-lived and are best grown as annuals. Choose from pink, white, purple, and red blossoms. Plant in full sun in any well-drained soil.

Yucca
(Yucca spp.)

ZONES: 3–10
HEIGHT: 3'–30' (.9–9m)
BLOOMING SEASON: Early summer to autumn, depending on species

An impressive spike of white, bell-shaped flowers stands like a sentinel over the yucca's straplike evergreen leaves. This very tough, drought-resistant plant likes full sun and average or sandy well-drained soil. Some species need protection in winter in colder climates.

Vines, Shrubs, and Trees

Some of the most favored blossoms of hummingbirds are those of vines, shrubs, and trees, which also provide shelter for resting, roosting, and nesting. If you can, make room in your garden for one or more of these beauties.

VINES
Many of these vines, having densely packed foliage, are ideal homes for hummingbirds.

Morning-glory
(*Ipomoea* spp.)

Zones: Grown as annuals
Blooming season: Midsummer through autumn

These twining vines with their blue, lavender, pink, or white flowers will wrap themselves around just about anything — and will also grow in just about anything, including poor, dry soil. Grow in full sun.

Scarlet runner bean
(*Phaseolus coccineus*)

Zone: 10
Blooming season: Midsummer to frost

Annuals everywhere but tropical climates, scarlet runner beans make everyone happy — hummingbirds for the nectar in the clusters of flowers, humans for the beans. Grow in full sun against a trellis to appreciate fully the brilliant red flowers.

Trumpet creeper
(*Campsis radicans*)

Zones: 4–9
Blooming season: Midsummer through autumn

This vigorous, twining perennial vine with its bold, trumpet-shaped (hence the name) scarlet flowers prefers full sun and a rich, moist, well-drained soil. It will need strong supports in your garden.

Trumpet honeysuckle
(*Lonicera sempervirens*)

Zones: 4–9
Blooming season: Early to late summer

Rich orange, scarlet, or yellow clumps of blossoms punctuate this deciduous or semi-evergreen vine (depending on your climate); in Zones 4 and 5, it needs protection. Grow in cool, semishady areas, in porous, well-drained, fertile soil.

SHRUBS

Azalea
(*Rhododendron* spp.)

Zones: 5–8
Blooming season: Spring

In colder climes, grow this decorative species of the classic rhododendron as a houseplant and put it outdoors after the last frost. Give it a rich, moist soil — an azalea needs lots of water — and shade.

Bearberry
(*Arctostaphylos uva-ursi*)

Zones: 2–10
Blooming season: Mid- to late spring

The drooping clusters of blossoms on this low-growing evergreen shrub give way to brilliant red berries. This species prefers soil that is sandy or acidic, but will grow in almost any type of soil. Prefers full sun but will tolerate some shade.

Butterfly bush
(Buddleia davidii)

ZONES: 5–9

BLOOMING SEASON: Midsummer to autumn

Also known as summer lilac, butterfly bush — which obviously also attracts butterflies — has profuse white, pink, red, or purple blossoms in long clusters. Grow this and other Buddleias in any soil in full sun.

Cape honeysuckle
(Tecomaria capensis)

ZONES: 9–10

BLOOMING SEASON: Year-round

Those in more tropical climes can enjoy the scarlet blossoms of this evergreen all year long. This beautiful shrub, which will reach 8 feet, should be grown in fertile soil in full sun.

Flowering quince
(Chaenomeles spp.)

ZONES: 4–9

BLOOMING SEASON: Spring

The showy flowers on these deciduous shrubs, not the fruit, are the main attraction for both hummingbirds and humans — although if the yield is bountiful, you can make preserves from the fruit. Plant in fertile soil in a sunny spot.

Hibiscus
(Hibiscus spp.)

ZONES: 5–10, depending on species

BLOOMING SEASON: Mid- to late summer

Hibiscus are often thought of as strictly tropical shrubs, but they also include some hardier species such as rose-of-Sharon *(Hibiscus syriacus).* Grow in a sheltered, sunny spot in any well-drained soil and enjoy masses of pink, purple, orange, yellow, or scarlet blossoms, depending on the species.

Honeysuckle
(Lonicera spp.)

ZONES: 4–9

BLOOMING SEASON: Late spring to early summer

These bushy shrubs have tubular blossoms in creamy white, pale yellow, pink, and even hot pink, depending on the species. Honeysuckles generally prefer well-drained soil and full sun to partial shade.

Lantana
(Lantana camara)

ZONES: 8–10

BLOOMING SEASON: Year-round

This 6-foot-tall evergreen shrub produces compact clusters of orange-yellow, orange, red, or red-and-white flowers. Grow in any well-drained soil in full sun.

Rosemary
(*Rosmarinus officinalis*)

ZONES: 6–10
BLOOMING SEASON: Early spring

The stems of the fragrant herb we get at our green-grocers are actually branches of an evergreen shrub that grows to 7 feet tall — yet another plant that satisfies the needs of both humans and hummingbirds. The latter appreciate the lovely lilac-blue flowers. Rosemary grows best in light, well-drained soil in a warm, sunny spot.

Weigela
(*Weigela florida*)

ZONES: 4–9
BLOOMING SEASON: Spring

This hardy shrub is generally easy to cultivate. It has tubular or funnel-shaped flowers in all shades of pink from deep carmine to almost white. Weigela thrives in any moist, well-drained soil in full sun.

TREES
Trees don't usually come to mind when we're thinking of flowers for hummingbirds, but many species have spectacular blossoms.

Chinaberry
(*Melia azedarach*)

ZONES: 7–10
HEIGHT: 30'–40' (9–12m)
BLOOMING SEASON: Late spring

This member of the mahogany family produces lovely sprays of lilac-colored flowers. A good shade tree, it grows best in full sun. Chinaberry is often considered a weed species, as its wood breaks easily during heavy storms.

Cry-baby tree
(*Erythrina crista-galli*)

ZONE: 10
HEIGHT: 15' (5m)
BLOOMING SEASON: Late summer

This small to average-size tree produces clusters of dark red, waxy flowers. It prefers moist but well-drained soil. Plant in full sun.

Dwarf Poinciana
(*Caesalpinia pulcherrima*)

ZONE: 10
HEIGHT: 15'–20' (5–6m)
BLOOMING SEASON: Summer

This fast-growing small tree (or shrub) is a member of the pea family. Beautiful clusters of white or yellow pealike flowers with prominent red stamens are framed by delicate fronds. Grow in full sun in well-drained, dryish soil.

Eucalyptus
(*Eucalyptus* spp.)

ZONES: 9–10
HEIGHT: 30'–100' (9–30m)
BLOOMING SEASON: Winter to summer

Eucalyptus provide both nectar and shelter for hummingbirds. These Australian imports have flowers that range from white to showy red and for the most part prefer full sun in moist soil.

Flowering crabapple
(*Malus* spp.)

ZONES: 2–6
HEIGHT: 15'–25' (5–8m)
BLOOMING SEASON: Mid- to late spring

This is another species that benefits both hummingbirds (nectar) and humans (fruit for preserves — if the blue jays don't eat them first). Flowers range in color from white to pink to bright red. Grow in any well-drained, fertile soil in full sun.

Red horse chestnut
(*Aesculus* x *carnea*)

ZONES: 3–7
HEIGHT: 30'–40' (9–12m)
BLOOMING SEASON: Late spring to early summer

As its name implies, the large clusters of blooms on this spectacular tree have rose red panicles that can reach 6 to 8 inches in length in the spring. Grow in moist, well-drained soil in full sun to light shade.

Siberian peashrub
(*Caragana arborescens*)

ZONES: 2–7
HEIGHT: 15'–20' (5–6m)
BLOOMING SEASON: Spring

Lovely yellow flowers dress up this tree's feathery leaves. It does well in all soil types and prefers full sun.

Silk tree
(*Albizia julibrissin*)

ZONES: 6–9
HEIGHT: 20'–35' (6–11m)
BLOOMING SEASON: Late spring to late summer

This small tree, also called mimosa tree, produces beautiful bristly clusters of flowers — looking like so many bottle brushes — that are white at the base and bright pink at the tips. Grow this member of the sun-loving pea family in full sun; it does well in all soil types.

Tulip tree
(*Liriodendron tulipifera*)

ZONES: 4–9
HEIGHT: Can grow to 200 feet (60m)
BLOOMING SEASON: Spring to early summer

This tall, stately tree, also known as tulip tree, produces — no surprise — tuliplike greenish yellow flowers lined with orange. Grow in rich, moist soil in full sun.

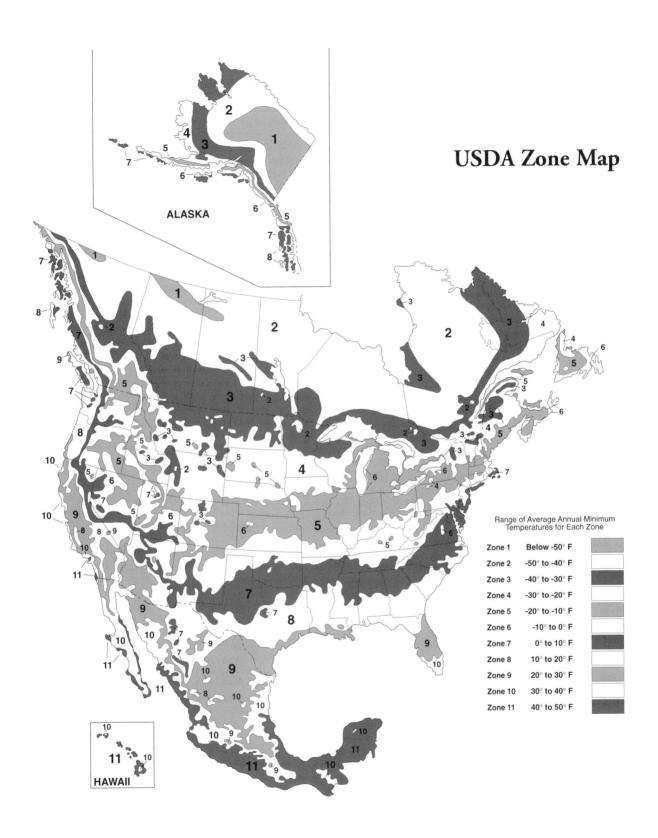

USDA Zone Map

ALASKA

HAWAII

Range of Average Annual Minimum
Temperatures for Each Zone

Zone 1	Below -50° F
Zone 2	-50° to -40° F
Zone 3	-40° to -30° F
Zone 4	-30° to -20° F
Zone 5	-20° to -10° F
Zone 6	-10° to 0° F
Zone 7	0° to 10° F
Zone 8	10° to 20° F
Zone 9	20° to 30° F
Zone 10	30° to 40° F
Zone 11	40° to 50° F

323

Illustration Credits

Polly Alexander: 57

Cathy Baker: 15, 62 (top left) , 63 (top left), 65 (bottom right), 66 (top), 88 (top right), 177 (middle), 261 (left), 261 (right)

Carolyn Bucha: 249, 251, 269, 272, 279, 280, 287

Judy Eliason: 2, 62 (bottom left), 62 (bottom right), 62 (top right), 63 (bottom left), 64 (bottom right), 64 (left), 65 (top right), 66 (bottom), 88 (bottom left), 88 (bottom right), 88 (top left), 89, 109, 110, 112, 118, 124 (right), 177 (bottom), 177 (top), 198, 225, 226, 241 (bottom), 262

Brigita Fuhrmann: 24, 37, 44 (left), 45, 53 (top), 100 (left), 133, 138, 139 (right), 141 (right), 142, 143 (bottom), 145 (left), 181 (right), 236, 237 (left), 282

Regina Hughes: 128

Nancy Hull: 85 (right), 94, 97, 104 (right), 215 (bottom right), 217 (bottom right), 218 (right)

Charles Joslin: 40, 42, 46, 137, 141 (left), 145 (right), 146, 147, 148 (left), 149 (left), 150, 151, 153, 154 (right), 155, 156 (left), 157, 158 (left), 159 (left), 160 (right), 161, 162 (left), 164 (left)

Carl Kirkpatrick: 124 (left), 281 (top)

Alison Kolesar: 22, 61 (left), 119 (top), 125 (left), 125 (middle), 136, 140, 143 (top), 222, 289, 292, 295, 301, 305, 307, 311, 312, 314

Mallory Lake: 135, 148 (right), 152, 158 (right), 159 (right), 162 (right), 163 (left), 164 (right), 211 (bottom right), 212 (top right), 212 (left), 213, 214 (top right), 214 (bottom right), 214 (left), 215 (left), 217 (top right), 217 (left), 218 (left), 232, 233, 234, 235, 237 (right), 241 (top), 245 (left), 246, 313, 315, 316, 319, 320

Michael Lamb: 56

Susan Berry Langsten: viii, 103 (left), 117

Doug Paisley: 1, 4 (left), 13, 33 (right), 36 (left), 43, 44 (right), 63 (bottom right), 70, 72 (left), 74 (right), 75 (left), 76, 78, 80 (left), 85 (left), 90 (left), 91 (left), 92 (right), 105 (right), 107 (right), 116, 116, 139 (left), 149 (right), 154 (left), 156 (right), 160 (left), 163 (right), 168, 169 (bottom), 171, 182, 187, 188, 200, 201, 211 (left), 211 (top right), 212 (bottom right), 215 (top right), 220, 221, 245 (right), 247, 252, 253, 258, 278, 284, 285

Louise Riotte: 65 (left), 244

Melody Sarecky: 64 (top right)

Ralph Scott: 165

Elayne Sears: v, 1 (screen), 3, 4 (right), 6, 11, 13 (screen), 20, 21, 23, 29 (screen), 30, 33 (top left), 33 (bottom left), 34, 35, 36 (right), 38, 39, 41, 49, 49, 50, 51, 52, 53 (bottom), 54, 55, 58, 59 (bottom), 59 (top), 61 (right), 69, 71, 72 (right), 73, 74 (left), 75 (right), 77, 79, 80 (right), 81, 83, 84, 91 (right), 92 (left), 93, 95, 96, 98, 99, 100 (right), 101, 102, 103 (right), 104 (left), 105 (left), 106, 107 (left), 111, 113, 114, 115, 119 (bottom), 122, 125 (right), 166, 169 (top), 170, 179, 180, 181 (left), 189 (left), 190, 191, 209, 216, 219, 224, 227, 230, 231, 239, 240, 242, 243, 254, 257, 259, 281 (bottom), 283, 286, 298

Mary Thompson: 63 (top right), 260

INDEX

Page references in *italic* indicate maps;
those in **bold** indicate charts.

Other Storey Titles You Will Enjoy

Seed Sowing and Saving: Step-by-Step Techniques for Collecting and Growing More Than 100 Vegetables, Flowers, and Herbs, by Carole B. Turner. From Storey's Gardening Skills Illustrated Series. 224 pages. Paperback: ISBN 1-58017-001-3. Hardcover: ISBN 1-58017-002-1.

Pruning Made Easy: A Gardener's Visual Guide to When and How to Prune Everything, from Flowers to Trees, by Lewis Hill. From Storey's Gardening Skills Illustrated Series. Paperback: ISBN 1-58017-006-4. Hardcover: ISBN 1-58017-007-2.

Secrets to Great Soil: A Grower's Guide to Composting, Mulching, and Creating Healthy, Fertile Soil for Your Garden and Lawn, by Elizabeth P. Stell. From Storey's Gardening Skills Illustrated Series. Paperback: ISBN 1-58017-008-0. Hardcover: ISBN 1-58017-009-9.

Year-Round Gardening Projects: From Horticulture magazine's monthly "Step-by-Step" Column, illustrated by Elayne Sears. Organized by season and appropriate for experts and beginners, a complete collection of 86 of the original articles. Written in a clear concise style by seven different gardening experts and illustrated in beautiful and detailed line drawings by Elayne Sears. 224 pages. Paperback. ISBN 1-58017-039-0.

The Big Book of Gardening Skills, by the Editors of Garden Way Publishing. A comprehensive guide to growing flowers, fruits, herbs, vegetables, shrubs, and lawns. Organized by topic to help plan, plant, and maintain beautiful and productive gardens. Includes skills for garden basics, plant selection, safe organic growing, and a garden equipment guide. 352 pages. Paperback. ISBN 0-88266-795-5.

Just the Facts! Dozens of Gardening Charts — Thousands of Gardening Answers, by the Editors of Garden Way Publishing. An excellent reference tool for the home gardener, with information about every aspect of gardening. 224 pages. Paperback. ISBN 0-88266-867-6.

The Organic Gardener's Home Reference, by Tanya Denckla. Detailed information on how to grow, harvest, and store vegetables, herbs, fruits, and nuts. 288 pages. Paperback. ISBN 0-88266-839-0.

From Seed to Bloom: How to Grow over 500 Annuals, Perennials & Herbs, by Eileen Powell. Easy-to-understand plant-by-plant format that includes information on hardiness zones, sowing seeds indoors and out, germination times, spacing, light and soil needs, care, and propagation techniques. 320 pages. Paperback. ISBN 0-88266-259-7.

These books and other Storey books are available at your
bookstore, farm store, garden center, or directly from
Storey Publishing, Schoolhouse Road, Pownal, Vermont 05261,
or by calling 1-800-441-5700. Visit our Web site at www.storey.com.